KISSINGER AND LATIN AMERICA

KISSINGER AND LATIN AMERICA

INTERVENTION, HUMAN
RIGHTS, AND DIPLOMACY

STEPHEN G. RABE

CORNELL UNIVERSITY PRESS
Ithaca and London

Visit our website at cornellpress.cornell.edu.

First published 2020 by Cornell University Press

Library of Congress Cataloging-in-Publication Data

Names: Rabe, Stephen G., author.
Title: Kissinger and Latin America : intervention, human rights, and diplomacy / Stephen G. Rabe.
Description: Ithaca : Cornell University Press, 2020. | Includes bibliographical references and index.
Identifiers: LCCN 2019032667 (print) | LCCN 2019032668 (ebook) | ISBN 9781501706295 (cloth) | ISBN 9781501749476 (pdf) | ISBN 9781501749469 (ebook)
Subjects: LCSH: Kissinger, Henry, 1923– | United States—Foreign relations—Latin America. | Latin America—Foreign relations—United States.
Classification: LCC F1418 .R237 2020 (print) | LCC F1418 (ebook) | DDC 327.730092 [B] —dc23
LC record available at https://lccn.loc.gov/2019032667
LC ebook record available at https://lccn.loc.gov /2019032668

Granddaughter Emma Clare
Born 15 November 2018
May her life be filled with peace and joy

Contents

Abbreviations

CIA	Central Intelligence Agency
CF	Confidential File
CO	Country File
DH	*Diplomatic History*
DoS	Department of State
DSB	*Department of State Bulletin*
FAOHC	Foreign Affairs Oral History Collection
FRUS	*Foreign Relations of the United States*
GPO	Government Printing Office
GRFL	Gerald R. Ford Presidential Library
HAK	Henry A. Kissinger
KTC	*Kissinger Telephone Conversations*
NIE	National Intelligence Estimate
NSA	National Security Archive
NSC	National Security Council
NSDM	National Security Decision Memorandum
NSSM	National Security Study Memorandum
NYT	*New York Times*
OAS	Organization of American States
OH	Oral History
PDB	President's Daily Brief
POF	President's Office Files
RAC	Rockefeller Archive Center
RMNL	Richard M. Nixon Presidential Library
RG	Record Group
SRG	Senior Review Group
UN	United Nations
WH	White House
WHCF	White House Central File

KISSINGER AND LATIN AMERICA

Introduction

The Case for Henry Kissinger and Latin America

Kissinger and Latin America: Intervention, Human Rights, and Diplomacy provides an opportunity for interpreting U.S. policies toward Latin America during a critical period of the Cold War. Except for the issue of Chile under Salvador Allende, historians have largely ignored inter-American relations during the presidencies of Richard M. Nixon and Gerald R. Ford. The book also offers a way of adding to and challenging the prevailing historiography on one of the most preeminent policymakers in the history of U.S. foreign relations. Scholarly studies on Henry Kissinger and his policies between 1969 and 1977 have tended to survey his approach to the world, with an emphasis on initiatives toward the Soviet Union and the People's Republic of China and the struggle to extricate the United States from the conflict in Southeast Asia. Other scholars have focused on Kissinger's role in bilateral relations with countries such as Pakistan and Iran. This book offers something new: analyzing U.S. policies toward a distinct region of the world during Kissinger's career as national security adviser and secretary of state.

The Ambitious Kissinger

Students and scholars might ask, Why open a book about Henry A. Kissinger and Latin America? That question might be asked because the prevailing assumption has been that Kissinger and the Richard M. Nixon and Gerald R. Ford administrations had no interest in the region and left relations with Latin America to career diplomats. The only significant issue was the U.S. opposition to the election of Salvador Allende (1970–1973) to the presidency of Chile, because of Allende's alleged ties to the international communist movement. This study challenges the notion that Henry Kissinger dismissed relations with the southern neighbors. The energetic Kissinger devoted more time and effort to Latin America than any of his predecessors or successors who served as national security adviser or secretary of state during the Cold War era (1945–1989). He waged war against Salvador Allende and successfully destabilized a government in Bolivia. He resolved nettlesome issues with Mexico, Peru, Ecuador, and Venezuela. He launched critical initiatives with Panama and Cuba. Kissinger also bolstered and coddled murderous military dictators who trampled on basic human rights. South American military dictators committed international terrorism in Europe and the Western Hemisphere.

In their memoirs, Presidents Nixon and Ford and Kissinger himself did their best to leave the impression that Republican administrations dismissed relations with Latin America. In *RN*, Nixon wrote a monumental memoir of over a thousand pages. The only substantial discussion of inter-American relations revolved around Vice President Nixon's tour of South America in the spring of 1958. Nixon faced violent protests over the Dwight D. Eisenhower administration's support for authoritarian rulers in the region and was almost killed by a howling mob in Caracas, Venezuela. The point Nixon wanted to make was that he remained calm and brave in the face of danger. On Allende and Chile, Nixon penned one innocuous page in which he conceded that the United States financed anti-Allende groups but only in response to communist Cuba's financial backing of Allende. He observed that the Chilean military overthrew Allende because of his inefficiency. Nixon had a few pages on the alleged plan by the Soviet Union to build a base for submarines in Cuba. But this incident was included to prove that his diplomacy was superior to President John F. Kennedy's rash approach to the Cuban Missile Crisis of 1962. President Ford largely ignored Latin America in his autobiography.[1]

Compared to their foreign-policy partner, Nixon and Ford proved concise writers. Henry Kissinger produced a three-volume memoir over two decades that amounted to over 3,800 pages in length. In all three volumes, Kissinger offered lengthy, legalistic defenses of his role in the overthrow of Allende and the subsequent embrace of the brutal Chilean dictator General Augusto Pinochet (1973–1990). Kissinger's defense could be summarized as, "I was not deeply engaged in Chilean matters." In any case, Kissinger reiterated Nixon's argument that Allende fell because of his own incompetence.[2] The problem for Kissinger was that the last volume of his memoirs was published in 1999, as President Bill Clinton was ordering files on covert U.S. activities in Chile to be opened and before the declassification of the transcripts of Kissinger's telephone conversations on Chile with President Nixon. Both men took credit for Allende's overthrow in an astonishing conversation that mixed talk of the Washington Redskins football team with a celebration of the demise of Chilean constitutionalism and democracy.[3]

Beyond Chile, Kissinger had nothing to say of significance about Latin America until his last volume, when he devoted eighty-five pages of text to the region. His approach was selective. He skipped his role in orchestrating the overthrow of the Bolivian government of Juan José Torres in 1971 and the implicit approval he offered in 1976 to the Argentine military's plan to carry out wholesale murder against political leftists. He thought, however, that by "Latin American standards," Brazil's military rulers were "remarkably benign." He made the factually incorrect statement that in Brazil "the opposition went into exile, rather than to prison or death."[4] Kissinger had received in April 1974 a top-secret report from the director of the Central Intelligence Agency (CIA) that revealed that Brazilian presidents authorized the summary execution of political prisoners.[5] On the other hand, Kissinger did not take credit in his memoirs

A jovial Secretary of State Henry A. Kissinger in Mexico City in 1976. Kissinger enjoyed interacting with Latin Americans and had many Mexican friends. He especially liked to relax in Acapulco. United States Information Services (USIS) photo.

for his successful negotiations with Mexico, Peru, and Ecuador over challenging treaty, trade, and investment issues, and he was modest about his role in negotiating a treaty to transfer sovereignty of the Panama Canal back to Panama. Perhaps the most intriguing assertion in Kissinger's memoirs was his self-discovery that he grew fond of Latin Americans and that he received "warmth and affection [he didn't] get anyplace else—including Europe."[6]

The documentary record sustains the finding that Henry Kissinger directed inter-American relations between 1969 and 1977. Scholars have long noted the irony that the secretive Nixon-Kissinger team was more open to study than previous governments. For three years, President Nixon taped his conversations with administration officials in various settings in the White House. Scholars have had available to them the 3,700 hours of the "White House Tapes." Kissinger further aided scholars by ordering aides to listen in and transcribe 15,000 of his telephone conversations. His conversations have been placed on the internet and are easily accessible through search engines. In recent years, the Historical Office of the Department of State has released perhaps 10,000 documents on inter-American relations during the Kissinger years in its prestigious *Foreign Relations of the United States (FRUS)* series. The Historical Office also produced separate volumes for 1969 to 1977 on U.S. relations with Chile and negotiations with Panama over the canal. In 2016, the CIA released the "President's Daily Briefs" (PDBs), some 2,500 documents, for the Nixon-Ford years. These were intelligence briefings on key international developments that the two presidents received on a daily basis. Kissinger claimed in his memoirs that the Nixon administration rarely focused on Allende's Chile. The PDBs demonstrate that Nixon received approximately 300 briefings on Chile from the CIA. Finally, President Barack Obama emulated Clinton's action on Chilean records, ordering the declassification of U.S. documents related to human rights abuses committed in Argentina during the military dictatorship. In April 2017, President Trump presented documents to Argentine President Mauricio Macri, who was on an official visit to Washington, DC. Vice President Joseph R. Biden Jr. had previously carried documents on U.S. knowledge of torture in Brazil to Brasília and presented them to President Dilma Rousseff.

Compared to the records of previous presidential administrations, the records for the Kissinger years are extraordinary. Kissinger ordered aides, such as Peter Rodman, to prepare verbatim accounts of his conversations with Latin American officials or his unfettered debates at the National Security Council (NSC). State Department and NSC records typically are summaries of discussions and are characterized by dry, bureaucratic language. But Kissinger's memorandums of conversations contain frank, even raw language and indicate when Kissinger raised his voice in anger. His endless jokes and jests, some of which are hilarious and others of which are grubby and mean, are also recorded. More important, the records demonstrate that Kissinger dominated the making of policy with Latin America, especially after he became secretary of state and after Gerald Ford became president. His legendary work ethic is on display in these records. He often spent two hours with individual Latin American foreign ministers in discussions on bilateral issues. By comparison, his notable predecessors—Dean Acheson, John Foster Dulles, Dean Rusk—assigned their assistant secretaries the duty of consulting with Latin American officials. He traveled to Latin America more often than his predecessors, and he sat though sessions of inter-American conclaves such as those in Mexico City (1974) and Santiago (1976). Secretary of State Dulles insulted Latin Americans by immediately leaving an inter-American conference in Caracas (1954) after he had obtained an anticommunist resolution aimed at Guatemala and President Jacobo Arbenz Guzmán (1950–1954). Kissinger remarkably stayed overnight at the residences of Latin American leaders. After his February 1976 visit at the country home of Alfonso López Michelsen (1974–1978), the erudite president of Colombia, Kissinger reported that he had "long philosophical talks" in the evening and morning. He continued: "I confess I rather like it this way, particularly when the talks are with someone as acute as President López."[7]

Like his predecessors, Kissinger judged relations with Western Europe, the Soviet Union, and China as strategically more important than relations with Latin America. And like Dean Rusk, he was consumed by the war in Vietnam. But Kissinger launched noteworthy initiatives, such as the attempt to normalize relations with Cuba and to transfer the canal to Panama. The Kissinger years were also historically significant for Latin Americans. Constitutional rule in South America had been under assault in the 1960s. In January 1969, Chile, Colombia, Ecuador, Uruguay, and Venezuela retained constitutional systems. But the Brazilian military's overthrow of President João Goulart (1961–1964) had established a dangerous precedent in the region. In 1969, military men ruled in Argentina, Bolivia, Brazil, Paraguay, and Peru. The right-wing military dictatorships in Brazil and Paraguay were especially repressive. The Argentine military permitted a democratic election in 1973. The newest military dictators were in Peru, where left-wing military officers seized power at the end of 1968. By January 1977, only Colombia and Venezuela had constitutional governments. The 1970s represented the most violent period in the history of post-independence (1825) South America. Argentina's military rulers, who again seized power in March 1976, set a goal of murdering 50,000 citizens. Uruguay, traditionally a placid and stable land, had more political prisoners on a per capita basis than any other nation in the world. Future democratic leaders—Michelle Bachelet of Chile, José Mujica of Uruguay, Dilma Rousseff of Brazil—were subjected to torture and abuse at the hands of military thugs. Central America was also descending into the chaos and violence. Widespread resistance followed Anastasio Somoza Debayle's rigging of an election in 1972 designed to perpetuate the Somoza family dynasty in Nicaragua. The Sandinista movement would feed on this discontent and triumph in 1979. In Guatemala, where political violence had reigned since the CIA's 1954 covert intervention against the Arbenz government, military rulers intensified the horror, sponsoring right-wing death squads that assassinated members of the democratic opposition.

In the case of Guatemala, Kissinger, then the national security adviser, ruled in 1971 that there would be no discussion of curtailing covert assistance to the regime of Carlos Arana Osorio (1970–1974), even though both aides and the CIA had informed Kissinger that President Arana directly participated in the drawing up of "death lists."[8] U.S. complicity in the political violence in Guatemala points to the reality that any discussion of Kissinger and Latin America inevitably raises the "war criminal" allegation that has dogged him for decades. In 2001, while staying at the Ritz Hotel in Paris, he received a summons to appear before Judge Roger Le Loire to answer questions about his knowledge of "Operation Condor," an international assassination project, and about five French nationals who had disappeared in Chile under General Pinochet. Kissinger ignored the summons and immediately left France. A Chilean court asked Kissinger for help in the cases of two "missing" U.S. citizens, Charles Horman and Frank Teruggi. The two men were the subjects of the award-winning film *Missing* (1982), starring Jack Lemmon and Sissy Spacek and directed by Costa-Gavras. Jurists in Spain, Argentina, and Uruguay also wanted to speak to Kissinger. Kissinger's lawyers responded to international jurists by noting that the former secretary of state wanted to be helpful but that his memory of events in the 1970s in South America was dim.[9]

Although the aged Kissinger no longer traveled extensively, an appearance by him in the Southern Cone countries of Argentina, Brazil, Chile, and Uruguay in the twenty-first century would unquestionably spark popular demonstrations and demands that the government detain him. The four countries, especially Argentina, have prosecuted war criminals who terrorized their respective populations in the 1970s. In 2010, Argentina sentenced General Jorge Rafael Videla (1976–1981) to life imprisonment for murder and the systematic kidnapping of children. Argentines bitterly recall that Kissinger came to Argentina in 1978 to attend the World Cup soccer tournament. President Videla escorted Kissinger, and Kissinger warmly praised the dictator. During the so-called dirty war (*la guerra sucia*), which started in 1976 and lasted until 1983, the Argentine military murdered 30,000 Argentines. Military officers also "appropriated" 500 children from their murdered parents. Argentine Jews disproportionately suffered at the hands of the military. In 1976, Kissinger was informed by the U.S. embassy in Buenos Aires and his staff that the military was targeting Argentina's Jewish population, "with anti-Semitic fury by defiant local Nazis, apparently with policy connections and even some official tolerance."[10]

An analysis of Kissinger and Latin America requires scholarly balance. I have learned through my teaching experience at universities in Argentina, Brazil, Colombia, and Ecuador that the very mention of Henry Kissinger's name agitates Latin Americans. Latin Americans hold Kissinger responsible for the tragedy of Chile. In a lecture in November 2016 at the Universidad Nacional in Bogotá, I suggested that Kissinger often backed Latin American countries in disputes with U.S. corporations. He judged, for example, that the International Petroleum Corporation, a subsidiary of Standard Oil of New Jersey, had violated standard business practices during its time in Peru. While in Lima in 1976, Kissinger informed Peruvian officials that economic issues should not disrupt relations between governments. He added, "I do not like us to act as lawyers for private companies."[11] Such information prompted an able Colombian graduate student to remark that Kissinger must be "schizophrenic." Harsh assessments of Kissinger are not limited to educated Latin Americans. Colleagues who teach Latin American history in the United States have told me at scholarly conferences that they could not study Kissinger and Latin America with detachment.

Both Kissinger's contested reputation and his importance to the history of the Western Hemisphere provide the most compelling answers to the question "Why write a book about Kissinger and Latin America?" The recent declassification of U.S. documents allows for a comprehensive investigation of the foreign policies of the Nixon and Ford administrations toward Latin America and Kissinger's central role in formulating and implementing those policies.

Kissinger Historiography

An examination of Kissinger and Latin America must be grounded in the copious Kissinger literature. Jussi Hanhimäki coined the term "Kissingerology" to label the historiography of the Kissinger years. Studies of Kissinger tended to break two ways. Authors either focused on "Dr. Kissinger," the erudite, skilled practitioner of diplomacy, realpolitik, and détente, or on "Mr. Henry," the devious, power-hungry war criminal. Kissinger was the "most admired and hated" diplomat in U.S. history.[12] Respected scholar Barbara Keys bluntly characterized the debate as "the Kissinger wars: the high-stakes contest over how to appraise the record of America's most controversial statesman."[13] In his magisterial study *The Flawed Architect*, Hanhimäki tried to break out of the intellectual straitjacket. Kissinger had significant triumphs in managing the Soviet-American relationship and working to reduce the chances of nuclear conflict. But Kissinger's belief in the centrality of bilateral Soviet-American relations blinded him to Third World issues and left him "too willing to view them as mere test cases for the 'rules' of Soviet-American détente." Kissinger's and Nixon's overreaction to the election of Salvador Allende was an example of this traditional "Cold War logic." In attacking Allende, Kissinger and Nixon had carried on the policies of the Eisenhower, Kennedy, and Johnson administrations when they perceived leftist movements in Guatemala, British Guiana, or Brazil as existential threats to U.S. national security. Hanhimäki hoped that future scholars would understand that if Kissinger was a war criminal, most foreign-policy makers in the Cold War were criminals. Hanhimäki pleaded for scholars to place Kissinger in historical context and analyze why U.S. officials failed "to grasp the intrinsic significance of local and regional circumstances to the unfolding of the Cold War." Hanhimäki conceded, however, that future research on Kissinger's policies toward Africa, the Middle East, and Latin America would inevitably highlight the dark "Mr. Henry" side of Kissinger.[14]

Mario Del Pero, Walter Isaacson, Jeremi Suri, and Niall Ferguson among others have offered Dr. Kissinger–style interpretations. Taking a European perspective, Del Pero dubbed Kissinger an "eccentric realist." Like Hanhimäki, he credited Kissinger for the opening to China, détente, and ending the war in Vietnam. Kissinger also understood "realism" in international relations— "being cognizant of power realities, the unalterable features of the international system, the rules and practices of such a system, and placing the national interest above any other concern." But Kissinger's realism "lacked, ultimately, the necessary dose of realism." Del Pero agreed with Hanhimäki that Kissinger adhered to a "rigid bipolarism." He interpreted the growth of leftist political movements in Portugal and Italy as gains for the Soviet Union and the international communist movement. The "entirely bipolar horizon" of his thoughts and policies led to intervention in Chile. Kissinger often spoke of practicing a "nuanced" foreign policy but rarely followed his own dictum.[15]

The journalist Walter Isaacson penned in 1992 a popular and compelling biography of Kissinger that was reissued in 2005 with a new introduction. Isaacson had special access to Kissinger but fell out of the diplomat's good graces because of his critical approach. Kissinger cared "obsessively" about his public standing. Like Hanhimäki and Del Pero, Isaacson pointed to a tragic flaw in Kissinger's diplomacy. His substantial achievement of triangular diplomacy with the Soviet Union and China was undermined by his fondness for secrecy. The public came to doubt Kissinger's diplomacy. Kissinger had fallen under Nixon's "dark" tutelage. The two men distrusted the national security bureaucracy, Congress, and the public. They conducted international relations through "back channels," more because "it suited their personalities than because it suited the security interests of the nation." The two had "a romantic view of themselves as loners." Knowledge was power, and power was not to be shared. In the view of veteran diplomat and future secretary of state Lawrence Eagleburger, Kissinger and Nixon took "a conspiratorial approach to foreign-policy management."[16] The back channel that Kissinger established in early 1969 with Ambassador Anatoli Dobrynin of the Soviet Union became well known. Nixon also ordered Kissinger in 1971 to establish a back channel with Emílio Garrastazú Médici (1969–1974). Nixon and Kissinger preferred that the Brazilian president take the lead in destabilizing governments in Bolivia, Chile, and Uruguay and keep the United States' hand hidden.[17]

Jeremi Suri presented a unique interpretation within the "Dr. Kissinger" framework. Suri judged Kissinger "a good man" who believed in the moral significance of his adopted country. Kissinger had witnessed the collapse of democracies in Europe during World War II. The Jewish Kissinger and his family had fled the Nazi menace, and Kissinger had returned to war-torn Europe as a soldier in the U.S. Army. Suri theorized that Jewish immigrants endorsed the preservation U.S. power, because a formidable United States would protect them from the hatred and violence they had suffered in Europe. In Kissinger's words, he "had seen evil in the world," and this historical experience led him to believe "that there are some things you have to fight for, and that you can't insist that everything be to some ideal construction you have made." Suri agreed that Kissinger "entered politics for moral reasons, and he worked feverishly to make the world better." Kissinger believed that he acted within the bounds of a moral compass, although he declined to elaborate on his moral principles in interviews with Suri. Although sympathetic to Kissinger, Suri conceded that Kissinger's diplomacy "did not always contribute to the world of greater freedom and justice." Suri absolved Nixon and Kissinger from orchestrating the overthrow of Allende, but the two "did encourage and facilitate" the action. To his credit, Suri became the first Kissinger scholar to point out that the secretary of state seemed indifferent to mass killings in Argentina in 1976. During the Cold War, most presidential administrations worked with anticommunist dictators. Suri admitted that Kissinger made support for dictators central to U.S. policy.[18]

Compared to Niall Ferguson, Suri had written a critical account of Kissinger's public life. Ferguson's first volume of a projected two-volume study analyzed Kissinger's life from 1923 to 1968. Ferguson argued that in his years as a soldier, student, and university professor, Kissinger had developed a knowledge and philosophy of history that most strategic options involved choosing between greater and lesser evils and that it was an inherently moral act to choose the lesser evil. Scholars had erred in dubbing Kissinger a "realist." Ferguson wrote, "In aspiring to loftier ends, I believe the young Kissinger was indeed an idealist." Although focusing on Kissinger's intellectual, moral, and philosophical development, Ferguson took on with relish the "war criminal" thesis both in his opening chapter and in response to reviews of his book. If Kissinger acted criminally, so too did Eisenhower and Dulles when they attacked Guatemala in 1954. Guatemalan security forces murdered at least 200,000 people over the next four decades. General Pinochet presided over the murder of only 3,279 Chileans. Perhaps Ferguson might have elaborated that the Pinochet regime tortured 100,000 Chileans and forced 200,000 into exile, a staggering number of victims in a country of 10 million. Kissinger chose to confront the "hostile and heavily armed" Soviet Union, Marxism-Leninism, and the international communist movement—the transcendent evils. In any case, Ferguson continued, "arguments that focus on loss of life in strategically marginal countries—and there is no other way of describing Argentina, Bangladesh, Cambodia, Chile, Cyprus, East Timor—must be tested against this question: how, in each case, would an alternate decision have affected U.S. relations with strategically important countries like the Soviet Union, China, and the major Western European powers?"[19] An Argentine *abuela* (grandmother) whose pregnant daughter was slaughtered after giving birth and still searches for her now middle-aged *apropriado* (appropriated) grandchild might object to Ferguson's prioritizing scheme. So too, an Argentine Jew, if he had survived, might wonder why his humiliation, which included having swastikas painted on his back and being forced to say, "Heil Hitler," facilitated Cold War victory. Military thugs saved the cruelest form of death for Argentine Jews—using a recto scope to release a rat in an anus or vagina. The rat would eat his way through the person's organs seeking escape. The "idealistic" Kissinger averted his eyes from what scholars have labeled "genocide."[20]

In quantity, if not quality, most Kissinger studies have been on the "Mr. Henry" side of the equation. John Lee Anderson, Gary J. Bass, Robert K. Brigham, Robert Dallek, Ariel Dorfman, Greg Grandin, Seymour Hersh, Christopher Hitchens, Barbara Keys, Tim Naftali, and a plethora of historians of twentieth-century Latin America have written critical studies of various intensities on Kissinger. An exploration of the ideas of Hitchens, Bass, and Grandin can serve as a representative sample. Perhaps the most influential of the "Mr. Henry" books has been Hitchens's *The Trial of Henry Kissinger*. In a relentless style, Hitchens indicted Kissinger for war crimes in Bangladesh, Chile, Cyprus, East Timor, and Indochina. Hitchens held Kissinger responsible for the assassination of General René Schneider, the top Chilean military officer who opposed subverting the Chilean constitution to prevent Allende from becoming president in 1970. In Hitchens's words, Kissinger had engaged in "the personal suborning and planning of murder, of a senior constitutional officer in a democratic nation—Chile—with which the United States was not at war." In the Chilean case, Kissinger displayed his "contempt for democracy."[21] Thoughtful scholars such as Hanhimäki preferred to say that Kissinger was guilty of the crime of "short-sighted" policies for viewing local and regional developments within the prism of the Soviet-American confrontation. But as indicated by Ferguson's lecture on the strategic irrelevance of Argentina and Chile, every Kissinger scholar has seemed obligated to respond to Hitchens.

Hitchens could not have chosen a more effective prosecuting attorney than Gary Bass. His book on Nixon and Kissinger's roles in the "forgotten genocide" in Bangladesh (East Pakistan) in 1971 has garnered acclaim and book prizes. On 28 March 1971, the U.S. consul in Dacca, Archer Blood, went outside the normal chain of command in sending an extraordinary cable to Washington with the subject line "Selective Genocide." The Pakistani government in Islamabad had cracked down on its restive Bengali population, targeting the Hindu minority and killing 200,000 people. Another ten million people fled to India. For both strategic and humanitarian reasons, India, led by Indira Gandhi, went to war in December 1971 against Pakistan to save the people of Bangladesh. Most global citizens applauded Prime Minister Gandhi's rescue mission. Nixon and Kissinger, however, downplayed the horrific events in Bangladesh, trashed the career of Consul Blood, and secretly and illegally armed Pakistan. The U.S. leaders had a visceral dislike of Indians and spoke of their prime minister as a "bitch" and an "old witch." Presumably, the administration's "moral" choice of the lesser of two evils was to preserve the balance of power. Pakistan was allied with the United States and opposed both India and its patron, the Soviet Union. Pakistan had also aided the Nixon administration in its opening toward China. In Bass's judgment, Nixon and Kissinger bore "responsibility for significant complicity in the slaughter of the Bengalis." Their "biggest success" in promoting themselves as "heroes" of diplomacy "has been the historical oblivion that surrounds the killing campaign in Bangladesh."[22]

Greg Grandin has also taken on the role of informing the public of Kissinger's perfidy. In *Kissinger's Shadow*, he argued that Kissinger had remained influential within the universe of conservative policy makers. Kissinger's "long reach" included providing the intellectual justification for the invasion of Iraq in 2003. Kissinger's philosophy of history was that "risk is a requirement of real statesmanship, that initiative creates its own reality, and that political leaders shouldn't wait on facts to seize the initiative." The United States would create its own reality when it overthrew Saddam Hussein.[23] It mattered not whether weapons of mass destruction existed in Iraq. Whereas it might be problematic to reason that the George W. Bush administration thought deeply about Kissinger's ideas, Grandin's analysis of Kissinger's sway demonstrated the intensity of disdain that Kissinger engendered among scholars. Barbara Keys characterized Grandin as the standard bearer for the "Kissinger-as-evil-mastermind camp."[24] Grandin, who served as a consultant to Guatemala's Historical Clarification Commission, the international body that investigated the abuses of human rights in Guatemala from 1954 to 1996, included a brief, damning section on Kissinger and Latin America in *Kissinger's Shadow*.

Although Kissinger's career has generated an enormous scholarly output, Kissinger served under Presidents Richard Nixon and Gerald Ford. Yet historians have focused on Kissinger, because his relationships with his bosses were peculiar. Nixon and Kissinger took pains in their respective memoirs to portray themselves as the sole architect of U.S. foreign policy and to downplay the other's contribution. Listening to the two men talk on tape has led analysts to offer nuanced interpretations of the relationship. Kissinger endlessly and unctuously flattered Nixon. Nixon, on the other hand, used Kissinger as a sounding board for some of his bizarre ideas. As Suri put it, "In his daily behavior and rhetoric, Nixon acted more like a gangster than a statesman."[25] Douglas Brinkley and Luke Nichter, who edited two volumes of the Nixon tapes, agreed that "Nixon was a ruthless political operator."[26] They emphasized, however, that Nixon kept full control of the White House's foreign-policy agenda. Studies by John A. Farrell and Tim Weiner on Nixon have tended to second the findings of Brinkley and Nichter.[27] Suri took a distinctive approach, suggesting that Kissinger tied himself to Nixon, because "he could never escape the nightmare of anti-Semitism." He sought the protection of a powerful figure because he feared losing everything, even as he endured Nixon's anti-Semitic rants.[28] Presidential historian Robert Dallek conversely saw the men as "partners in power," with Kissinger serving as "a kind of co-president." Dallek asserted that the two men "had few qualms about making a bargain with the devil."[29] Tom Blanton agreed, characterizing the relationship as "the gangster den."[30] In his review of the relationship, Robert Schulzinger resorted to popular psychology, using terms like "exceptionally needy" and "complex co-dependency." Nixon and Kissinger developed a bunker mentality, perceiving that they were surrounded by adversaries, enemies, fools, and knaves.[31]

Whereas Nixon and Kissinger may have clung to one another, it did not signify that they admired one another. In his memoirs, Nixon cited Secretary of State William Rogers's judgment that Kissinger was "Machiavellian, deceitful, egotistical, arrogant, and insulting." Nixon did not dispute Rogers's analysis of Kissinger. He also disparaged Kissinger in conversations with White House Chief of Staff H. R. Haldeman. Kissinger "is a terribly difficult individual to have around," Nixon lamented. He wanted to be national security adviser, secretary of state, and de facto secretary of defense. Kissinger would become "a dictator." Kissinger had a "personality thing." For his part, Kissinger disparaged Nixon's stability in telephone conversations with Rogers and Secretary of Defense Melvin R. Laird, noting the president's penchant for wanting to bomb countries on the flimsiest of pretexts. Kissinger indicated in his memoirs that Nixon was obsessed with Chile and Cuba. In a telephone conversation with Kissinger, Nixon sustained that judgment. He told Kissinger, "Probably only you know how strongly I feel about the Cuban business." The president promised to write "an eyes only" memorandum for Kissinger on Cuba and Allende's Chile, explaining, "so you will know in the future how far I am willing to go."[32]

Kissinger's thirty-month relationship with Gerald Ford has not been the subject of psychological analysis. President Ford relied on Kissinger for foreign policy and strategy, accepting Nixon's recommendation that Kissinger was "absolutely indispensable." Although loyal to Kissinger, Ford ordered Kissinger to relinquish his national security adviser position when, in November 1975, he carried out a major restructuring of his cabinet. Ford believed he needed to strengthen his position with political conservatives. Governor Ronald Reagan of California, who challenged Ford for the Republican presidential nomination in 1976, criticized Kissinger for both his détente policies with the Soviet Union and for negotiating over the future status of the Panama Canal.[33] Kissinger offered respectful comments about Ford in his memoirs. He claimed that "I was close to the president," that there was "a mood of mutual confidence," and that their interactions were "cordial and businesslike." He further noted that Ford detested gossip; Kissinger and Nixon had gossiped endlessly. In private, Kissinger may have taken a different tone toward his boss. Joseph Sisco, a friend and adviser to Kissinger on the Middle East, remembered that Kissinger judged Ford "a decent man, but he did not give him very high grades intellectually."[34] When Ford assumed office in August 1974, Kissinger told him not to be just a caretaker but to run for the presidency in 1976. Kissinger had confidence that a victorious President Ford would keep him on as secretary of state. Kissinger informed Latin Americans that he planned to shepherd a new treaty with Panama through Congress in 1977.

Declassified records demonstrate that Kissinger had more freedom to conduct policy with Latin America under Ford than under Nixon. But Kissinger had his way in both administrations. Nixon deemed himself an expert on global affairs, and he issued directives on Latin American policy. Both as national security adviser and later as secretary of state, Kissinger had little trouble with Nixon's dictums. Neither man cared whether democrats or military dictators ruled in individual countries. They cared about fighting communism. Kissinger's hatred of Salvador Allende may have surpassed that of Nixon's. Nixon reflexively defended U.S. multinational corporations in Latin America. On investment, trade, and treaty issues, Kissinger temporized, even circumvented, Nixon's harsh views through all manners of diplomatic subtleties. Nixon had a visceral hatred of Fidel Castro, and these feelings slowed Kissinger's desire to explore an accommodation with Cuba. Once Ford assumed office, Kissinger took complete charge of inter-American relations, including contacting Cubans. Ford confined himself to hosting pleasant Oval Office meetings with visiting Latin American officials. Ford interjected himself only in relations with the oil-producing nation of Venezuela. He pleaded with President Carlos Andrés Pérez to use his influence within the Organization of Petroleum Counties (OPEC) to moderate oil prices.[35] High gasoline and fuel oil prices in the United States were jeopardizing President Ford's electoral prospects.

The lack of access to the archival record had kept scholars from exploring the topic of Kissinger and Latin America. As Mark Atwood Lawrence lamented in a bibliographic essay, no book directly addressed inter-American issues between 1969 and 1977.[36] In 1988, political scientist Michael J. Francis wrote a sound article that surveyed Kissinger's approach to the region. He concluded that the Nixon and Ford administrations wanted to accommodate Latin Americans on nonstrategic issues. But if the issue was perceived as having Cold War significance, then Kissinger and his presidents "were willing to play very rough." The attack on Allende and the subsequent U.S. support for General Pinochet proved that point. Francis concluded, however, that Nixon, Ford, and Kissinger displayed "a fundamental lack of interest in Latin America."[37] In preparing his article, Francis had no access to archival materials or primary sources other than congressional hearings conducted in 1975 by Senator Frank Church (D-ID) on the U.S. intervention in Chile.

Both in his bibliographic essay and in an essay in an edited collection on U.S. foreign relations, Lawrence surveyed inter-American relations. Like Francis, he concluded that "Latin America ranked at the bottom" of U.S. global priorities. Lawrence focused on a few flash points—the Soviet submarine base at Cienfuegos, the overthrow of Allende, and Operation Condor, the assassination project of South America's dictators. Lawrence ended his cursory review by noting that scholars needed to move beyond talking about the tragedy of Allende's Chile. Further research would show "that Chile was only the most egregious example of an approach practiced across the hemisphere." Lawrence predicted that with new scrutiny the reputations of Nixon and Kissinger were "likely to sink further still."[38]

As Lawrence indicated, scholars have produced strong analyses of the U.S. intervention in Chile because they have had available to them since 1999 the U.S. archival record. Democratic Chile has also assisted historical research by opening records and conducting public trials of the Pinochet-era abusers of human rights. Tanya Harmer produced in *Allende's Chile and the Inter-American Cold War* an authoritative study that places Chile within an international context. Jonathan Haslam dissected Allende's baffling economic policies that created a sense of crisis within the nation. And Peter Kornbluh of the National Security Archive published documents that contradicted what Kissinger had publicly said and written about his relationship with General Pinochet.[39] Prior to the mass declassification of documents that began in 2015, the National Security Archive used the Freedom of Information Act (FOIA) to release documents on inter-American relations during the Kissinger years. These studies informed bilateral studies on U.S. policies toward Argentina, Brazil, and Cuba.[40]

What retarded studies on U.S. policies toward Latin America from 1969 to 1977 was not solely the incomplete documentary record. Scholars have assumed they would find nothing historically significant if they embarked on a study. Mark Lawrence wrote, for example, that neither Nixon nor Kissinger went south of Mexico. In fact, Secretary of State Kissinger traveled throughout South America. Lawrence and others have also cited the principals' disdain for the region. Nixon declared on tape in 1971 that "the only thing that matters in this world is Japan and China, Russia and Europe."[41] Two years previously, Kissinger had famously told the Chilean foreign minister that "nothing important can come from the South" and that "history has never been produced in the South." He added, "The axis of history starts in Moscow, goes to Bonn, crosses over to Washington, and then goes to Tokyo."[42] Those who have quoted Kissinger have probably not placed his rudeness in context. Kissinger's insult followed a contentious conversation between Foreign Minister Gabriel Valdés and Nixon over foreign aid. In any case, it would be foolish to challenge the conventional wisdom on the foreign policy priorities of the Nixon and Ford administrations. Nonetheless, the two presidential administrations conducted foreign policies in Latin America. The exercise of U.S. power had both positive and dire ramifications for Latin Americans in the 1970s. And in his interactions with Latin American officials, Kissinger perhaps revealed more about his philosophy of government and international relations than he did in either his memoirs or in his interviews with scholars.

Chapter Themes

This book takes a topical approach and does not progress in a strictly chronological manner. Chapter 1 outlines the state of inter-American relations in the middle of the Cold War. President Nixon came to office in 1969 in the aftermath of the Alliance for Progress, the ambitious ten-year, $20 billion economic aid program announced by President Kennedy in March 1961. Richard Nixon had strong views about the shortcomings of the Alliance for Progress. Unlike Kissinger, who had limited familiarity with Latin American thought, culture, and society, Nixon judged himself knowledgeable about Latin America. Nixon directed Kissinger to develop a comprehensive review of the U.S. policies toward Latin America. Kissinger threw himself into the exercise with enthusiasm, perceiving the review of trade, investment, aid, and security issues as a learning experience. Nixon also dispatched his political rival and Kissinger's mentor, Governor Nelson Rockefeller (R-NY), on a fact-finding mission to Latin America.[43]

The first crisis for the new administration came with the news that leftist Salvador Allende had captured a plurality of the vote in the September 1970 presidential election. Chapter 2 reviews the U.S. role in destabilizing the Allende government. The historical literature tends to give scant attention to the United States and Chile after 11 September 1973. To recount the complete story about the U.S. role in Chile demands investigating not only the war against Allende but also the myriad of ways that the Nixon and Ford administrations and Secretary of State Kissinger bolstered the Pinochet dictatorship. Chapter 2 also analyzes Kissinger's lead role in encouraging the overthrow of President Juan José Torres (1970–1971), the socialist political and military leader of Bolivia.

Torres's overthrow leads to a discussion of Kissinger's relationship with military dictatorships. In Chapter 3, U.S. policies toward Paraguay, Brazil, and Uruguay are analyzed. What is evident is that the secretary of state was comfortable and loquacious in the presence of men who authorized mass murder, torture, and terrorism. His most revealing memorandums of conversations on political philosophy are with military dictators and their minions.

Argentina emulated its South American neighbors when the military seized power in March 1976. Argentina's military rulers thought it would be in the nation's best interest to eliminate 50,000 Argentines. Secretary Kissinger was made aware of the Argentine military's campaign of murder by U.S. officials in Washington and Buenos Aires. His aides further warned him that Argentina's murderers and torturers targeted Argentina's Jewish population. Chapter 4 further examines Secretary Kissinger's response to Operation Condor, a conspiracy of South American military dictatorships that perpetrated international assassinations and terrorism.

Chapter 5 shifts the focus from South America and explores U.S. relations with Central America during the Kissinger years. In the 1980s, civil wars in El Salvador, Nicaragua, and Guatemala frightened the Reagan administration into reasoning that the Cold War had come to the doorstep of the United States. The civil wars in El Salvador and Nicaragua erupted during Kissinger's tenure (in 1972 and 1974, respectively). Wholesale political violence carried out by "death squads" continued to characterize life in Guatemala in the 1970s. Examining the U.S. response to the mounting right-wing oppression in Central America provides historical background to the crisis of the 1980s and deepens an understanding of Kissinger's worldviews. Whereas Kissinger may have been impervious to Central American violence, he acted boldly toward Panama, pushing both of his presidents to renegotiate U.S. control of the canal and the Canal Zone.

Security concerns did not always dominate Kissinger's approach to relations with Latin America in the 1970s. Chapter 6 demonstrates that Kissinger engaged in resolving inter-American trade, investment, and treaty disputes. He responded imaginatively to Latin American grievances over water rights, tuna fishing, multinational corporations, and oil prices.

The last chapter examines two major initiatives of Kissinger that ended in failure. Kissinger proved amenable to discussing reforms to the international economic order but abruptly concluded that such hemispheric discussions shifted the balance of power against the United States. He also worked on a plan to break out of the diplomatic stalemate with Fidel Castro's Cuba. He reasoned that if the United States could open a relationship with the People's Republic of China, it could also do so with communist Cuba. Kissinger believed, however, that Cuba had to accept a subordinate position in the global order. Fidel Castro declined to become subservient to the United States.

The concluding section of the book offers a judgment of Kissinger in Latin America. The customary approach for historians is to ask first the "change and continuity" question. Scholars sympathetic to Kissinger were troubled by Kissinger's actions in Latin America and fell back on the argument that his policies were no different than those of his predecessors or successors. Critical scholars assumed that Kissinger's actions in Chile and throughout Latin America were unprecedented in their depravity. What cannot be ignored is that the gross violation of human rights that marked life in the 1970s was unprecedented in the history of Latin America in the national period. Responsibility for the murders, disappearances, and tortures must be assigned.

The assessment of the thoughts and policies of Henry A. Kissinger toward Latin America will also add to prevailing historiography or "Kissingerology." Kissinger pointed to the "warmth and affection" that he received from Latin Americans. Perhaps this sense of well-being and comradery led Kissinger to be remarkably candid about his philosophy of life, government, and international relations in his extended conversations with Latin American democrats and dictators.

CHAPTER 1

Getting Started

A Year of Study

When it assumed office on 20 January 1969, the Nixon administration had the pressing task of extricating the United States from the debacle of the war in Vietnam. President Nixon and his national security adviser, Henry Kissinger, also wanted to build on the progress that had been made by the previous two presidential administrations on improving relations with the Soviet Union. The new administration seemingly would also embark on new initiatives with Latin America. President Nixon had more experience in inter-American affairs than any of his predecessors in the White House. He ordered Kissinger to conduct a systematic review of inter-American relations. He simultaneously dispatched Governor Nelson A. Rockefeller of New York to conduct a fact-finding mission throughout the region and to present recommendations to him. As revealed in his only major address on inter-American affairs, however, Nixon decided against focusing on relations with Latin America. Only after the Bolivians and Chileans placed leaders in office who challenged U.S. global policies did the Nixon administration, led by Kissinger, demonstrate sustained interest in relations with Latin American nations.

The Alliance That Lost Its Way

In January 1969, in the middle of the Cold War, U.S. policymakers and citizens could have judged relations with the twenty Latin American nations as stable and satisfactory, both from strategic and economic perspectives. Except for Fidel Castro's Cuba, Latin American nations continued to accept U.S. leadership in the confrontation with the Soviet Union. Latin American delegates at international fora such as the United Nations reliably backed U.S. positions on Cold War issues. Even Cuba no longer seemed much of a threat to U.S. hegemony in the region. Dependent on the Soviet Union's economic largess, Castro had acceded to Soviet demands that he give up talk about promoting revolution in Latin America. The communist parties of Latin America similarly followed the cautious line dictated by Moscow.[1]

U.S. traders and investors continued to profit in Latin America. The recovery of Western Europe and Japan under the Marshall Plan and the postwar promotion of global prosperity under the aegis of the World Bank, the International Monetary Fund, and the General Agreement on Tariffs and Trade, the so-called Bretton Woods system, had diminished Latin America's economic importance to the United States. In 1950, for example, trade with Latin America amounted to 29 percent of U.S. trade, and 38 percent of U.S. direct investments were in Latin America. Twenty years later, the global economy had grown enormously. Global trade had increased by more than 400 percent, and U.S. businesspeople conducted much of their trade and investment with the advanced industrial nations. Nonetheless, Latin America remained important to the United States. Trade with Latin America amounted to 13 percent of U.S. trade. U.S. citizens purchased coffee from Brazil and Colombia, raw materials from Mexico, and fuel oil from Venezuela. The United States had a healthy surplus of trade with Latin America, even as balance-of-trade deficits were increasingly characterizing U.S. trade with other regions of the world. The value of U.S. direct investments in Latin America nearly tripled from 1950 to 1970, although they now represented 16 percent of U.S. investments. U.S. companies had $2.6 billion invested in Venezuela, principally in oil production.[2]

In 1969, Latin Americans did not share the same favorable assessment of the state of relations within the Western Hemisphere. Latin Americans called for a new international economic order, pointing to sluggish economic growth and declining terms of trade. In May 1969, delegates at an inter–Latin American conclave, held at a seaside resort in Chile, produced the "Consensus of Viña del Mar." Latin Americans called for "a fairer international division of labor that will favor the rapid economic and social development of the developing countries, instead of impeding it as has been the case hitherto." Inherent in that language was the conviction among Latin Americans that the international economy worked against them. Their export-oriented economies depended on the sale of primary food products and raw materials. But throughout the 1960s, the prices they received for their coffee, cacao, lead, zinc, copper, and oil stagnated or even declined. The price of oil, for example, fell from $2.35 a barrel in 1957 to $1.81 in 1969.[3] Latin American economies grew at a measly rate of less than 2 percent a year in the 1960s. The impoverished majority of the population in countries such as Haiti, Honduras, Nicaragua, Bolivia, and Paraguay lived outside of a cash economy. The relatively wealthy Latin American country of Argentina had a gross domestic product (GDP) per capita of $1,323 in 1969. By comparison, the GDP per capita in the United States was $4,803. Rapid population growth compounded the problems of poverty. The population of the twenty countries in Latin America rose from 218 million to 285 million in the 1960s. Brazil's population rose from 70 million to 95 million, with the largest increase in the desperately poor northeastern region of the country.[4]

Latin Americans would not have been expressing dismay in 1969 if Latin America's political and economic history had followed the plans of the Kennedy administration. On 13 March 1961, less than two months after his inauguration, President Kennedy announced a grandiose plan for Latin America's socioeconomic development, the Alliance for Progress. The United States would replay the success of the past; it would now have a "Marshall Plan for Latin America." The United States would provide $20 billion in economic aid to the region. Combined with an expected $80 billion in internal investment, Latin America would reach the "take-off" stage for self-sustaining growth, as outlined in Walt Whitman Rostow's influential treatise *The Stages of Economic Growth: A Non-Communist Manifesto* (1960). The 1960s would be "the decade of development." Kennedy administration officials opined that the region was "set for miracles." U.S economic aid would spur an annual economic growth of 2.5 percent a year. Administration officials posted a readily attainable growth rate; they privately expected a much higher annual growth rate. Socioeconomic advancement would follow economic growth. Rural citizens would have access to potable water, and their children would attend school. In the words of Teodoro Moscoso, an administrator of the Alliance for Progress, the United States was determined to undermine the status quo "of a society made up of the few who have much and the many who have little."[5]

In an article penned in 1967 in the establishment journal *Foreign Affairs*, President Eduardo Frei Montalva of Chile highlighted how the Alliance for Progress "lost its way."[6] Alliance planners had enumerated ninety-four goals to mark progress in Latin America. None were attained. The Alliance made imperceptible progress in achieving its objectives of adding five years to life expectancy, halving the infant mortality rate, eliminating adult illiteracy, and providing access to six years of primary education for every school-age child. During the 1960s, the number of unemployed Latin Americans actually rose from 18 million to 25 million, and agricultural production per person declined. More than half of the population of the region continued to live on an annual per capita income of $120. Only in three democratic countries—Colombia, Costa Rica, and Venezuela—could measurable socioeconomic progress be found.[7]

The Alliance failed for a myriad of reasons. Latin America had formidable obstacles to change. Elites resisted land reform, equitable tax systems, and social programs that changed the balance of power in communities. The declining terms of trade undercut socioeconomic progress. In Chile, for example, President Frei of the Christian Democratic Party used his Alliance money wisely, resettling 27,000 families on their own farms and building 400,000 homes for low-income Chileans. But Frei had counted on having more financial resources based on a rising Chilean economy. The price of copper, Chile's major export, fluctuated wildly in the 1960s. Between 1966 and 1970, the Chilean economy grew at an annual rate of only 1.3 percent. The Marshall Plan experience also served as a poor guide to solving the problems of a region that was far different from Western Europe and Japan. Europeans and the Japanese had the requisite education, skills, and social order to operate a "modernized" society and economy. They needed U.S. money to "rebuild" after the devastation of World War II. In his last address on inter-American affairs, President Kennedy conceded that the Marshall Plan analogy did not work for Latin America. What was required in Latin America was "to create a basic new foundation, capable of re-shaping the centuries-old societies and economies of half of a hemisphere."[8]

President Kennedy was sensitive to misery and injustice in Latin America. But the Alliance for Progress was rooted in national security concerns. Kennedy often dubbed the region as "the most dangerous area in the world."[9] The years between 1958 and 1964 were the crisis years in inter-American relations. U.S. leaders persuaded themselves that the Soviet Union's master plan for global domination now included Latin America. Until 1958, President Dwight Eisenhower gave his secretary of state, John Foster Dulles, primary responsibility for inter-American affairs. Dulles was content to bolster Latin American tyrants who professed to be anticommunist. The Eisenhower administration awarded the Legion of Merit, the nation's highest award for foreign personages, to Manuel Odría of Peru (1948–1956) and Marcos Pérez Jiménez of Venezuela (1952–1958), two of the region's most odious military dictators. President Eisenhower denied that the United States had given up on democracy and constitutionalism in Latin America. In 1955 at an NSC meeting, he rebuked Treasury Secretary George Humphrey for arguing that dictatorship in Latin America was in the best interests of the United States. Eisenhower pointed out to NSC members that he "firmly believed that if power lies with the people, then there will be no aggressive war."[10] Nonetheless, Eisenhower authorized the CIA to destabilize the constitutional president of Guatemala, Jacobo Arbenz Guzmán. Eisenhower and Dulles judged that President Arbenz was a communist, soft on communism, or blind to the communist conspiracy. After President Arbenz fled the country in June 1954, U.S. intelligence agents scoured Guatemalan archives looking for evidence of a communist conspiracy. Secretary Dulles especially was disappointed to learn that no Guatemalan leader had any connection to Moscow. The CIA, on the other hand, was so proud of its subversion of Guatemalan constitutionalism that it produced a manual on the operation, which carried the code name "PBSUCCESS."[11] The manual served as a guide for future operations against constitutional governments in British Guiana (Guyana), Brazil, and Salvador Allende's Chile.

The public dismay that followed Vice President Nixon's tumultuous tour of South America in the spring of 1958 led Eisenhower to reassess U.S. policies. South Americans jeered, spit, threw rocks, and attacked Nixon's limousine in the streets of Caracas, because they were furious about the state of inter-American affairs. The United States had reneged on promises made to Latin American allies during World War II to assist their postwar development. The minuscule nations of Belgium, Luxembourg, and the Netherlands received more economic aid from the United States from 1946 to 1958 than did Latin America. That crowds assembled to confront Nixon was a sign of remarkable change within the region. Between 1956 and 1960, ten dictators fell from power in a process journalist Tad Szulc dubbed the "twilight of the tyrants."[12] The protestors knew that the United States had proffered medals and military support to these dictators. In 1955 during a tour of the Caribbean and Central America, the vice president had been photographed embracing Rafael Trujillo (1930–1961), the murderous strongman of the Dominican Republic, and, in a toast in Havana, he compared Fulgencio Batista (1952–1958) to Abraham Lincoln. Once he returned safely back to Washington, Nixon adjusted to the new inter-American realities, proposing a new policy on hugging. Nixon told the public the U.S. approach should hereafter be "a formal handshake for dictators; an *embraso* [sic] for leaders in freedom." Eisenhower accepted Nixon's idea, overruling Dulles who warned Eisenhower that Latin Americans were not prepared for popular rule. The president openly backed the new Venezuelan president, Rómulo Betancourt (1958–1964), and condemned Trujillo for interfering in Venezuelan affairs and attacking Betancourt. The president also persuaded the U.S. Congress in 1960 to put $500 million into the Social Progress Trust Fund to assist socioeconomic development in Latin America.[13]

The catalyst for meaningful change was not, however, unhappy Latin Americans hurling rocks at U.S. officials. The Cuban Revolution led by Fidel Castro would prove to be the momentous event in the history of the Cold War in Latin America. The triumph of Castro's guerrilla army at the beginning of 1959, Castro's increasingly anti-American stance through 1959, his economic opening to the Soviet Union in February 1960, his diplomatic break with the United States in early January 1961, and his pledge at the end of 1961 to follow the dictates of Marxism-Leninism until the day he died created a sense of mounting crisis about inter-American relations. Latin America now seemed ripe for revolution, because the United States had "neglected" the region since 1945. The United States also had pursued the shortsighted policy of supporting despots. Desperate, impoverished, alienated Latin Americans would now entertain the false promises of radical leftists. "Castro-communism" might sweep through the region, tilting the global balance of power toward the Soviet Union. President Eisenhower responded by authorizing in March 1960 a project to overthrow Castro. This planning culminated in the disastrous Bay of Pigs invasion in April 1961 under President Kennedy. Eisenhower had previously told the president-elect that the United States could not live with Castro. Eisenhower simultaneously imbibed in the new wisdom that support for dictators was counterproductive, for it pushed Latin Americans toward extremism. When Trujillo ignored U.S. demands to retreat into exile, the CIA launched plots to assassinate him. On 30 May 1961, Dominican dissidents, who carried weapons supplied by the CIA, ambushed and assassinated Trujillo. Both Eisenhower and Kennedy had a general understanding of the plot.[14]

The Alliance for Progress aimed to undercut the appeals of Castro and communism through socioeconomic development within the framework of democracy. As presidential aide Arthur Schlesinger Jr. put it, the Alliance represented "enlightened anticommunism."[15] President Kennedy accepted the insight that promoting "decent democrats" who carried out land and tax reforms was the most effective way to respond to Fidel Castro. Under the aegis of the Alliance for Progress, between 1961 and 1965 the United States provided Betancourt's Venezuela $340 million in loans and credits to underwrite projects such as building homes for the urban poor. Kennedy also sharply criticized Jorge Alessandri (1958–1964), the conservative, constitutional president of Chile, for ignoring the needs of Chile's poor. Kennedy made no secret of his hope that Eduardo Frei would win Chile's 1964 presidential election. Between 1962 and 1964, the CIA funneled $2 million into campaign coffers of Frei's Christian Democrats. In addition to visiting Venezuela and participating in a land redistribution ceremony there, Kennedy went to Costa Rica and Colombia to demonstrate his support for constitutional leaders committed to progressive change. During the Alliance years, Colombia was the second-highest U.S. aid recipient in Latin America, receiving $762 million. U.S. officials judged that Colombian leaders dedicated U.S. money to worthy development projects.[16]

President Kennedy hedged, however, the U.S. commitment to democracy. He turned against constitutional leaders who did not break with Cuba and join his war against Fidel Castro. Beyond permitting the Bay of Pigs operation to go forward, Kennedy authorized in late 1961 Operation Mongoose, a massive sabotage and terrorist campaign against Cuba run by the CIA from Florida. Assassination plots against Cuban leaders including Castro, which had begun under Eisenhower, continued under Kennedy. Attorney General Robert F. Kennedy, the president's brother, was briefed about the assassination plots. Rómulo Betancourt earned Kennedy's gratitude, because he offered to assist in the assassination of Castro. President Lyndon Johnson eventually shut down the covert war against Castro, concluding that it would not spark a popular uprising against the popular leader. Johnson would later recall in an interview that "we were running a damned Murder Incorporated in the Caribbean."[17]

Latin American democrats who did not share the U.S. obsession with Castro's Cuba found that the Kennedy and Johnson administrations would be indifferent, even hostile, to their political fortunes. President Arturo Frondizi (1958–1962) of Argentina was a constitutional leader who enthusiastically embraced the goals of the Alliance for Progress. But Frondizi maintained relations with Cuba and hosted Che Guevara. On 29 March 1962, the Argentine military physically removed Frondizi from office. Three months previously, Frondizi had complained to President Kennedy in a meeting at the president's vacation home in Palm Beach, Florida, that he suspected the pressure from the armed forces for more emphatic action against Cuba "is accentuated by stimulation [from] US intelligence sources."[18] The Kennedy administration destabilized the government of Guatemala in 1963, because it feared the former president of Guatemala, Juan José Arévalo (1944–1950), would be permitted to run again. The administration also launched a massive covert campaign against another leftist democrat thought soft on Cuba, Prime Minister Cheddi Jagan of British Guiana (1961–1964).[19] Most important, the administration turned against President João Goulart of Brazil (1961–1964), who was thought oblivious to the Castro-communist menace. The CIA ran a destabilization campaign against Goulart based on the Guatemalan model of 1954. In April 1964, the Brazilian military forced Goulart out. The Johnson administration had developed a comprehensive contingency plan to assist the Brazilian military if it encountered resistance. The Brazilian military would hold power for two decades and back U.S. Cold War objectives in Latin America, such as the U.S. invasion of the Dominican Republic in 1965. Authoritarian Brazil was the highest recipient of U.S. economic aid during the Alliance years, receiving $1.833 billion.[20]

The Kennedy administration further qualified its support for democracy in Latin America by enhancing ties with security forces. In the name of "continental defense," the Eisenhower administration had transferred $400 million in heavy military equipment—combat aircraft, warships, tanks—to Latin America during the 1950s. No military analyst expected the Soviet Union to invade the Western Hemisphere. The primary purpose of the aid was to ensure that the United States retained the confidence of the armed forces of Latin America. Even after he announced in 1958 a new approach to Latin America, Vice President Nixon was confidentially urging President Eisenhower to preserve military aid programs. In Nixon's view, military officers were "a great stabilizing force" and were essential in protecting governments from "the highly trained subversive cadres maintained by the Communists."[21] Nixon retained those views during his presidency. President Kennedy quietly agreed with Nixon, although he changed the direction of U.S. military aid in Latin America. The threat was not the Red Army but guerrilla forces inspired by the Cuban Revolution. The United States began to train Latin Americans in the art of counterinsurgency, sending officers and enlisted personnel to war schools such as the School of the Americas in the Panama Canal Zone, and select personnel to the U.S. Special Forces training camp at Fort Bragg in North Carolina. On average, 3,500 officers and enlisted personnel annually trained in U.S. war schools in the 1960s. Military aid initially increased by 50 percent a year over the Eisenhower years to $77 million. In the mid-1960s, military aid amounted to over $100 million a year. The Kennedy administration also initiated in 1962 a police training program to combat urban guerrillas, bringing over 3,000 Latin American officers to schools such as the new International Police Academy in the Georgetown section of Washington, DC. It would be subsequently revealed that U.S. instructors taught Brazilian and Uruguayan police how to use torture to interrogate suspects. The United States spent $43.6 million on the Latin American police. In the 1960s, more U.S. technicians worked on police projects than on health and sanitation programs.[22]

The Kennedy and Johnson administrations failed to build prosperous, socially just, democratic societies in the Western Hemisphere. But from a Cold War perspective, the two administrations had waged a successful foreign policy. Neither the Soviet Union nor Cuba had expanded their reach in the region. Latin America was no longer "the most dangerous area" in the world. The Latin American military and police waged effective counterinsurgency campaigns against leftist guerrillas in countries such as Venezuela. The Somoza family dynasty (1937 1979) continued to dominate Nicaragua. All 5,000 personnel in Nicaragua's National Guard had trained in the Canal Zone and easily contained the leftist Sandinista movement in the 1960s. The United States had also helped create an authoritarian Brazil eager to wage Cold War against any future radical movement in South America. In any case, after the Cuban Missile Crisis, leaders of the Soviet Union demanded that Cubans cease promoting agitation in the region. The Cubans largely submitted to their benefactors, focusing instead on promoting revolution in Africa, not Latin America. As such, the new Nixon administration found anticommunists of various persuasions, democrats and dictators, leading nineteen Latin American nations. What united them was discontent about Latin America's place in the international economic order.

Nixon and Kissinger

Richard M. Nixon had more prior experience with Latin America than any other person who took the presidential oath of office in U.S. history. Perhaps only John Quincy Adams, who as secretary of state authored the Monroe Doctrine and negotiated trade treaties with the newly independent Latin American nations, could rival Nixon's background and experience. In his memoirs, Nixon said nothing about his 1955 tour of Central America and the Caribbean. He embarrassed himself and the United States by heaping praise on dictators Fulgencio Batista and Rafael Trujillo. He also propagated the Cold War myth that Guatemala had been rescued from communism. He posed for photographs with Colonel Carlos Castillo Armas, the U.S. man in Guatemala City, inspecting purported communist literature. In truth, the best the U.S. team that combed the Guatemalan archives after the overthrow of President Arbenz could find was an invoice for $22.95 revealing that Guatemala's small communist party had purchased books from a Moscow bookstore.[23] However dubiously Nixon acted, he was carrying out the policies of Secretary of State Dulles. His tour of South America in 1958 proved a political windfall. He emerged from the melee in Caracas as a national hero. President Eisenhower welcomed him and his spouse, Patricia Nixon, at Washington National Airport. He and Pat received standing ovations whenever they appeared publicly for weeks thereafter. He pulled even with Senator Kennedy in presidential polls. The South American trip became part of his popular political autobiography, *Six Crises* (1962). Tellingly, Nixon did not repeat in his 1978 memoirs his 1958 formula for how the United States should distinguish between Latin American dictators and democrats.[24]

Fidel Castro's turn toward the Soviet Union and communism strengthened Nixon's lack of faith in political progress in Latin America. He blamed the State Department and especially R. Richard Rubottom, assistant secretary for Latin American affairs, for foolishly abandoning Fulgencio Batista. In 1958, the Eisenhower administration cut off arms shipments to Batista's Cuba and tried to persuade the Cuban strongman to leave the island nation, as it haphazardly looked for a "third way" between him and Castro. In Nixon's view, Cubans had substituted a right-wing dictator for a left-wing one. Batista had been allied with United States, whereas Castro became "an implacable and dangerous enemy."[25] Nixon's public feelings about abandoning Batista were often repeated to Henry Kissinger in private. Nixon was further convinced that the Cuban issue had deprived him of victory in the 1960 presidential election. The Democrats paid the Republicans back for alleging during the 1952 campaign that the Truman administration had "lost" China to communism. Now the Republicans bore responsibility for "losing" Cuba. Kennedy even implied that the United States should invade Cuba and overthrow Castro. Kennedy's reckless campaign charge frustrated Nixon, because he knew of Eisenhower's project to overthrow Castro but could not disclose the secret plans.[26]

Nixon engaged in revisionist history when he suggested that he always recognized that Castro was a danger to the United States. The vice president was the highest-ranking U.S. official ever to have a meaningful conversation with Castro during the period of his leadership of Cuba (1959–2016). In April 1959, Castro came to the United States at the invitation of the American Society of Newspaper Editors. Castro stayed eleven days in the United States and Canada, giving speeches and media interviews and meeting with government officials. President Eisenhower declined to invite Castro to the White House in protest over the Cuban Revolution's summary trials and executions of Batista's henchmen. Nixon spent three hours with Castro. Although Nixon later claimed he immediately urged a forceful policy toward Cuba, his report of the conversation revealed that Nixon seemed remarkably sympathetic to the new Cuban leader. He found Castro too easily swayed by the crowd. He debated with Castro the efficacy of the free enterprise system. He noted that Castro wanted socialism for Cuba, but he did not believe that Castro was a communist. Instead, Castro was naïve and uniformed about communism: "He sounded almost exactly like Sukarno had sounded to me when I visited Indonesia in 1953." Castro also had those "indefinable qualities which make him a leader of men," and the prescient Nixon predicted that he was "going to be a great factor in the development of Cuba and very possibly in Latin American affairs generally." Given Castro's appeal, the vice president recommended that the United States try "to orient him in the right direction."[27]

The United States found it impossible to point Castro in the "right direction" or to retain its traditional hegemony over Cuba. In a meeting in the Oval Office on 20 April 1961, Nixon found himself consoling President Kennedy after the failure at the Bay of Pigs. He urged Kennedy to redouble his efforts and find a pretext to launch an invasion of Cuba. He recommended to Kennedy that the administration "do whatever is necessary to get Castro and communism out of Cuba." When, according to Nixon, Kennedy demurred, worrying that the Soviet Union might retaliate against Berlin, Nixon reminded him of the monolithic nature of communism. "The Communist threat was indivisible, and unless it was resisted everywhere there was no point in resisting it anywhere."[28] Although Kennedy would receive fulsome public praise for forcing the Soviet Union to withdraw its nuclear-tipped missiles from Cuba in October 1962, Nixon continued to be privately critical of Kennedy's Cuba policy. Soviet Premier Nikita Khrushchev had outsmarted Kennedy by using the fear of war to secure a presidential pledge that the United States would foreswear a future invasion of Cuba.[29]

Prior to launching his second presidential bid, Nixon toured Latin America in May 1967, accompanied by his devoted friend, Charles "Bebe" Rebozo, a Cuban-American banker from Florida. Nixon sensed the keen disappointment in the region over the Alliance for Progress. The program "had raised expectations too high" and had not given proper attention to the role of private foreign investment. Nixon visited Peru, Chile, Argentina, Brazil, and Mexico City over a twelve-day period. Unlike his 1958 tour of South America, this trip was pleasant and did not generate international controversy. He met with presidents and citizens, including the Brazilian *fútbol* superstar Pele. Displaying the common touch, Nixon was photographed embracing poor children from the favelas of Rio de Janeiro. These photo opportunities underscored Nixon's critique of the Alliance. The United States needed to work with Latin Americans in improving the region's social and economic infrastructure—telecommunications, roads, agriculture, and education. Too much time and money had been wasted pushing socioeconomic reforms such as land redistribution. Nixon also welcomed Mexico's emphasis on self-reliance and its plans for trade expansion.[30]

Within Latin America, Nixon managed to generate news. Ever the cold warrior, Nixon tied a U.S. victory over Viet Cong guerrillas in South Vietnam to the fate of Latin America. In a conference with Brazilian journalists, Nixon observed that "should the Cuban government feel the U.S. is weakening on the matter of guerrillas, they would stimulate subversion all over Latin America." Although still promoting the notion of a global communist conspiracy, Nixon had tacitly renounced his tenuous 1958 commitment to democracy in

Latin America. He praised the "total liberty" of the press in Brazil. He denied that the country was a military dictatorship and said that General Artur da Costa e Silva (1967–1969) was more a civilian than a military officer.[31] In fact, a year later, in December 1968, Costa e Silva issued Institutional Act No. 5, which abolished Congress and transformed Brazil into a military dictatorship. Criticism of government became a national security issue subject to military justice. On 14 May 1967, one Brazilian columnist bravely responded to Nixon by asserting that "the political system is a prospective dictatorship, not a democracy." Brazil now had "fascist laws." He noted that his prosecution for exercising his free speech "depends on bad or good humor of those in power."[32] Nixon took the same approach in Buenos Aires, calling the ruler of Argentina, General Juan Carlos Onganía (1966–1970), "a very strong leader who respects free institutions" and had "reverence for the law." Nixon argued that "a new breed of military leaders has arisen in Latin America dedicated to progress rather than protecting the status quo." Latin America needed strong leaders like Charles de Gaulle in France. Nixon asserted that inter-American dialogue had been marked by too much courtesy and not enough sincerity. Nixon's sincerity included telling journalists in Argentina and Brazil, "A U.S. style democracy cannot function in Latin America. If I had to choose a system for South America it would be a democracy in the style of de Gaulle." Nixon hoped that the military regimes of Argentina and Brazil succeeded, for "this would have a strong impact on other South American countries."[33]

President Nixon avoided such blunt talk about Latin America in his public pronouncements in the United States. Nixon wanted to be a foreign-policy president, and he organized his policy-making process so that it left him alone or with Henry Kissinger when he made major decisions. Vice President Nixon had disliked the foreign-policy organization of President Eisenhower. Eisenhower used the NSC to set policy for the Cold War. Attending 339 of these often-lengthy meetings, he encouraged open debate, normally waiting until the end of the meeting to offer his views and decide on policy. Nixon wryly noted in his memoirs that Eisenhower "allowed discussions to ramble on as if it were his duty to be bored for his country as well as lead it."[34] Scholars known as the "Eisenhower revisionists" have found much to admire in Eisenhower's approach to decision-making and his stewardship of U.S. foreign policy in the nuclear age. Before the NSC met, a the Policy Planning Board had prepared detailed policy options. NSC members appreciated the open debate, and the process enhanced their sense of loyalty to the president and the policy adopted. After Eisenhower ruled, the Operations Coordinating Board monitored the implementation of the policy. To coordinate national security policy and diplomacy—the day-to-day conduct of international relations carried out by the State Department—Eisenhower, aided by his staff secretary, gathered regularly with foreign policy officials. The president also often met with Secretary Dulles in the late afternoon for cocktails and philosophical discussions on foreign policy. These formal mechanisms and informal arrangements left Eisenhower in the center of the decision-making process.[35] Nixon was not alone in rejecting Eisenhower's organizational approach. President Kennedy preferred meeting with a small, shifting group of advisers on foreign-policy matters. Both Nixon and Kennedy concluded that Eisenhower's way of doing things was slow and ponderous.

Nixon had the right to be confident over his ability to manage international relations. During his time as vice president and as a New York–based lawyer and consultant to multinational corporations in the 1960s, Nixon had traveled to most regions of the world and met most of the main players in global affairs. In addition to visiting Latin America, Nixon's 1967 foreign-study trips included journeys to Western and Eastern Europe, the Soviet Union, Asia, Africa, and the Middle East. He published his reflections on what he found in *Foreign Affairs*. Nixon delighted in displaying his grasp of foreign policy to the press corps and the public by delivering statements without notes. He boasted, "I can do toasts and arrival statements better than anybody in the world. I have traveled all over the world."[36] Nixon once instructed Kissinger to remind the press corps that he had conversed with seventy-three heads of state and never once used notes. Nixon recalled that "when he met with [Soviet Premier Nikita] Khrushchev in 1959 in the seven-hour luncheon at the dacha, neither he nor Khrushchev had a note and yet discussed matters of the greatest consequences in covering many areas."[37] Nixon's biographers agree that Nixon had exceptional ability, intelligence, and vision, as well as a capacity for hard work. As demonstrated in his prediction of Fidel Castro's future, Nixon was also a shrewd judge of the ambition and character of international figures. Biographers also agree that Nixon lacked moral scruples and was determined to win at any cost, which included engaging in extensive lying.[38]

In his interactions with Latin American leaders, Nixon acted professionally. Unlike John Kennedy, who hosted presidents, foreign ministers, economic ministers, military officers, and Latin American scholars, Nixon usually met only with heads of state from Latin America. His first extensive meeting was with President Carlos Lleras Restrepo (1966–1970), the constitutional president of Colombia. President Lleras had the honor of being the first to visit the Oval Office, because U.S. relations with Colombia had been salutary for several decades and past U.S. presidents, such as Franklin D. Roosevelt and Eisenhower, had developed warm relationships with Colombian leaders. As he normally did in his presidential-level meetings, Nixon opened the conversation by "inviting President Lleras to bring up whatever topic he desired." Nixon listened and then reacted to issues of concern. Nixon especially enjoyed speaking with officials who had a conservative philosophy of life. President Lleras complained about social activism by the Roman Catholic clergy, believing it bordered on Marxism. The previous year, Latin American bishops had gathered in the Colombian city of Medellín and set the church on a new course. Roman Catholic clergy should demonstrate "a preferential option for the poor" and teach that hunger and poverty were not the will of God. Nixon asked Lleras to submit an analysis to him in writing about this new direction.[39] Nixon would later claim that he was "the strongest pro-Catholic who is not Catholic" and decried "the deterioration of the attitude of the Catholic Church." He calculated that one-third of Latin American Catholics were now "Marxists."[40]

Although Nixon acted properly in the presence of constitutional leaders such as Lleras and President Gustavo Díaz Ordaz (1964–1970) of Mexico, he continued to doubt the abilities and significance of Latin Americans. He declined to schedule a presidential trip to the region, noting that "it was too goddamn dangerous" for him to travel there. Military governments were best for Latin Americans; they could not "afford the luxury of democracy." All "Latin" countries—Spain, Italy, and Latin American nations—needed "strong leadership."[41] Notably, the Latin American president that Nixon enjoyed hosting in Washington was General Emílio Garrastazú Médici (1969–1974), the most repressive of Brazil's military dictators. Nixon had already decided in 1967 that the military dictators would transform Brazil into a regional power. Nixon instructed aides to tell Médici that "with only very few chiefs of state had he developed so quickly a close relationship."[42]

Henry Kissinger displayed a different style than his boss in his interactions with Latin American officials. Nixon appointed Kissinger as his national security adviser shortly after interviewing him on 25 November 1969. The two men had met only once before at a social occasion. Nixon knew about Kissinger's career. Dr. Kissinger, the academic, had focused his scholarly studies on diplomacy in Central Europe in the nineteenth century. He had served as a consultant and unofficial envoy for both the Kennedy and Johnson administrations and advised his patron, Governor Nelson Rockefeller. Kissinger had come to the attention of foreign-policy elites and the educated public with his book *Nuclear Weapons and Foreign Policy* (1957), which challenged the Eisenhower administration's nuclear deterrence strategy. Kissinger also participated in a pre-election study group at Harvard University on the need for a revived and reorganized NSC. Allegations have surfaced that during the 1968 presidential campaign Kissinger curried favor with the Nixon campaign by passing intel-

ligence about the status of U.S. peace negotiations with Vietnamese communists, which were taking place in Paris. Kissinger and sympathetic biographers
have denied the allegation.[43]

Kissinger had more than just a scholarly background in international affairs.
As a young man, he had served in the U.S. Army during World War II in his
native Germany. He thereafter traveled extensively in Europe, meeting lumi-
naries such as Chancellor Konrad Adenauer. He also served as a consultant to
Henry Cabot Lodge Jr., ambassador to South Vietnam. Through the 1960s,
he would think and write about the U.S. entanglement in Southeast Asia. Kissinger neither studied Latin American history nor had much practical experience with the region. At the suggestion of the State Department, he gave a
lecture in May 1962 at the National Defense University in Brazil. He met Brazilian officials, generals, and Gilberto Freyre, the eminent scholar of racial relations in Brazil.[44] Although he lacked experience in Latin America, Kissinger
had an attribute that Latin Americans would appreciate. Kissinger often noted
that he knew little and cared even less about foreign economic policy. Prior to
1969, he had not served U.S. corporations. He heard out Latin Americans when
they charged that U.S. investors and corporations had exploited the region
throughout the twentieth century. President Nixon rejected out of hand these
Latin American protests.

Kissinger came to dominate the making of U.S. policy toward Latin America, because he was intelligent, diligent, shrewd, and ambitious, and because
he served his masters, President Nixon and Ford, well. The locus of his power
was the NSC, the 40 Committee, the Senior Review Group (SRG), the Washington Special Action Group (WSAG), and, after 1973, the State Department.
Kissinger chose what recommendations were presented to the president. He
easily controlled the NSC, because Nixon disliked attending full meetings.
Under Kissinger, the NSC's budget grew from $700,000 in 1968 to $2.2 million in 1971, and the size of the staff and administrative personnel nearly doubled. Kissinger chaired the 40 Committee, which oversaw covert operations.
The SRG and WSAG were small committees of foreign-policy principals that
analyzed major issues. The WSAG focused on crises.[45] Although the State Department was represented in these organizations, its influence on key inter-
American issues was limited. Secretary of State William P. Rogers (1969–1973),
the nominal vicar of U.S. foreign policy, played no major role in inter-American
relations. President Nixon ran foreign policy from the White House, and he
relied on Kissinger to enforce his wishes. As Nixon once observed to Kissinger,
Secretary Rogers and his colleagues "do like to think they run foreign policy.
They don't." Key issues went through the NSC, the 40 Committee, the SRG,
and the WSAG. Rogers, who seemed to lack energy and motivation, limited

himself to Middle Eastern affairs. In his memoirs, Kissinger conceded that he excluded Rogers "from key decisions on almost all issues except the Middle East."[46] Only after he became secretary of state did Kissinger permit a larger voice for the State Department. The day after Nixon resigned his presidential office, Kissinger appointed William D. Rogers, a liberal Democrat who had worked as a coordinator of the Alliance for Progress, assistant secretary of state for inter-American affairs. Kissinger trusted Rogers, and they became lifelong friends.

Kissinger's interactions with Latin Americans could not have been more different than Nixon's. Nixon's crisp, businesslike meetings with Latin American presidents lasted thirty minutes to an hour. Kissinger's encounters with Latin American ambassadors, foreign ministers, and presidents often rambled on for more than two hours, especially after he became secretary of state. Perhaps making an effort at multitasking, Kissinger frequently scheduled his discussions with Latin Americans during mealtimes. In the vernacular, many of these soirées could be characterized as over the top. Kissinger habitually spoke first, telling a self-effacing joke or relating humorous stories about his difficulties with Congress or the Washington bureaucracy. He congratulated the Venezuelan foreign minister for reading his books, for as "a *London Times* reviewer

President Nixon, Secretary of State William P. Rogers, and Kissinger in Key Biscayne, Florida, in 1969. The president and Kissinger curbed the secretary of state's influence. Rogers had limited impact on policies toward Latin America. Nixon Library.

years ago pointed out that is not a question of Henry Kissinger being a great writer, but that he requires great readers." He assured the Peruvian foreign minister that he wished he could travel more to Latin America and less to the tempestuous Middle East, because "compared to the Arabs, Latin Americans have a Scandinavian temperament." He added, "You are colder than the Arabs but warmer than we are. I like the Latin temperament." As conversations progressed, Kissinger joshed and bantered with Latin American officials, accusing, for example, the Mexican foreign minister of angling to retake Texas. He used Assistant Secretary Rogers as his punching bag, telling Latin Americans that Rogers, the Democrat, "is our specialist in surrender."[47] Beyond creating a relaxed atmosphere, Kissinger's approach inevitably made him the center of attention. Conversations were as much about him and his value to the world as about bilateral or regional issues. His ample sense of self-worth was constantly on display. When Juan Perón returned to power in Argentina in 1973, Kissinger relayed his positive reaction to the Argentine foreign minister. Kissinger "stated that in all frankness he preferred to deal with big people rather than small people."[48]

Whereas the distinctions between Nixon and Kissinger's personal interactions with Latin Americans were apparent, the differences in their policies toward the region were more of degree than of kind. When the taped recordings in the White House began to be released in mid-1974, U.S. citizens were shocked to hear their president use vile language in his characterizations of various ethnic, national, racial, and religious groups. Nixon perhaps reached his most uncivilized point in his 8 April 1971 discussion with Douglas MacArthur II, ambassador to Iran, and General Alexander M. Haig Jr., a presidential assistant. During the twenty-five-minute conversation, Nixon managed to denigrate just about everyone living in Asia, Africa, Latin America, and the Middle East. The Philippines was "a can of worms," and Burma was "always in a mess." "Miserable little countries" were Morocco, Tunisia, Libya, Algeria, Sudan, and the United Arab Republic. Except for the military dictatorship in Brazil, Latin America was "chaos." Nixon reserved his worst for the new African nations. As he told Ambassador MacArthur, "Those Africans, you know, are only about 50–75 years from out of the trees, some of them."[49] Nixon's racist rant was to justify his conviction that developing nations were incapable of living under a constitutional system and upholding democratic civic life.

Unlike Nixon, Kissinger did not engage in endless contemptible talk about Latin Americans or anyone else. To be sure, the documentary record reveals Kissinger occasionally speaking of Latin Americans in patronizing, condescending ways. He thought that Latin American officials were too inclined to give grandiloquent speeches in multilateral settings, that they were overly formal, and that they were reluctant to make decisions. He judged Latin American foreign ministers as "an ineffectual lot." He liked them personally but "efficiency was not their strong point."[50] In a telephone conversation with Assistant Secretary Rogers, he noted, "I think it is a basic principle that we cannot look like Latin Americans. When we say we will have an answer on Thursday, we do it."[51] He also repeatedly claimed that he could sway officials with flattery. He assured President Gerald Ford that "the Latins and Arabs are two places [sic] where with flattery you can get more than you anticipated."[52] Latin Americans were not, however, strangers to the flattery game. Kissinger became good friends with Mexican Foreign Minister Emilio Rabasa. They spoke often on the telephone. Rabasa had a home in Acapulco that he made available to Kissinger and his family. And Kissinger adored the sun and atmosphere of the Mexican coastal resort. Whenever Rabasa wanted something from Kissinger, he opened the conversation with a tribute to Kissinger's wisdom and diplomatic triumphs.[53]

Kissinger implicitly adopted, however, Nixon's thesis that military dictatorship was in the best interest of Latin America and the United States. He may not have accepted Nixon's reasoning that Latin American thought, history, and culture were incompatible with constitutionalism and democratic civil life. But authoritarian, anticommunist rule suited the national security interests of the United States during the Cold War. Kissinger was unmoved by reports that military dictators in Brazil and Guatemala sanctioned summary executions and extralegal "death squads." He rejected suggestions from aides that he press the longtime dictators of Nicaragua and Paraguay to liberalize their regimes. He participated in the destruction of constitutionalism and democratic processes in Chile and Uruguay, two countries that had long, proud histories of peaceful, open political processes. He also turned a blind eye to the horrifying practices of the Argentine military dictatorship. State Department officers in Washington and Buenos Aires warned Kissinger that the Argentine despots were engaged in the mass murder of civilians and the persecution of Argentine Jews. Kissinger promoted democracy and respect for fundamental human rights in his speeches. But the documentary record provides little evidence of Kissinger recommending democracy to military dictators and their representatives in private conversations.

First-Year Studies

At the outset of his presidency, Nixon initiated two full-scale reviews of inter-American relations. On 3 February 1969, Nixon ordered, under the aegis of

National Security Study Memorandum (NSSM) 15, a wide-reaching review of U.S. policies toward Latin America. Topics to be analyzed included U.S. recognition policy, regional security issues, the future of the Alliance for Progress, trade problems, and the role of the Organization of American States (OAS). During his first year in office, Nixon remained engaged with the process. He attended, in July and October, two NSC meetings devoted to Latin America. The president also peppered the NSC with memoranda containing his thoughts on inter-American relations. For example, he made it clear he was not interested in using economic aid to promote socioeconomic reform—the leitmotiv of the Alliance for Progress. He informed Kissinger and the NSC that aid for public housing amounted to "welfare handouts." Nixon wanted both to reduce aid and redirect the remaining aid to "tangible" projects, such as the completion of the Pan American Highway. In his 1967 tour of the region, Nixon had told Latin Americans that he favored investing U.S. money in economic infrastructure projects. The United States also sharply reduced economic assistance to the region; aid to Latin America in 1971, for example, was $463 million, 50 percent less than in a typical year in the 1960s.[54]

Henry Kissinger oversaw the review of inter-American policies. He conducted the NSC meetings like a professor in a graduate seminar, asking large,

Guillermo Sevilla-Sacasa, the senior Latin American diplomat in Washington, presents a book to Richard Nixon to honor the new president. Kissinger and Chief of Protocol Emil "Bus" Mosbacher look on. Ambassador Sevilla-Sacasa represented the Somoza family dictatorship in Washington from 1943 to 1979. Nixon Library.

probing questions about the nature of the "special relationship" between the United States and Latin America. Admitting the obvious, Kissinger noted that he was "not a Latin American expert." He informed the NSC Review Group that the "principals were more concerned with other areas of the world but that the President was more insistent on specific answers concerning our goals in Latin America." Discussions actually focused on issues of significance to Latin Americans—the terms of trade, whether Latin American exports should be given preferential tariff treatment in the U.S. market, and the issue of "tied" foreign aid. During the 1960s, Latin Americans had not been permitted to spend U.S. foreign aid on goods outside of the United States. Notably, the NSC did not devote much time to international security issues. Intelligence analysts testified that neither the Soviet Union nor Cuba had launched any new initiatives in the region. The apocalyptic language that had characterized policy papers on inter-American relations in the Kennedy-Johnson years was now gone. No longer was Latin America, as President Kennedy characterized it, "the area of greatest danger to us."[55]

Whereas national security analysts focused on foreign economic policy issues in discussions about NSSM 15, they also addressed two issues of concern to President Nixon—the role of the Roman Church in Latin America and the purpose of U.S. military aid to Latin America. Recalling his conversation with President Lleras of Colombia, Nixon asked the CIA to study the church, because "he thought it was no longer promoting stability." Both the CIA and U.S. embassies in Latin America presented nuanced, intelligent analyses of the post-Medellín church. Pressure for change came from both Rome and from within Latin America. Both Pope John XXIII (1958–1963) and Pope Paul VI (1963–1978) believed that the teachings of Jesus Christ mandated that clergy identify with the poor. Conservative prelates in the bureaucracy in Rome impeded the popes' progressive teachings. Many church leaders in Latin America preferred to separate religion from politics, but they were aware that young priests and nuns believed that religion could not be divorced from daily life. The embassy in Asunción judged Archbishop Aníbal Mena Porter a moderate man, who rejected achieving political change through violence. But the archbishop had grown tired of the repression of the Paraguayan strongman Alfredo Stroessner (1954–1989) and had implicitly criticized him. The archbishop also favored birth control in his impoverished country. The CIA reasonably concluded that advocacy by Catholic clergy for social reforms could produce instability and even spur revolution. Anti-American sentiment could rise if the United States was identified with the elite's resistance to change. On the other hand, the CIA noted that socially progressive clergy remained a minority segment in the region, "facing an ambivalent Vatican and traditional Latin American conservatism."[56] Such conclusions did not come as welcome news to President Nixon. He instructed Kissinger to relay the information to speechwriter, conservative Catholic, and ideologue Patrick Buchanan, with the idea that Buchanan might publish some "think pieces" on the new Catholic Church.[57]

On 9 July 1969, Nixon asked the Joint Chiefs of Staff (JCS) to prepare a report on the issue of military aid to Latin America. The president noted that military assistance should promote stability or be cut. Pointing, however, to Indonesia in 1967 "as a possible cautionary historical precedent," Nixon further observed that "the military prevented the country from falling to the communists."[58] During fiscal years encompassing 1962 to 1969, the United States had sent $478 million in grant military assistance to enhance the internal security and counterinsurgency capabilities of Latin American armed forces. On a bipartisan basis, U.S. legislators increasingly questioned whether military aid was compatible with the Alliance for Progress's goal of promoting democracy. During the Alliance years, sixteen extraconstitutional changes of government rocked the region. Legislators began to cut military aid and place restrictions on it. Grant military aid fell to $7 million in 1970.[59] Representative Silvio Conte (R-MA) sponsored the Conte Amendment, which called for a cut in economic aid to any Latin American country that purchased expensive weapon systems such as jet aircraft. The growing congressional resistance to military aid also reflected the assumption that outside forces no longer threatened U.S. hegemony in the region.

The internal review of military assistance lamented congressional interference in the prerogatives of the executive branch. The United States should continue a robust military assistance program. Latin American military officers were key political actors, and the United States needed to court them. The embassy in Montevideo reported that Uruguayan officers who trained in the United States "retain a very pro-U.S. attitude." One change advocated was to cut the "visible presence" of the U.S. military in Latin America. In 1968, there were 791 U.S. military advisers in Latin America. Nixon approved of the idea, remarking at a NSC meeting, "We must lower our profile." By the end of 1970, the number of U.S. military personnel had been reduced to 325, with the goal of lowering the number to 236.[60] Nixon agreed that the administration needed to maintain contact with the Latin American military officers. As he underscored, "We should do it but not appear to be doing it." He also reminded the NSC that he harbored doubts about the capabilities of civilian, democratic leaders. Nixon opined, "There are not very many leaders among political scientists. The military are bad but political scientists are worse." Nixon ordered the NSC to resist cutting off contact between the U.S. military and Latin American armed forces. After all, "they may run the place someday." Nixon was knowledgeable and prophetic. A 1976 Defense Department study demonstrated that of the Latin American military officers who had served on the Inter-American Defense Board (1942) in Washington, fifteen had become heads of state, 144 had held cabinet positions, 153 had become chiefs of staff of their armed services, and twenty-eight had served as ambassadors. Beyond knowing the past, Nixon assisted the evolution of Latin America's history. He remarked, "We should get away from the knee-jerk reaction that a democratic government in Chile is to be more admired than another."[61] Within three years of Nixon's remark, U.S. military advisers would begin to cultivate General Augusto Pinochet of Chile.

The final report for NSSM 15 that Kissinger compiled took seriously Latin American concerns about trade and aid. The United States should loosen restrictions on how foreign aid could be spent and give special preferences to imports from developing regions such as Latin America. The report recommended that the United States should encourage long-term economic development and "foster a Latin American system of independent, self-reliant states." To be sure, the study continued to see Latin America as part of the U.S. sphere of influence, asserting, "We would feel, as a nation, that our power had been greatly diminished in the world were Latin America to slip out of our orbit—and so would other nations."[62] Nonetheless, one veteran State Department officer who had been assigned to the NSC noted, "We constructed and articulated a conceptual framework for Latin American policy which was (I believe) realistic and reasonable—even historic."[63] The officer, Viron V. Vaky, had a reputation of being critical of U.S. policies, having denounced the U.S. role in human rights abuses in Guatemala in the mid-1960s.

While Henry Kissinger and the NSC were quietly reviewing U.S. policies and learning about President Nixon's jaundiced view of Latin Americans, international attention was fixated on Governor Nelson Rockefeller's tour of the region. Nixon had not mentioned inter-American affairs in his inaugural address. Galo Plaza, the former president of Ecuador (1948–1952), secretary-general of the OAS (1968–1975), and a friend of Rockefeller, advised Nixon at a reception on Inauguration Day that he redress the slight by dispatching Rockefeller on a goodwill and fact-finding tour of the region. Referring to Rockefeller, the diplomat noted that "his name is still magic" in Latin America. During World War II, Rockefeller had successfully served as the coordinator of inter-American affairs, helping keep the region allied to the United States. Fluent in Spanish and with a good knowledge of Portuguese, Rockefeller had in the postwar years developed businesses and promoted scientific agriculture in Brazil and Venezuela. He also owned a large hacienda in Venezuela and had financed the impressive Ávila Hotel in Caracas.[64] He had supported the Alliance for Progress and imbibed in the Western Hemisphere ideal that the United States and Latin America had a common history and destiny. The opening statement of his report—"We went to visit neighbors and found brothers"—reflected that idealism.[65] Rockefeller had an excellent reputation among U.S. educated Latin Americans like Galo Plaza. But his family's wealth came from Standard Oil of New Jersey, which was perceived by many Latin Americans as an exploitative enterprise. The company's history in countries such as Mexico, Peru, and Venezuela had been controversial. The Rockefeller name was also commonly associated by Latin American leftists with interventionism and imperialism.

President Nixon respected his political rival. After he decided to resign, Nixon recommended to Vice President Ford that he appoint Rockefeller as vice president. But Nixon almost immediately regretted following Secretary-General Plaza's advice, worrying that the energetic Rockefeller would propose "extravagant spending programs." The NSC feared that Rockefeller would propose "Grand Designs."[66] Indeed, Rockefeller assembled a large study team, often taking more than twenty people with him to individual countries. This team, which included educators, scientists, and businesspeople, wrote lengthy reports, often exceeding 200 pages, on each country. Nancy Maginnes, who married Henry Kissinger in 1974, served as a staff member. The records of the Rockefeller mission fill hundreds of archival boxes at the Rockefeller Archive Center in New York. For a few months in 1969, Rockefeller was the de facto secretary of state for Latin American affairs, calling on heads of state and foreign ministers. He made himself available to Latin American journalists, and he testified before the U.S. Congress. He had direct access to Henry Kissinger and often sent notes to Nixon. Indeed, Rockefeller's judgment was that his mission and Latin America were so important that the State Department should create the new position of under secretary of state for Latin America. The person holding that title would outrank the assistant secretaries for Asia, Europe, the Middle East, and elsewhere and would have direct access to the president. The proposal was not new, as Adolf A. Berle Jr., an adviser to Franklin D. Roosevelt, had proposed the same to President Kennedy in 1961. The State Department bureaucracy could be counted on to resist such an innovation.

Rockefeller's high-profile venture, which included four trips and twenty countries in 1969, proved as tumultuous as Nixon's tour of South America in 1958. Three countries—Chile, Peru, and Venezuela—cancelled Rockefeller's visit, fearing demonstrations and in protest over U.S. trade and investment policies. Demonstrations often ended in violence, ranging from a student being shot in Honduras to Brazilian security forces armed with machine guns invading university campuses and arresting thousands of students even as they were attending class. Rockefeller's meeting with President Jorge Pacheco Areco (1967–1972) of Uruguay was moved from Montevideo to the seaside resort of Punta del Este to shield Rockefeller from discontent and danger. A General Motors showroom in Montevideo was bombed, a bomb exploded outside of the Bolivian/American Center in La Paz, and seventeen "Minimax" grocery stores in Buenos Aires were firebombed. The stores were operated by the International Basic Economy Corporation, a Rockefeller enterprise. Only in two countries—Haiti and Paraguay—did Rockefeller receive a warm, enthusiastic welcome, complete with cheering crowds. As Rockefeller observed in a letter to Nixon, apparently without irony, the two countries represented "the best organized dictatorships we visited."[67] In Haiti, however, Rockefeller ended up with negative publicity, as he was photographed arm-in-arm with President François "Papa Doc" Duvalier (1957–1971), the malicious, kleptomaniacal oppressor of the poorest nation in the Western Hemisphere.[68]

As Nixon had in 1958, Rockefeller reflexively blamed outside agitators for the hostility he encountered. But Rockefeller wanted the United States to maintain its "special relationship" with Latin America, and he understood that the tensions in the region revolved around slow economic progress, barriers to trade, rapid population growth, and disappointment with the Alliance for Progress. He also informed President Nixon that the United States needed to address contentious bilateral issues, such as the status of the International Petroleum Corporation, a subsidiary of Standard Oil of New Jersey, in Peru and disputes over tuna fishing by U.S. commercial boats off the coasts of Ecuador and Peru. Rockefeller also confidentially told his advisers that he understood that President Nixon was not interested in agricultural, economic, financial, or health issues. What Nixon was interested in hearing about was military assistance and the U.S. attitude toward dictatorships.[69] Rockefeller mainly chose to follow his own perceptions. His report called on the United States to support Latin America's development and ameliorate the concerns about barriers to trade raised at the Latin American conclave at Viña del Mar. As such, the Rockefeller Report echoed many of the proposals on trade in NSSM 15.

Although Rockefeller differed with the president on the importance of Latin America to the United States, he implicitly adopted Nixon's stance on democracy and dictatorship. He did not raise issues of democracy, constitutionalism, or human rights with military dictators in Argentina, Brazil, Guatemala, or Nicaragua. He did not protest the wholesale roundup of university students in Brazil. As had Nixon in 1967, Rockefeller fulsomely praised the rule of General Costa e Silva of Brazil and Lieutenant General Onganía of Argentina. He also did not react when Costa e Silva implied that Brazil planned to foment a military takeover of power in Uruguay or when the Brazilian general predicted that the United States would need its own military seizure of power within five years.[70] He attended a reception for General Anastasio Somoza Debayle (1967–1979), the latest in the Somoza family dynasty (1936–1979) at the U.S. embassy in Managua that excluded all of the family's political opponents. Pedro Joaquín Chamorro, the editor of the Nicaraguan opposition newspaper *La Prensa*, warned one of Rockefeller's aides that such actions fueled anti-Americanism and identified the United States with the "annihilated, rotten, and obsolete system."[71] As he wrapped up his mission, Rockefeller told Henry Kissinger that he wanted the United States to focus on enhancing the "quality of life" in Latin America, with the hope that democratic practices would eventually follow economic growth. Kissinger agreed with his patron, noting that "the history of the last decade and a half should have taught us the limits of our ability of direct social engineering."[72]

What captured public notice and became a central feature of the Nixon-Kissinger approach to Latin America was the remarkable assertion in the Rockefeller report that military rule could be in the best interests of Latin America. A "new military man" was "prepared to adapt his authoritarian tradition to the goals of social and economic progress." This new military man would be "a major force for constructive social change in the American republics."[73] In its internal memoranda and reports to Washington, the Rockefeller team noted that the U.S. military had friendly relations and influence with the Latin American armed forces, because the United States had supplied training and weapons and brought Latin American officers to study at U.S. war colleges. As one report asserted, no other agency of the U.S. government had "a comparable rapport or integration in its sphere of activity."[74] This was true for a large country like Brazil or a small one like Nicaragua. These points were made repeatedly by the military representative on the team, retired General Robert W. Porter Jr., the former commander in chief of the Southern Command. But Porter and others offered new arguments. They theorized that the Latin American officer corps was no longer composed of sons of wealthy owners of haciendas and plantations. Latin American officers were now urban men, drawn from the middle class, educated, and possessing technical expertise. In General Porter's words, "They are dedicated to nation-building and improvement in the living conditions and capabilities of the lower classes."[75] Rockefeller seconded the general. In an address to the Center for Inter-American Affairs,

Rockefeller explained, "None of these dictators down there—the military dictators so-called—that I saw are the old-style dictator, the pawn of the oligarchy. These guys are all coming from the people and are sympathetic toward and concerned about the people." In a radio interview with the esteemed journalist Sam Donaldson, Rockefeller predicted that the Latin American military, by establishing stability and order and taming chronic price inflation, would be in a position to carry out the reform goals of the Alliance for Progress.[76]

General Porter and Governor Rockefeller's theories had some support from academic scholars and by developments in the 1960s. John J. Johnson of Stanford University, among others, predicted that technically trained, scientifically oriented military officers would help "modernize" Latin America and help fulfill Walt Rostow's grand theories on economic development.[77] The Kennedy administration put the theory into practice, funding "civic-action" programs in Bolivia, which consisted of having the military build public-works projects in rural areas. The thoughts behind the program were that Bolivia's economic infrastructure would improve and that the military would learn from direct experience about the problems of rural folk. The effect of the civic-action projects was to encourage the Bolivian military to dominate the nation's political system.[78] But what especially excited those who promoted the virtues of military rule was the "Brazilian miracle." After they seized power in 1964, Brazil's military rulers focused on reducing price inflation, which was at 92 percent in 1964 but fell to 28 percent in 1967. Under the guidance of Minister of Finance Delfim Neto, a young economics professor from São Paulo, the Brazilian economy thereafter boomed, with an annual growth rate of 10.9 percent from 1968 to 1974.[79] Progress seemingly followed the establishment of order.

The course of Latin American history raised serious questions about the enthusiasm for military rule in Latin America expressed by Richard Nixon, Henry Kissinger, and Nelson Rockefeller. U.S. leaders were implicitly embracing the doctrine of positivism, which was popular among Latin American elites in the late nineteenth century. Historical progress theoretically went through an evolutionary process, with order and stability a prerequisite for economic growth. Once a nation enjoyed economic growth, the good things in life—constitutionalism, civic life, and democracy—would inevitably follow. The Brazilian flag, adopted in 1889, encapsulated positivism with the emblazoned motto "Ordem e Progresso" ("Order and Progress"). But between 1889 and 1945, Brazil's political and socioeconomic progress had been, at best, uneven. Perhaps the most notable laboratory for positivism had been Mexico under the authoritarian General Porfirio Díaz (1876–1911). During the "porfiriato," orderly Mexico became a hospitable place for foreign and domestic investors. But the Mexican people suffered repression and survived in a grossly unequal society.

In 1910, the nation exploded into ten years of revolution that ultimately produced a Mexican constitution that guaranteed regular elections, term limits, and mandates for social justice.

U.S. leaders needed not to have been students of Latin American history to realize the dubious value of military rule. Within the Rockefeller team, David Bronheim dissected the prevailing wisdom on the advantages of military rule. Bronheim, who had served in the U.S. Agency for International Development, argued that military aid, with its emphasis on internal security and counterinsurgency, caused the Latin American military to become impatient with civilian rule. In Bronheim's words, "They now have a tendency to see Communists everywhere and equate all opposition with subversion and the Communist threat."[80] Proof of Bronheim's analysis could be found in the Brazilian generals' issuing Institutional Act No. 5, which equated criticism of the government with treason. The embassy in Montevideo added that it could find no evidence that the Uruguayan military was prepared to advance economic development. The courses taught in military academies were strictly military, with little emphasis on the humanities. The schooling of officers fostered "patriotism and loyalty to established authority."[81] The impact of military rule on South America was becoming evident in 1969 and would be manifest in the 1970s. The military governments of Argentina, Bolivia, Brazil, Chile, and Uruguay increased spending on the military and imprisoned, tortured, and murdered those who dissented. Uruguay would have, on a per capita basis, more political prisoners in the mid-1970s than any other country in the world. The Argentine military slaughtered 30,000 citizens.

The Big Speech

In a news conference in Honduras, Nelson Rockefeller noted that the fate of his report depended on "what the President does with this—and what success he has in Congress."[82] Upon the advice of Secretary of State Rogers, Nixon decided in July 1969 to give a major speech on inter-American affairs "to highlight the President's desire to cultivate a special relationship with the region." Kissinger recommended the speech be delivered in October 1969 so that it could incorporate Rockefeller's ideas. Nixon informed Rogers and Kissinger that his speech "would stress realism, not generalities or platitudes, while not admonishing the region to implement United States–style democracy."[83] The president wanted to deliver a big speech, telling Kissinger that "this 31 October speech must not be dud stylistically." He ordered Chief of Staff H. R. "Bob" Haldeman to make a maximum effort to generate favorable publicity. Nixon wanted "a heavy advance job done on Latin experts in the press." Haldeman should work with Kissinger on garnering favorable publicity from Latin American leaders. As Nixon put it, "What I am primarily interested in here is to get favorable statements by the heads of government in these foreign countries the day after the speech is made." Kissinger followed directions, lobbying Galo Plaza to persuade OAS members to react favorably to the president's speech, for a "receptive response would be most useful to us in moving things in the right direction."[84] In a career marked by cynicism and opportunism, Nixon outdid himself in hoping for love from Latin Americans. Two weeks before the speech, he told the NSC, "The Latins know they are not special. When you say they are, they like it." He opposed giving Latin Americans increased decision-making power in the Inter-American Development Bank (IADB), because "Latin Americans don't have competence. It would be money down a rat hole."[85]

Richard Nixon delivered the only major statement of his presidency on inter-American relations to the Inter-American Press Club in Washington on 31 October 1969. His speech incorporated central recommendations of NSSM 15 and the Rockefeller Report on foreign economic policy. The United States would work in international fora to create a generalized system of preferences to promote the export of finished goods by developing nations. Nixon also announced that he was issuing an executive order to untie partially U.S. foreign aid to Latin America. Latin Americans would now be able to spend U.S. money in other Latin American countries. Latin Americans wanted to purchase capital goods in industrial Western Europe and Japan, however, not just the United States. Nixon further announced that he would ask the U.S. Congress to create the new position of undersecretary of state for Latin America. Nixon understood that U.S. legislators would ignore the proposal. Nixon envisioned a "mature partnership" for the inter-American community. He had previously asked his administration's "word merchants" to think of the new term. The United States would no longer pursue the "illusion" that it alone could remake continents. The dramatic success of the Marshall Plan had created "overweening confidence in the rightness of our own prescriptions." Nixon was, of course, implicitly criticizing President John F. Kennedy and his Alliance for Progress. Nixon announced no specific commitment of economic aid and spent considerable time extolling the merits of direct private investment. Nixon's call for humility also signified that he would not raise issues of democracy, constitutionalism, civic life, or human rights with Latin Americans. As he observed, "We must deal realistically with governments in the inter-American system as they are." Perhaps sensing that his speech was less than inspiring, Nixon added, "We do care. I care."[86]

Nixon's prosaic, workmanlike speech did not earn the plaudits that he desired. Only President Lleras of Colombia responded in an especially favorable way. Editorial writers in the United States expressed disappointment, with the *Washington Post* characterizing the administration's agenda for the region "so unambitious as to be embarrassing."[87] More important, Nixon did little to fulfill his own promises. NSC staff member Vaky complained to Kissinger that the United States was "betraying" the promises made in NSSM 15 and the Nixon speech by inaction.[88] Perhaps sensing what was developing, Rockefeller proposed to Kissinger that a White House advisory committee of "knowledgeable people" consisting of himself, General Porter, and veteran diplomat Sol Linowitz be formed to help on inter-American affairs. Rockefeller wrote that "it might be very useful" to have a committee "who could follow with you some of the hot situations, which with the pressure of events elsewhere sometimes cannot get the full attention it deserves."[89] The administration ignored Rockefeller's recommendation. For the rest of 1969 and early 1970, President Nixon focused on signing waivers to permit Argentina, Brazil, Chile, and Colombia to purchase jet aircraft and thereby avoid the penalties of loss of economic aid imposed by the Conte Amendment. Responding to entreaties from domestic producers, Nixon declined to raise import limits on Latin American meat and textiles.[90]

A year into office, President Nixon had changed his mind on his foreign-policy priorities. In a 2 March 1970 memorandum to Haldeman, presidential assistant John D. Ehrlichman, and Kissinger, Nixon concluded that he and Kissinger were spread too thinly. His study of history and his personal experiences taught him that "what really matters in campaigns, wars, or in government is to concentrate on big battles and win them." He and Kissinger would hereafter focus on East-West relations, the Soviet Union, the People's Republic of China, the influential countries (France, Germany, the United Kingdom) in Western Europe, Vietnam, and the Middle East. He ruled that he did not want matters submitted to him in regard to "all of Latin America and all countries in the Western Hemisphere with the exception of Cuba and anything else that may be concerned with the East-West conflict." He advised Kissinger that he would have to be subtle in resisting pressures from his staff and "members of the establishment" to pay attention to Latin America.[91]

President Nixon's March 1970 directive seemingly confirmed what would become the common historical wisdom that he and Kissinger did not take inter-American affairs seriously. Nearly a year's worth of study and debate within the NSC on U.S. relations with Latin America had been summarily discarded. Governor Rockefeller's copious reports on individual countries were fated to be consigned to his family's private archive. But within months after the March directive, inter-American issues would be back on Nixon and Kissinger's agenda. First in Chile and then in Bolivia, leftist politicians committed to far-reaching socioeconomic change would assume presidential power. Nixon and Kissinger would direct the destabilization of both Bolivia and Chile and encourage military dictatorship in Uruguay.

CHAPTER 2

Overthrowing Governments
Chile and Bolivia

Six months after being told by his president that Latin America was not worth his time, Henry Kissinger again turned to inter-American affairs. In September 1970, Salvador Allende, a politician who professed a belief in Marxism, won a plurality of votes in an open and free election in Chile. A month later, General Juan José Torres, who had ties to political leftists, took power in Bolivia. Anger and panic swept through the White House. Kissinger feared that Chile could become the "worst failure" of the Nixon administration. It might develop into "our Cuba."[1] President Nixon and Kissinger would not countenance Marxist governments in the traditional U.S. sphere of influence. It would take three years to overthrow the Allende government but less than a year to oust General Torres. The Bolivian campaign would be kept from public knowledge. But the U.S. war against Salvador Allende has long been a central feature of the debate about the character and policies of Henry Kissinger.

La Vía Chilena

Chileans traditionally considered themselves citizens of a special country. The country is peculiar geographically, stretching 2,360 miles along the Pacific Coast but averaging only 100 miles in width. Most Chileans, 9.3 million in 1970, lived in the center of country in an area stretching less than 300 miles. Santiago, the capital, and the port of Valparaiso were the major urban areas. Chileans pointed with pride to their history. They had largely maintained a constitutional system since 1833, with the gradual enfranchisement of adults. Chileans had political conflicts but had kept their disputes within constitutional boundaries. Chileans also perceived themselves as living in an urbane, literate society that took art, literature, and philosophy seriously. Poets Gabriela Mistral (1945) and Pablo Neruda (1971) won the Nobel Prize in literature. The nation also had a European-style social welfare system that came into being during the administration of President Arturo Alessandri Palma (1920–1925).

The socioeconomic realities of Chilean life did not sustain the self-perception that Chile was "the Switzerland of South America." The population was growing rapidly with a 2.2 annual percent increase in the 1960s. The country could not feed itself and had to rely on expensive imports of food. As a legacy of the colonial past, 7 percent of the population controlled 80 percent of the land and often held much of the land in fallow. Most of Chile's 400,000 rural households were landless. Rural folk were migrating to urban centers in search of work and living in shantytowns known locally as *callampas*, or "mushrooms." Perhaps 25 percent of Chile's burgeoning population lived in absolute poverty.

In the mid-twentieth century, Chile's prosperity depended on the sale of copper abroad. U.S. mining companies Anaconda and Kennecott produced and marketed Chilean copper. Sales of copper accounted for 60 to 75 percent of export income and 10 to 15 percent of national income. But the companies employed only 17,000 Chileans, for the companies processed the copper in the United States. Copper prices had also fallen since World War II, although the price of copper rose from 40 cents to 60 cents a pound in the late 1960s because of U.S. demand for copper engendered by the war in Vietnam. With the economy barely growing from the 1950s on, Chilean leaders resorted to monetary expansion, deficit spending, and international borrowing to finance imports and to underwrite social welfare. The predictable result of those policies was annual inflation rates of 30 to 40 percent. Then, in 1960, Chile suffered a destructive earthquake in the Puerto Montt region that created more than $200 million in damages.

Economic instability contributed to political division. In the mid-twentieth century, the Chilean polity divided roughly into thirds. Conservative Chileans voted for candidates who believed in the political economy of the past. Chile would earn the income to finance its social welfare state by welcoming foreign investment and engaging in international trade. Chileans also were more socially conservative than many Latin Americans, opposing laws that would permit divorce, birth control, and abortion. The leader of conservative Chileans was Jorge Alessandri Rodríguez, the son of President Arturo Alessandri. "Don Jorge," a confirmed bachelor, was a parsimonious, ascetic man who was admired for his rectitude and dignity. In the middle of the Chilean political spectrum were the Christian Democrats, who emulated the Christian Democrats of West Germany and Italy. Christian Democrats took their inspiration from the teachings of Pope Leo XIII (1878–1903) and his encyclical *Rerum novarum* (1891). Christians had the responsibility to work for a fair and justice society that ensured that industrial workers had decent wages and housing and the right to join labor unions. In calling for evolutionary reform and social change, Pope Leo rejected class conflict and Marxism. Eduardo Frei Montalva was the most prominent Christian Democrat in Chile. A pragmatic, shrewd politician, Frei's slogan was "Revolution in Liberty." Frei promised to enact land, tax, and educational reform but also to protect private property. Communists and socialists led by Salvador Allende Gossens in the Frente de Acción Popular (FRAP), or Popular Action Front, promised Marxist solutions for Chilean problems. Allende favored the nationalization of the copper industry and the redistribution of land, and he spoke favorably of Fidel Castro and the Cuban Revolution. But Allende also emphasized that change would occur through parliamentary procedures and within the framework of the Chilean constitution. A medical doctor and a politician with over thirty years of experience in the Chilean legislature, the handsome Allende was a bon vivant, with a good sense of humor. His repeated unsuccessful runs for the presidency led him to joke that the epitaph on his tombstone would read, "Here lies the future president of Chile."

Presidential elections demonstrated the political divisions of Chile. In 1958, Allende nearly won, finishing only 3 percent, or 34,000 votes, behind Alessandri. Frei finished third. Alessandri won only 31.6 percent but became president (1958–1964) because the Chilean legislature customarily ratified the election of the presidential candidate who received a plurality of votes. Such a procedure was part of *la vía Chilena*, "the Chilean way."

The Kennedy and Johnson administrations believed Chileans had erred when they elected Jorge Alessandri. Both administrations believed that Eduardo Frei and the Christian Democrats would fulfill the promises of the Alliance for Progress. Alessandri failed to curb inflation or develop a plan for socioeconomic reform. President Kennedy pointedly noted to Alessandri in an Oval Office conversation that the Chilean's father had promoted social welfare when he was president in the 1920s. Kennedy planned to visit Chile in 1964 to promote the Alliance and by implication Frei for the upcoming presidential election.[2] The United States accepted Frei's proposed "Chileanization" of the copper industry. Chile would purchase part ownership of the companies; the companies, in turn, would be expected to use the proceeds of the sale to increase production and establish processing and fabricating facilities in Chile. Chile would thereby increase export earnings, and workers would find new employment opportunities.

The United States campaigned for Frei and the Christian Democrats. Between 1962 and 1964, the CIA spent $4 million on polling, posters, and radio and television advertisements for Frei and his party. On a per capita basis, the CIA spent more money on the 2.4 million registered Chilean voters than did the two major candidates, President Lyndon Johnson and Senator Barry Goldwater (R-AZ), in the 1964 U.S. presidential election. U.S. public spending on Chile exceeded the covert campaign. The U.S. embassy in Santiago approved "impact projects" like repairing a school building or equipping a mobile health unit for electorally significant areas. Spending on these impact projects amounted to $30 million in 1963 alone. U.S. officials also carried out a propaganda campaign—flags, lapels, pins, films, photo exhibits, comic books— to ensure that Chileans understood U.S. foreign aid helped poor Chileans and that the Christian Democrats embraced the Alliance for Progress.[3]

The United States not only wanted to boost Eduardo Frei, the Christian Democrats, and the Alliance for Progress but also to derail the campaign of Allende and the FRAP. The Kennedy and Johnson administrations accepted the judgment of Ambassador Charles Cole that FRAP would end democratic government in Chile and "would be so dangerous for U.S. interests in Chile and in all Latin America that U.S. policy should strive to prevent it."[4] Cole's successor, Ambassador Edward M. Korry, held similar views. And between 1970 and 1973, Kissinger would repeatedly make the same argument, alleging that Allende's "long-standing goal [was] to establish an irreversible dictatorship."[5] Nothing in Allende's political career prior to 1970 could sustain those fears. Beyond telling themselves that they were saving Chilean democracy, U.S. officials reasoned that the Soviet Union interfered in Chilean politics. In July 1964, the executive secretary of the 303 Committee, which oversaw covert operations, noted, "We assume the Commies are pouring in dough, we have no proofs. They must assume we are pouring in dough, they have no proofs. Let's pour it on and in." Like other communist parties in the region, the Chilean communists received an annual subsidy, $275,000 in 1965, from Moscow. Allende also accepted cash from Soviet agents. These amounts were miniscule compared to the U.S. effort in Chile.[6]

The embassy and the CIA celebrated the Christian Democrat's landslide victory in 1964. Frei took 56 percent of the vote, whereas Allende won 39 percent, and Julio Durán of the Radical Party earned only 5 percent. Frei had been aided by the decision of conservative Chileans to vote for him and not Durán. Although badly defeated, Allende and FRAP could take some solace in the electoral results. Allende had increased his share of the electorate from 5 percent in 1952 to 28 percent in 1958 to 39 percent in 1964.

In his memoirs, Kissinger fatuously suggested that President Frei was unaware of the massive covert intervention in Chilean politics. In fact, in 1964, candidate Frei joshed with U.S. diplomats about the sources of his campaign funds.[7] The Johnson administration continued to supply President Frei and the Christian Democrats with campaign funds. In March 1969, for example, when asked by Ambassador Korry whether he could find funds in the future to support his party, Frei "candidly" replied that "politicians with good causes never have difficulty finding friends with funds."[8] In the previous months, the CIA had spent $350,000 to underwrite the campaigns of twelve "moderate" candidates in Chilean legislative elections. As the 303 Committee now chaired by Kissinger noted, the United States had invested wisely, for ten of the twelve candidates supported by the CIA had won in the March 1969 elections.[9]

The Johnson administration generally approved of President Frei's performance in office. During the 1960s, Chile received $743 million in Alliance funds, the third-highest amount in Latin America. Chile also had access to an annual line of credit of $200 million to $300 million from U.S. commercial banks.[10] The Frei administration built low-cost housing, purchased fallow land and redistributed it to 25,000 landless families, and purchased 51 percent of Kennecott Copper, the smaller of the two U.S. mining enterprises in Chile. But by the end of the 1960s, President Frei was in political trouble at home and had frayed relations with the United States. The economy grew a measly 1.3 percent a year, which was well below the modest 2.5 percent target rate of the Alliance for Progress. Inflation remained stubbornly high, and the nation had a staggering public external debt of $2 billion. Frei's political coalition began to dissipate, with many conservatives thinking he was moving too rapidly, whereas more leftist Christian Democrats thought he should nationalize the foreign copper companies. The Christian Democrats garnered only 30 percent of the vote in the 1969 legislative elections. The military also grew restive, complaining about low salaries and the lack of new military equipment. In October 1969, a hotheaded general, Roberto Viaux, led a brief military insurrection against the government. Contributing to the turmoil were about 300 members of a leftist group, Movimiento Izquierida Revolucionaria (MIR). They perpetrated violence, carrying out bank robberies, kidnappings, and land seizures in the name of revolution.

Frei irritated the Johnson administration by opposing the U.S. invasion of the Dominican Republic in 1965 and by publicly criticizing the direction of the Alliance for Progress in a famous article in *Foreign Affairs*. Against the wishes of Secretary of State Dean Rusk, President Frei also established diplomatic and trade relations with the Soviet Union. Relations with the United States deteriorated further when the Nixon administration took power. President Nixon resented Frei's decision not to allow Nelson Rockefeller to visit Chile during his mission to Latin America. On 11 June 1969, Foreign Minister Gabriel Valdés bluntly criticized U.S. foreign economic policies in the presence of President Nixon and an assembled group of Latin American ambassadors to the United States.[11] Ambassador Korry asked Frei to restrain his foreign minister. Nixon further disliked President Frei's new plans to curtail the role of the copper companies. Taking advantage of the spike in copper prices, Frei raised the taxes of the companies. He also proposed that the government buy a 51 percent share of Anaconda Copper. Chileans were also angered when the *Washington Post* reported in October 1969 that the CIA knew of General Viaux's plot weeks before he attacked the government. The disclosure underlined how deep CIA contacts were within the Chilean military.[12]

Despite the turmoil and discontent, Chileans adhered to their constitution and self-perceptions and held a peaceful presidential election on 4 September 1970. President Frei was constitutionally barred from seeking immediate reelection. The 1970 election was a reprise of the 1958 election, with three major candidates. Former president Alessandri was the presumed front runner, as he hoped to capture the votes of Chileans who believed that Frei had been too extreme. Radomiro Tomic led the Christian Democrats. Tomic alienated President Frei by pushing a leftist agenda that called for the nationalization of the copper companies and extensive land and labor reforms. Salvador Allende led a new coalition of the socialists, communists, and four small parties in the Unidad Popular (Popular Unity). Allende pledged to nationalize major industries and to foster a socialist society in Chile through the parliamentary process. He also promised to establish diplomatic relations with Cuba. The election evoked interest in the country, with 2.9 million Chileans voting, comprising 83 percent of registered voters. In this election, Allende won a narrow plurality, with 36.6 percent of the vote. Alessandri finished second with 35.3 percent, and Tomic trailed with 28 percent. With no candidate securing a majority, the Chilean congress would have the constitutional duty to choose the president on 24 October 1970.

Spoiling the 1970 Presidential Election

Salvador Allende's victory was a surprise, but not a major upset in the context of Chilean politics. The Nixon administration was, however, stunned by the results. Henry Kissinger later recounted that President Nixon "was beside himself" and desperate to do "something, *anything* that would reverse the previous neglect."[13] Beginning in 1969, the embassy in Santiago and the CIA and other U.S. intelligence agencies analyzed the Chilean political milieu with an eye toward the 1970 presidential elections. Ambassador Korry found all three candidates wanting and lamented that Frei could not continue as president. Korry added that it was in the vital interests of the United States to keep Allende from winning, for an Allende government "might be worse" than the Castro regime.[14] Nonetheless, as late as 30 July 1970, five weeks before the election, the consensus of the CIA and intelligence organizations in the Departments of State and Defense and the National Security Agency was that Alessandri was in the lead and might approach 40 percent of the vote. Indeed, Korry met Frei at his home for three hours on the day before the election and assured the worried, "morose" president that Alessandri would capture 38 percent of the vote and that Allende could not exceed 35 percent.[15] The ambassador and intelligence analysts made their predictions, knowing that the United States had again covertly intervened in Chilean politics. On 25 March 1970, the 303 Committee approved the expenditure of $125,000 as a "spoiling" operation. Money would be spent on propaganda discrediting Allende and his coalition. On 27 June, the committee on covert operations, now renamed the 40 Committee, approved the expenditure of an additional $300,000 to boost other candidates. The 40 Committee further established a contingency fund of $500,000 to be used to bribe Chilean legislators not to vote for Allende, for the time when the election inevitably reached the Chilean legislature. The CIA was also authorized to contact Chilean officials and military officers to discuss extraconstitutional measures they would support in the unlikely event that Allende received a plurality of the vote.[16] These contingency measures would provide the basis for the CIA's plan of action between 4 September and 24 October, dubbed Track I and Track II under the code name Project FUBELT.

The course of the Chilean election demonstrated that political campaigns matter in a free society. Alessandri started 1970 with the support of 45 percent of the electorate. But "Don Jorge" was seventy-four years old and displayed little energy or drive, lacked a cohesive party apparatus, and performed poorly on television. Radamiro Tomic confused his Christian Democrats by delivering full-blown attacks on the capitalist system. Christian Democrats, like President Frei, traditionally believed in a reformed capitalism. Allende, on the other hand, campaigned well and vigorously. The normally restrained Chileans were attracted to Allende's dashing style. As U.S. intelligence analysts later ruefully noted about Allende, "A taste for expensive sports cars, liquor, clothes, and women have indeed tended to add luster to his image rather than damage him politically."[17] The revolution that Allende called for would seemingly be accompanied by fine Chilean wine. Although the United States intervened in the local contest, no other power did. Viron Vaky reported to Kissinger that the Soviet Union maintained "a strict and aloof neutrality during the elections, apparently because it [was] not willing to jeopardize relations with a possible Tomic or Alessandri government, despite the tempting prospect of a Marxist electoral victory."[18]

In his shifting accounts of his actions toward Allende and Chile in his three volumes of memoirs, Kissinger claimed that he was not well informed on Chile.[19] But he chaired the 303 and 40 Committees that authorized the covert interventions in 1970. His aide for Latin America on the NSC, Viron Vaky, sent him updates on the Chilean elections. With his formidable intelligence and work ethic, Kissinger was always conversant on foreign-policy issues, whether major or minor. Kissinger blamed the Latin American section of the State Department for not embracing the Alessandri candidacy. Perhaps Kissinger was thinking of the department officers who opposed Anaconda Copper's suggestion that the company send money to the Alessandri campaign.[20] The department's man on the scene, Ambassador Korry, thought Alessandri the best of bad choices, but he despaired of Alessandri's performance. Kissinger further protested that the United States "acted in the most minimal and ineffectual fashion prior to the Chilean election." To be sure, the $425,000 allocated for campaign spending in Chile in 1970 was only about 15 percent of what the CIA spent between 1962 and 1964. Richard Nixon added in his one-page summary of Chile in his memoirs that the money was dispatched to counter heavy Cuban spending on Allende.[21] Cuban intervention is not raised in the declassified documentary evidence on covert activities, and Kissinger does not raise in his memoirs the presentation he gave in April 1971 to a graduate seminar on inter-American relations at Georgetown University. In response to a question about the relationship between Allende and Fidel Castro, Kissinger responded, "The election of Allende was an indigenous product; Castro had nothing to do with it. The competence of Allende's opponents had more to do with it!"[22]

In the aftermath of Allende's electoral triumph, Nixon and Kissinger launched their campaign to keep Salvador Allende from being inaugurated in November 1970. Scholars have had for two decades a first-rate understanding of the Nixon administration's intervention in Chile from 1969 to 1973. In the mid-1970s, the Senate Foreign Relations Committee, chaired by Senator Frank Church (D-ID), released two major studies on the intervention.[23] In 1999, President William Jefferson "Bill" Clinton authorized the declassification of 20,000 documents on Chile through the "Chile Declassification Project." Many of these key documents appeared in compilations released in 2014 and 2015 by the Historical Office of the Department of State. The documentary record has not sustained Henry Kissinger's repeated, laborious attempts to downplay his role in the destabilization of Allende's Chile.

Nixon was filled with fury in September and October 1970. As one veteran State Department officer recalled, the White House "had gone ape about this—ape." When he heard that a reporter for CBS television had characterized the election as "a victory not only for Marxists but also for Chilean democracy," the president demanded that aides find out the name of the reporter (George Natanson). Nixon immediately concluded that Allende's victory was a repeat of the Castro fiasco of 1959–1960, which he perpetually believed led to his electoral defeat in the 1960 presidential election. In a telephone conversation with Kissinger on 12 September, he actually suggested that Ambassador Korry, "a Kennedy Democrat," had been disloyal to him.[24] Nixon learned, however, that Korry was virulently anti-Allende. Korry, who had been a journalist for *Look* magazine before entering the diplomatic world, sent daily telegrams filled with florid prose about the need to stop Allende. He returned to Washington in mid-October to plot with Kissinger and Nixon. At a session in the Oval Office, an enraged Nixon startled the ambassador by striking his fist against his open palm and swearing that he would "smash" that "son of a bitch Allende."[25] Kissinger displayed the emotion of gloom. At the initial 40 Committee meeting to review what had happened, Kissinger called for a "cold-blooded assessment" of whether the United States could stimulate a military intervention to keep Allende from office. He expressed "considerable skepticism that once Allende is in the presidency there will be anyone capable of organizing any real counterforce against him."[26]

The Nixon administration declared war on Allende on 15 September 1970. Director of the CIA Richard Helms's handwritten notes of his meeting with President Nixon have become famous.[27]

- 1 in 10 chance perhaps, but save Chile!
- worth spending
- not concerned risks involved
- no involvement of embassy
- $10,000,000 available, more if necessary
- full-time job—best men we have
- game plan
- make economy scream
- 48 hours for plan of action

Kissinger would later claim that his president was prone to making "grandiloquent statements" and that historians should not focus on his tirade with Helms.[28] Helms later testified, however, that "if I ever carried a marshal's baton in my knapsack out of the Oval Office, it was that day."[29] Helms appointed Thomas Karamessines, the deputy director of planning, to assume responsibility for FUBELT. Veteran CIA officer David Atlee Phillips became chief of the task force in Washington.

The outrage expressed by Nixon and Kissinger—self-described foreign-policy "realists"—to an Allende presidency seemed out of proportion to conceivable national security threats. The Soviet Union subsidized communist parties throughout Latin America. But its support of Cuba cost more than $1 million a day, draining Soviet coffers. Chile was about as far away from the Soviet Union as it could possibly be. Concerns about the survival of democracy in Chile rang hollow. Nixon did not consider the region suitable for democracy, and Kissinger happily cooperated with Latin American dictators such as the Brazilian generals. In any case, Allende and his Unidad Popular coalition would be unable to destroy liberty in their country. Chile was a pluralistic society with independent centers of power—the security forces, the Christian Democrats, elements of organized labor, the Chilean legislature, the judiciary, and the Catholic Church. As one State Department officer noted, "To equate an Allende victory with a 'Castro-type dictatorship' assigns insufficient weight to Chile's profound differences from Cuba."[30] National Intelligence Estimates (NIEs), the combined work of the intelligence agencies, made similar points both before and during the Allende presidency. Viron Vaky repeatedly warned Kissinger that the United States would damage its international reputation if it were caught trying to subvert the democratic process.[31] Assistant Secretary of State for Latin America Jack Kubisch, who had extensive experience both in the foreign service and business world, informed Kissinger that the United States had no vital national security interests in Chile.[32]

In a peculiar way, Kissinger agreed with critics of the Nixon administration's assault on Salvador Allende. He famously jibed, "Chile was a dagger pointed at the heart of Antarctica."[33] Chile produced copper, but the United States was not dependent on Chilean copper. Trade with Chile amounted in 1970 to $457 million, far less than trade with Argentina, Brazil, Colombia, Mexico, and Venezuela. U.S. direct investments in Chile were not growing, because the Christian Democrats were establishing majority Chilean control of the copper companies. Nixon and Kissinger interpreted Allende's election within symbolic terms, asserting that Allende's victory imperiled the credibility of the United States in the region and throughout the world. A new version of the hoary domino theory would evolve if political radicals were permitted to gain power through constitutional means. Allende's election would encourage the communists in France and Italy to believe that there was a peaceful road to power. Kissinger warned, "The imitative spread of similar phenomena elsewhere would in turn significantly affect the world balance and our own position in it."[34] President Nixon drew similar conclusions. In 1971, he ordered CIA Director Helms to develop "a tough program, ask for plenty of money to do the job" to influence elections in Italy. As Nixon saw it, "Italy is a Latin country," adding, "I don't want to let this get screwed up like Chile."[35]

What the Nixon administration perpetrated in Chile between 4 September and 24 October had elements of both farce and tragedy. Track I was a daft scheme to prevent the Chilean congress from certifying Allende's victory. It involved bribing Chilean legislators and enlisting President Frei, Jorge Alessandri, and the Chilean military in a bewildering series of constitutional gambits. But as David Phillips of the CIA later conceded, the plan had no chance. His experience in Chile taught him this: "You might get away with bribing one Chilean Senator, but two? Never. And three? Not a chance. They would blow the whistle. They were democrats and had been for a long time."[36]

La via Chilena also undercut Track II, which aimed at a *golpe de estado* with the Chilean military seizing power. Between 5 and 20 October 1970, the CIA made twenty-one contacts with Chilean military and police officers. The CIA provided gas grenades, machine guns, and $50,000 to conspirators. CIA agents also worked to create a "coup climate," a sense of political crisis and confrontation, by spreading propaganda, waging "psychological warfare," and encouraging U.S. businesses not to spend money in Chile. The CIA even fed anti-Allende material to the popular news magazine *Time*.[37] The administration also deferred international loans to Chile and asked commercial banks to deny credit. Nixon and Kissinger were the driving forces behind Track II. At meetings of the 40 Committee and SAG, Kissinger informed attendees that "higher authority" or his "client" (Nixon) "had no intention of conceding before the 24th; on the contrary, he wanted no stone left unturned."[38] On 14 October, a U.S. military attaché in Santiago was instructed to inform two "trusted" Chilean officers that "high authority in Washington has authorized you to offer material support short of armed intervention to Chilean Armed Forces in any endeavors they may undertake to prevent the election of Allende on October 24, his inauguration on 4 [sic] November, or his subsequent overthrow."[39] For his part, Kissinger ridiculed studies such as NIE-97 that argued that the United States could live with an Allende government. The imaginative Kissinger foresaw Allende spreading communist revolution throughout Latin America, if not the world.[40]

The administration went forward, even though it was advised that Chile's military leaders would defend the constitution. For example, the CIA reported from sources that on 6 September, two days after the election, high-ranking military officers had privately met and that General René Schneider and General Carlos Prats, the commanders of the army, opposed a military strike.[41] Track II collapsed with the shooting on 22 October and subsequent death of General Schneider. Military conspirators had tried to kidnap Schneider, and when the general resisted, they shot him, hitting him in the spleen. It was Chile's first political assassination in 130 years, leaving citizens shocked and outraged. Two days after the shooting, Allende received more than 75 percent of the congressional vote.

The assassination of General Schneider has long marred Henry Kissinger's international reputation and has become a central feature of the "war criminal" scenario. He has struggled to escape responsibility. Men associated with General Roberto Viaux, who led the 1969 attack on the Frei administration, assassinated Schneider. On 15 October, Kissinger decided to end urging Viaux to launch a military *golpe*, because Viaux was, in Ambassador Korry's words, "unpredictable," and because Karamessines, the CIA deputy director of planning, estimated Viaux's chances of success as one in twenty.[42] As Kissinger lamented to Nixon on the telephone, "Nothing would be worse than an abortive coup."[43] But Nixon and Kissinger did not give up on Track II on 15 October. The message sent by the CIA to its station in Santiago on 16 October urged Viaux to preserve his assets and to join with other plotters, such as General Camilo Valenzuela. The Nixon administration remained committed to a "firm and continuing policy that Allende be overthrown by a coup."[44] Money and weapons were passed to General Valenzuela. His men twice unsuccessfully tried to kidnap Schneider. During the 48 hours between Schneider's assassination and Allende's inauguration, the CIA hoped General Valenzuela, who now controlled the Santiago garrison, would launch a *golpe*.[45] A military court in Chile subsequently found Generals Valenzuela and Viaux responsible for the assassination of General Schneider.

The question of U.S. responsibility for General Schneider's death can be related to a previous presidential entanglement with assassination. President John Kennedy did not order the assassination on 1 November 1963 of President Ngo Dinh Diem of South Vietnam. Kennedy took responsibility, however, for initiating a course of events in August 1963 that led to President Diem's assassination. Neither Nixon nor Kissinger adopted Kennedy's conviction that U.S. officials must be held accountable for their actions. Nixon does not mention General Schneider's death in his memoirs. He sent a grotesque letter to President Frei, calling the attack on Schneider "a repugnant event" and "a stain on the pages of contemporary history."[46] In his memoirs, Kissinger expressed no sorrow over Schneider's death. He offered the dubious proposition that the

CIA misunderstood his instructions. Kissinger claimed he wanted to end all military plots, not just Viaux's plot.[47] No document has surfaced in which Kissinger subsequently raised questions with the CIA about its activities in Chile between 16 and 24 October 1970.

The Cool but Hardly Correct Policy, 1971–1972

The failure of Operation FUBELT and the tragic death of General Schneider had not dissuaded the Nixon administration from its goal of smashing Salvador Allende. Nixon started off by being petty, declining to congratulate Allende on his ascension to the presidency. After a lengthy NSC meeting on Chile, the president issued National Security Decision Memorandum (NSDM) 93. The United States would take a "correct but cool" policy toward Allende. Public hostility toward Allende would provide the Chilean leader with an opportunity to rally domestic and international support. Although it would be publicly civil, the administration vowed "to maximize pressures on the Allende government to prevent its consolidation and limit its ability to implement policies contrary to U.S. and hemispheric interests." The directive also called on the United States to cultivate "friendly military leaders" in the hemisphere, particularly those in Argentina and Brazil. Harsh talk at the NSC meeting informed NSDM 93.[48] Both Secretary of State William Rogers and Secretary of State Melvin Laird agreed that "we have to do everything we can to hurt him [Allende] and bring him down." The president ranted, vowing, "No impression should be permitted in Latin America that they can get away with this, that it is safe to go this way. All over the world it is too much the fashion to kick us around." Nixon added that he was unconcerned about how democratic countries in Latin America would react to U.S. policies. The "game" was to keep military leaders of Argentina and Brazil closely aligned to the United States.[49]

Prior to the NSC meeting, Kissinger and General Vernon A. Walters had hardened the president's resolve. Walters was close to Nixon. Walters had an amazing capacity with languages, fluently speaking his native English as well as French, Italian, Portuguese, Spanish, and German. He also acquired a basic knowledge of other several other languages. He was the U.S. military adviser to the Brazilian expeditionary force in Italy in World War II. He translated for Presidents Harry Truman and Dwight Eisenhower and was with Nixon on his stormy tour of South America in 1958. Walters served as a U.S. military attaché in Brazil from 1962 to 1964 and was the contact with the Brazilian generals, who with U.S. support seized power in April 1964. A conservative, devout Catholic, Walters shared Nixon's disdain for activist priests and nuns in Latin

America. Walters served as an aide to Kissinger at the Paris peace talks. At Nixon's request, he kept in close contact with the Brazilian military dictators, whom Walters admired. Brazil would aid the U.S. campaign against Allende. In 1972, the president appointed Walters the deputy director of the CIA. On 3 November, the day Allende was inaugurated, Walters sent an apocalyptic warning to Nixon and Kissinger, proclaiming that the United States was engaged in a "mortal struggle" over the future of the world and that "there is no acceptable alternative to holding Latin America." Walters urged that the administration work with South American military forces to promote development within a non-Marxist framework. In response, Nixon wrote on the margin of the memorandum, "This is my preference." Nixon returned the memorandum to Kissinger with the notation "K[issinger]—Read the Walters memo again + see that it is implemented in *every* respect."[50]

Kissinger offered Nixon a similarly grim assessment of the forthcoming Allende presidency. He wrote, "[Allende] poses for us one of the most serious challenges ever faced in this hemisphere. . . . Your decision as to what to do about it may be the most historic and difficult foreign affairs decision you will have to make this year." Kissinger would subsequently absolve himself of what would happen by claiming, after the failure of Operation FUBELT, "I was not

In May 1972 in the Oval Office, President Nixon promoted Vernon Walters and named him deputy director of the CIA. Walters, who retired with the rank of lieutenant general, would serve as the Nixon and Ford administrations' contact with South American dictators and security officials. Nixon Library.

deeply engaged in Chilean matters." The documentary record demonstrates that his aides on the NSC kept him apprised of developments and that he participated in major decisions on covert activity. As Kissinger rationalized, "I don't see why we have to let a country go Marxist just because its people are irresponsible."[51]

In practice, "cool but correct" meant running a dual foreign policy. The administration recalled Ambassador Korry, who would advise on anti-Allende activities in Washington. Nixon and Kissinger decided to keep Korry occupied until the U.S. presidential election, because they feared he might talk to someone about Operation FUBELT. As Kissinger put it to Nixon in a telephone conversation, "[Korry] just knows too damn much. He's emotionally highly unstable."[52] Nixon appointed Nathaniel Davis, a career diplomat, to be the U.S. ambassador in Santiago. Davis did not involve himself intimately in plotting, as had his predecessor. He kept a tight control over embassy staff, signing off on each cable and requiring that he be present at every meeting with members of Allende's Cabinet. Davis later conceded that he was aware of spending by the CIA on opposition parties and the virulently anti-Allende newspaper El Mercurio, which was published by Augustín Edwards, a media mogul and friend of President Nixon. He also has noted that he was fully aware of Nixon and Kissinger's antipathy toward Allende.[53] But Ambassador Davis was either obtuse or disingenuous in claiming he knew nothing else. Foreign service officers in the embassy became friends with CIA agents in Chile and learned from them details of U.S. covert activities. Harry Shlaudeman, the deputy chief of mission, was especially well informed about covert activities, according to embassy personnel. Shlaudeman, a veteran diplomat, was probably Kissinger and the 40 Committee's man in Santiago.[54] Shlaudeman, who was recalled from Chile just before the fall of Allende, was subsequently richly rewarded by Secretary of State Kissinger. Shlaudeman was named an ambassador to Venezuela in 1975 and then assistant secretary of state for Latin America in 1976. In the 1980s, he worked with Kissinger on Ronald Reagan's National Bipartisan Commission on Central America.

Under the aegis of NSDM 93, officials in Washington and agents in Chile carried out the policy of undermining the new government. The United States conducted economic warfare against Chile. U.S. economic aid, which had been $260 million in 1967, amounted to only $7.4 million in 1972. Economic aid was restricted to institutions judged as centers of anti-Allende viewpoints, such as the Catholic University in Santiago. The Export-Import Bank denied commercial loans and credits, making it nearly impossible for Chileans to obtain replacement parts for their U.S.-made vehicles and machinery. The United States used its voting power to delay or deny loans to Chile. The Inter-American

Development Bank provided Chile with $46 million in loans in 1970s but only $2 million during the Allende presidency.[55] U.S. officials defended these policies by pointing out that Chile violated norms of international commerce, nationalizing U.S. properties and suspending payments on international loans. But the policy was the fulfillment of President Nixon's directive to CIA Director Helms to make the Chilean economy "scream."

The CIA admitted to spending $7 million in Chile between 1970 and 1973, although the agency may have channeled additional funds into the country through third parties. Financed by the CIA, *El Mercurio* and the television and radio stations of Agustín Edwards denounced the government on a daily basis and began to suggest in 1972 that the Chilean military seize power. The CIA also funded conservative parties and the anti-Allende wing of the Christian Democrats. Officials in Washington and Ambassador Davis justified the spending as a means to preserve democratic freedoms. In April 1971, in a meeting in the president's hideaway office in the Executive Office Building, Kissinger opined to Nixon that Allende would follow the "German strategy" of Adolf Hitler of gradually eliminating dissent to create a "fascist" state. In June, speaking in the Oval Office, Kissinger and Nixon took turns denouncing Allende, with Nixon demanding a "harder line" on Chile. Kissinger agreed, claiming that the Chilean leader was gaining control over the press and police and isolating the military. Chile would "never have a free election," lamented Kissinger. Ironically, Nixon and Kissinger discussed in detail the results of the free and open elections that took place in Chile between 1971 and 1973 and decried the growing electoral strength of Allende's coalition, Unidad Popular.[56]

Nixon and Kissinger's anxieties about freedom in Chile cannot, of course, be taken seriously. Salvador Allende practiced parliamentary democracy. All Chileans, wherever they stood in the political spectrum, were free to speak, shout, or write their own hysterical versions of events. Ambassador Davis acknowledged that Chile remained an "open society" until 11 September 1973. Davis found Allende an attractive, relaxed person with a puckish sense of humor. He also noted that Allende rejected violence. Economist Samuel F. Hart, who was attached to the U.S. embassy from 1971 to 1975, related that Allende was no "flaming revolutionary" but "essentially a bourgeois, gradualist kind of person."[57] To be sure, political violence and terrorist acts led to the deaths of a hundred citizens in Allende's Chile. But scholars who have investigated the mayhem have found that right-wing extremist groups bore responsibility for the violence. CIA money went to a fascist paramilitary group, Patria y Libertad (Peace and Liberty), that perpetrated terrorism.[58]

As foreign-policy realists, Nixon and Kissinger presumably would focus on Allende's international initiatives. Since the Peace of Westphalia (1648), which ended the European wars of religion known as the Thirty Years' War, the cardinal imperative of realism has been respect for the principle of sovereignty. Countries judged other governments by how they acted in the international arena and not on how they ruled at home. After becoming secretary of state, Kissinger would constantly cite the principle when he resisted congressional efforts to impose human rights conditions on aid to South America's military dictators. Allende tried to assuage the Nixon administration's mortal fears of him. In 4 November, he passed a note to a State Department officer attending his inauguration, pledging that Chile would never allow its soil to be used by a power hostile to the United States.[59] Allende was obviously referring to the Cuban Missile Crisis. Chile conducted normal diplomatic relations with Cuba and the People's Republic of China. Fidel Castro came to Chile for a month in 1971 and overstayed his welcome. Allende ignored Castro's unsolicited advice to supersede constitutional principles and to arm workers. He also repudiated the schemes of the Cuban embassy in Santiago to arm Chilean extreme leftists, the MIR. The CIA produced no evidence of Chilean support for insurgencies in Latin America. In late 1972, Allende journeyed to Moscow, seeking economic aid. His mission failed. The Soviets found his economic strategies to be incomprehensible. And as CIA Director Helms reminded President Nixon, the Soviets were burdened by their daily $1 million subsidy to Cuba. In any case, Moscow practiced détente; it was not interested in alienating Nixon and Kissinger by challenging the United States in its traditional sphere of influence. The big prize for the Soviet Union was to have the West recognize its suzerainty in Eastern Europe and the permanent division of Germany. This was achieved with the Helsinki Accords (1975).[60] In August 1971, an NIE aptly summarized Allende's foreign policy. Allende was not challenging the Cold War balance of power. Allende saw "no advantage in needlessly antagonizing the United States in such a sensitive manner as Western Hemisphere security." The Chilean followed an "independent nationalist course," not wanting to alienate the noncommunist world.[61] Chile received economic assistance from Western nations, such as Sweden.

Meanwhile, Over in Bolivia

The plethora of documents available on Chile have absorbed scholars and perhaps caused them to miss what happened in Bolivia during the Allende years. Records on U.S. relations with Bolivia were also classified until 2015. Scholars had speculated that the United States played a role in the overthrow of President Juan José Torres in August 1971 but were uncertain of the facts.[62] Indeed, in a campaign directed by Henry Kissinger, the United States aided the over-throw of a purported leftist government. The discreet U.S. intervention in Bo-livia was connected to the war against Allende and served as a dress rehearsal for the final assault on Allende.

The landlocked nation of Bolivia has traditionally been characterized as a land with problems. In 1970, the country had deep socioeconomic and racial inequities. It was the poorest country in South America and, aside from Haiti, the poorest country in the Western Hemisphere. Per capita income for Bo-livia's 3.8 million people was under $200 a year. Life expectancy was below fifty years of age. The poorest and most repressed of Bolivians were indige-nous people, who represented over 20 percent of the population. Most Boliv-ians were mixed-blood *mestizos*, with many identifying with and living in indigenous communities. Many indigenous people did not speak Spanish but rather communicated in native languages, such as Quechua, the language of the ancient Inca Empire. What would become Bolivia was highly valuable to both the Incas and Spanish colonialists because of its mineral wealth—gold and silver. Bolivia's earth continued to produce mineral bounty, with tin and oil being exploited in the twentieth century and natural gas in the twenty-first century. Most accounts raise the issue of political volatility, with Bolivia, which became independent in 1825, having more presidents than years of independ-ence. The CIA's online *World Factbook* (2017) notes that since 1825 "much of its subsequent history has consisted of a series of coups and countercoups." Such a patronizing view obscures both the awesome beauty of Bolivia and the vibrancy of its culture. The country's topography ranges from the Andes Moun-tains, to the Atacama Desert, to the salt flats of Salar de Uyuni, to the rainfor-ests of the Amazon Basin, to the smooth waters of Lake Titicaca. The ancient capital city of La Paz is situated on the Andes Altiplano at an altitude of 12,000 feet. Indigenous people have preserved for millennia their rich, ritualized cul-ture, which emphasizes the community over the individual.

The epoch historical event for Bolivia in the twentieth century was the rev-olution of 1952. In April 1952, in a bloody uprising, the Movimiento Naciona-lista Revolucionario (MNR), or National Revolutionary Movement, took control of Bolivia. In 1951, the MNR's candidate, Víctor Paz Estenssoro, had been elected president, but the Bolivian army had disallowed the election and seized power. The MNR represented a vast array of disaffected Bolivians, including middle-class intellectuals, small entrepreneurs, junior military officers, the ru-ral poor, and mine workers. They judged that Bolivia's traditional rulers—large landholders, senior military officers, and mine owners—were incompetent and corrupt. Led by President Paz Estenssoro (1952–1956, 1960–1964), the MNR set out to topple the nation's oligarchic socioeconomic structure. It purged the army, established its own militia, enfranchised illiterate Bolivians, nationalized tin mines, and redistributed land.

The Eisenhower administration embraced the Bolivian Revolution. Between 1953 and 1961, the United States gave Bolivia $192.5 million in economic assistance, $178.8 million of that in grants. On a per capita basis, Bolivia received more economic aid from the United States than any other country in the world. In 1957, the Eisenhower administration supplied nearly 40 percent of Bolivia's national budget. Eisenhower and his advisers perceived Estenssoro and his successor, Hernán Siles Zuazo (1956–1960), as noncommunist reformers. This judgment that Bolivian leaders were at heart reformers and not revolutionaries was reinforced by Bolivia's able ambassador in Washington, Víctor Andrade. Ambassador Andrade frequently played golf with President Eisenhower. The Eisenhower team used the U.S. largess to curb political radicalism and economic nationalism. Support for the Bolivian presidents was intended to undermine the left wing of the MNR led by Juan Lechín, the leader of the mine workers. The United States also insisted that the government compensate the tin mine owners, implement U.S.-designed economic stabilization plans, and adopt legislation that permitted foreign companies to look for oil. Gulf Oil, a U.S. concern, began to drill in Bolivia.[63] The United States also recommended that Bolivia rebuild a professional army and not rely on militias loyal to the MNR and the Bolivian Revolution for security. As Ernest V. Siracusa, a State Department official overseeing relations with Bolivia from Washington, reasoned, a reconstituted army would serve as "insurance" against "extreme circumstances."[64] Direct U.S. military assistance began in 1958. Siracusa would serve as the U.S. ambassador in La Paz from 1969 to 1973.

The Kennedy administration, under the aegis of the Alliance for Progress, continued to use foreign aid to manage Bolivia's political life. U.S. aid remained substantial, constituting 20 percent of Bolivia's economy. Between 1953 and 1970, the United States provided Bolivia with over $500 million in aid.[65] Kennedy and his advisers respected President Paz, but they became exasperated by the president's reluctance to crush political radicals and by his refusal to break diplomatic relations with Castro's Cuba. Bolivia also entertained offers of economic assistance from the Soviet Union as means of inducing the United States to provide more money. Paz eventually succumbed to U.S. pressure, brutally suppressing striking miners, disarming the peasant militias, and closing the Cuban embassy in La Paz in 1964. Paz also permitted the United States to sponsor military "civic-action" programs in Bolivia. Military units went into the countryside, building roads, installing water pipes, and providing medical services. The rationale was that economic development and modernization in rural areas would ensure that communists could not build bases of support in the countryside, as they had in China in the 1930s and Cuba in the 1950s. Officers who oversaw these projects had attended U.S. war schools in the United States and the Panama Canal Zone. Such experiences stimulated the belief among the new, modernized Bolivian military that it had the capability and expertise to govern the country.[66]

Twelve years of civilian rule ended in 1964 when General René Barrientos Ortuño (1964–1969), the commander of the air force, overthrew the Paz government in November 1964. The *golpe* followed five months after the military seized power in Brazil, Bolivia's powerful neighbor to the east. President Paz had weakened the MNR coalition through his authoritarian actions. Political leftists cheered his overthrow. Bolivians also objected to Paz's *continuismo*, a third term as president. General Barrientos had political appeal and talent. He was identified with MNR, having piloted the plane that brought Paz back to Bolivia from exile in 1952. General Barrientos oversaw many of the civic-action projects. He cut a dashing figure, parachuting out of planes in public ceremonies. He also spoke Quechua. U.S. officials in Bolivia admired Barrientos and were not alarmed when he replaced Paz.[67] Barrientos proved to be an ally of the United States and a friend of U.S. businesses in Bolivia. He worked with the CIA and U.S. Special Forces in capturing Che Guevara in southeastern Bolivia in 1967. Major Ralph "Pappy" Shelton of the Green Berets, a decorated combat veteran, trained a Bolivian ranger battalion that joined the hunt for Guevara. A CIA operative, Felix Rodríguez, organized an intelligence network in the countryside and briefly interrogated the captured Guevara. Bolivians disliked having Guevara, a native of Argentina, disrupting their country, and campesinos reported on Guevara's movements to authorities. Guevara found to his surprise that the rural folk spoke the indigenous language of Guaraní and not Spanish.[68] Barrientos perished in a helicopter crash in April 1969. The helicopter had been given to Barrientos by Gulf Oil.

Bolivia seethed with discontent about the United States when Ambassador Siracusa arrived in La Paz in late 1969. Bolivians deplored foreigners meddling in their country, whether they were Guevara and his band of Cuban guerrillas or the CIA. Allegations had arisen that Barrientos had been on the CIA payroll. Larry Sternfield, the CIA station chief, later boasted that until Barrientos's death, "nothing happened in Bolivia without our involvement."[69] Bolivians were disappointed with the achievements of the Alliance for Progress. The visible presence of so many U.S. officials also irritated Bolivians. U.S. officials had been vetoing proposed cabinet appointments.[70] General Alfredo Ovando Candía (1969–1970), the commander of the armed forces, took over the government in September 1969. The always complicated country had become politically complex. The MNR had broken into factionalism. Various military officers vied for power. A homegrown guerrilla group, Ejército Liberación Nacional (ELN), or the National Liberation Army, attracted university students to its cause of a revolution in the countryside. Bolivian campesinos were predictably unimpressed with what urban young people had to offer them.

General Ovando, who was nationalistic but anticommunist, tried to curry popular favor by expropriating Gulf Oil. Bolivians of all political persuasions believed that Gulf had a privileged legal position in Bolivia and competed unfairly against the national oil company. Ovando also established ambassador-level relations with the Soviet Union, hoping for aid and new markets for Bolivian tin. The aggressive Ambassador Siracusa faced down General Ovando. Siracusa was a career service officer; Bolivia was his first ambassadorial assignment. Although he professed to admire indigenous culture, Siracusa defamed Bolivians for their "violent past" and "penchant for violence." Cabinet ministers were "paranoically anti-American." He characterized General Ovando as a "somewhat senile old general." Born in 1918, Ovando was fifty-two years of age in 1970 and lived until 1982. Siracusa became the Nixon administration's favorite ambassador in Latin America. Both Nixon and Kissinger found Siracusa's sarcastic dispatches about Bolivian political culture to be amusing. Nixon sent him a note of congratulations for defending the role of the United States in Latin America in a speech before the Bolivian–North American Business Council in La Paz. Siracusa returned the compliment, noting that he "found President Nixon to be very interested in Bolivia and well informed on Latin America in general."[71]

Siracusa employed bullying tactics and economic pressure to force Ovando to succumb to U.S. policies. At two meetings in Ovando's home in December 1969 and January 1970, Ambassador Siracusa used a "hard and direct" tone deploring the "hate campaign" against the United States in Bolivia. Deploying "all the emphasis and clarity at my command," Siracusa informed the Bolivian president of the "national psychosis" about the CIA in Bolivia. The ambassador had been angered by graffiti linking him to the CIA he had seen on walls along a road linking the airport to the capital. Siracusa threatened to leave his post, presenting Ovando with an ultimatum: "Did he or did he not want an American ambassador in Bolivia?"[72] Siracusa's threats were accompanied by tangible pressures. Washington instructed Siracusa to identify "moderate elements in the Bolivian power structure" but "without giving the impression the Embassy was interfering in Bolivian affairs." The Nixon administration also slowed the flow of economic and military aid to Bolivia. By September 1970, the government agreed to settle with Gulf Oil, awarding it

$78 million in compensation. Ambassador Siracusa celebrated with Ovando and his cabinet but cautioned Washington that "this being Bolivia, it is always possible that tomorrow's news may disrupt today's."[73]

Ambassador Siracusa proved prophetic. Political factions within the military and in the civilian population judged Ovando's initiatives as either too moderate or too radical. His appeasement of Ambassador Siracusa and the Nixon administration frustrated Bolivians. In a confusing day that saw various factions within the military reach for power, General Juan José Torres Gonzales (1970–1971) claimed leadership on 4 October 1970. Torres, unlike Ovando, was committed to far-reaching reform. He had been born poor and had been influenced by the spirit of the Bolivian Revolution. Hardworking and loyal, he had risen through the ranks of the new Bolivian military. Torres would establish a Popular Assembly, "an organ of workers' and popular power," that would presumably serve as a more authentic voice of the people than the Bolivian legislature. The new body would approve resolutions calling for a workers' university, the nationalization of all mining enterprises, and the ousting of the Peace Corps. Although such a people's forum seemed something out of the French Revolution, dispassionate analysts noted that the assembly had no real power. Assistant Secretary of State for Latin America Charles A. Meyer even opined that members of the assembly had shown "responsible" leadership.[74] The rise of General Torres came during the Track I and II period, with the Nixon administration scheming to prevent Salvador Allende from gaining the presidency in Chile. An alarmed Kissinger predicted to Nixon on 7 October that General Torres would be "ultra-nationalistic, leftist and anti-US."[75]

A week after his initial warning to the president, Kissinger sent a more optimistic memorandum to Nixon suggesting that Torres was not a replica of Allende but might be a classic Latin American caudillo, or strongman, in the mold of a Juan Perón of Argentina or Anastasio Somoza of Nicaragua. If the United States signaled support, Torres might pursue a moderate course. Nixon thereafter decided to postpone sales of U.S. stockpiles of tin, for a sale would inevitably drive down the price of Bolivian tin and hurt export earnings.[76] By May 1971, however, Nixon and Kissinger had decided to do away with Torres. Nixon had met for an hour with Ambassador Siracusa at the White House. Siracusa had expected only a five-minute courtesy visit with the president. Siracusa had been reporting from La Paz that Torres was transforming Bolivia into another Cuba and that the Soviet Union was assigning more personnel to its embassy. After the meeting in a telephone conversation with Kissinger, Nixon said of Siracusa, "He's just one of a few tough hard-line ambassadors."[77] A month later, on 11 June, Nixon and Kissinger discussed on the telephone on how to remove Torres. Kissinger informed Nixon that he had ordered the

CIA's deputy director of planning, Thomas Karamessines, the man who oversaw Operation FUBELT in Chile, to "crank up an operation post-haste." Nixon rued that "we gave those goddamn Bolivians that tin." The next week, Kissinger decided to woo the Bolivian military with an immediate delivery of $1 million in military aid, with the promise of $6 million more. As he remarked to Deputy Secretary of Defense David Packard, the $1 million aid package "is worth the gamble." Kissinger also ruled that new economic aid would not be forthcoming and that the United States would take steps to delay international loans to Bolivia. Such tactics were also being used against Allende. On 23 June, in NSDM 114, the president signed off on Kissinger's policy.[78]

The U.S. plotting against Torres accelerated in July. The 40 Committee, with Attorney General John Mitchell serving as acting chair, approved an expenditure of $410,000 in covert funding to be directed at military leaders and moderates within the MNR. Ambassador Siracusa seemed to have second thoughts, labeling the covert funding "coup money" and recommending that the United States try economic aid as a way to increase influence with General Torres. Siracusa also worried that the plot might be "exposed." The 40 Committee was, however, operating under the influence of Siracusa's dispatches, which warned that the Soviet Union had 150 people in its embassy in La Paz and might take over Bolivia.[79] What seems not to have been influential was the CIA's analysis of the Soviet's Union's role in Bolivia. Since establishing relations in 1969 and having an ambassador arrive in 1970, the Soviets had concluded minor trade deals, proposed various cultural exchanges, and offered forty scholarships for Bolivian students to study in the Soviet Union. CIA analysts saw the Soviets as being "fairly low key" in their approach to the Torres government. The Soviets could possibly take advantage of the chaos in Bolivia. The CIA reasoned, however, that "it is highly doubtful" that "the USSR desires to become deeply committed in so inherently unstable a political situation."[80]

Disorganization and factionalism within the military and society created the context for an inexpensive and rapid, albeit violent, overthrow of Torres. Precautions were taken. Ambassador Siracusa sent his family home in June 1971 and then received a "Personal Security Unit" to protect him in La Paz. The ambassador in Saigon was the only other U.S. ambassador to have such a security detail. In August, Siracusa returned home for vacation.[81] Whether part of the plan or not, Siracusa's absence exonerated the embassy of any complicity in the *golpe*. Ambassador Davis would be similarly out of Chile when the Chilean military moved against Allende. CIA money was initially used to discourage unreliable military officers from attacking the government. The U.S. man for La Paz was Colonel Hugo Banzer Suárez, who was in exile in Argentina. Banzer had been involved in an effort in January to overthrow Torres.

The CIA depicted Banzer as "avowedly anti-Communist" and one who would reverse the leftist policies of Generals Ovando and Torres.[82] The U.S. military knew Banzer well, for he had taken military courses at Fort Hood in Texas and at the School of the Americas in Panama. Major Robert J. Lundin apparently served as the U.S. contact with Banzer. Lundin, who served as an adviser to the Bolivian Air Force School in Santa Cruz, communicated frequently with Banzer and met with him in Santa Cruz, Banzer's home city, when the colonel clandestinely slipped back into Bolivia. Major Lundin arranged for Banzer to use U.S. military communications to maintain contact with rebel units in La Paz.[83] Banzer received financing for the *golpe* from private business groups in Bolivia. On 21 August, in the daily briefing he received from the CIA, President Nixon was informed that the situation in Bolivia was "murky." Kissinger, however, radiated confidence, telling aides, "Let's just relax and see what happens."[84] Banzer had full control of the government by 23 August. The Torres government had lasted ten months.

Brazil's military rulers also assisted Colonel Banzer's seizure of power. The Brazilian generals, especially Emílio Garrastazu Médici (1969–1974), perceived themselves as the guardians of Christianity and Western civilization. During Torres's tenure, the Brazilian ambassador in La Paz openly assisted right-wing attempts to overthrow Torres. The government subsequently deported the Brazilian ambassador.[85] When President Nixon hosted General Médici in Washington in December 1971, he was surprised but was "very happy" to learn that Brazil had assisted in the campaign against Torres. Nixon knew and approved of Brazil's efforts to encourage military rule in Uruguay. The president instructed Kissinger to open a back-channel communication with Brazil's foreign minister. The United States and Brazil would work together to overthrow Salvador Allende, with the United States providing money and "other discreet aid." As Nixon observed, "There were many things that Brazil as a South American country could do that the U.S. could not."[86] For his part, Banzer would ally Bolivia with Brazil and join with Brazil in Operation Condor, the international assassination project organized by Chile in the post-Allende years.

While contemplating the day that Allende would be overthrown, the Nixon administration took immediate steps to bolster the Banzer regime (1971–1978). The steps taken in Bolivia would be repeated in Chile. Bolivia was granted an emergency $10 million aid package. Kissinger overruled State Department officials who thought aid should not be granted until a plan for Bolivia's long-term development had been designed. In all, Bolivia received $63 million during the Banzer regime's first year in power. Bolivia would continue to be showered with U.S. munificence during the Kissinger years. Kissinger asked the rhetorical question "Why are we always so tough with friends?" to officials in

Washington who questioned the spending.[87] Ambassador Siracusa, who rushed back to La Paz two days after the *golpe*, agreed with Kissinger. He fawned over President Banzer. The Bolivian was an "attractive," "sympathetic," and "coura-geous" leader and a "typically Catholic family man" who had given the United States the gift of a "victory over communism."[88] The ambassador hoped President Nixon could honor Banzer by hosting him in Washington in 1973. Although that did not happen, Secretary of State Kissinger made a surprise visit to his friend, traveling to Banzer's home in Santa Cruz in June 1976. Link-ing Bolivia to military rule in Chile, Kissinger told Banzer, "We understand your problem."[89] Siracusa was not at the meeting; a grateful Nixon and Kiss-inger had assigned him to Uruguay to oversee the consolidation of military rule in that traditionally democratic nation.

Ambassador Siracusa conceded that the new regime had taken "many po-litical prisoners" but added that the government had no "intent" to be repres-sive. He also excused abuses of prisoners, noting that Bolivia lacked the resources, tradition, and capability of conducting orderly and fair trials.[90] Re-pression marked life in Bolivia during the Banzer years. The regime arrested 15,000 people, tortured 8,000, and "disappeared" 155 citizens without a trace. Another 19,000 Bolivians fled the country.[91] One of those was General Torres, who had sought refuge in Argentina in 1971 and was assassinated shortly after the Argentine military took power in March 1976. When interviewed in 1989, Siracusa protested that he personally liked Torres and that his death was an unsolved mystery.[92] The ambassador apparently had forgotten about Opera-tion Condor.

That Chilean Guy May Have Some Problems

Upon hearing from Henry Kissinger on 26 August 1971 that "a right-wing gov-ernment" had replaced General Torres, President Nixon pointedly asked, "What about Chile?"[93] Having successfully developed tactics on how to overthrow a Latin American government and bolster a new military dictatorship, the Nixon administration prepared its final assault on Salvador Allende. The administra-tion would accelerate its efforts to destabilize the Chilean government in the aftermath of legislative elections in March 1973. Chile in early 1973 was po-litically and economically tumultuous. Scholars such as Jonathan Haslam have made the case that the Allende government had taken measures that were eco-nomically unviable and that economic collapse was in the offing. The govern-ment had raised wages for low-income workers and lowered prices on basic food necessities. It had increased consumption without a matching increase in production. The result was price inflation that hit 500 percent in 1973. The escudo, the Chilean unit of currency, was officially pegged to the U.S. dollar at 46 to 1. On the black market, a dollar claimed 280 to 300 escudos. Haslam coined the term "assisted suicide" to characterize the Allende years, recognizing that the $7 million the CIA spent added to political polarization and that U.S. maneuvers to block Chile's access to international loans contributed to the economic turbulence.[94] Notwithstanding the disorder, Allende and Unidad Popular retained significant support among urban workers, who saw their standard of living rising; among campesinos, who were becoming landowners; and among young Chileans, who admired Allende's socialist vision.

The Nixon administration, the CIA, and Chilean conservatives looked forward to the March 1973 legislative elections. The hope of conservatives was that anti-Allende parties would gain an overwhelming majority in the Chamber of Deputies and the Senate and be in a position to impeach Allende and remove him from office. On 26 October 1972, the 40 Committee assigned $1,427,666 for the support of four anti-Allende political parties. In February 1973, the CIA requested and received an additional $200,000 for campaign spending. Of the more than $1.6 million, all but $25,000 would be spent. The CIA set a more modest goal than Chilean conservatives, envisaging that 60 percent of the legislators elected would be opposed to Allende and Unidad Popular.[95] Electoral results disappointed the Nixon administration. Legislators pledged to Unidad Popular received 43.3 percent of the vote, an increase from the 36.6 percent of the vote garnered in 1970. Unidad Popular would have two additional senators and four additional deputies, albeit not a governing majority. The CIA concluded that the candidates it supported had been energetic and organized. The results showed, however, "a conviction on the part of lower income groups and younger voters that their interests lie with Allende and his Popular Unity forces."[96] The result further suggested that Unidad Popular might retain the presidency in the 1976 election.

President Allende radiated this political strength when Secretary of State William Rogers called on him at the Chilean embassy in Buenos Aires on 29 May 1973. Both men were attending the inauguration of President Héctor Cámpora and the restoration of constitutional rule in Argentina. Rogers wanted to talk about compensation for the copper companies. Allende deflected Rogers, responding truthfully that the expropriation of the copper companies had overwhelming support among Chileans. He added that the companies had made "fabulous, almost incredible profits" and had never built manufacturing or processing industries in Chile. Chile thus "remained simply a producer of raw materials." Allende's predecessor, President Eduardo Frei, held similar beliefs. Allende further noted that "as a Socialist and as a man who believed in democratic freedom and pluralism," he sensed a desire for change in Latin America and hoped the United States would not block or frustrate those sentiments. Saying he hoped this was strictly between him and the secretary of state, Allende related to Rogers the advice he had received from his friend of twelve years, Fidel Castro. Castro had said, "Don't get into fights with the US unnecessarily, and watch your dollars." Allende judged that "very sound advice."[97]

In the summer of 1973, U.S. officials debated where to put another $1 million of covert funding into Chile. Assistant Secretary of State Kubisch resisted more funding, believing that national security issues were not at stake and that Chile had the responsibility "to save itself." Ambassador Davis favored the continued funding of political parties and the media on the demonstrably false premise that Allende was destroying civic life in Chile. The latest NIE on Chile again noted that the opposition still controlled the legislature and was influential "in the judiciary, the news media, the educational system, organized labor and some sectors of the economy." Davis opposed the desire of the station chief of the CIA in Santiago to fund private groups, however, because such entities were urging the military to overthrow Allende. The ambassador thought it was U.S. policy not to be involved in a *golpe*. Deputy Chief of Mission Shlaudeman, who had been recalled to Washington, knew very well what U.S. agents were doing in Chile, explained, "The important step was to keep clear of any role in which we were attempting ourselves to engage in operational activities."[98] Shlaudeman's formula was put into practice. Knowing that military plotters were conspiring with private groups who planned a nationwide truckers' strike beginning on 25 July, the CIA passed covert money to intermediaries who transferred the money to the strikers.[99] The strike went on through August; it paralyzed the economy and plunged Chile into crisis.

What mattered most were the views and actions of Nixon and Kissinger and high-ranking Chilean military officers. On 4 July, just before relaxing for the holiday, Nixon telephoned his national security advisor and engaged in a circumlocutious conversation. Nixon opened by saying, "You know I think that Chilean guy may have some problems." Kissinger agreed: "He has definitely massive problems." Nixon added: "If only the Army could get a few people behind them." The two then discussed the recent failure of a renegade Chilean Air Force commander to overthrow the government. The CIA knew the details of the plot a month before it was launched. Kissinger related, "That coup last week—we had nothing to do with it but still it came off prematurely." Noting that in the aftermath of the failed *golpe* Allende had not yet added military officers to his cabinet, Nixon pointed out, "Those military guys are very proud down there and they just may—right?" Kissinger again agreed with his boss: "Yes, I think he's definitely in difficulties."[100]

Relying on the military to overthrow a leftist government in Latin America had been the standard operating procedure of U.S. presidential administrations during the Cold War. With U.S. encouragement and support, military officers had overthrown constitutional governments in Guatemala and Brazil and the regime of General Torres in Bolivia. The numerous efforts between 1961 and 1965 to overthrow Fidel Castro, such as at the Bay of Pigs, failed because Castro and Guevara had dismantled the Cuban armed forces and fashioned a military that was loyal to the Cuban Revolution. The Nixon administration took care to cultivate the Chilean military, providing more than $33 million in aid and equipment between 1971 and 1973, a more than 40 percent increase over the previous three years. More than 600 junior officers and non-commissioned officers attended U.S. war schools in the Canal Zone. The CIA funded an anti-Allende newsletter for military officers. It also kept in contact with senior Chilean officers, reporting, for example, that General Augusto Pinochet had kept his political thoughts to himself at a dinner party in August 1971. In 1972, a CIA source within Pinochet's entourage reported that the general now believed that "Allende must be forced to step down or be eliminated." While in the Canal Zone to negotiate the purchase of U.S. tanks, General Pinochet was told by U.S. military officers that the "U.S. will support coup against Allende 'with whatever means necessary' when time comes."[101]

On 11 September 1973, the Chilean armed forces overthrew the Allende government. Jets strafed and bombed the presidential palace, La Moneda, pinpointing Allende's offices. Allende made a historic radio broadcast beginning at 9:10 a.m., with "my last words." The address is cherished by contemporary Chileans for its dignity. The president proclaimed, "I have faith in Chile and its destiny." Those words are inscribed under the impressive statue of Allende that Chileans would ultimately place in front of La Moneda. Allende committed suicide. General Pinochet had developed a scheme to assassinate Allende if he was captured alive.

U.S. officials anticipated the dramatic events of 11 September. On 13 August 1973, David Phillips, who oversaw CIA operations in Latin America, reported that sources estimated that Allende would not last six weeks, with the economy collapsing because of the strike by truckers. Officials in Washington calculated that the resignation of General Carlos Prats as commander in chief of the army on 23 August "removes from the armed forces the most effective opponent to coup-minded military plotters." General Pinochet assumed command. Both in Washington and in the embassy in Santiago, U.S. officials prepared to aid the golpistas, positioning riot-control gear, tear gas, and food in the Canal Zone. CIA agents monitored military plotting and knew an attack

The statue of President Salvador Allende is located between the presidential palace and the Ministry of Justice in Santiago. Author's photo.

was imminent on 11 September.[102] Adhering to the Shlaudeman formula, the CIA did not participate in the operations of the *golpe*.

In his memoirs, President Nixon simply noted that after three years of inefficiency and crippling strikes, the Chilean military overthrew Allende. Kissinger felt it necessary to defend himself repeatedly in the three volumes of his memoirs, decrying the "mythology" that the United States had "relentlessly assaulted" Allende between November 1971 and September 1973. The vindictive Kissinger also assaulted the character of President Allende, retelling the canard that the Chilean leader "tried to throttle free expression."[103] Ambassador Davis and his embassy staff placed blame on Allende's mishandling of the economy for the military's seizure of power.[104] Scholars have also absolved the United States for the *golpe*, holding Allende accountable for the chaos and disorder that prompted the military to act.[105] To make such arguments is to engage in counterfactual reasoning, for the Nixon administration pursued policies to prevent Allende from assuming office and then fomented political polarization and economic instability in the country. The counterfactual approach also raises ironic contemporary issues. Ariel Dorfman, the renowned Argentine-Chilean novelist and playwright who fled Pinochet's terror, noted the irony of the CIA—"the very agency that gave not a whit for the independence of other nations"—deploring Russia interference in the U.S. presidential elections of 2016. Nikki Haley, President Donald Trump's ambassador to the United Nations, said in an October 2017 forum hosted by President George W. Bush, "I will tell you that when a country can come interfere in another country's elections, that is warfare."[106] Political analysts and scholars can exhaust themselves trying to parse out the international and domestic dimensions of the tragedy that would engulf Chile. U.S. officials inadvertently highlighted the complexity of the issue. Harry Shlaudeman conceded, "Our activities may have contributed to—probably did contribute to the atmosphere in which the military moved, but the military moved on their own, for their own reasons." On 25 August 1973, in the context of a recommendation to pass money to private groups collaborating with the Chilean military, CIA Director William E. Colby reported to Kissinger that his agents would not be plotting directly with the armed forces of Chile. But "realistically, of course, a coup could result from increased opposition pressure on the Allende government."[107]

Richard Nixon and Henry Kissinger should have the last word on the question of U.S. responsibility for the events of 11 September. On Sunday, 16 September, the two had a telephone conversation. Kissinger sought to block the release of a transcript of the conversation for thirty years. After first discussing his plan to attend a Washington Redskins football game, Kissinger celebrated the end of the Allende government, lamenting that the media did not share his joy over what had happened in Chile. Conceivably thinking about the covert interventions in Iran and Guatemala, Kissinger added, "In the Eisenhower period we would be heroes." Nixon responded, "Well we didn't, as you know—our hand doesn't show on this one though." "We didn't do it," Kissinger declared, "I mean we helped them—created the conditions as great as possible." Nixon agreed: "That is right. And that is the way it is going to be played."[108]

The Government Is Better for Us

The Nixon administration's first task was to manage public discussion of the U.S. covert role in Chile and "to deny any CIA involvement." Kissinger met with CIA Director Colby to ensure that U.S. officials spoke from the same script.

U.S. officials also engaged in squalid talk about Salvador Allende's death. President Nixon insisted that no U.S. officials attend Allende's funeral. Kissinger informed Nixon that Allende was drunk on the fateful day. CIA Director Colby labeled Allende a "boozer" who had ten drinks by morning and "was loaded" by noon. One official suggested that Allende killed himself so as to achieve martyrdom. Kissinger retorted that "losers don't become martyrs in Latin America." Kissinger joked that the death of Allende and the destruction of Chilean constitutionalism had come at an inopportune time for him, because events in Chile had complicated his confirmation hearings to be secretary of state.[109]

The Nixon administration wasted little time signaling its support for the Pinochet dictatorship. By focusing on the campaign to destabilize the Allende government, historians have not given sufficient attention to the sustained U.S. effort to bolster the new Chile. The Nixon administration followed the playbook it developed for bolstering General Banzer's regime in Bolivia. On 13 September, in a cable from the White House Situation Room, the embassy in Santiago was instructed "to make clear its desire to cooperate with the military junta and to assist in any appropriate way." On the next day, the administration advised Chileans to dispatch a delegation to the United Nations to defend the *golpe* from mounting international criticism. The United States subsequently responded favorably to a Chilean request for one thousand flares and one thousand steel helmets for soldiers engaged in suppressing those who protested the loss of freedom in Chile. On 24 September, the United States extended diplomatic recognition to the Pinochet regime. The administration waited two weeks to resume relations, because Kissinger believed the Johnson administration had committed a faux pas when it immediately recognized the military government of Brazil in April 1964. The immediate recognition left the impression that the United States knew of the impending coup against President João Goulart and assisted the Brazilian military. As the 13 September cable noted, "It is best initially to avoid too much public identification between us."[110]

Brazil wanted to be the first nation to establish relations with the Chilean military rulers. President Médici kept his December 1971 promise to President Nixon that he would enlist in the war against Allende. Brazilian military officers exchanged information with their Chilean counterparts and sent intelligence officials to Santiago. Brazil also opposed Allende's Chile in international fora. Between 11 September and the end of October, the military dictatorship provided the Pinochet regime with medical supplies, food, and $100 million in credits.[111] The United States funneled some of its initial aid to Chile through Brazil. Brazilian officers helped with the interrogation and torture of the thousands of prisoners held in the National Stadium in Santiago. Brazilians gave courses to Chilean security forces on methods of interrogation. The Brazilians were passing on the techniques of interrogation and torture they had learned from the Office of Public Safety Program (1962–1974), which was funded by the U.S. Agency for International Development (USAID).[112]

The United States surpassed its junior partner in the bounty it bestowed on General Pinochet and his minions. In October and November 1973, the Nixon administration granted Chile $48 million in commodity credits to purchase wheat and corn. Between 1974 and 1976, Chile received $132 million in Food for Peace (P.L. 480) grants. Kissinger proudly informed the Chilean foreign minister that his nation received two-thirds of the total food assistance for Latin America. Chile also received $30 million for housing. President Nixon had once label housing assistance "welfare." The rest of Latin America received only $4 million in housing aid. Loans and credits also flowed from international lending agencies. During its first three years, the military government received $238 million in loans from the Inter-American Development Bank, whereas the Allende government had received only $11.6 million. The Chilean military went on a buying spree, ordering $100 million in new equipment and spare parts. With purchases of jet airplanes and tanks, Chile emerged as the fifth-largest customer in the world for U.S. military hardware. In 1974–1975, nearly 900 Chileans trained at the School of the Americas in Panama.[113]

The Nixon administration, especially Secretary of State Kissinger, embraced Pinochet's Chile even as the military dictator plunged the nation into the darkness of a Nazi Germany. In the immediate aftermath of the *golpe*, the regime arrested 50,000 citizens. Summary executions were carried out in the National Stadium. Before murdering Víctor Jara, a renowned folk singer and guitarist, soldiers first broke the bones in his hands and then taunted him to play the guitar. Two U.S. citizens, journalists Charles Horman and Frank Teruggi, were executed at the National Stadium. Teruggi's body had seventeen bullet wounds. Chilean jurists would subsequently conclude that U.S. agents, especially Navy Captain Ray E. Davis, a U.S. military attaché in Santiago, were complicit in the deaths of Horman and Teruggi.[114] High government officials, such as Orlando Letelier, were shipped off to Dawson Island in the extreme south of the country in the frigid, windy Straits of Magellan. The political prisoners lived in filth and were forced into hard labor. A hideous fate awaited the perhaps 5,000 incarcerated Chileans sent to the Villa Grimaldi detention center, a walled estate on the outskirts of Santiago. One detainee, Gladys Díaz, a radio broadcaster and member of MIR, survived Villa Grimaldi and recounted her ordeal. She and her husband were forced to watch each other being tortured. Her husband was later taken away and "disappeared." She was subjected to electrical shocks and drugs, and her head was plunged into toilet water in a technique

known as "the submarine." A karate expert broke her hip. Diaz was also made
to witness two murders—one a beating by chains, the other by shooting. Female detainees were routinely subjected to gang rape by security forces. Michelle Bachelet, the future president of Chile, and her mother suffered abuse
at Villa Grimaldi. President Bachelet's father, Air Force General Alberto Bachelet, a constitutionalist and supporter of Allende, died in detention after torture.[115] In the twenty-first century, the bodies of Nobel Laureate Pablo Neruda
and President Eduardo Frei were exhumed and autopsied. Forensic evidence
indicated that the Pinochet regime poisoned the two men while both were
seeking medical care in hospitals.[116]

Chilean fact-finding commissions would later charge the regime with 3,197
recorded murders. Some 36,000 Chileans testified to their torture or the torture of a family member. Scholars judged that official findings were too conservative. Credible detention estimates were 150,000 to 200,000 citizens, with
more than 100,000 Chileans suffering torture while in the custody of state
agents. The human rights organization Amnesty International reported that
the "real purpose" of the torture was not to extract confessions from innocent Chileans "as to induce conformity by terror, dehumanization, and the destruction of the will by prolonged pain." More than 200,000 Chileans, 2 percent
of the population, went into exile in more than a hundred countries.[117] Chileans spread out because they knew the regime would try to hunt them down
and kill them. In 1974, Chilean agents assassinated General Carlos Prats, the
former commander of chief of the armed forces, who was living quietly in
Buenos Aires. Like General Schneider, General Prats had been faithful to the
Chilean constitution and *la vía Chilena*. Chilean agents, part of a secret police
organization established by General Pinochet and known by the acronym
DINA, devised a car bomb attack against Prats. The general was thrown out
of his car and killed instantly, whereas his wife, Sofia Cuthbert, was trapped
in the burning car and carbonized.[118] General Pinochet made the absurd claim
to U.S. diplomats that he was saving the country, alleging that Allende planned
to kill a million Chileans. He also assumed the mantle of Chile's messiah. The
attack on Allende had been God's work, and Pinochet pledged himself to
the "heroic struggle" to carry out a "moral cleansing" in order "to extirpate the
root of evil from Chile."[119]

Secretary of State Kissinger took no issue with Pinochet's savagery. As the
leader of both NSC and the Department of State, Kissinger had control of U.S.
foreign policy in the period after 11 September 1973. Engulfed by the Watergate political scandal, a distracted President Nixon saw his power and influence
ebbing day by day. Kissinger made every major decision on Chile in the year
after the death of Allende. As tales of horror emanated from Chile, Kissinger,

on 1 October, told his staff, "We should understand our policy—that however unpleasant they act, the Government is better for us than Allende was." Meeting Pinochet's foreign minister, Admiral Ismael Huerta, for the first time, he told him that "the Department of State used to tell other countries how to run their business but that he had abolished that policy and now the Department conducted foreign and not domestic policy." He signed off on Chilean requests for military equipment, no matter how excessive. As he reasoned, "It seems to me that military governments are going to buy equipment and cannot be denied equipment by our conception of what their country requires."[120] Most famously, Kissinger erupted when he heard that his new ambassador in Santiago, David H. Popper, a career diplomat, raised issues of democracy and human rights with Chilean officials. "Tell Popper to cut out the political science lectures," he scrawled over a cablegram. Ambassador Popper subsequently received a formal complaint letter from Kissinger's Department of State.[121]

Throughout the Allende years, Henry Kissinger justified U.S. covert activities by asserting that the United States was preserving democracy in Chile and that a socialist Chile was a danger to U.S. national security. The secretary of state raised no objection to Pinochet's destruction of Chilean democracy. By September 1974, analysts in the CIA and State Department predicted that Pinochet would hold dictatorial power for an additional five years. In fact, Pinochet terrorized the nation for seventeen years (1973–1990). The embassy also reported that the Pinochet regime seemed intent on eliminating moderate political parties such as the Christian Democrats.[122] The regime abolished all political institutions other than the courts. So profound was the regime's contempt for the trappings of liberal democracy—freedom of speech, freedom of association, open elections—that it prohibited private groups, including professional associations, mothers' centers, and sports clubs, from holding elections for officers. The Pinochet dictatorship also proved a danger to the United States, perpetrating the first state-sponsored terrorist attack on U.S. soil in modern history. In September 1976, DINA agents triggered a remote-control bomb that killed former Foreign Minister Letelier and his assistant, Ronni Moffitt, and wounded her husband, Michael. The married couple were U.S. citizens. Letelier had his legs blown off. Ronni Moffitt had her carotid artery and windpipe severed by shrapnel. She drowned in her own blood. The threesome was traveling in a Chevrolet Chevelle in an area known in Washington as "Embassy Row."[123]

The hypocrisy and irony inherent in U.S. policy was apparently lost on Kissinger. The CIA was left with nearly $1 million in unexpended funds for the war against Salvador Allende. In June 1974, with Kissinger's approval, the 40 Committee decided to give the Christian Democrats a $50,000 severance payment, even as the dictatorship was eliminating political life in Chile and murdering, incarcerating, and torturing Christian Democrats. The 40 Committee also authorized a final payment of $176,000 to the media empire of Agustín Edwards. *El Mercurio* went from being an anti-Allende organ to serving as the regime's mouthpiece, publishing lies and disinformation on the assassinations of political figures. Pinochet's minions lied when they claimed that political leftists killed one another in internecine warfare.[124]

Within Cold War terms, the Nixon administration, led by Henry Kissinger, had major triumphs in Latin America during Nixon's first term. Nixon and Kissinger had bonded with Brazil's military dictators, especially the most repressive of the lot, General Emílio Médici. With Brazil's help, the Nixon administration destabilized the leftist governments of Bolivia and Chile. More important, the administration quickly and effectively sustained the anticommunist military dictators in the two countries with substantial economic and military assistance packages. But Kissinger's work was not done. By the end of Ford administration in January 1977, military dictators ruled throughout the southern cone of South America. Although these anticommunists followed the U.S. lead in international affairs, they would present problems for the secretary of state. Their barbaric behavior so alarmed civilized society that it ultimately forced a reluctant Kissinger to confront the issue of human rights. And the plans of dictators to assassinate political figures around the world, including U.S. legislators, compelled Kissinger to address matters of international law.

CHAPTER 3

Kissinger and Friends
Paraguay, Brazil, and Uruguay

When Henry Kissinger arrived in Washington in January 1969, violent, right-wing military dictators controlled Brazil and Paraguay. Military despots operated in Argentina and Bolivia, but neither government engaged in gross violations of basic human rights. In Chile and Uruguay, civilians ruled their historically stable, constitutional countries. By the time Kissinger left office in January 1977, military extremists who perpetrated wholesale incarceration, torture, and murder ran the six countries of southern South America. The six countries also formed into Operation Condor, an international terrorist organization. The United States aided the military takeovers of Bolivia, Chile, and Uruguay. And Secretary of State Kissinger encouraged the murderous thugs who seized power in Argentina. The mayhem created by these military ideologues forced Kissinger to confront the issues of human rights and international terrorism. Kissinger's intellectual defense of military extremism, his reluctant embrace of human rights matters, and his policies toward the military dictatorships revealed fundamental tenets about his character and his concept of international relations.

El Stronato

The United States did not create Alfredo Stroessner Matiauda, the crafty, ruthless general who terrorized Paraguay for more than three decades (1954–1989). Stroessner's Paraguay was a poor, landlocked country with a small population. It has traditionally been a tough place to make a living. Paraguay, which is about the size of California, lacks valuable natural resources, and only about 10 percent of the land is arable. Most of the population lives east of the Río Paraguay, which runs north and south. The eastern area, which borders Brazil, has forests, grassy hills, and adequate rainfall. A minuscule percentage of the population lives in the Gran Chaco, which is west of the Río Paraguay and constitutes 60 percent of the country's territory. The Gran Chaco is flat and arid, with dry forests and thorny scrubs. Most of the population survived as subsistence farmers or workers on larger agricultural estates. Paraguay's population in 1970 was only 2.5 million. Annual per capita income was $220. The capital city, Asunción, which is located on the Río Paraguay, had 250,000 residents. The mainly mestizo population was bilingual, speaking Guaraní and Spanish. Reflecting perhaps both wonderment and haughtiness, a Peace Corps volunteer who arrived in Paraguay in 1967 remarked that "Paraguay seemed to epitomize the small, rural backwater country that many people imagined Latin America to be."[1] Paraguay's strategic value was that it bordered Bolivia, Argentina, and Brazil. But disputes with its neighbors had been detrimental to the nation's socioeconomic progress. Paraguay had engaged in costly conflicts in the War of the Triple Alliance (1865–1870) against Argentina, Brazil, and Uruguay and in the Chaco War (1932–1935) against Bolivia. The country's geographic location proved valuable in one area of life: Paraguayans traditionally engaged in smuggling—electronic goods, whiskey, cigarettes, narcotics—to Argentina and Brazil.

Alfredo Stroessner was not a typical Paraguayan. His father was a German immigrant who worked as an accountant in a brewery. His mother came from a wealthy Paraguayan family of creole Spanish heritage. U.S. diplomats in Asunción often noted that Stroessner disdained Paraguayans for not having Northern European virtues. He constantly complained that "he was a good German trying to get things done in a Latin country and he couldn't get people to do work."[2] Ambassador George Landau characterized Stroessner as "methodical, punctual, and punctilios" and one who looked like a *"braumeister."*[3] Stroessner, who was born in 1912, entered the Paraguayan military as a teenager and distinguished himself in the Chaco War. He moved through the officer ranks, securing the rank of general and taking care to build alliances with other officers and influential politicians of the Colorado Party. He studied in Brazil during World War II and met Colonel Vernon Walters, the U.S. liaison with the Brazilian Expeditionary Force. In the postwar period, he took military courses at Fort Leavenworth and met officers at the U.S. Southern Command in the Panama Canal Zone.[4] Reverential of military power, Stroessner would align his country with the United States and Brazil and away from Paraguay's traditional friend, Argentina. Stroessner carried out a military *golpe* in May 1954, just as the Eisenhower administration was plotting to overthrow the government of Guatemala. The United States played no role in General Stroessner's seizure of power.

Stroessner was a caudillo, a Latin American strongman, but one who avoided the limelight. He lacked charisma and disliked public speaking. Money for him was a source of power, not opulence. He worked endlessly. A common saying was that "a sparrow would not drop from the tree without Stroessner knowing about it."[5] Because he seemed self-effacing, his political opponents underestimated his cunning and his brutality. He employed the usual carrots and sticks to hold on to power. He transformed the Colorado Party into a political machine. Employment, social services, and free medical care were dependent on membership in the party and loyalty to Stroessner. Military officers had access to government positions, with opportunities for graft and corruption. Ambassador Robert E. White testified that "the Stroessner regime was in essence a military mafia."[6] Incarceration, torture, and death awaited those who opposed Stroessner. For the thirty-five years known as *el Stronato*, the country was in a "state of siege" or under martial law because of alleged threats from subversive communists. Authorities had the power to arrest people with impunity and hold them without trial. Pastor Coronel, Stroessner's chief of police in the 1970s, favored interviewing inmates while they sat in a bath of excrement. The regime murdered 3,000 to 4,000 citizens, with perhaps 500 of them being "disappeared"—little wonder that the records of Operation Condor, "the Archives of Terror," would be found in the 1990s in a suburb of Asunción.

In order to keep his political and military machine well oiled, Stroessner needed international support and money. Perhaps only rivaled by Rafael Trujillo (1930–1961), the odious dictator of the Dominican Republic, Stroessner proved a master at ingratiating himself with the United States.[7] From 1954 to 1977, he slobbered over every U.S. official he ever met. The country without a sea coast ironically became the "USS Paraguay." In 1956, at an inter-American conclave in Panama, Stroessner told President Eisenhower that his country had "two great resources—the Paraguayans and the land." He pledged both to Eisenhower in case of World War III, adding that Paraguay was "one-hundred percent anti-communist and would continue to be so."[8] Paraguayan officials repeatedly encouraged the United States to build military bases in their country. Richard Nixon did not have to confront furious, rock-throwing students when he visited Asunción in early May 1958, as part of his tour of South America. Instead, cheering government workers and citizens lined the streets to welcome the vice president. The relieved Nixon declared, "I do not know of any other nation which has arisen more strongly against the threat of communism. And this is one reason why I feel especially happy here." In 1961, Stroessner tried to hug Adlai Stevenson, who was in Paraguay in preparation for the Alliance for Progress. In 1967, the Paraguayan president presided over a grand ceremony welcoming the first Peace Corps volunteers.[9]

Stroessner backed his rhetorical enthusiasm for U.S. foreign policies with tangible measures. He supported the U.S. occupation of the Dominican Republic in 1965 by dispatching 200 troops there. He startled U.S. officials when he offered in 1968 to join the U.S. war effort in Vietnam. At international fora, the Paraguayan delegate reliably followed the U.S. lead. In 1968–1969, Paraguay held the Latin American seat on the U.N. Security Council. No other nation on the council voted more often with the United States.[10] By the mid-1970s, many Latin American nations were reestablishing diplomatic relations with Cuba and calling for Cuba's readmission to the OAS. Paraguay stayed with the United States in judging Cuba a "pariah" nation.[11] Stroessner also remembered his Brazilian friends. He permitted Brazilian agricultural colonies in eastern Paraguay. And he struck a deal with Brazil on the construction of the Itaipu Dam on the Río Paraná on the Brazilian-Paraguayan border. (The hydroelectric power plant now produces the most energy of any in the world.) The new power sparked economic growth in Paraguay in the 1970s.

U.S. policies served the regime's interests. Between 1954 and 1961, the U.S. aid package for Paraguay amounted to $6 million a year, which represented almost 30 percent of the national budget. Stroessner perpetually complained that neighboring Bolivia received more money and that as South America's most dedicated anticommunist he should be favored. During the Alliance for Progress years, the United States continued to thank Stroessner, with U.S. aid representing 5 percent of the total Paraguayan economy. Stroessner focused the aid on infrastructure projects, building farm-to-market roads, paving highways, and establishing telecommunications systems. He reliably showed up for every ribbon-cutting ceremony for a new project. The aid improved life in the countryside and strengthened Stroessner's political standing with campesinos. The aid also provided opportunities for patronage and graft within the Colorado Party. The United States did not forget Paraguay's military. U.S. military aid to Paraguay from 1954 to 1969 accounted for as much as 17 percent of the nation's defense budget. Paraguayan officers were invited to attend U.S.

war schools in the Canal Zone. The Alliance for Progress was designed to promote democracy and socioeconomic development. Stroessner would respond to criticism about his dictatorship by making token efforts to liberalize political life. When U.S. officials turned to other matters, Stroessner reinstated bans on political activity. U.S. officials could comfort themselves with the finding that Paraguay's economy expanded in the 1960s, exceeding the 2.5 percent annual growth target of the Alliance for Progress.[12]

Stroessner was pleased that his friend Richard Nixon won the presidency in 1968. Given Nixon's publicly stated faith in military government for Latin Americans, U.S. policy aimed at preserving the Stroessner-imposed stability. An initial country analysis prepared in February 1969 by the embassy in Asunción noted that the goals were to maintain Paraguay's support for U.S. leadership and see the country develop "under conditions of internal security and political stability." The report judged President Stroessner as "the only man indisputably capable of holding the country together." A year later, the embassy reiterated those goals but noted the obvious when it added that "the significance of Paraguay to the United States is less than that of most independent countries of South America." U.S. direct investment amounted to only $20 million, and Paraguay had no vital natural resource to sell to the United States. The embassy focused on keeping Paraguay from being a "trouble-spot."[13]

Stroessner's unceasing repression created some political turmoil in the 1970s, with dissidents rallying around the leadership of the archbishop of the Roman Catholic Church. The archbishop excommunicated several of the dictator's brutal ministers. In turn, the regime expelled eight priests from Paraguay from 1969 to 1973. The CIA provided updates to Nixon on the protests but concluded that "the government retains the support of the real sources of power—the armed forces and the Colorado Party."[14]

Two issues briefly marred the harmony with Paraguay. During its first year, the Nixon administration proposed reducing the visible U.S. military presence in Latin America. Stroessner protested directly to Nixon, warning that Paraguay was surrounded by "Castro-trained Communist guerillas." Never wasting an opportunity to ingratiate himself with a U.S. official, Stroessner reminded Nixon that he was the "best friend" of the United States and further suggested that the United States open an air base in the Chaco region.[15] Henry Kissinger agreed that Paraguay should not suffer reductions in military aid. He met with the Paraguayan ambassador to the United States and later wrote on the memorandum proposing the military cut the sarcastic observation "I bet we have laid into Paraguay with particular relish."[16] Stroessner need not have fretted. By December 1970, the administration dropped the proposal to reduce military aid in the aftermath of the election of Salvador Allende and the rise to power in Bolivia of General Juan José Torres. The embassy celebrated the decision, remarking that military aid ensured that the United States would continue to have easy access to Stroessner and the armed forces, "the principal prop for the regime."[17]

Stroessner miscalculated when he gave refuge to Auguste (André) Ricord, an international drug trafficker, who was popularly identified as the kingpin of the "French Connection." Ricord's organization was responsible for 50 to 75 percent of the heroin smuggled into the United States. The illegal activity provided financial opportunities for key Stroessner allies in the military and the Colorado Party. President Nixon had declared in June 1971 his "War on Drugs," labeling the drug trade "public enemy number one." Nixon demanded the extradition of Ricord, assigning the issue to the State Department. Kissinger never showed interest in the international narcotics issue. When Stroessner balked at extraditing Ricord, Nixon dispatched in August 1972 Nelson Gross, the deputy assistant secretary of state for international narcotic matters, to Asunción to deliver an ultimatum to Stroessner that threatened suspension of economic and military aid and economic sanctions against Paraguay. Within forty-eight hours, Ricord was extradited to the United States, where he was sentenced to twenty years of imprisonment.[18] Paraguay thereafter complied with U.S. counternarcotics efforts. U.S.-Paraguayan relations returned to the status that had existed since 1954.

As dictatorship spread throughout southern South America, the Stroessner regime's violations of basic human rights intensified. In February 1975, a military unit entered the northern village of Jejuí, where a peasant commune had been founded. The troops fired on inhabitants, killing eight, and then beat survivors, raped women, and torched homes. In April-May 1976, the regime arrested nearly two thousand students and rural activists, murdering many and torturing others.[19] U.S. Ambassador George Landau received no directives from Secretary of State Kissinger to protest the grotesque brutality. But Landau raised issues about the incarceration of individual Paraguayans with Stroessner and was persistent enough to secure the release of some of them. Ambassador Landau was aided by Representative Donald Fraser (D-MN), who chaired the House Foreign Affairs Subcommittee on International Organizations and Movements. Representative Fraser sent letters about Paraguay to the ambassador. Between 1975 and 1976, Fraser held forty hearings on human rights issues in countries such as Argentina, Brazil, Chile, Cuba, El Salvador, Haiti, Nicaragua, Uruguay, and Paraguay.[20] Cognizant of Ambassador Landau's work on human rights, President Jimmy Carter dispatched him to Pinochet's Chile in 1977. Robert E. White replaced Landau and, with the backing of the new presidential administration, pressured Stroessner to improve human rights in Paraguay. Ambassador

White made a show of visiting the relatives of those abused by the regime. The number of political prisoners fell from several hundred to three during the period between 1977 and 1979. A Paraguayan told an embassy official that during the Carter years, "the hall of justice in this country [was] centered in this Embassy."[21]

In the mid-1970s, President Stroessner became an active participant in Operation Condor and an ally of Chile's Pinochet. The two dictators had a lengthy meeting when they attended in 1974 the inauguration of Brazil's latest dictator. Pinochet asked his Paraguayan friend to assist him in the planned assassination of Orlando Letelier. Using the pretext of the need for an undercover operation to check for irregularities on the Codelco Corporation, a Chilean state agency that marketed copper in the United States, Pinochet asked Stroessner to issue Paraguayan passports to two agents. The agents were Michael Vernon Townley, a U.S. citizen, and Armando Fernández Larios, a Chilean military officer. They operated under the control of Colonel Manuel Contreras, the head of DINA, the Chilean secret police. In 1974, Townley had participated in the mission to assassinate General Carlos Prats and his wife in Buenos Aires. The new mission was to recruit anti-Castro Cubans who would assassinate Letelier. Townley and Larios applied for U.S. visas with their Paraguayan passports. Ambassador Landau suspected something nefarious and retained photos of the two men. The photos ultimately proved vital in helping U.S. federal prosecutors uncover who assassinated Foreign Minister Letelier and Roni Moffitt.[22]

Brazil Is Destined for Greatness

Whereas the character of Stroessner's Paraguay did not dominate Henry Kissinger's thinking, the national security advisor and secretary of state reflected and talked often about Latin America's largest and most populous nation, Brazil. Relations between Brazil and the United States had been cordial between April 1964 and the end of 1968. Prior to the military's seizure of power, the United States had taken steps to destabilize the constitutional government of João Goulart (1961–1964). Alliance for Progress money had been directed to state governors who were anti-Goulart. The CIA spent $5 million in 1962 on anti-Goulart political candidates. Using the tactics of "controlled penetration," the CIA had encouraged demonstrations and strikes against the government by labor unions. Colonel Vernon Walters, a U.S. military attaché, kept in contact with the military officers he had served with in Italy during World War II. Walters was especially close to General Humberto de Alencar Castello Branco, who would lead the military conspiracy against Goulart. The Johnson administration positioned war matériel and readied a U.S. naval task force for duty off the coast of Brazil in case the generals encountered resistance.[23] After immediately recognizing the new regime, the Johnson administration bolstered the Castello Branco regime (1964–1967) with an emergency package of $50 million in aid. Between July 1964 and June 1968, the United States provided $1.2 billion in loans and grants to Brazil. The United States did not press the Brazilian regime to carry out socioeconomic reform, as called for in the Alliance for Progress.[24] Ambassador John Tuthill (1966–1969) admitted that Colonel Walters remained the most influential U.S. official in the country. As Tuthill observed, Walters was "an extremely conservative, military-oriented guy and had the all the weaknesses of the military. . . . He was against the university, against journalists, and trade unions." Walters also excused the regime's repression. Against Ambassador Tuthill's advice, the CIA began recruiting informants in unions, the military, and among student groups. Tuthill found that if he met with labor leaders who opposed the regime, the leaders would subsequently be "beaten up." The Castello Branco regime tried to create the façade of democracy, permitting an "official" opposition party and "safe" labor union leaders.[25] When Brazilian democrats continued to protest, the newest military leader, General Artur da Costa e Silva (1967–1969) issued Institutional Act No. 5 in December 1968, which outlawed political activity. The new act had no expiration date.

Institutional Act No. 5 shocked the outgoing Johnson administration. For four years, Washington had deluded itself, believing that Brazil's anticommunist military would guide the country back toward democracy and development. State Department officers noted that the "Brazilian regime appears to have stripped itself of any disguise as military dictatorship." Declaring "We are clearly unhappy with events and do not intend [to] sound happy," the administration sharply reduced economic assistance for Brazil.[26] U.S. diplomats in Brazil predicted that waves of unrest, violence, and terrorism would follow the declaration of military dictatorship. Political counselor Richard E. Johnson argued that by suppressing "liberal sentiments in politics," the regime was transforming students into terrorists. He explained: "They were college kids who had liberal aspirations and were not necessarily Marxists or anarchists or anything, but they just resented the pressure the military regime was keeping on, and partly it was this refusal to allow them to form liberal organizations of any kind of student groups that led them to violence."[27] Johnson might have been thinking about an incident in 1968 when military units violently broke up a demonstration in Rio de Janeiro by university students who were protesting the poor quality of cafeteria food. One student died. The military commander explained that the army must treat student protestors like "an enemy attacking the fatherland's territory and threatening the nation's basic institutions." Along with cafeteria food, the role of women in society became a national security issue for the Brazilian regime. The military dictators found women's rights, feminism, and even birth control and oral contraceptives politically and sexually deviant. Female activists, who were denounced as *putas communistas* ("communist whores"), were subjected to appalling abuses—torture and rape—at the hands of the Brazilian military and police. The torturers reveled while delivering electrical shocks to the sexual organs of female university students.[28]

In late 1970, an NSC study group agreed with counselor Johnson, reporting that by closing the political system, the military dictatorship had "helped stimulate urban terrorism, the kidnapping of foreign diplomats, including U.S. officials, and other clandestine political activity."[29] Brazilian terrorists kidnapped U.S. Ambassador C. Burke Elbrick in Rio de Janeiro in 1969, wounded Consul Curtis C. Cutter in Porto Alegre in 1970, and murdered a U.S. army captain who was studying at the Universidade de São Paulo. Brazilian authorities would justify their subsequent mass incarceration, torture, and murder as a way to protect U.S. citizens in Brazil and exterminate communism.[30] The course of events in Brazil was replicated in the other five military dictatorships—Argentina, Bolivia, Chile, Paraguay, and Uruguay. Leftist groups, who often resorted to bombing, kidnapping, and robbery, rose in rebellion against military repression. Security forces easily crushed the rebels. Seeking international credibility and respect, the dictatorships justified their grotesque violations of human rights by boasting that they were defending Western civilization from terrorism inspired by the international communist movement.[31]

Brazilian security forces had been trained by the United States to combat political crimes. Between 1962 and 1974, the United States operated the Office of Public Safety (OPS), a police training program. OPS provided $337 million in training, equipment, and advisers to Third World police. In Brazil, OPS spent $10 million and trained 100,000 police. The public goal of OPS was to reduce crime and promote civic life in Latin America by teaching police how to act in a legal, rational, and professional manner. Critics of OPS argued that the program contributed to authoritarianism by turning U.S. national security fears about communism into an obsession of Latin American security forces. OPS trainers also encouraged the bureaucratic innovation of placing military men in charge of police units, thereby, in one scholar's view, "militarizing the police and inculcating a war model of social control." Brazilian police officers took courses at the International Police Academy in Washington on subjects such as "prisons as schools for terrorists" and "subversive manipulation and domestic intelligence." OPS also offered a course near the border town of Laredo, Texas, on manufacturing and using explosives. Brazilian authorities actually contemplated blowing up gas lines in Rio de Janeiro, which would have caused mass casualties, and then blaming the tragedy on political leftists.[32]

U.S. officials denied that they encouraged Brazilian police to torture and murder. But one OPS adviser, Daniel A. "Dan" Mitrione, helped Brazilians organize a "shock unit" of tall Brazilian military and police officers who patrolled the night in Rio's poor neighborhoods and practiced a "shoot to kill" policy. OPS officers reported favorably about Operacão Bandeirantes, a joint military-police operation in 1969 in São Paulo that perpetrated murder and torture. Critics compared the Brazilian operation to the Phoenix Program, the U.S. assassination program in South Vietnam that eliminated more than 26,000 suspected Viet Cong. Theodore Brown headed the Phoenix Program immediately after concluding his tenure as director of OPS in Brazil.[33]

The United States did not need to teach Brazilians torture tactics. Brazilian police had tortured criminal suspects in the past, using a technique called *pau de arara* ("parrot's perch"). The victim was suspended upside down and naked on a horizontal pole and subjected to beatings and electrical shocks. Dilma Rousseff, the future president of Brazil (2011–2016), was repeatedly subjected to such horrors between 1970 and 1973, her years as a political prisoner. Torturers also favored the *geladeira*, or "refrigerator," a five-foot-square windowless cubicle equipped with loudspeakers, strobe lights, and heating and cooling units. Inside the *geladeira*, political prisoners were subjected to high-technology attacks on their senses. Brazilian security forces also proved adept at spreading fear and terror throughout society.[34] Cardinal Paulo Evaristo Arns, the archbishop of São Paulo, regularly received in the archdiocesan office twenty to fifty people every week, all trying to discover the whereabouts of their apprehended relatives. In one case, a young woman informed Cardinal Arns that she had found her husband's wedding ring on her doorstep. She was uncertain whether this meant he was dead or whether she should continue searching for him. Cardinal Arns had no answer for her. He understood that the pain was unimaginable for those who saw their loved ones vanish behind prison bars. He wrote for the young wife, "Deep darkness covers the earth, as it did when Jesus died."[35]

U.S. officials and OPS and CIA officers knew about the abuses of human rights in Brazil. In June 2014, Vice President Joseph Biden, who attended the World Cup soccer tournament in Brazil, delivered forty-three documents to President Rousseff. The documents revealed that U.S. officials had detailed knowledge of torture techniques such as the *geladeira* and that they understood that off-duty police officers served in *escaudrãos da morte* ("death squads"), murdering Brazilian dissidents.[36] Ambassador William M. Rountree (1970–1973) downplayed human rights issues during his tenure. Rountree, who had never served in Latin America, did not speak Portuguese, was unhappy living in the new capital city of Brasília, and was near retirement. But other diplomats kept Washington apprised of the brutality in Brazil. Ambassador John H. Crimmins (1973–1976) confirmed that reports of widespread torture were accurate. In the ambassador's words, "This wasn't just electrical shocks; this was the medieval stuff." Crimmins angered the Brazilian military when he publicly protested the torture of a U.S. missionary in the Recife area. Consul Cutter recalled that he was taken on a tour of torture facilities in Porto Alegre, shown "The Tank," where prisoners were held underwater, and told about the "Mad Dentist." Prisoners were strapped into a chair and operated on with drills by a person who had failed dental school. Cutter delivered reports about what he saw to Ambassador Rountree's embassy but concluded they were never sent on to Washington.[37]

The documents that Vice President Biden brought to Brazil were transferred to Brazil's National Truth Commission, which delivered a lengthy, detailed report to President Rousseff in December 2014. The Brazilian president had established the commission in 2011 to investigate abuses during the military dictatorship. It was modeled after "truth commissions" in Argentina, Chile, El Salvador, and Guatemala. Prior to 2014, only Cardinal Arns had prepared an extensive report on human rights issues during the military dictatorship.[38] Rousseff, who rarely showed emotion in public appearances, broke down in her speech at the report's launch ceremony in Brasília. She expressed the hope that "this report prevents ghosts from a painful and sorrowful past from seeking refuge in the shadows of silence and omission." The report documented over 400 murders and identified over 300 security personnel who violated human rights. The report's authors, who focused on provable cases, conceded that many more had died at the hands of the military. Estimates are that over 3,000 citizens were murdered during the twenty-one years of military dictatorship (1964–1985). The report added grisly detail, revealing that torturers crucified some victims, beating the palms of their hands with sticks as they hung on the walls of interrogation centers. The report implicated the United States in the savagery. More than 300 members of the Brazilian military studied at the School of the Americas in the Canal Zone. While there, attendees "had theoretical and practical lessons of torture, which would be later replicated in Brazil."[39]

The "deep darkness" that spread over Brazil did not trouble Presidents Nixon and Ford, Henry Kissinger, or General Walters. When he toured South America in 1967, Nixon had been impressed by the order that the military had imposed on Brazil. During the presidential transition, Kissinger received a forceful memorandum from Walters. The general dismissed concerns about Institutional Act No. 5, asserting that "there is no harsh repression in Brazil and the President has stated that he neither desires nor will tolerate a dictatorship." But Brazil, Walters opined, was not ready for civilian, democratic government. The Costa e Silva government was "friendly and cooperative," whereas the regime's opponents "are largely hostile to the United States." Walters concluded his memorandum with the apocalyptic warning: "If Brazil were to be lost it would not be another Cuba. It would be another China."[40]

Nixon and Kissinger followed Walters's lead in 1969–1970. The president directed the NSC to undertake a thorough review of U.S. policy toward the South American giant. Reversing the December 1968 decision to punish Brazil, Nixon approved arms sales, technical assistance, food aid, and program loans for the military dictatorship. Nixon and Kissinger rejected the advice of Viron Vaky of the NSC that "close identification with the Médici regime will alienate other sectors of Brazilian society in which in the longer term may be more important to [the] achievement of a constructive U.S.-Brazilian relationship."[41] General Médici, the most repressive of Brazil's dictators, had replaced the ineffective Costa e Silva in 1969. Nixon signaled his approval of the new direction in Brazilian political life, instructing the pliable Ambassador Rountree "to assure the Brazilian government and Brazilian military do not get the impression that we are looking down our noses at them because of their form of government."[42] Rountree thereafter squashed reports of human rights abuses that he received from U.S. diplomats stationed throughout Brazil. Kissinger made sure that any references to torture in Brazil were removed in reports about global human rights abuses.[43]

The new alliance with Brazil was cemented in December 1971 when Nixon hosted General Médici at the White House. Nixon and Kissinger were almost giddy speaking about Médici on the telephone. Kissinger and Nixon agreed that the general was "really impressive." Kissinger reported that Médici was "really most anxious to establish that special arrangement." Nixon responded, "It will be done. That is the big thing I will hit tomorrow."[44] The big thing was establishing a back-channel communication between Kissinger and the Brazilian foreign minister for "private and delicate matters." Private and delicate matters included, of course, conspiring with the United States to destabilize Allende's Chile and then bolstering the regime of General Pinochet and instructing Chileans on the latest in torture styles. The Brazilians had already earned gratitude from the United States for helping General Hugo Banzer come to power in Bolivia and helping rig an election in Uruguay. Nixon subsequently lauded Brazil to Prime Minister Edward Heath of the United Kingdom for Brazil's covert intervention in Uruguay.[45] Through the Kissinger years, Brazil could be counted on to help the United States in blocking Cuba's readmission to the OAS. The Brazilians also apparently encouraged the Argentine military to seize power. In a conversation with Kissinger, the Brazilian foreign minister lamented that the Argentine military was "bashful." General Walters, now deputy director of the CIA, kept in close contact with his Brazilian military friends. General João Baptista Figueiredo, the chief of intelligence services, told Walters that "the Argentine Armed Forces were inhibited by a failure complex." Nixon remarked to Secretary of State William P. Rogers that he wished that General Médici "was running the whole continent."[46] The president had planned to visit Brazil in 1974.

In the aftermath of the overthrow of Allende, Kissinger and Foreign Minister Gibson Barboza celebrated Brazilian-American relations. As Ambassador Rountree had observed in his last report from Brasília, "Relations have probably never been better." Kissinger flattered the foreign minister, predicting "that over the next 25 years Brazil would become a superpower."[47] During Kissinger's tenure as secretary of state, relations with Brazil remained cordial. Issues

President Nixon hosts President Médici, the military dictator of Brazil, in December 1971. Nixon bonded with the Brazilian general, because he helped the United States destabilize civilian governments in Bolivia and Chile and rig an election in Uruguay. Nixon professed that military rulers would keep Latin America safe from communism. Nixon Library.

did arise over trade, nuclear proliferation, and new directions in Brazilian foreign policy. The two countries' leaders did not, however, debate the issue of human rights.

Brazil's economic fortunes sank after the Arab oil embargo of 1973 and the subsequent rapid increase in the price of oil. The "Brazilian Miracle," which had seen annual economic growth rates of over 10 percent since 1968, could not be sustained. Economic growth had been based on the import of inexpensive oil, which amounted to over 700,000 barrels a day. The U.S. economy also staggered under the impact of high energy prices, plunging the United States into a deep economic recession in 1974–1975. Domestic pressures arose to do something about the expanding U.S. trade deficit, with 1971 being the last year that the United States had a trade surplus. In 1974, the Treasury Department proposed countervailing duties on the import of Brazilian footwear, charging that Brazil was underpricing or "dumping" shoes in the U.S. market. Taking his characteristic stance that economic issues should not damage bilateral relations, Kissinger informed Treasury Secretary William Simon that "we paid a horrendous price in Brazil" for the countervailing duties. Kissinger used diplomacy to resolve the issues, establishing a consultative commission. In 1976, President Ford decided not to provide relief to the domestic footwear industry. In turn, Brazil promised to phase out a subsidy policy for leather goods. Kissinger informed Foreign Minister Antonio Silveira, with whom had a warm relationship, that he was "delighted" that the two countries no longer needed to be "preoccupied" by the issue.[48]

The proliferation of weapons of mass destruction mattered more than the price of shoes. In 1975, Brazil had signed an agreement with West Germany to obtain nuclear equipment, materials, and technology, including reprocessing and enrichment capabilities. Ambassador Crimmins charged that military officers "indirectly admitted" to him that Brazil's goal was to enrich the uranium and develop nuclear weapons. As the ambassador interpreted it, Brazil believed it needed nuclear weapons to fulfill its "destiny" as a great power and to offset any progress Argentina may have made in the production of nuclear weapons. Crimmins's view was sustained by Brazil's refusal to sign the international Non-Proliferation Treaty (1969) "on the grounds that it limited Brazil's sovereignty." Crimmins further believed that Secretary Kissinger did not take the nonproliferation issue seriously.[49] In June 1975, Kissinger wrote a "Dear Antonio" letter to his friend Silveira, merely expressing the hope that the issue would not "affect the present cordial and constructive relationship between our two countries." The secretary stated that he wanted to avoid nuclear proliferation but added, "We understand and support Brazil's desire to expand its use of nuclear energy as a tool of development." He also regretted public debate had arisen over Brazil's intentions.[50] Presidential candidate Jimmy Carter raised the question of Brazil's nuclear intentions, and President Carter would send his diplomats to Brasília to press the issue. The military dictators continued, however, to pursue their covert plan to develop nuclear weapons. In 1990, the civilian government of Fernando Collor de Mello (1990–1992) dismantled the program, and in 1998 Brazil acceded to the Non-Proliferation Treaty.

Brazil's covert nuclear weapons program highlighted a subtle shift in Brazil's foreign and domestic policies. Brazilian democrats and dissidents no longer had a place of refuge in southern South America. The military generals had helped create virulent anticommunist military regimes throughout the region. With the home front secure, the new regime of General Ernesto Geisel (1974–1979) began to broaden the nation's global contacts, including establishing relations with the socialist world. Brazil envisioned being a global leader, and the decline in the economy mandated that Brazil seek new commercial opportunities. Brazilian leaders proclaimed the formulas of "ecumenism," "responsible pragmatism," and "no automatic alignments" in their approach to foreign affairs.[51] Foreign Minister Silveira interpreted the Helsinki Accords as an attempt by the United States and the Soviet Union to continue to rule the world and exclude the rising nations from the southern half of the globe from meaningful leadership roles. Kissinger responded to his friend that his essential foreign policy goal was to prevent a catastrophic war in Central Europe. He assured Silveira that "Brazil should be one of the leading forces in any search for a truly global order." But Kissinger seemed surprised when Brazil demonstrated independence in international affairs.[52] He was disappointed that Brazil recognized in 1975 Angola's first independent government, the Marxist MPLA, and offered no support for the U.S.-backed UNITA movement. As Assistant Secretary of State William D. Rogers explained to Kissinger, the recognition of the MPLA was "consistent with Silveira's general policy of ignoring ideology and trying to improve relations with everyone." In any case, Silveira told Kissinger over the telephone that "we know very well that the leadership of the (free world) is in the hands of the United States."[53]

At home, General Geisel pronounced his new policy of *abertura*, or "opening." Geisel pledged a relaxation of censorship, the end of political detentions, restrictions on intelligence agencies, and the prospect of elections. National Intelligence Chief General Figueiredo assured Walters that political "decompression" would be "measured and cautious." Figueiredo added, "The opposition and others will have to behave in a responsible manner."[54] The embassy under Ambassador Crimmins saw limited change. An opposition candidate was permitted to contest the 1974 presidential election. The embassy labeled the affair "a rubber-stamping exercise and a "charade." In January 1976, Crimmins reported that "Brazil's best-known human rights problem is, of course, the arbitrary arrest and mistreatment of people suspected of subversion or of links with organizations deemed to be subversive."[55] The ambassador did not know, however, of a crucial meeting among Brazilian leaders on 30 March 1974. CIA Director William Colby informed Kissinger of the meeting on 11 April. The secretary of state would have been hard-pressed not to grasp the significance of Colby's memorandum, for the subject title read, "Decision by President Ernesto Geisel To Continue the Summary Execution of Dangerous Subversives Under Certain Conditions." Geisel met with officers of the Army Intelligence Center and General Figueiredo. President Geisel was told of the "extra-legal methods" that had been used against the "terrorist and subversive threat" during the Médici regime. In the "past year or so," the intelligence center had summarily executed 104 suspects. General Figueiredo urged that the execution policy be continued. On 1 April, Geisel accepted Figueiredo's recommendation, with the caveat that "great care should be taken to make certain that only dangerous subversives were executed." Geisel directed that General Figueiredo, who served as president from 1979 to 1985, would hereafter approve summary executions.[56]

Secretary of State Kissinger never raised the issue of summary executions with Brazilian officials. A direct reference to the memorandum would have perhaps compromised the source the CIA had within Brazil's military high command. But Kissinger avoided discussing human rights issues in his numerous meetings, letters, and telephone conversations with Brazilian officials. By the mid-1970s, some U.S. officials were, however, cautiously raising the issue of human rights in Brazil. Since 1964, there had been a small but growing movement of academics, artists, clerics, and human rights activists that had raised awareness about repression in Brazil. The military regimes had forcibly retired globally prominent academics such as Celso Furtado and Fernando Enrique Cardoso. Furtado, who was also stripped of his political rights, had written about economic development and had established SUDENE (1959), a government agency dedicated to overcoming poverty in the northeastern region of the country. President Kennedy had discussed economic development issues with Furtado at the White House. Cardoso, who lost his position at the Universidade de São Paulo, challenged classical economic theory with his *dependencia*, or "dependency," school of economic interpretation. Cardoso would later become president of Brazil (1995–2003). The military dictatorship further outraged the international community by forcing into exile the great, innovative recording artists Caetano Veloso and Gilberto Gil. Veloso and Gil had earned the ire of the regime because of their dedication to the new movement,

Tropicalismo, which fused Brazilian pop with rock and roll and avant garde music.[57] Gil would subsequently serve as Brazil's minister of culture (2003–2008). Concern in the United States about repression in Brazil intensified in the aftermath of the overthrow of Salvador Allende and the onset of the Pinochet dictatorship. In 1974, the U.S. Congress attached to the Foreign Assistance Act the proviso that required the president to reduce or terminate assistance to any country that engaged in a consistent pattern of gross violations of human rights. Legislators such as Representative Donald Fraser began to ask the State Department about specific cases of human rights violations. In March 1975, Washington authorized the embassy to approach Brazilian authorities about the status of specific individuals.[58]

Kissinger's greatest opportunity to address state-sanctioned violence through "quiet diplomacy" came when he visited Brasília in February 1976. He had intended to visit in 1975 but postponed his trip because of the collapse of South Vietnam. The embassy had previously recommended that he raise the issue of human rights with General Geisel. Words like "flatterer," "sycophant," "toady," and "fawner" could not adequately characterize how Kissinger acted in Brazil. Geisel raised the issue of human rights, lamenting, "Our image is an image of dictatorship and violence." Kissinger responded, "Since my trip here in 1962, I have been profoundly convinced that Brazil is destined for world greatness." As for dictatorship and violence, he remarked, "As far as we are concerned, its domestic organization is Brazil's concern. We have trouble enough conducting our own domestic policy, without trying to conduct yours." Geisel agreed but remarked that not everyone in the United States shared Kissinger's opinion. Kissinger acknowledged, "There are a lot of frustrated missionaries in my country."[59]

In his report to President Ford, Kissinger celebrated the "warmth" of his reception during his two-day trip. He boasted, "Other ambassadors here have concluded that the welcome was an order of magnitude warmer, and the press coverage ten times more extensive, than that accorded the French and German foreign ministers who were recently here." Brazil was "a big country, with a big heart and a faith in its greatness and its future." Kissinger conceded to President Ford that Brazil was a military government, but added that "no one wears a uniform to the office." Brazil, the secretary found, had moved from dictatorship to authoritarianism. Democracy would come; "the question is how fast, not whether." Kissinger gave this description of President Geisel: "protestant, gentle in the Brazilian mode, but firm, a real father figure, and I think, incapable of cruelty or of tolerating cruelty." CIA Director Colby's memorandum about Geisel approving summary executions had apparently slipped Kissinger's mind. The secretary concluded, "I confess I really like the Brazilians."[60]

Secretary of State Kissinger in the modernistic city of Brasília in February 1976. United States Information Services (USIS) photo.

Kissinger bonded with some Brazilians, but he studiously avoided contact with distinguished opponents of the regime. When he journeyed to Brazil in March 1978, President Jimmy Carter asked for an audience with Cardinal Arns, the revered leader of the resistance. The previous year, Notre Dame, the prestigious Catholic university in the United States, had awarded honorary degrees to both the president and the cardinal. Not wanting to anger Brazilian authorities, the U.S. embassy arranged a meeting for Carter with a group of Brazilians of various political persuasions that included Arns. At the conclusion of the session, Carter publicly embraced the cardinal and arranged a private interview by insisting that Arns accompany him on the automobile ride to the airport. The two leaders had forty minutes of private conversation.[61] When Kissinger returned to Brazil in 1982 as a private citizen, he encountered some of the Brazilians he missed in 1976. His speech at a university in Brasília was shut down by a large group of students, who banged on air-conditioning vents outside the auditorium. The noise became so loud that Kissinger could not be heard. They students were outraged that they had been excluded from the speech. The audience was limited to prominent government and university officials. The students jeered Kissinger as he was hustled away from the university by Brazilian police.[62]

I Wouldn't Bet the Democratic Process Would Survive Another Twenty Years

Whereas Henry Kissinger never professed his love for the people of Uruguay, he appreciated their turn toward military authoritarianism. Along with Chile, Uruguay had traditionally been considered a fortunate country, another "Switzerland of Latin America." Sandwiched between Argentina and Brazil, Uruguay had been an export-oriented agricultural nation, taking advantage of its arable land of rolling plains, temperate climate, and access to the Río de la Plata and the South Atlantic Ocean. About the size of the U.S. state of Washington, Uruguay has always had a small population. In 1970 the population was 2.8 million. In the twenty-first century, Uruguay is the least populous nation of the twenty Latin American nations, with only 3.5 million people. Although the nation's economy revolved around the export of meat, wool, and grains, Uruguay developed in the twentieth century into an urban nation. Situated at the meeting of the Río de la Plata and the ocean, the city of Montevideo, with its lovely and lengthy coastal avenue known as La Rambla, came to dominate the nation's life. An educated, literate nation, Uruguay developed a prestigious university system. Along with its large neighbor, Argentina, Uruguay had one of the highest per-capita incomes in Latin American. Since the early twentieth century, political life had been stable, with the Colorado and Blanco Parties competing for power under constitutional guidelines. The ideological differences between the two parties were minor. Both parties indulged in political patronage. In the international arena, Uruguay promoted democracy, constitutionalism, and respect for human rights. A charter member of the United Nations, Uruguay was an original signatory to the U.N. Universal Declaration of Human Rights (1948). During the early Cold War, Uruguay also promoted the Larreta Doctrine in the Western Hemisphere. Named after Uruguay's foreign minister Eduardo Rodríguez Larreta, the Larreta Doctrine called on the inter-American community to consider multilateral action against member nations that violated elementary human rights.

Despite its admirable past, Uruguay did not escape the turmoil and violence that rocked the other nations of southern South America in the 1960s and 1970s. The vagaries of the global economy placed unbearable stress on Uruguay's political system and socioeconomic order. In the post–World War II period, the economies of agricultural nations stagnated; the prices of meats and grains that they exported failed to keep up with the prices of manufactured and finished goods that they imported. Uruguay's export earnings fell from $254 million to $129 million in the 1960s. Hard times also hit U.S. farmers over the "parity" issue, leading to a decline in family farming, the consolidation of agricultural enterprises, and the migration of rural folk to cities in search of work in the manufacturing and service sectors of the economy. Uruguay, however, did not have the type of diverse economy that could absorb new migrants to the cities. The decline in export earnings also made it difficult for the nation to maintain its educational standards and social safety network. In truth, Uruguay's leaders failed to respond adequately to the new challenges of the international trading order. Political leaders did not push for the modernization of the agricultural sector, and they did not trim the bloated governmental bureaucracy. Perhaps 25 percent of the labor force worked for the government, accounting for almost 60 percent of government expenditures. The government borrowed and spent money it did not have, leading to annual inflation rates of 40 to 50 percent. Uruguay's excellent universities continued to turn out doctors and lawyers, but not business managers, scientists, engineers, mathematicians, or technicians. By the 1960s, Uruguay had a sizeable population of educated young people with limited employment prospects.

Restive, idealistic young people joined the Movimiento Nacional de Liberación, (National Liberation Movement) popularly known as the Tupamaro movement. Although inspired by other radical political and social movements of the 1960s, the Tupamaros were uniquely Uruguayan. As one member of the U.S. embassy noted, they were "prodigious writers and pamphleteers" who were intent on raising the "revolutionary consciousness" of common folk, whom they perceived "as easily led and sheep-like." The Tupamaros viewed "the Soviet Union as too bourgeois."[63] They drew their name from Túpac Amaru II, the famed eighteenth-century leader of an indigenous rebellion in Peru. The leader of the Tupamaros was Raúl Sendic, a labor leader. Another prominent member was José Mujica, who would later serve as president of Uruguay. The Tupamaros initially cultivated a Robin Hood image, stealing from the wealthy and robbing banks, and then distributing the money to the poor. Although the Tupamaros would eventually become the public face of the insurgency in Uruguay, they were part of much larger political and social movements. In 1968, laborers, government workers, teachers, and students were constantly engaged in protest marches and strikes. The government of President Jorge Pacheco Areco (1967–1972) responded by unleashing the police and military. The armed forces used shrapnel bombs against the demonstrators and occupied the universities and secondary schools. Students and workers were killed and wounded. The events of 1968 shocked Uruguayans. As one protestor recalled, "In Uruguay you just thought that sort of thing was impossible."[64] The government crackdown created extreme political polarization and led to five years of urban violence. The government operated under a "state of siege" mandate, permitting arbitrary arrest and detention.

International observers began to pay attention to the small nation when, on 31 July 1970, the Tupamaros kidnapped Dan Mitrione, who now headed the OPS program in Uruguay. They alleged that Mitrione taught torture tactics, especially the uses of electric shock, to Uruguayan security forces. The Tupamaros, who conducted lengthy interrogation sessions with Mitrione, apparently intended to release the U.S. official after Uruguay released political prisoners. But when negotiations with the government broke down, they executed Mitrione with two shots to the head, leaving his body in a parked car on a street in Montevideo.[65] The renowned filmmaker Costa-Gavras depicted the Mitrione episode in his famous film *State of Siege* (1972). Although the film would earn condemnations from the Nixon administration for alleging that the United States encouraged torture, the film was equally critical of the Tupamaros for resorting to murder. Mitrione was the father of nine children. Mitrione's assassination became a cause célèbre in the United States, with entertainers Frank Sinatra and Jerry Lewis holding a benefit concert in Richmond, Indiana, for Mitrione's family.

From 1970 to 1973, security forces ruthlessly crushed dissidents. Government-sponsored death squads roamed the streets of Montevideo. As President Carter's ambassador to Uruguay, Lawrence Pezzulo (1977–1979), would later observe, security forces easily "rolled up" the Tupamaros, "who were not very good as guerrillas." By 1973, the Uruguayan military took over the government, keeping President Juan María Bordaberry (1972–1976) as a figurehead. The military command became, in Ambassador Pezzullo's words, the "cleansers of a society that really didn't need so thorough a cleansing."[66] "Cleansing" included shutting down fine arts departments at universities and destroying 20,000 library books in order to purge secondary schools of politically unacceptable texts. The military dictators also declined to participate in 1975 in U.N. activities for the "Year of the Women," claiming that a "Marxist conception of state and society" informed the focus on women. The human rights group Amnesty International charged in reports from 1974 to 1976 that, under military dictatorship, Uruguay had more political prisoners per capita than any other country in the world. Political prisoners were routinely tortured.[67] José Mujica, who fired shots at police, was held in custody for thirteen years in subhuman conditions, including being confined for two years at the bottom of an emptied horse-watering trough. Uruguay also joined Operation Condor.

Neither the United States nor Brazil was an innocent bystander to the unfolding tragedy in Uruguay. Between 1964 and 1968, the Johnson administration lamented the "lack of leadership and drift" in "model" Uruguay. The administration confessed that it had no ideas on how to make democracy work in Uruguay, hoping only that the "remarkable recuperative power" of Uruguayan society would come to the fore. U.S. economic aid to Uruguay had been modest, averaging less than $2 million a year in the 1960s. The administration decided against increasing economic aid for Uruguay, reasoning that economic conditions were so chaotic that additional aid would prove of little use. The Johnson administration did not judge the international communist movement responsible for Uruguay's sad plight.[68]

President Nixon and Henry Kissinger rejected the Johnson administration's assessment that communism posed no immediate threat to Uruguay. Governor Nelson Rockefeller had first raised the alarm in reporting back in 1969 to Nixon about his visit to Uruguay. He had met President Pacheco in a hotel room in the seaside resort of Punta del Este because of the mayhem in Montevideo. The display room of the General Motors automobile company had been bombed, with urban guerrillas justifying the action by alleging that General Motors sold to the police a hundred automobiles. Rejecting the U.S. embassy's assessment that the Tupamaros were home-grown radicals who disdained the Soviet Union, Pacheco claimed that there was a "highly organized and effective Communist penetration" of his country, with communists controlling the teachers' union and "80 per cent of all other unions." The Uruguayan president asserted that the Soviet embassy in Montevideo, with 300 personnel, directed the insurgency. Noting he had to retain the support of the police and armed forces, Pacheco pleaded for more U.S. military aid. The authoritarian Pacheco added that he hoped "President Nixon will pay attention to his small friend—who is struggling to save his nation from disaster through democratic means."[69] Rockefeller further reported that President Costa e Silva of Brazil was alarmed about Uruguay. Brazil had acceded to the request of Pacheco to purchase $10 million in wool to help in the fight against communism in Uruguay. Rockefeller relayed to Nixon the Brazilian president's pledge that "the United States could regard Brazil as a friend and agent in Latin America to keep Uruguay from going Communist."[70] The governor repeated his concerns about Uruguay to his protégé, Henry Kissinger. In a 9 July 1969 telephone conversation, Rockefeller complained that the administration had not yet acted on his recommendations. He warned, "If our house falls down here, you will have Communists in there." Kissinger responded that "this is a very delicate situation and one which he didn't want to discuss on [the] telephone."[71]

During the period from 1953 to 1962, the United States had supplied Uruguay with $27 million in grant military aid, when the U.S. goal was to arm and train the Uruguayan military for external defense. During the period from 1963 to 1970, the U.S. reduced military aid to $16 million. But the new goal was to orient the armed forces toward internal security. The United States now transferred vehicles and small arms instead of expensive naval ships.[72] The

Uruguayan military had traditionally stayed out of domestic politics. The mission of internal security inevitably brought the military into the political arena. As Horace Y. "Tex" Edwards, a diplomat serving in the U.S. embassy, observed, "[The civilian government] made the mistake of turning over to the Army the responsibility of combatting the terrorism. The Army grew stronger and stronger and decided it liked what it had. It liked the power and so kept it."[73] As it had in Brazil, the U.S. government bolstered the Uruguayan police. It dispatched Dan Mitrione to Montevideo to head the OPS. Mitrione's ostensible mission was to improve the crowd-control and intelligence-gathering capabilities of the Uruguayan police.

President Nixon became directly involved in relations with Uruguay after Mitrione was kidnapped. He wrote twice directly to Pacheco, asking the Uruguayan president to "spare no effort" to secure Mitrione's safe return.[74] In demanding the release of political prisoners, the Tupamaros were surely thinking of their leader Raúl Sendic, who had just been apprehended by the police along with eight other high-ranking Tupamaros on 7 August 1970. On 9 August in a highly classified cable, Secretary of State William P. Rogers instructed U.S. Ambassador Charles Adair to meet the Uruguayan foreign minister. U.S. authorities "assumed that the government of Uruguay has considered the use of threat to kill Sendic and other key MLN prisoners if Mitrione is killed." If not, Ambassador Adair was ordered to "raise it with GOU at once." Uruguayan Foreign Minister Jorge Periano Facio rejected the U.S. advice, noting that "his type of government did not permit such an action." Periano added, however, that a threat was made that members of the Escuadrón de Muerte (Death Squad) would take action against the relatives of the prisoners if Mitrione was killed.[75] Uruguayan police found Mitrione's body early in the morning of 10 August. Sendic would be confined in jail until 1985. The killing of Mitrione undermined the international and domestic credibility of the Tupamaros. The killing also strengthened the forces of repression. By the afternoon of 10 August 1971, the Uruguayan General Assembly had suspended civil liberties in the nation.

The Uruguayan democratic political system tried to regenerate itself in 1971. National elections were scheduled for 28 November. Jorge Pacheco of the Colorado Party wanted to run again but failed in a referendum to persuade the public to change the constitution and permit his immediate reelection. Juan Bordaberry, the minister of agriculture, became the standard bearer of the Colorados. Senator Wilson Ferreira Aldunate led the Blancos. Frustrated members of the two traditional parties joined with a variety of leftist groups, including the Communist Party, into the Frente Amplio (Broad Front). Their presidential candidate was a retired general and politician, Liber Seregni Mosquera.

The State Department informed National Security Adviser Kissinger that Seregni was a "moderate leftist" who avoided taking extremist positions and was not controlled by the Communist Party.[76] In results announced in early 1972, Bordaberry and the Colorados won 41 percent of the vote, barely edging out Senator Ferreria and the Blancos, who garnered 40.2 percent. Frente Amplio had 18.3 percent of the vote, although a Gallup poll of potential voters conducted in late November 1971 had indicated that General Seregni's coalition might win about 25 percent of the vote.[77] President Bordaberry took office in 1972 but turned over control of the government to military commanders the next year. Senator Ferreira thereafter fled into exile and made it his life's work to inform the world about the nature of his country's dictatorship. The military government ordered General Seregni to prison, where he would stay until 1984. Bordaberry would eventually face justice in a democratic Uruguay ruled by civilians. In 2011, Bordaberry died under house arrest, having received in 2010 a thirty-year sentence for his role in murders conducted under the aegis of Operation Condor.

The United States and Brazil vowed not to permit a free and open election in Uruguay. Frente Amplio, in the view of U.S. and Brazilian leaders, smacked of Unidad Popular in Allende's Chile. Brazilian archives are closed, and some U.S. records on Uruguay for 1971–1972 remain surprisingly classified. But there are enough clues in the open documentary record to demonstrate that both nations intervened covertly in the 1971 election, sustaining Nixon's comment to Prime Minister Heath that Brazil helped "rig" the election. In August 1971, the State Department asked its embassies in Buenos Aires and Brasília to assess how Argentina and Brazil would react to a strong showing by Frente Amplio in the upcoming election. Ambassador to Argentina John Davis Lodge responded that the intelligence agencies of Argentina and Brazil had discussed events in Uruguay. Argentina was reluctant to intervene covertly in the election but would urge President Pacheco to seize dictatorial power, an *autogolpe*, if Frente Amplio won the election. Lodge added that Argentina had just played a role in overthrowing the government of Juan José Torres in Bolivia.[78] Argentina had probably assisted in secreting General Hugo Banzer back into Bolivia. While the State Department was collecting information, Kissinger's NSC instructed the embassy in Montevideo to develop a strategy "to increase support for democratic parties in Uruguay and lessen a threat of a political takeover by the *Frente*." Among numerous proposals for closer cooperation with Uruguay was the recommendation that the United States collaborate "overtly and covertly with those media elements which compete with those of the *Frente*." The embassy also called for a strengthening of OPS in Uruguay and sending twenty-five to thirty Uruguayan security personnel for training abroad.[79]

Unlike in the cases of Bolivia and Chile, there are not declassified minutes of meetings on Uruguay by the 40 Committee chaired by Kissinger. But the 40 Committee had authorized $400,000 in mid-1971 to undermine the Torres government and was spending millions of dollars on anti-Allende groups and media outlets. In the 1960s, the United States had covertly intervened in elections in Brazil, Chile, the Dominican Republic, and Guyana. It would strain credulity to believe that Nixon and Kissinger relied solely on the military governments in Argentina and Brazil to influence the results of the Uruguayan presidential election. The CIA may have funded the Colorados and the Blancos. Almost certainly, the CIA underwrote the costs of media outlets that attacked Frente Amplio. During the last month of the presidential campaign, General Seregni repeatedly charged that the United States was intervening in the election. Seregni cited the tactics of "psychological warfare" and "misinformation." Frente Amplio further alleged that CIA agents were operating in Uruguay under the cover of the U.S. embassy and that the embassy bore responsibility for violent attacks on Frente political clubs by extremist, right-wing groups. On 4 December, after the election, Uruguayan newspapers carried an unsigned advertisement that depicted Uruguay having shattered the Soviet boot that had trampled Chile.[80] The allegations of interference made by Seregni and his party seemed authentic, because such tactics had been used throughout Latin America since 1954. Based on its success in Guatemala, the CIA had developed a playbook on how to destabilize governments and influence elections.[81]

The discussions in early December 1971 in Washington between General Médici and Nixon and Kissinger served as a postmortem on the Uruguayan election. U.S. officials celebrated the electoral results, although Médici lamented that Frente Amplio had received even 18 percent of the vote. A happy Nixon remarked to Secretary Rogers that Médici was "quite a fellow" and on "the Uruguayan thing, apparently he helped a bit there." In his private meeting with the Brazilian, Kissinger was unusually restrained, noting, "In areas of mutual concern such as the situations in Uruguay and Bolivia, close cooperation and parallel approaches can be very helpful for our common objectives."[82] In addition to praising Brazil for its intervention in Uruguay, the president told Prime Minister Health, "There are forces at work which we are not discouraging."[83]

The covert intervention and the "forces at work" were not about saving constitutionalism and democracy in the model Latin American country. President Bordaberry, who had campaigned on "law and order" issues, declared in April 1972 a "State of Internal War" after the Tupamaros gunned down four government officials. The armed forces were granted powers to transfer suspected terrorists to military jurisdiction and to suspend constitutional guarantees. The military was now completely in charge of the antiterrorist campaign. The military destroyed the Tupamaros by "a push to capture as many members as possible, by rapid and forceful interrogations, and by hunting down Tupamaro weapons caches and hiding places." The CIA had previously reported to the president of the formation of a counterterror unit in the security apparatus that carried out "extralegal activity." In his daily briefing of 15 November 1972, President Nixon learned from the CIA that "in less than seven months the military [had] managed to wreck a terrorist organization that earned the envy and respect of guerrilla groups throughout the Western Hemisphere."[84]

Whereas the legendary guerrillas of Cuba may have admired the Tupamaros, Cuba was playing no tangible role in Uruguay. On 28 January 1972, the CIA reported to Nixon about the lack of revolutionary effort by Cuba in Latin America. Cuba was seeking to extend its influence through the conventional pursuit of closer political and economic ties. To be sure, Castro had angered the Pacheco government by saying in 1971 that "violence was the only road to power in Uruguay."[85]

In early 1973, the triumphant Uruguayan military commanders subordinated President Bordaberry to their dictates. During his first year in office, Bordaberry had launched no initiatives to resolve the nation's economic crisis. As the CIA reported, the generals decided they could not leave the Uruguayan "mess" in the hands of civilian politicians.[86] They also decided that politicians such as Wilson Ferreira, Senator Jorge Batlle, and Jorge Periano, the former foreign minister, were corrupt and should be arrested. Senator Batlle, who would serve as a constitutional president (2000–2005), had the temerity to criticize the growing involvement of the armed forces in the country's political life. In March 1973, military leaders preempted radio and television broadcasting to denounce the government's "moral deterioration" and congressional obstruction to the economic recovery plans of the armed forces. Like the military rulers in Bolivia, Brazil, Paraguay, and Peru, and those that would follow in Chile and then in Argentina, the Uruguayan generals professed the faith that their reputed efficiency and expertise would rescue the nation from communism and put the economy on the path of prosperity. And like other Latin American military men, the Uruguayan generals perceived themselves in semireligious terms. As the U.S. embassy noted, the admirals and generals "proclaimed in often messianic terms that they are saving Uruguay" and were "drawing a line for a new morality and new approach to the country's problems."[87]

The Nixon administration predictably did not object to the latest *golpe* in South America. The administration transferred the president's favorite ambassador in Latin America, Ernest V. Siracusa, from General Banzer's Bolivia to

Uruguay. Siracusa, who presented his credentials in September 1973, would spend his more than three years in Montevideo defending the generals from "the carping and criticism along with the popular flow stimulated by 'human rights' activists in Washington and elsewhere." For good measure, the ambassador denounced the film *State of Siege* for poisoning the world against the United States.[88] Ambassador Siracusa was not, however, present to bloviate about the military's seizure of power. The embassy, under the direction of Deputy Chief of Mission Frank V. Ortiz, provided Washington with an accurate appraisal of developments. There had been no change in the institutional structure of government; the "locus of power" simply had moved from President Bordaberry to the military. CIA analysts concurred with the embassy's assessment, finding that Bordaberry "remains in the presidency only at the sufferance of the armed forces." The State Department informed the NSC that there were "no immediate policy implications," because both Bordaberry and the generals accepted U.S. global leadership on Cold War issues. Remaining silent about the latest *golpe* in South America would also have the advantage of keeping the United States from being "party to the demise of Uruguay's democratic constitutionalism."[89] But with the military closing down the legislature, dissolving unions, and violently breaking labor strikes and popular demonstrations over food shortages, Ortiz asked Washington on 2 July 1973 whether it would be appropriate to mention to Uruguayan officials a "common commitment to democratic ideals" at the Fourth of July party hosted by the embassy. Deputy Secretary of State Kenneth Rush rebuked Ortiz, ordering him in a 3 July telegram to "not indicate that US shares with Uruguay common institutions and commitment to democratic ideals." Ortiz should follow the policy set forth by President Nixon in his 1969 Pan American speech that the United States would "deal realistically with governments in the inter-American system as they are."[90] As James L. Tull, an embassy political officer who left Montevideo in July 1973, lamented, "As always, the embassy took its official line from Washington, but on a private and personal basis I think many of us believed [we] might have been able, if not [to] save democracy in Uruguay, at least to have prevented many of the horrors and excesses which took place over the following decade." During the period from 1969 to 1973, Tull never heard "a single negative word out of Washington" about the growing repression in Uruguay.[91]

If there ever was a rejection of U.S. identification with constitutionalism, democracy, and human rights, it came on 10 May 1975 in Secretary of State Kissinger's conversation in Washington with Foreign Minister Juan Carlos Blanco (1972–1976). Kissinger scholars would be hard-pressed to find a more outrageous set of statements from their subject and perhaps a more revealing insight into his thoughts on government than Kissinger's forty-five-minute rant with the Uruguayan foreign minister. Ambassador Siracusa was present for the conversation, and Kissinger first praised him to Blanco for the "excellent reports" he had sent from Bolivia. Kissinger was upset that Congress and U.S. interest groups were raising human rights issues. Congressional meddling in his stewardship of foreign policy "was the biggest problem in our country." Kissinger informed Blanco that he had a study done that revealed that, during his tenure as secretary of state, he "met 116 times with Congressional groups including meetings with the Congressional leadership on human rights, Jewish questions, etc." Blanco, the representative of a military dictatorship, commiserated with the secretary, noting that contemporary legislatures were incapable of dealing "with so many modern, complex problems." The U.S. Senate had no constitutional right, Kissinger asserted, "to give its advice and consent on policy." The Senate could only "wreck things" and never do anything constructive, because it could never achieve consensus. "The House is even worse," Kissinger continued. "It's a rabble with more than 400 members, and even the leaders don't know what to do." Blanco responded that he had recently met with Senators Jacob Javits (R-NY) and Henry Jackson (D-WA), two legislators who raised issues of human rights and the emigration of Jewish people from the Soviet Union. Kissinger shot back: "What did they want, free emigration of Jews from Uruguay?" "As a historian," Kissinger predicted to Blanco, "I wouldn't bet that the democratic process would survive another 20 years, at least not in Western Europe. Maybe that doesn't apply here."

The two foreign policy chiefs extended their discussion to global affairs. Blanco explained that Uruguay was "trying to develop [its] own solutions to the political crisis facing Western civilization," which included "the problem of subversion and terrorism." Kissinger responded that the United States would soon have similar problems. Blanco blamed Cuba for the Tupamaros. Kissinger assured the foreign minister that if the United States ever established relations with Cuba, it would insist that Castro cease promoting subversive activities in Latin America. Kissinger then moved on to a topic for future discussion between friends. He opined that "left-wing and the intellectuals are demoralizing public opinion on every issue." On television in Western Europe, including the United Kingdom, he continued, "nothing favorable about the United States is being shown. The Viet Cong are depicted as heroes, the United States as an ogre." Blanco agreed with Kissinger's view that "the left-wing extremists are demoralizing public conceptions." Kissinger ended the discussion by thanking Blanco for his "strength and courage."[92]

Foreign Minister Blanco, the strong and courageous one, would be repeatedly indicted in the twenty-first century by jurists and courts in Uruguay and in Europe for orchestrating the murder of Uruguayan legislators, Tupamaros, and international citizens. Kissinger had discussed the end of democracy with an official who represented a country that held thousands of political prisoners between 1973 and 1977. Amnesty International documented that twenty-two prisoners had died under torture in 1975. Two legislators, Zelmar Michelini and Héctor Gutíerrez Ruiz, fled Uruguay and were murdered in Buenos Aires in May 1976. Michelini had been a long-time member of the Colorado Party who joined Frente Amplio. Gutíerrez Ruiz, a Blanco, had been speaker of the Chamber of Deputies but resigned his position after the military seized power in 1973. Blanco was also a high official in a government that planned to assassinate the chief critic in the United States of the military dictatorship—Representative Edward I. "Ed" Koch (D-NY).

The ongoing human rights abuses and the plot against Ed Koch forced Secretary Kissinger, the State Department, and Ambassador Siracusa to explain U.S. policies toward Uruguay. By 1975–1976, an international uproar had arisen over the small country. Amnesty International, which was awarded the Nobel Peace Prize in 1977, drew the world's attention to Uruguay with a series of reports it issued in the mid-1970s. In 1976, it presented a petition with 350,000 signatures to the United Nations calling for an independent inquiry into the use of torture in Uruguay. Amnesty International charged that there were at least 5,000 political prisoners in Uruguay and perhaps as many as 8,000. In 1976, it estimated that one of every 500 Uruguayan citizens was a political prisoner and that one of every fifty citizens "had been through a period of imprisonment, which for many included interrogation and torture." Security forces arrested Uruguayans without a warrant and held them in wretched prisons for months, even years, without informing relatives of their status or location. This was an assault on the urban middle class—teachers, professors, lawyers, judges, journalists, government workers, and union leaders. There were so many doctors in prison that they were expected by their jailers to provide medical services to the other inmates. Twenty military officers, including two generals, rotted in prison, because they had committed the criminal act of pledging their loyalty to the constitution. Captain Carlos Arrarte violated the nation's martial laws when in 1972 he tried to stop military colleagues from torturing a prisoner. Amnesty International's meticulous reports were supplemented by the testimonies of citizens who fled the terror. Wilson Ferreira, the former presidential candidate, lobbied officials in Western Europe and the United States to help restore freedom and democracy in Uruguay. The other presidential candidate, Liber Seregni, could not, of course, assist Ferreira, because he was one of the two generals in prison.[93]

In the aftermath of the military dictatorship, Uruguayans opened in 2007 the Museo de la Memoria on the outskirts of Montevideo to commemorate the victims of human rights abuses. This exhibit presents the images of citizens who were tortured, murdered, and "disappeared" by the military government. Author's photo.

From his post in Montevideo, Ambassador Siracusa engaged in an unceasing campaign to defend the honor of the military dictatorship. He informed the desk officer for Uruguay stationed in Washington that the embassy could not investigate violations of human rights "without jeopardizing our larger mission." There was "some torture of prisoners," and a prisoner had died under torture on 31 July 1975, but Siracusa dismissed this: "We believe it to be an isolated case and absolutely contrary to policy and intent." Expressing his "sympathy and understanding" of Uruguay's problems, Siracusa denigrated Amnesty International in discussions with Foreign Minister Blanco, finding "the style of some AI reports to be propagandistic in tone rather than judicious and even-handed, and their content, as regard Uruguay, sometimes shockingly exaggerated." The ambassador did not object, however, when Blanco presented his defense of Uruguay's gross violations of human rights with the preposterous argument that Uruguay was engaged in the "Third World War" against the "international Communist apparatus." Siracusa also repeatedly asked that the State Department not speak with Wilson Ferreira, because Ferreira had "taken to sniping at the Uruguayan government in a most irresponsible fashion." In mid-1976, he added that Ferreria's "broad, sweeping charges" were without foundation and were calculated "to involve USG, the Ambassador, and this Embassy in Uruguayan internal affairs and to further his own political interests."[94] In fact, Ferreira had excellent sources, presenting accurate information to U.S. officials on the circumstances surrounding the deaths in Argentina of Juan José Torres, the former president of Bolivia, and of the two Uruguayan legislators. Siracusa retired from the foreign service in 1977 after being recalled from Montevideo by the new Carter administration. In retirement, Siracusa continued to defend himself and his authoritarian Uruguayan friends. He declared that President Bordaberry and Foreign Minister Blanco both upheld "Uruguayan principles of democracy" and both ranked "high in my opinion for honesty and integrity among all leaders I have met in my long career in Latin America."[95] Siracusa, who died in 2000, did not live to see both Bordaberry and Blanco prosecuted by Uruguayan civilian courts.

Henry Kissinger's State Department did not rebuke Siracusa, because he was carrying out U.S. policy. In a 11 June 1976 letter to Representative Koch, Acting Assistant Secretary of State Hewson A. Ryan conceded that "there have undoubtedly been cases of serious violations of human rights" in Uruguay. Ryan argued, however, there had been fewer abuses of human rights since the 1972 war against the Tupamaros. Private representations by the U.S. government were having the "positive" effect of "strengthening the Uruguayan government resolve to improve the human rights situation in that country." Ryan then added the absurd assertion that "it is inaccurate to describe the Uruguayan Government as a military dictatorship."[96] The day after Ryan sent his letter, the armed forces ousted President Bordaberry for a new figurehead, Alberto Demicheli. On 16 June 1976, the CIA predicted to President Ford that the military would soon pick "another figurehead."[97] Less than three months later, the generals ejected the eighty-year-old Demicheli for another civilian sycophant, Aparacio Méndez (1976–1981).

Representative Koch had earned the ire of the State Department and Ambassador Siracusa because he added to the Foreign Assistance Act of 1976 an amendment that banned military aid to Uruguay. Koch had met with Uruguayan exiles, including Wilson Ferreira. Representative Thomas Harkin (D-IA) sponsored an amendment that called upon the executive branch to vote against international loans, such as from the Inter-American Development Bank, to nations that engaged in gross violations of human rights. The congressional rebellion against the policy toward the generals of southern South America prompted Secretary of State Kissinger to meet on 11 June 1976 with Foreign

Minister Blanco at an inter-American conclave in Mexico City. Kissinger assured Blanco that he understood the "pressures" on Uruguay "but suggested that unless certain minimum standards were observed the pressures in the United States would become unmanageable" and the United States would be unable to assist Uruguay. Kissinger hastened to add, however, that he would lead no "crusade" against Uruguay. Kissinger and Blanco then immediately turned to a more pressing topic than the subject of human rights, which was "a wide-ranging discussion concerning the motivation of the present generation of well-educated, middle-class origin terrorists."[98]

The prospect of Uruguayan military officers assassinating U.S. legislators concentrated the minds of U.S. officials in the latter part of 1976. Ambassador Siracusa initially denied that Uruguay participated in an international assassination scheme. On 7 June 1976, he informed Washington that Uruguay had nothing to do with the murder of the exiled legislators and two other Uruguayans in Buenos Aires. A "source" close to President Bordaberry "told us that speculation in the palace was that an official Argentine group killed the four acting independently" of the Argentine government.[99] But in July 1976, a CIA source or perhaps a CIA agent had overheard two Uruguayan military officers from the army intelligence unit, Colonel José Fons and Major José Gavazzo, talking about assassinating Representative Koch.[100] Both officers were scheduled to be assigned to Washington. Prominent critics of the government, such as Wilson Ferreira, also seemed vulnerable. The FBI subsequently warned Koch about the threat against his life. Anxious officials in Washington, led by Assistant Secretary of State for Inter-American Affairs Harry Shlaudeman, recommended to the secretary of state that Ambassador Siracusa be empowered to warn Foreign Minister Blanco against fomenting international assassination plots and that Shlaudeman would deliver the same message to the Uruguayan ambassador in Washington. On 16 September 1976, Secretary Kissinger, who was in Lusaka, Zambia, "declined to approve message to Montevideo and has instructed that no further action be taken on this matter."[101] Five days later, the Chileans assassinated Orlando Letelier in Washington. State Department officers resorted to informing Montevideo in December 1976 that Fons and Gavazzo could not take up their respective positions on the Inter-American Defense Board and as a military attaché in the Uruguayan embassy. The department had determined that Fons was involved in Operation Condor. The Uruguayans protested, and Ambassador Siracusa supported their protest, asking that Fons be issued a visa. On 31 December 1976, Shlaudeman informed Under Secretary of State for Political Affairs Phillip Habib that "we would be buying trouble" if a visa were issued to Fons. Shlaudeman further advised Habib that the director of the Uruguayan Defense Intelligence Service had "gone out of his way" to promise that his officers would engage only in legitimate activities in the United States. Shlaudeman archly noted that the Uruguayan assurance of good behavior "gives me some pause."[102]

The United States took a different approach to Uruguay during the administration of Jimmy Carter. When he arrived in Montevideo, Ambassador Lawrence Pezzulo endured a three-hour tirade from three generals who protested that the United States did not understand communism and that it had abandoned Uruguay. The ambassador responded that world opinion was against Uruguay and that the regime had engaged in arbitrary actions against citizens. In the ambassador's judgment, reasoned pressure on the issue of human rights led to results. By the time he headed for a new assignment in Nicaragua in 1979, the regime had closed two torture centers, the number of political prisoners had declined from 4,700 to less than 1,000, and there was talk of political liberalization.[103] Democracy and constitutionalism did not return to Uruguay until 1985, however. Before relinquishing power, the military secured an amnesty law, Ley de Caducidad, that barred the prosecution of military personnel for violations of human rights. In 2011, the law was declared invalid. Since 1985, citizens have consistently voted for politicians who were imprisoned and parties that were proscribed during the long period of authoritarianism and military dictatorship. The Frente Amplio has won three national elections. President José Mujica (2010–2015), the former Tupamaro, earned international renown for his simple ways, earning the sobriquet as "the world's poorest president." His presidential "limousine" was a 1987 Volkswagen Beetle. The Argentine-born Pope Francis (2013–) embraced Mujica in the Vatican. Mujica helped President Barack Obama by agreeing to take six inmates from the U.S. prison in Guantánamo Bay, Cuba. In the twenty-first century, the Uruguayan economy began to show impressive growth rates, as the nation embraced globalism and took an aggressive approach to marketing its primary products. The model Latin American country had emerged from the nightmare that the Nixon administration and Henry Kissinger helped create and perpetuate.

In an 8 October 1976 conversation about human rights with State Department officials in Washington, Uruguayan Foreign Minister Blanco pleaded for fairness and relativism. Blanco pointed out that "if Uruguay had simply killed the terrorists and dumped them into the Río de la Plata nothing would have been heard from human rights organizations."[104] What the foreign minister was implying was that the military dictators in Uruguay were more restrained those in neighboring Argentina. Argentina's military rulers had launched *la guerra sucia* ("dirty war") against their citizens, with plans to murder 50,000 Argentines. Argentines were indeed being dropped from planes and helicopters into the Río de la Plata and the South Atlantic Ocean. But the foreign minister was inaccurate when he suggested that the Argentine security forces were tossing bodies out of aircraft. The victims were still alive. During his final years as secretary of state, Henry Kissinger would be forced to encounter the issue of mass murder and rampant anti-Semitism in Argentina. He would also have to return to the issue of Chile. General Pinochet and his minions were spreading their brand of terror around the world.

CHAPTER 4

Mass Murder and International Assassination

Argentina and Chile

The military regimes of Bolivia, Brazil, Paraguay, and Uruguay tortured and murdered political opponents and trampled on the civil rights of citizens. However appalling the human rights records of these regimes, they paled in comparison to the grotesque policies of the military commanders of Argentina and Chile. The Argentine military launched in 1976 a campaign euphemistically labeled *el Proceso* ("the Process") to cleanse the nation of unwelcome ideas by murdering 50,000 Argentines. In Chile, General Augusto Pinochet continued in 1975–1976 his mission to preserve Western civilization by accelerating the detainment and torture of ordinary citizens. The Chilean dictator also founded Operation Condor, an organization of countries of southern South America dedicated to assassinating political exiles wherever they could be found. The murderous policies pursued by Argentina and Chile intensified national and international criticism of Henry Kissinger's approach to military dictatorship in Latin America. Officers within the U.S. State Department joined in the denunciation of the secretary of state's resistance to defending basic human rights in Argentina and Chile. Any fair analysis of Kissinger's foreign-policy record must assess his rationale for his sanguine approach to Argentina and Chile.

The Dilemma of Argentina

An NSC analysis conducted in 1969 for the new Nixon administration labeled Argentina "a conservative, status quo, 'have' nation." The study elaborated on that assessment by accurately noting, "Judged by such economic and social criteria as per capita income, class structure, literacy, longevity, and degree of urbanization and industrialization, Argentina is already the most advanced nation in Latin America."[1] The NSC study could have added that the country had been endowed by history and nature. It is the ninth-largest country in the world, with excellent natural resources and climate. Argentina has the basic minerals, except for coal. It has been largely self-sufficient in petroleum. Its agricultural bounty, the vast plains known as the Pampas, are unsurpassed for the raising of livestock and harvesting of grains. Argentines consume enormous quantities of *bife lomo* and *bife chorizo*, the most luscious beef steaks in the world, accompanied by superb malbec wines made with grapes harvested from the provincial vineyards of Mendoza and Salta. The vibrant, elegant capital city of Buenos Aires often invokes comparisons to Paris. Argentina has also profited from the contributions of the waves of immigrants who have come since the late nineteenth century. Such happy developments have contributed to the Argentine self-perception of being special people. Argentines are not surprised that the first Latin American pope came from Argentina. Jorge Mario Bergoglio (1936–), the son of an Italian immigrant father and mother of Italian heritage from Buenos Aires, became a Jesuit priest, bishop, and cardinal before being elevated in 2013 to the papacy in Rome. Pope Francis knows well the exuberant, boastful nature of Argentines, especially the residents of Buenos Aires, known as *porteños*. Pope Francis has gentle fun with his people by repeating the revealing Argentine maxim that "God is everywhere, but He keeps office hours in Buenos Aires."

Despite these natural and assumed heavenly blessings, Argentina has been politically and economically chaotic since 1930. Argentina has also exerted minimal influence in the international arena. To be sure, the nation has held on to its constitutional democratic system since 1983, and it has become a global leader in promoting the rights of gay, lesbian, and bisexual people. But libraries are filled with books by scholars and pundits trying to explain why Argentina has been politically unstable and unable to produce an Australian or Canadian quality of life. In the period from 1870 to 1914, the country seemed to be on the move. It pursued liberal trade and investment policies, selling its agricultural products in European markets and welcoming foreign investment. Argentina's economy grew at an annual rate of at least 5 percent, which was one of the highest growth rates ever recorded. Foreign investment underwrote the building of a modern railroad system and the introduction of electricity in urban areas. Immigrants from Spain, Italy, and Greece were welcomed. The country's population grew from 1.7 million in 1869 to 7.9 million in 1914. By 1914, Buenos Aires was being favorably compared to New York City.

Argentina's export economy depended upon a peaceful, open world. But World War I, the Great Depression of the 1930s, World War II, the Cold War, and various international financial crises disrupted the free flow of international trade. Twentieth-century Argentines began to question the wisdom of the principles of Adam Smith in his *Wealth of Nations* (1775), even when trade flowed freely. As espoused by the economist Raúl Prebisch, Argentines embraced the theory of "unequal exchange," which was related to the "parity" issued raised by U.S. farmers. The prices of agricultural exports were not keeping up with the prices of imported manufactured goods. Prebisch recommended the economic strategy of "import substitution," using the revenue gained from agricultural exports to purchase plants, equipment, and technology for an industrial base. But whether the home market, with a population of 22 million in 1970, would be large enough to sustain Argentina's "infant industries" remained a key question. An import substitution policy further meant that Argentina would have less money to invest in agricultural modernization and the upgrading of the economic infrastructure—highways, ports, harbors, and telecommunication systems. Argentines further doubted whether they wanted international investors playing prominent roles in their economy. In 1948, the nation bought the British-owned railways. In sum, since 1930 Argentines have bitterly debated the issue of whether they wanted to pursue nationalistic economic policies or return to the halcyon era of liberal trade and investment practices. The numerous, abrupt changes in economic strategies that have subsequently marked their policies have retarded Argentine economic growth and development and bewildered international observers.

Oligarchic rule characterized political life in the era of liberal trade practices. Argentina was undemocratic and economically unequal. The gradual extension of the franchise and continued immigration brought working-class adults into the political process who wanted power and economic justice. Their champions were Juan Perón (1946–1955), a military officer, and his charismatic wife, Eva Perón. Both, but especially "Evita," publicly identified with the *descamisados* or "shirtless ones." They built a base of political support with trade unions. Although his economic policies were inconsistent and inchoate, Juan Perón seemed to take a nationalist and redistributionist approach, although he tempered those approaches after Eva Perón died of cancer in 1952. The politicization of historically marginalized groups terrified the traditional arbiters of power. Moreover, the economic surplus that had accumulated through the selling of beef and wheat to the Allies during World War II had been dissipated during the Perón years. The Argentine military, which had dominated political life from 1930 to 1946, overthrew President Perón in 1955. Thereafter, they banned Perón from returning to Argentina and devised various schemes to proscribe the labor union movement. From 1958 to 1966, the military permitted civilian presidents from the middle class to govern, but overthrew them when they took the natural step of trying to reintegrate the Peronist movement into Argentina's political life. Political instability, labor unrest, and economic stagnation became the conspicuous features of Argentine life.

The United States had not deeply engaged with Argentina prior to 1969. Trade had been limited, because both countries were exporters of meats and grains. Argentina traditionally looked to Western Europe for its cultural models. During World War I, the country stayed neutral, although it readily sold its foodstuffs to Great Britain and France. Argentine jurists took up the cause of Central American and Caribbean nations, who were occupied by U.S. Marines under the aegis of the Roosevelt Corollary (1904–1933) to the Monroe Doctrine. The Drago Doctrine (1902) held that it was a violation of international law to invade a country to collect unpaid debts. Argentina also supported the invaded nations of Latin America at an inter-American conference held in Havana (1928). Through most of World War II, Argentina reasserted its traditional neutralist stance and again happily sold its agricultural products to the embattled British. Under U.S. pressure, Argentina eventually declared war against Nazi Germany so that it could be a charter member of the United Nations. A U.S.-Argentine confrontation erupted at the end of the war, when the Truman administration, and especially its bombastic ambassador, Spruille Braden, decided that Colonel Perón had fascist sympathies. In 1946, Braden, who had been promoted to assistant secretary of state, interfered in the Argentine election by issuing a "Blue Book," a study that purported to document the fascist proclivities of prominent Argentines. Perón cleverly seized upon Braden's impolitic behavior and successfully turned the election into a campaign against Yankee imperialism.[2] Relations improved in the early 1950s, with Secretary of State John Foster Dulles ruling that Perón's anticommunism was his saving grace.[3] The Kennedy administration had high hopes for President Arturo Frondizi (1958–1962), perceiving in him a middle-class reformer who would carry out the goals of the Alliance for Progress. But Frondizi angered the administration by conferring an award on Argentina's native son, Che Guevara, and refusing to break relations with communist Cuba. The Kennedy administration undermined the central goal of the Alliance—promoting democracy—by welcoming the overthrow of Frondizi by the Argentine military. One important postwar development was that U.S. traders and investors had replaced Europeans as the principal international business people in Argentina. In 1970, U.S. direct investments amounted to $1.28 billion, and the United States had a substantial trade surplus with Argentina.[4]

In January 1969, Lieutenant General Juan Carlos Onganía (1966–1970) was the latest military dictator in charge of Argentina. Military officers had been suitably impressed by what Argentina's neighbor and rival, Brazil, was accomplishing under military dictatorship and planned to provide the order and technical efficiency that would undergird economic progress. Onganía proscribed political parties, outlawed labor strikes, and purged universities of professors and students who had unwelcome ideas. In May 1969, citizens were shocked when troops opened fire on antigovernment protestors and strikers in the city of Córdoba. Unpaid wages in the sugar industry, the elimination of Saturday as a day of rest in the automobile factories, and a fivefold price increase in meal tickets at university cafeterias were principal issues. The Cordobazo became an infamous event and a turning point in Argentine history. In a closed political system, governmental violence predictably engendered retaliatory violence by union groups, students, and political leftists. Kidnappings, robberies, bombings, and urban terrorism disrupted life from 1969 to 1976. In the aftermath of the Cordobazo, new armed groups—Fuerzas Armadas Peronistas (Armed Peronist Forces), the Movimiento Peronista Montonero (Peronist Movement–Montonero), and the Ejército Revolucionario del Pueblo (Revolutionary Army of the People, or ERP)—espoused various forms of socialism and vowed to topple the military dictators. Military officers would subsequently charge that such groups killed 495 uniformed personnel, military and police, between 1960 and 1989. Right-wing paramilitary groups, often tied to government officials, waged war on these leftist organizations.

Candidate Richard Nixon approved of General Onganía's dictatorship and pronounced the unsuitability of democracy for Argentina when he visited in 1967. In turn, Onganía expressed his high regard for Nixon. Governor Nelson Rockefeller was also enthusiastic about military rule when he met with Onganía for a two-hour conversation in Buenos Aires. The general blamed the turmoil in Córdoba on communists. Rockefeller found Onganía to be "decisive," a friend of the United States, and one who vowed to restore a democratic, progressive society in Argentina within ten years. Onganía, however, first had to "re-order the country to achieve national integration" by eliminating political parties.[5] Between 1969 and 1972, U.S.-Argentine relations were orderly and noncontroversial, although the U.S. ambassador, John Cabot Lodge (1969–1973), was perceived as incompetent, both in Washington and Buenos Aires. Lodge, the brother of Henry Cabot Lodge, Nixon's running mate in 1960 and a former Republican governor of Connecticut, spoke Italian and Spanish and wanted an ambassadorship in Italy. In March 1969, Henry Kissinger judged that "a terrible idea." He wanted to make Lodge the U.S. representative to OAS but eventually accepted the idea of dispatching him to Buenos Aires.[6] The embassy staff ridiculed the unhappy and uninformed ambassador. The labor attaché, John T. Doherty, noted that Lodge "thought Peronists were Communists and he was shocked to find out that a lot of them were National Socialists and right wingers." Political officer Dan W. Figgins added, "The labor unions were anti-communist but he saw labor unions as being dangerous and subversive or even communist."[7] Argentine officials saw in Lodge another Spruille Braden and declined to attend social functions with him. By 1971, the news got back to Washington that the embassy held Lodge in contempt, and Kissinger asked the president to address the situation. Nixon decided to leave Lodge in Argentina, explaining, "He is surrounded by competent people."[8] Nixon replaced Lodge in 1973 with Robert C. Hill, an archconservative from New Hampshire, who had both political and diplomatic experience. During his tenure as ambassador, Lodge opposed the return of representative democracy in Argentina, predicting that the Peronists would win a free election. He continued to believe that some Peronists were aligned with Fidel Castro.[9]

Military men overthrew General Onganía on 9 June 1970. Onganía had lost credibility because of public outrage over the Cordobazo. A debate had also broken out among military commanders on whether a timetable should be established for elections and the return of civilian rule. General Alejandro Agustín Lanusse (1971–1973) emerged as the new military strongman. General Lanusse calculated that the Peronists could be defeated in an open election. He legalized the party and even permitted Juan Perón to return to Argentina, after seventeen years in exile, in late 1972. The aged leader stayed for a month. General Lanusse also scheduled an election for March 1973. Lanusse needed U.S. help to accomplish his plan. In order to curry favor with workers, Lanusse implemented an expansionary spending policy to promote the economy. He asked the United States for $500 million to $1 billion in economic aid in July 1971. The mayor of Buenos Aires even suggested that the United States grant Argentina $5 billion. Lanusse tried a carrot-and-stick approach with the Nixon administration. He recalled that Argentina helped with the overthrow of Juan José Torres in Bolivia in August 1971. He also suggested that Argentina might look to the Soviet bloc for help if the United States turned him down.[10]

The Nixon administration showed sympathy toward General Lanusse but offered him no money. Henry Kissinger recommended to President Nixon that the United States immediately recognize and congratulate Lanusse when he seized power in March 1971. The administration believed that military rulers could be counted on to side with the United States in the international arena. The president also dispatched a personal representative, Assistant Treasury Secretary John Petty, to explain why the United States had no money for Argentina. Nixon was in the midst of devising his "New Economic Policy" to revive the stagnant U.S. economy in preparation for his reelection campaign in 1972. In his two-hour meeting with Petty at the presidential residence, Quinta de Olivos, Lanusse explained that he needed the money to provide "a margin of safety" to "bring about a return of a politically-based system." The best that Petty could offer was a pledge to support the Argentine cause at the International Monetary Fund. Kissinger subsequently asked the Treasury Department to recommend Argentina to the "New York banking community" for commercial loans.[11]

Lanusse stuck to his electoral plan, with free elections being held on 11 March 1973. His candidate was his minister of social welfare, Francisco Manrique, a former naval officer. Perón was prohibited from running, but he chose a stalking horse, Héctor Cámpora, a Peronist legislator in the 1950s, to lead his party. The third major candidate was Ricardo Balbín, a lawyer and politician, who represented the middle-class Radical Party. Over 85 percent of eligible voters participated in the election. Cámpora won 49.6 percent of the vote, barely missing the 50 percent required to take office. Balbín, who finished second, conceded the obvious and petitioned for cancellation of the second round of voting. Cámpora took office on 25 May. But the Argentine minuet continued. Perón returned to Argentina a month later, Cámpora resigned, and new elections were scheduled. On 23 September 1973, twelve days after the overthrow of Salvador Allende, Juan Perón, who was seventy-seven years old, swept to victory with 60 percent of the vote. His running mate was his spouse, María Estela Martínez, known as Isabel Perón, who was born in the northern Argentine province of La Rioja. Perón met his third wife in Panama, brought her to Madrid, and married her in 1961. Isabel Perón, who was born in 1931 and was considerably younger than her husband, had a limited formal education. She assumed the Argentine presidency on 1 July 1974 when her husband died from a heart attack after less than one year in office.

The Nixon administration watched but did not interfere in these astonishing Argentine political developments. On 2 February 1973, the CIA's deputy director for plans, Thomas H. Karamessines, recommended to Kissinger that the United States not interfere in the March 1973 elections, for a covert intervention "would involve a relatively high-risk factor in the present highly-charged, volatile political climate in Argentina."[12] Beyond being an arrogant affirmation of U.S. hegemony in the Western Hemisphere, the CIA recommendation pointed to the assessment that a Peronist government would pose no threat

to U.S. interests. Thereafter, high administration officials made several conciliatory gestures toward Argentina. Secretary of State William P. Rogers attended
Cámpora's inauguration and had a cordial, private meeting with the new president.[13] President Nixon sent warm messages of goodwill after both elections
of 1973. Kissinger, now secretary of state, met in October 1973 in New York
City with Alberto Vignes, Perón's foreign minister. Kissinger lavished praise
on President Perón, observing that "a leader who has been in exile for twenty
years who returns to his country and gets 65% of the vote is a man of historic
importance." Implicitly suggesting that he too was a man of significance, Kissinger added "that in all frankness he preferred to deal with big people rather
than small people." Vignes would subsequently refer to "his good friend Henry
Kissinger." Discussions would subsequently ensue about Perón coming to the
United States and meeting President Nixon.[14] The Argentine president was always too weak and sick to travel. The U.S. embassy hoped that Secretary of
State Kissinger would pay a visit to Buenos Aires.

U.S. intelligence agencies produced a series of papers speculating on what
the restoration of Peronist rule meant for Argentina and U.S. foreign policy.
Like other international observers, U.S. analysts were befuddled by the conun-
drum of why a potentially wealthy country suffered endless political turmoil.
In a study recommended to Kissinger by Deputy Director of the CIA Vernon
Walters, the Office of Current Intelligence noted that Argentina had "created
for itself a way of life and a philosophy of living that has no equal in the Western Hemisphere." It was a European country that happened to be attached to
the land mass of South America. Yet Argentines perceived the pursuit of pleasure as a worthy life goal, rejecting the "Calvinist work ethic" associated with
Europe. The richness of the Pampas had "permitted Argentina to operate on
the brink of economic failure for many years, while its people eat well and
enjoy TV sets and cars—what one economist calls mini-prosperity with macro-
chaos."[15] But Argentines wanted to escape the chaos and had come to the conviction, in the embassy's words, that "Perón is the only person who can save
Argentina at this point."[16] The problem was that Perón's electoral coalition was
unsustainable. In an NIE produced on 31 January 1974, U.S. analysts pointed out
that conservative union members, Marxists, proto-Nazis, young people, business executives, professionals, and some of the intelligentsia had voted for
Perón. Argentina, a country of immigrants, had Latin America's largest Jewish population. A large segment of the Jewish financial community supported
Perón, "despite the anti-Semitic overtones of Perón's policies during the 1940s."
Working in Perón's favor was the temporary withdrawal of discredited military
officers from Argentine politics. The military high command understood that
the civilian population held them responsible for many of Argentina's problems.[17]

In exile, Perón had taken an increasingly populist and leftist stance. In practice, he was a conservative authoritarian. Even after the elections of Cámpora and Perón, Argentina continued to be plagued by bombings, kidnappings, and murders by political extremists. Foreign business executives were kidnapped, held for ransom, and sometimes murdered by leftists. Ford Motor Company threatened to leave Argentina if its executives were subjected to further violence. Perón responded to the ongoing violence by authorizing conservative unionists to purge leftists from their ranks. He also quietly directed paramilitary groups, staffed by retired military personnel, to wage war on the young leftists. Vice President Isabel Perón also cooperated with the extralegal death squads.

During her twenty-two months in office, President Isabel Perón intensified Argentina's extreme political polarization. She lacked the background and political experience to lead the tumultuous nation. She was bedeviled by health issues. Isabel Perón also lacked the common touch of an Eva Perón that had so inspired everyday Argentines. She predictably encountered disdain because of her sex, with opponents dismissing her as "Isabelita," or "little Isabel." These sexist attitudes carried over to Washington. In briefing Kissinger about Isabel Perón's ascension to power, Assistant Secretary of State Jack Kubisch referenced her sixth-grade education and former career as a nightclub dancer. Kubisch added that the new president "is a rather sad, very feminine person, and is really sort of bewildered by it all."[18] Without doubt, President Perón chose her advisers poorly. She fell under the sway of a former associate of her husband's, José López Rega, the minister of social welfare. The papal nuncio, Pope Paul VI's diplomatic representative in Argentina, informed the CIA that she was under the "complete dominance" of her minister.[19] López Rega, who dabbled in the occult, urged the president to wage war against political leftists through paramilitary groups and death squads. In November 1974, Perón declared a "state of siege," suspending normal legal safeguards for suspected terrorists. López Rega led the Alianza Anticomunista Argentina (Argentine Anti-Communist Alliance or "Triple A"), an especially vicious death squad responsible for numerous assassinations. The U.S. embassy estimated that over 2,000 Argentines died in political violence between 1973 and March 1976. The various armed leftist groups continued to glorify violence and assassinated prominent politicians and military leaders, but most of the victims of political violence were students, unionists, and leftist politicians engaged in legitimate political activity.[20] Right-wing death squads and the increasingly authoritarian government perpetrated most of the mayhem. The state-supported terrorism that would result in perhaps 30,000 deaths in Argentina can be properly said to have begun during the Perón years.

Secretary Kissinger and the U.S. embassy in Buenos Aires neither encouraged nor discouraged the military *golpe* against President Perón, which took place on 24 March 1976. Kissinger met with Argentine foreign ministry officials a remarkable six times during Isabel Perón's presidency. The status of her presidency was not a subject of conversation, and Kissinger never spoke of the need to honor the results of elections or to uphold constitutional procedures. Kissinger bonded with Foreign Minister Vignes. Their meetings began with abrazos and were filled with banter from Kissinger. On the subject of the Malvinas (Falkland Islands), Kissinger wondered if he had a consulate there, believing an island in the stormy South Atlantic to be an excellent place to send State Department personnel that he disdained.[21] The embassy characterized the Kissinger-Vignes relationship as "the core factor" of Argentine foreign policy and the reason why bilateral relations "were as good as and probably better than they had been for many years."[22] Kissinger repeatedly assured Argentine officials that he ranked Argentina with Brazil and Mexico as the key Latin American countries. He planned to visit Buenos Aires in the spring of 1975 but had to cancel the trip when the government in Saigon, South Vietnam, collapsed in April 1975. Although he did not visit Argentina until 1978 during the World Cup *fútbol* tournament, Kissinger went out of his way to assist Argentine trade. President Cámpora had reestablished relations with Cuba, and the Argentines wanted to sell to the Cubans cars and trucks manufactured by U.S. subsidiaries and to ship the goods on Argentine bottoms. These plans violated U.S. laws on sanctions on Cuba and mandated penalties on Argentina. Using his bureaucratic skills, Kissinger worked out a variety of ways for the Argentines to skirt U.S. laws. His foreign-policy philosophy was to prevent economic issues from disrupting harmonious relationships. He also pointed out that U.S. subsidiaries, such as Ford Motor Company, should not be put in the untenable position of obeying U.S. trade restrictions by violating Argentine laws.[23]

Ambassador Robert Hill and his embassy diligently monitored the attitudes of the Argentine military command and discussed the political situation with generals and admirals. Embassy officials understood that the military was waiting for the political and economic collapse of Argentina so that the public would welcome the military's return to power after the Perón interregnum. As reflected in the daily briefings given to President Gerald Ford, the CIA was well connected to the plotters and accurately predicted when the military would strike against President Perón.[24] Ambassador Hill took a careful, diplomatic approach to the looming crisis, concluding one lengthy political analysis with the statement that "it is up to the Argentines to put their own house in order."[25] Hill deluded himself into believing that General Jorge Rafael Videla, the leader of the golpistas, was a "professional" man who would restrain the worst instincts of his military colleagues. The ambassador was not the only one to misjudge General Videla. Many Argentines, including Jorge Luis Borges, the celebrated literary figure, initially characterized Videla as a gentleman and patriot. A U.S. diplomat would later call on President Videla in his office and sarcastically observe, "He had his crucifix hanging on the wall behind his back. He gave us a line of bull about anarchists and so on."[26] Hill did have two indirect but chilling conversations with Air Force General Orlando Ramón Agosti and Admiral Emilio Eduardo Massera on what would be the U.S. reaction to violations of human rights. A month before the *golpe*, the embassy was warning Washington that "the presence of hard-line officers in the Armed Forces could lead to military rule for an extended duration and of unprecedented severity." In turn, on 13 March 1976, State Department officers in Washington informed the embassy that an Argentine military attaché was soliciting information on "Argentine nationals in the US who may be leftist or Communist sympathizers or former members of ERP," as well as seeking the whereabouts of individuals who worked for the Argentine government in the United States. The attaché, Major General Luis Miro, explained that the information was "required for possible recall of individuals in case of a military coup." The State Department declined the general's request.[27]

State-Sponsored Terrorism

Argentina's military dictatorship lasted from 1976 to 1983. The admirals and generals labeled their rule *Proceso de Reorganización Nacional* (National Reorganization Process) or simply *el Proceso* ("the Process"). Like the military dictators in Bolivia, Brazil, Chile, and Uruguay, Argentina's military men explained that they were waging the Third World War against international communism. Foreign Minister Juan Carlos Blanco of Uruguay was perhaps the most articulate spokesperson in southern South America for this national security doctrine. Although allied to the United States, the dictators sensed the United States had lost its way in the international arena. Some had doubts about whether the United States was too trusting of the communists in pursuing détente with the Soviet Union or in initiating contacts with the People's Republic of China. The Argentine military wondered if the United States had lost its nerve in permitting the collapse of South Vietnam and not confronting Cuba over its intervention in the African nation of Angola. The dictators further questioned why President Ford and Secretary Kissinger would permit the revelations about the CIA and the U.S. intervention against Salvador Allende in the congressional hearings chaired in 1975 by Senator Frank Church (D-ID).[28] The

Argentine military would give substance to this theory of a global war against communism when it began to assist right-wing groups in Nicaragua after the Sandinistas overthrew the Somoza family dictatorship in Nicaragua in 1979.[29]

The first official Argentine assessment of the death toll, which was contained in the study *Nunca Más* (1984), held the military responsible for 8,960 "disappeared" persons. The investigative commission, which was chaired by the distinguished novelist and scientist Ernesto Sábato, conceded that its findings were conservative.[30] Perhaps up to 30,000 Argentines died in the so-called dirty war, or *la guerra sucia*. There were not 30,000 subversive terrorists in Argentina. The military dictatorship, the paramilitary units, and the death squads killed people who believed in democracy, free speech, freedom of religion, and social justice. They tortured and murdered students, trade unionists, politicians, priests, nuns, journalists, and mothers who marched in the Plaza de Mayo in Buenos Aires. The military and associated thugs took a special delight in killing Argentine Jews. Military officers stole as many as 500 infants. Pregnant women who were incarcerated were permitted to give birth and then were slaughtered. Laura Carlotto was permitted to hold her newborn for five hours before she was shot in the head. The babies, such as Laura's son, Guido, were distributed to military officers and friends of the officers. A couple, José Liborio Poblete and his wife, Gertrudis Hlaczik, committed the subversive act of submitting a petition calling for affirmative action in the hiring of the disabled. The torturers taunted Poblete, who had lost his legs in an automobile accident, calling him *cortito* ("shorty") and turned him into a bowling ball, rolling him down flights of stairs. The couple's baby, Claudia, was renamed and given to a military family.[31]

The military's claim that they seized power in order to safeguard Christianity and Western civilization from communist barbarians was a fabrication. Military officers established dictatorships because they believed they could give their nations order, technical efficiency, and progress. The "Brazilian Miracle" was to be emulated, although ironically by the mid-1970s the Brazilian economy was collapsing under the weight of high energy prices and excessive borrowing from international banks. The military also acted to keep working-class citizens, students, and religious minorities, like Argentine Jews, from exercising power. A notorious Argentine sadist was Julio Simón, known as "Julián the Turk," who attached a big swastika to his watch chain. Simón, like many a Nazi SS officer, was an opera fanatic who would listen to operatic music before commencing his torture sessions. He favored pushing a stick up the victim's anus while shocking the victim with 220 volts of electricity. In the 1990s, Simón boasted of his work in an interview on Argentine television. Speaking directly to the camera, the unrepentant Simón said, "The norm was to kill everyone, and anyone kidnapped was tortured." He defended himself by asserting that he was fighting "terrorist hordes" and that "torture is eternal" and an "essential part of the human being."[32]

Julián the Turk was stating what his military superiors professed. A year before seizing power, General Videla declared that "if the Argentine situation demands it, all necessary persons must die to achieve the security of the country." General Luciano Menéndez, commander of the Third Army Corps in Córdoba, calculated that 50,000 "necessary persons" needed to die. On the general's list was Enrique Angelelli, the bishop of La Rioja, who was revered for ministering to the poor. The bishop, who was murdered on 4 August 1976, has been named by the Roman Catholic Church a "Servant of God" and designated a candidate for sainthood. Killing the innocent and the good did not trouble the officers. As Lieutenant Colonel Hugo Pascarelli put it, "The fight in which we are engaged does not recognize moral limits; it is beyond good or evil." General Ibérico Saint Jean, military governor of Buenos Aires Province, vowed that the "indifferent" and the "timid" would be killed along with subversives. As General Videla would have it, "One becomes a terrorist not only by killing with a weapon or setting a bomb but also by encouraging others through ideas that go against our Western and Christian civilization."[33] Evil ideas included agreeing with Catholic bishops who had resolved at their conclave in Medellín in 1968 to pursue a preferential option for the poor in their ministry. Threats to Western and Christian civilization apparently also included student activism. Sixty students from Manuel Belgrano High School in Buenos Aires were "disappeared" simply for having joined their student council. In September 1976, six high-school students from La Plata, the capital of Buenos Aires Province, were disappeared for having protested a rise in student bus fares. The infamous incident became known as La Noche de los Lápices ("The Night of the Pencils").[34] Such grotesque, odious assaults on the innocent and the young have increasingly led Argentines to reject the term *la guerra sucia* to label the years from 1976 to 1983. General Videla and his subordinates perpetrated state-sponsored terrorism against their citizens. The military rulers of Bolivia, Brazil, Chile, Paraguay, and Uruguay similarly used terror to force obedience to military dictatorship.

El Proceso most often took place at the Escuela de Mecánica de la Armada (ESMA), or Navy School of Mechanics, a set of handsome buildings on the 8100 block of Avenida del Libertador, one of the grandest boulevards in Buenos Aires. Security personnel in civilian clothes would snatch people off the streets and stuff them into Ford Falcons. A hood, *la capucha*, would be placed over the victim's head. Within thirty minutes of arrival at ESMA, the kidnapped would be tortured. Women would be raped. The torture took place in the base-

This handsome building, known by the acronym ESMA, sits in a smart neighborhood in Buenos Aires. It was the central venue for torture and murder during the period of the Argentine military dictatorship, 1976–1983. Author's photo.

ment of a building, where on the upper floors military personnel socialized and slept. After suffering weeks of torture, prisoners would be administered a sedative and transported to helicopters and airplanes. On 9 March 1995, Captain Adolfo Scilingo told an Argentine television audience what happened next. Scilingo participated in two of the weekly "death flights." Thirty drugged but alive people were dumped into the South Atlantic. Among the victims that Scilingo pushed out of the airplane included a senior citizen, a teenager, and two pregnant women in their early twenties. Of the 5,000 Argentines who were spirited into ESMA, only 150 survived to recount the horror.[35]

If There Are Things That Have to Be Done . . .

U.S. diplomats, both in Buenos Aires and in Washington, kept Henry Kissinger apprised of state-sponsored terrorism in Argentina. Despite receiving reports of gross violations of human rights, Secretary of State Kissinger defended the Argentine military to subordinates and encouraged the murderous behavior of Argentina's military rulers. As a private citizen, he signaled his approval of repressive military rule. Ambassador Robert Hill took on the role of speaking truth to power. As described by his immediate superior, Assistant Secretary of State Shlaudeman, Hill was "a very conservative Republican politician, by no means liberal or anything of the kind."[36] As a young man, Hill had worked for W. R. Grace, a shipping and chemicals company that had extensive business in Latin America. The young executive warned the Truman administration about the dangers of communism in Latin America. In 1953, President Eisenhower appointed Hill to be ambassador to Costa Rica. At the age of thirty-three, Hill was the youngest ambassador to represent the United States abroad in the history of the foreign service. Thereafter, he served as U.S. ambassador to El Salvador, Mexico, and Spain. Hill took pride in being the first U.S. diplomat to openly label Fidel Castro as a communist. Hill's service in Argentina during the tumultuous Perón years proved challenging. Fearful of a guerrilla attack, Hill traveled in a convoy with security guards. He and his wife gave up eating at restaurants in Buenos Aires, because Argentines, fearing that a kidnapping attempt might ensue, would immediately leave the premises. Although he had been unsettled by his conversations with Admiral Massera and General Agosti, Hill trusted that General Videla would steer Argentina onto a path of sanity, peace, and prosperity. He characterized the overthrow of Isabel Perón as "probably the best executed and most civilized coup in Argentine history."[37]

By the end April 1976, Hill began to be alarmed. The regime had conducted a mass arrest within one week of 1,500 Peronist politicians, including Carlos Menem, the governor of La Rioja Province and future president of the nation (1989–1999). By August, Argentina had 5,000 political prisoners. The "Triple A" death squad kidnapped Elida Messina, a member of the Fulbright Commission, the U.S.-Argentine educational exchange program. Tens of thousands of Bolivians, Brazilians, Chileans, Paraguayans, and Uruguayans had fled their respective military dictatorships to civilian Argentina. Exiled Uruguayan legislators were kidnapped and murdered. When the bodies of the Uruguayans were found in an abandoned automobile, they showed visible signs of torture, with eyes poked out, faces crushed, knuckles mangled, and burn scars. Juan José Torres, the former president of Bolivia, was shot dead. A U.N. official told Hill that photos of prominent Bolivian exiles had been posted in the northern city of Salta. The posters asked citizens to report the whereabouts of the Bolivians to the police.[38] On 23 June 1976, the CIA briefed President Ford that a Brazilian and a Chilean had been handed over to Chilean security forces. The embassy suspected the acquiescence or even "direct involvement" of Argentine security forces. In August, the embassy reported on the discovery of thirty bodies in a field near Pilar, a city in Buenos Aires Province, and held security forces responsible for the mass murder.[39] U.S. citizens were also being arrested and tortured. Between 1 September 1976 and 6 January 1977, embassy staff made thirty-one representations to the Argentine government about U.S. citizens. One of the arrested U.S. citizens was Father James "Santiago" Weeks, the supervisor of five Argentine seminarians of the La Salette order. The young seminarians, true to the new teachings of the Catholic Church, worked among the poor in Córdoba Province. Father Weeks was kept in solitary confinement, whereas the seminarians were repeatedly beaten. Public pressure from Catholics in the United States and the diplomatic efforts of Ambassador Hill led to the release of Father Weeks and eventually of the five seminarians, who were deported to the United States. Such representations led to new dangers for Ambassador Hill. He had to ride in a caravan with four lead cars and two behind, because he faced threats from paramilitary outfits and death squads allied with the government.[40]

Ambassador Hill's thinking about Argentina's military leaders evolved as terror and murder spread throughout the land. On 27 April 1976, he had a pleasant lunch with Admiral Massera and other Argentine officials. Massera projected an air of "balance and moderation" on human rights issues. But Hill left the luncheon uneasy, because Defense Minister Luís María Klix had insisted that "one must be a fanatic to defeat fanatics." On 27 May, Hill delivered a démarche to Admiral César Guzzetti, the junta's foreign minister, advocating "some sort of statement on part of GOA deploring terrorism of any kind, whether from left or right, and reaffirming GOA's resolve to enforce law and respect human rights." The ambassador lamented, "I did not have the impression that he [Guzzetti] got the point." By June, Ambassador Hill suggested to Washington that "hard-liners" in Southern Cone governments were conspiring to murder dissidents and exiles. The embassy asked itself whether General Videla possessed a "Machiavellian turn of mind" when he repeatedly proclaimed his respect for human rights. A ninety-minute conversation with Videla on 21 September left Hill "somewhat discouraged," for the general avoided answering his probing questions about human rights abuses. Yet Hill was still inclined to give Videla the benefit of the doubt, describing him as "a decent, well-intentioned man."[41]

General Videla was anything but uninvolved in terror and mass murder. In the postdictatorship years, Argentine jurists would unearth secret orders bearing Videla's signature that conclusively linked the general to state-sponsored terrorism. He would die in prison convicted of mass murder and the systematic kidnapping of children. The regime had devised a system that allowed Videla to appear as the reasonable face of the military junta and disassociated from the crimes. Videla would later claim, "I never killed or tortured anyone." Admiral Massera, however, participated in clandestine operations and in torture sessions. He also received a life sentence and died in custody. In an ongoing process, hundreds of Argentines have been sentenced to jail for the crimes they committed between 1976 and 1983. Perhaps the worst of the lot, General Menéndez, received twelve life sentences, an Argentine record. Between 2,500 and 3,000 Argentines disappeared from Córdoba, the province under General Menéndez's command.[42]

Ambassador Hill can be perceived as a victim of General Videla and his minions. Hill was especially distressed when the son of a thirty-year employee of the embassy disappeared. Argentine authorities, including Guzzetti and Videla, stonewalled him when he inquired about the student. When Patricia Derian, President Carter's new assistant secretary of state for human rights and humanitarian affairs, came to Argentina in March 1977, Ambassador Hill detailed to her his stubborn fight to protect human rights. Derian later recalled in an interview that Hill's experience in Argentina had unsettled his conservative political beliefs. In Derian's words, "After that happened I think he realized the whole weight and horror of what was going on, and that we were complicit in it."[43] The next year, Hill died prematurely of heart failure in the United States. A decade later, Assistant Secretary Shlaudeman, who would later serve as an ambassador to Argentina (1980–1983), praised Hill for reporting "quite effectively about what was going on, this slaughter of innocent civilians."[44]

Secretary of State Kissinger repeatedly undercut Ambassador Hill's diplomacy and was complicit in the "whole weight and horror" of Argentina's state-sponsored terrorism. Other than historian Michael Schmidli, scholars have missed the extraordinary lengths to which Kissinger went to defend the murderous Argentine generals from condemnation. Although he never discussed the impending military overthrow of President Perón, Kissinger signaled what his attitude would be when, on 28 September 1975, he met with Foreign Minister Ángel Robledo in New York and decried the "missionary instinct" of personnel in the Latin American Bureau. These State Department officers, Kissinger alleged, liked "to reform other countries, especially allied countries, because it is too dangerous to try to reform unfriendly countries."[45] Kissinger judged Videla and the military junta as friendly and allied. On 26 March 1976, two days after the *golpe*, Kissinger was unmoved by Assistant Secretary William D. Rogers's prediction "We've got to expect a fair amount of repression, probably a good deal of blood." Kissinger repeated to his staff several times that the success of the junta was in the United States' interest and that he wanted to "encourage" the officers. He said, "I don't want to give the sense that they're harassed by the United States."[46] The United States immediately extended diplomatic recognition to the junta and agreed to the release of a previously approved loan of $127 million from the International Monetary Fund. Thereafter, the Ford administration quietly authorized $49 million in security assistance for Argentina.[47]

Kissinger held an extraordinary sixty-five-minute meeting with Foreign Minister Guzzetti and other Argentine diplomats in Santiago on 10 June 1976. The secretary was in Chile to attend an OAS meeting. After several minutes of Kissinger jokes about *fútbol*, the foreign minister asked for U.S. "understanding and support" on internal security and economic aid. Argentina's main problem was "terrorism." Kissinger assured the Argentines that he wanted Argentina to "succeed" and that "we understand that you must establish authority." Kissinger repeated the words "succeed" or "success" four more times in the course of the conversation. He pledged to be sensitive to Argentina's economic needs and promised to call on banker David Rockefeller and his brother, Vice President Nelson Rockefeller, for their help with private sector loans. Kissinger reminded the Argentines that international criticism would mount about their war against terrorism. "If there are things that have to be done," he instructed, "you should do them quickly. But you must get back quickly to normal procedures." Kissinger reiterated that he did not want to "harass" Argentina and that he was prepared to be "harassed" for his Argentine policy. The secretary whined, "I have discovered that after the personal abuse reaches a certain level you become invulnerable." In the course of the discussion, Guzzetti committed a diplomatic faux pas. He claimed that 500,000 exiles from southern South America lived in Argentina and that 10,000 of them were terrorists. Argentina, he continued, was "encouraging joint efforts to integrate with our neighbors," which included Bolivia, Chile, Paraguay, and Brazil. In essence, Guzzetti informed Kissinger about Operation Condor. Kissinger pretended he did not understand that he had been told about an international assassination and kidnapping scheme. The note taker recorded that Kissinger "sharply" responded, "I take it you are talking about joint economic activities." Guzzetti quickly realized his mistake and agreed that economic stability and regional economic integration were the ways to defeat terrorism. The note taker then recorded that the "mollified" Kissinger replied, "That sounds like a good idea." At the end of the meeting, Kissinger and Guzzetti retired from the room for a private, unrecorded conversation that lasted four minutes.[48]

If there were questions among U.S. diplomats in Washington and Buenos Aires about his stance on human rights in Argentina, the secretary of state made his policy forcefully clear to Assistant Secretary Shlaudeman on 30 June 1976. Kissinger found out about a démarche to Argentina asking them to respect human rights. He was probably referring to the démarche delivered by Ambassador Hill in late May. The nature of the words he used in the transcript suggested that Kissinger was yelling at Shlaudeman over the telephone. "In what way" was the démarche "compatible with my policy." "What do you guys think my policy is?" Kissinger warned Shlaudeman, "You better be careful," and said that he would transfer the person responsible for the démarche. Shlaudeman was reduced to responding "Yes, sir." Nothing came of Kissinger's threat, for Under Secretary of State for Political Affairs Joseph P. Sisco, Kissinger's friend, had signed off on the démarche.[49]

Shlaudeman had not been intimidated by Kissinger's tirade. He had been Kissinger's man inside the U.S. embassy in Santiago when he served as deputy chief of mission during the Allende years. But perhaps Ambassador Hill's dispatches about kidnapping and mass murder in Argentina combined with the ongoing horror in General Pinochet's Chile led him to contest Kissinger on the issue of human rights. At Secretary Kissinger's staff meeting on 9 July 1976, Shlaudeman opened his remarks by saying, "It looks very much that this group for Videla in Argentina—the security forces are totally out of control. We have these daily waves of murder." Kissinger reacted by emphasizing the threat of leftist terrorists, pointing to their ability to assassinate the chief of the Argentine federal police force by putting a bomb under his bed.[50] Ambassador Hill also persisted. He had the opportunity to speak to Kissinger in July on an airplane flight back from San Francisco after both had attended a Bohemian Grove meeting, an annual summer camp for rich, influential, conservative men. In August 1976, Hill wrote directly to Kissinger, asking him to block an Inter-American Development bank loan to Argentina on human rights grounds. Kissinger ruled that Argentina would receive the loan. Hill called the decision a "mistake," believing it could result in "misinterpretations here concerning the seriousness with which the USG views this [human rights] problem."[51] By late September, a shocked Hill began to realize why Videla and Guzzetti did not take his protestations about human rights seriously. Both Argentine leaders pointed to the 10 June meeting with Kissinger in Santiago. As they saw it, the United States' overriding concern was not human rights but rather for Argentina to "get it over quickly."[52]

Ambassador Hill was further undercut by Kissinger's second meeting with Admiral Guzzetti, this time in New York City on 7 October 1976. Guzzetti had met the previous day in Washington with Deputy Under Secretary of State Charles W. Robinson, Shlaudeman, and Edwin M. Martin, who worked for the World Bank. Martin had previously been the assistant secretary of state for Latin America during the Kennedy administration and then ambassador to Argentina. Robinson commiserated with Guzzetti as he defended Argentina's war against leftist terrorists. Guzzetti now claimed the terrorists had substantial international support and had "their central control in Paris." The U.S.

diplomats challenged Guzzetti's ludicrous assertion, and Shlaudeman warned the foreign minister that the U.S. Congress would block future loans to Argentina over human rights questions. Ambassador Martin emphasized that "if members of religious groups violate the law it is essential that they not simply 'disappear.'" Martin added that the U.S. public did "not believe that religious men can act in a fashion that warrants summary treatment."[53] Foreign Minister Guzzetti received no warnings or lectures in his satisfying audience with Secretary of State Kissinger. Kissinger summarized his policy in a few sentences, noting, "Look, our basic attitude is that we would like you to succeed. I have an old-fashioned attitude that friends ought to be supported." Kissinger pointed out that U.S. citizens did not understand that Argentina was engaged in a civil war. The key for Argentina's international reputation was "The quicker you succeed the better." Kissinger assured Guzzetti that the United States would not "cause you unnecessary difficulties" and that "we have no intention" of voting against two pending international loans for Argentina.[54]

Ambassador Hill met with Guzzetti on 15 October 1976, the day after the foreign minister returned to Buenos Aires. In Hill's words, Guzzetti was "euphoric," "in a state of jubilation," as he "enthusiastically told me of the success of his visit." Guzzetti had "bounded into the room and greeted me effusively with an *abrazo*, which is not typical of him." The thirty-five-minute meeting in Guzzetti's private audience left Hill deflated and demoralized. Hill wrote that Guzzetti expected to receive "strong, firm, direct warnings" to cease human rights abuses. Instead, the foreign minister had discovered that the Ford administration had "no real problem" with Argentina. Guzzetti would be telling General Videla that criticism of Argentina was limited to biased and uninformed segments of the U.S. Congress and public. Hill concluded that it would hereafter be "unrealistic and ineffective" for the embassy to press the government to respect human rights. Hill also sent a back-channel message to Assistant Secretary Shlaudeman about his encounter with Guzzetti. As Shlaudeman informed Kissinger, the ambassador had "registered for the record a bitter complaint" about what happened in Washington and New York.[55]

Kissinger personally approved a response to his recalcitrant ambassador in Buenos Aires. Guzzetti allegedly "heard only what he wanted to hear." The foreign minister had been told "in detail" that the U.S. public reacted strongly to accounts of abuses in Argentina. But the foreign minister focused on what Kissinger told him on 7 October, which was a reiteration of their conversation in June in Santiago. The response to Hill did not raise the substance of the secretary's conversations with Guzzetti. Hill was empowered, however, to tell the Argentines that Kissinger had given, on 19 October, a speech on human rights to the Synagogue Council of America. Hill was not dissuaded by this misleading response. He retorted, "We continue to believe many in GOA maintain their illusions GOA has no serious human rights problems." He called for a State Department protest about mass murder in Argentina.[56]

In his speech to the Synagogue Council, Secretary Kissinger made the unimpeachable point that "no people has experienced more of man's exaltation—and man's depravity—than the Jewish people." He added, "The Jewish people know that survival requires unending struggle."[57] Argentine Jews certainly knew those truths during the time of military dictatorship. Although representing only 2 percent of the nation's population, Argentine Jews accounted for 10 percent of the murdered and disappeared. Once kidnapped, few Jews lived to tell their stories of humiliation and pain. Eyewitness accounts of what happened to Argentine Jews depended on Christian inmates who survived. An inmate recalled that "Jews were punished simply because they were Jewish." One torturer, who called himself the "Great Führer," forced Jewish inmates to shout "Heil Hitler," and stare at portraits of Hitler and Mussolini. Perpetrators painted Hitler mustaches on Jews and sprayed swastikas on their backs so they would be identified and punished as Jews. One female prisoner who survived testified that she was threatened that she would be transformed into soap.[58]

Director of Policy Planning Winston Lord informed Kissinger, and the U.S. embassy in Buenos Aires warned the State Department about the rise of anti-Semitism under the military dictatorship. National Security Adviser Brent Scowcroft briefed Vice President Nelson Rockefeller that the regime targeted Jewish dissidents.[59] Foreign Minister Guzzetti addressed the issue in his New York City meeting with Kissinger. According to Guzzetti, leftists were creating a distorted image of Argentina; the Jewish community was integrated into the country, anti-Semitic episodes were isolated, and "there has never been persecution." Kissinger accepted these assurances, observing, "On the Jewish situation, you know the sensitivities as well as I do. I have no reason to suppose your government is doing anything."[60] Other scholars have found evidence that Kissinger showed a similar lack of interest about the fate of Jews elsewhere. In May 1971, in a conversation with President Nixon and his aides, he suggested that the United States should not complain about the treatment of Soviet Jews, because the Soviets would retaliate by "making a public protest to us for the treatment of Negroes." In March 1973, he remarked to the president, "If they put Jews in the gas chambers in the Soviet Union it is not an American concern. Maybe a humanitarian concern."[61] Henry Kissinger had witnessed genocide. Kissinger's family fled Nazi Germany, and his family lost relatives in the Holocaust. In April 1945, Staff Sergeant Kissinger participated with his military unit in the liberation of a concentration camp at Ahlem, west of Hanover, Germany. The conditions in the camp were unspeakable, a "hell on earth," as described by a U.S. soldier. Kissinger informed one inmate, "You are free," and wrote a moving two-page tribute to the dignity and humanity to one of the other "skeletons in striped suits," Folek Sama.[62] Given these shattering encounters with the consequences of anti-Semitism, it has remained difficult to understand how a world leader could be uncurious about the disappearance of Argentine Jews.

After he left office, Kissinger defended both the Argentine military dictatorship and his diplomacy. In June 1978, he travelled to Buenos Aires for the first time to attend the World Cup and sat prominently in the presidential box with General Videla. The venue for the match was only a few blocks away from ESMA.[63] Kissinger also met alone for thirty minutes with Videla at the presidential residence. U.S. Ambassador Raúl Castro was excluded from the meeting. At lunch, which the ambassador attended, Kissinger cautioned that the Soviet Union and Cuba continued to target Latin America. On 24 June 1978, at a news conference, Kissinger congratulated Argentina for its "outstanding" job in eliminating terrorism. Kissinger added that the methods security forces had used should not be perpetuated. Kissinger also suggested to Ambassador Castro that he would speak out against the Carter administration's human rights campaign in Latin America. The unsettled ambassador reported back to Washington, "Kissinger's repeated high praise for Argentina's action in wiping out terrorism and his stress on the importance of Argentina may have gone to some considerable extent to his hosts' heads. There is some danger that Argentines may use Kissinger's laudatory statements as justification for hardening their human rights stance."[64] Reporting to his superior, Zbigniew Brzezinski, Robert A. Pastor of the NSC staff noted, "[Kissinger's] praise for the Argentine government in its campaign against terrorism was the music the Argentine government was longing to hear, and it is no accident that his statements were played back to us by the Southern Cone countries during the OAS General Assembly." As to Kissinger's dire warning of Soviet/Cuban designs on Latin America, Pastor labeled them "about 15–20 years out of date."[65]

Since the 1970s, Kissinger has been repeatedly challenged about his attitude and policies toward Argentina. The Carter administration, led by Assistant Secretary of State Patricia Derian, succeeded in pressuring the military dictatorship to reduce, albeit not eliminate, human rights abuses.[66] Derian went to Argentina twice in 1977, collecting stories from the relatives of the disappeared and challenging Argentine authorities. The formidable Derian nearly came to blows with one general before aides restrained them. General Videla protested that "he'd never been spoken to by anybody, let alone a woman, like she spoke to him." She met with Admiral Massera in the elegant ESMA building and told him that she knew that torture was taking place "in the bottom floor of this building."[67] Derian would, however, be beloved by Argentine democrats. She was an honored guest at the inauguration of President Raúl Alfonsín (1983–1989), and in 2006 she received Argentina's highest award for foreign personages. As one U.S. diplomat recalled, Derian conducted "in many ways a one-person crusade." Argentines did not forget that "she had fought for their freedom starting in 1977."[68]

The Carter administration also saved the lives of Argentines, notably newspaper publisher and journalist Jacobo Timerman, an Argentine Jew who endured thirty months of incarceration, torture, and extreme anti-Semitism. His moving memoir, *Prisoner without a Name, Cell without a Number* (1981), persuaded most readers that Nazi-like thugs ran Argentina. Kissinger dissented from that interpretation, reasoning that "there is no doubt that there are many anti-Semitic trends in Argentina, but not in the Nazi sense."[69] Perhaps Kissinger noticed that General Roberto Viola, Videla's successor, compared *la guerra sucia* to the wars waged by armies of Third Reich when he came to the United States in 1981 at the invitation of the Reagan administration.[70]

The gradual release of documents and telephone conversations has prompted Kissinger to defend his honor. After *The Nation* published in 1987 an article citing some of Ambassador Hill's dispatches and Kissinger's meetings with Foreign Minister Guzzetti, Kissinger was greeted with disdain in Europe. Kissinger wrote an angry letter to publisher Victor S. Navasky wondering, "How is it that a short article in an obscure journal such as yours about a conversation that was supposed to have taken place years ago about something that did or didn't happen in Argentina resulted in sixty people holding placards denouncing me a few months ago at the airport when I got off the plane in Copenhagen?"[71] In 2004, as more documents were released about his cordial relationships with Argentine and Chilean dictators, Kissinger claimed that he believed in human rights, had given two speeches on human rights, and had brought up the issue in private conversations with dictators and their representatives. He explained that he ruled out personal attacks on the leaders of the dictatorships.[72] Kissinger possibly believed that he would not live to see the release of the complete documentary record. These new documents, which became publicly available from 2015 to 2017, have undermined Kissinger's defense of his actions.[73] In March 2016, just before his visit to Buenos Aires, President Barack Obama ordered the "Argentine Declassification Project," to assist jurists in the prosecution of Argentina's war criminals.

Chile, Operation Condor, and "the Third World War"

In his memoirs, Secretary of State Kissinger did not address either the menace of Operation Condor or the assassination of Orlando Letelier, the former Chilean foreign minister, and his assistant, Ronni Karpen Moffitt, a U.S. citizen, on 21 September 1976 in Washington, DC. (Moffitt's husband of four months, Michael, was also injured in the car-bomb attack.) This was a remarkable omission in the more than 3,400 pages of reflection on Kissinger's stewardship of foreign policy. This was the first act of state-sponsored terrorism in the history of the nation's capital. Augusto Pinochet, the Chilean dictator, authorized the assassination of Letelier. Kissinger instead focused on justifying his relationship with General Pinochet: "Cold War reality impelled us to maintain a constructive relationship with authoritarian regimes of South America." Nonetheless, he continued, "we exercised our influence to advance the causes of democratic institutions so long as we could do so without damaging fundamental United States interests or unleashing the radical violent left." Kissinger explained that his method was to engage with regimes that supported U.S. national security interests and not to confront them, "as we were being urged."[74] Perpetrating terrorist attacks in the United States, Latin America, and Western Europe, as the military dictators of South Americans did in the 1970s, however, seemed incompatible with U.S. national security interests.

In 1975–1976, Chile had become a major political problem for the secretary of state. U.S. citizens and Western European allies intensified their anger about the loss of constitutional practices in Chile and the savagery of the Pinochet regime. The government would ultimately incarcerate 150,000 to 200,000 Chileans and torture perhaps 100,000. Many of the abused would flee to Europe and Latin America and tell their stories. In the Netherlands, for example, in response to lobbying by exiles, the government cancelled a loan to Chile and imposed a boycott on Chilean products. Western Europeans were further alarmed as the Pinochet regime proscribed the Christian Democratic Party and persecuted Roman Catholic clergy. Democratic governments in Europe and Latin America sponsored resolutions at the United Nations and the OAS demanding that Pinochet and his minions respect human rights. The regime responded by blocking visits by international human rights commissions to Chile and denouncing "biased and arbitrary" reports about what was happening in Chile.[75] By the end of 1975, the U.S. and international public also knew far more about the circumstances of the overthrow of Salvador Allende. The Democratic Party had been emboldened by the Watergate scandal and its massive electoral victories in 1974. Senator Frank Church (D-ID) headed investigative committees that revealed that the United States had intervened covertly in the Chilean political process in the 1960s and 1970s. The findings implicated Henry Kissinger in the destabilization of the Allende government. Citizens also learned that the United States had participated in plots to assassinate Patrice Lumumba of the Congo (1960), Rafael Trujillo of the Dominican Republic (1961), and Ngo Dien Diem of South Vietnam (1963), and that the CIA had repeatedly attempted to assassinate Fidel Castro in a variety of bizarre schemes. Church's committee implicated the Nixon administration and Kissinger in the tragic assassination of General Rene Schneider (1970) by right-wing Chilean military officers. In Kissinger's judgment, the reports issued by Senator Church's committees amounted to "a national disgrace" and "a nut house."[76]

Senator Edward M. Kennedy (D-MA) took the lead in imposing sanctions against Chile. He successfully attached to the Foreign Assistance Act of 1974 a ban on military aid and foreign military sales to Chile. Kennedy also took up the cause for a democratic Chile in speeches on the Senate floor. In 2008, President Michelle Bachelet would confer on Senator Kennedy the Order to the Merit of Chile Award, Chile's highest civilian award, for his efforts to restore democracy and respect for human rights. Bachelet took the extraordinary step of traveling to Kennedy's home in Hyannis Port to present the award to the ailing senator, who died in 2009. Secretary Kissinger was unimpressed with the senator's commitment to democracy, however, telling him on 1 October 1974 that his proposed amendment would have "unfortunate consequences." In a meeting with President Ford on 20 December 1974, he characterized the Kennedy amendment as "disastrous" and vowed "to do everything possible to get arms for Chile."[77] Over the next two years, Kissinger constantly badgered the foreign policy bureaucracy to find ways to circumvent the law and sell Chile $50 million to $100 million in military equipment. The Chileans especially wanted tanks and antitank weapons, because they claimed the Peruvians had military superiority over them. Officials in the State and Defense Departments responded to Kissinger that the law prohibited selling U.S. weapons to Chile.

Kissinger became unhinged over the linkage between arms sales and human rights. He convened meetings two to three times a month in 1975, ranting and raving over foolish restrictions on his foreign policy. Democrats such as Kennedy and Representative Donald Fraser were "crippling" his foreign policy. After all, he said, "you don't expect a military government to be without arms." He told aides, "There can be no doubt about my policy. I want to strengthen Chile. I don't want to drive them to despair." He predicted that "when a Portuguese-type government takes over in Chile, you will all sit around and wring your hands." "When we get a Portuguese government in power in Chile" became a constant Kissinger refrain. The secretary asserted that a repetition of the "Carnation Revolution" (1974), which brought about the transition to democracy in Portugal and the collapse of the imperial enterprise in Africa, "would be bad for Latin America." Helpless Chile was "being thrown to the wolves." He added, "We are experts at undermining our friends."[78] When his warnings and threats produced no results, Kissinger engaged in self-pity. Critics attacked his Chilean policy because they wanted to feel moral about themselves. As he told his staff, "They're going to attack me, and they're going to attack me on Chile anyway. That's part of the game now. And if the Department can't take some heat, then I feel sorry for it." Kissinger then compared himself to Winston Churchill, recalling that the anticommunist British prime minister, as a matter of national interest, allied with the Soviet Union during World War II.[79]

Whereas State Department officers may have been risk averse, the main issue was not their courage and fortitude but rather their opposition to Kissinger's Chilean policy. What took place in Argentina, with Ambassador Robert Hill condemning the military dictatorship's murderous behavior, also happened in Chile. Appalled State Department officers judged the Pinochet regime's behavior grotesque and contrary to civilized conduct. They found it impossible to defend Secretary of State Kissinger's policy of bolstering General Pinochet. Assistant Secretary of State William D. Rogers set the tone in 1974 when he replied with a simple yes to Kissinger's heated question that "I'd like to know whether the human rights problem in Chile is that much worse than in other countries in Latin America." A year later, Rogers told Kissinger, "Chile, I believe—although you may argue that Zaire is just as bad, is just as bad on the human rights as you can find." Kissinger shot back: "I doubt it."[80] In mid-1975, officers in the embassy in Santiago joined with the Policy Planning office of the Latin American section in penning a dissent to policy. They called "for cutting off all economic and military assistance to Chile." Despite the ban on military aid, the United States continued to supply Chile copious amounts of food and housing aid and supported Chilean requests for loans at international agencies. When he heard of the dissent, Kissinger vowed to "straighten out" the diplomats. Ambassador David Popper, who had previously been chastised by Kissinger, kept his reporting restrained but emphasized at the end of 1975 that Pinochet's "appearance now is of a personal dictator who returned from what he saw as a triumphal visit to Spain intending to impose a Francoist pattern on his country."[81]

State Department officers hoped that pressure would induce the Chilean government to improve its human rights record. But Kissinger was dismissive of human rights concerns in meetings with Chilean officials. In May 1975, he opened a conversation with Foreign Minister Patricio Carvajal by stating,

"I hold the strong view that human rights are not appropriate for discussion in a foreign policy context. I am alone in this." He would not use "the human rights issue to harass Chile." In any case, he stated, "Chile's record on human rights is improving." In a meeting with Carvajal on 29 September 1975, Kissinger ridiculed the briefing paper prepared for him, noting that "it was nothing but human rights." He lamented, "The State Department is made up of people who have a vocation for the ministry. Because there were not enough churches for them, they went into the Department of State." Chile suffered a "total injustice." Other violators of human rights, such as Idi Amin (1971–1979), the dictator of Uganda, did not receive similar global criticism. He reiterated that it was not in the interest of the United States "to turn Chile into another Portugal" and then immediately added, "I'll be in great trouble when this is leaked to the papers." In his meetings with the foreign minister, Kissinger noted that it would be helpful to the United States if Chile could make a gesture on human rights. But Kissinger assured Carvajal that he was not "making it a formal issue."[82]

In his memoirs, Kissinger defended his record on Chile and human rights by noting the strong actions he took when he journeyed to Santiago in June 1976 to deliver an address to the OAS General Assembly and to meet with General Pinochet. As he would in October 1976 in his speech to the Synagogue Council of America, Kissinger spoke eloquently about human rights in his address to the Latin American delegates. He instructed them that "technological progress without social justice mocks humanity; national unity without freedom is sterile; nationalism without a consciousness of human community—which means a shared concern for human rights—refines instruments of oppression." In his speech, Kissinger further noted that the OAS Commission on Human Rights had found that Chile violated human rights and that human rights issues had "impaired" the U.S. relationship with Chile. On 8 June 1976, before the human rights speech, Kissinger met with Pinochet in the dictator's office. As described by Kissinger, the meeting was formal, with Pinochet exhibiting "no special warmth either toward the United States or its representative." Kissinger alleged that he focused his conversation with Pinochet on the subject of human rights and asked him to list "the measures you are talking in the human rights field." As he explained in his memoirs, "As Secretary of State, I felt I had the responsibility to encourage the Chilean government in the direction of greater democracy through a policy of understanding Pinochet's concerns, without unleashing the forces on which Allende had relied for his revolution."[83]

Kissinger had quoted selectively from the memorandum of conversation of his meeting with Pinochet. The secretary had long expressed a desire to visit Chile and meet Pinochet. In the days before the meeting, he planned carefully. On 1 June 1976, he told his staff that, contrary to their wishes, he would not "launch a broad scale attack on Chile" and that he would make only a general statement on human rights in Latin America in his speech. He sarcastically dismissed his staff's concerns, noting, "Human rights make me love the State Department." He then asked, "Am I supposed to make a revolution in Chile?"[84] Two days later, in a telephone conversation with Assistant Secretary Rogers, he ruled that only he, Rogers, and a note taker would meet with Pinochet. Kissinger chose Anthony Hervas, because, he explained, Hervas was an "effective" note taker and because "I could work with him afterwards" in deciding on the content of the memorandum of the conversation. As Kissinger informed Rogers, "[I] would like to have a serious talk with him [Pinochet] and since I am not on the same wave length with you guys on this business. I am just not eager to overthrow these guys." Kissinger added, "I think that we are systematically undermining them." He also asked Rogers to arrange a meeting for him on the same day with Peruvian Foreign Minister Valle Miguel Ángel De La Flor: "I think it is a good idea to see a left-winger on the same day I see Pinochet."[85]

Kissinger was indeed restrained in his meeting with Pinochet. He was not the effusive, cheerful jokester that he was in the presence of Bolivian and Brazilian military dictators and the foreign ministers of the Argentine and Uruguayan military dictatorships. But he took the same approach with Pinochet that he took with Foreign Minister Carvajal. He did not use the word "democracy" or speak of the need for Chile to move to democracy, as he claimed he did in his memoirs. He told Pinochet, "We are sympathetic with what you are trying to do here" and "We wish your government well." He agreed with Pinochet that Salvador Allende "was headed toward communism." What Kissinger needed was a gesture from Chile on human rights so he could counter domestic critics and persuade Congress to fund military and economic aid for Chile. Kissinger emphasized, "I want you to succeed and I want to retain the possibility of aid." He explained that he had delayed his speech until after he met with Pinochet, because he wanted to assure the dictator that "the speech is not aimed at Chile" and "is not offensive to Chile." Pinochet complained that Chilean exiles, such as Gabriel Valdez, the former foreign minister of the Christian Democratic Party, had access to congressional critics of Chile. Kissinger responded, "I have not met a Christian Democrat for years." Pinochet also ominously observed that Orlando Letelier "has access to the Congress." Kissinger concluded the meeting by congratulating the dictatorship. Chile "did a great service to the West in overthrowing Allende" and preventing a second Cuba.[86]

Neither Kissinger nor Pinochet changed his approach to human rights after their June meeting. On 14 June 1976, Kissinger met with Cardinal Raúl Silva in Washington. Assistant Secretary Rogers had recommended that Kissinger meet with him because the Chilean cardinal was a prominent advocate for human rights and the meeting "would demonstrate Kissinger's sincere interest in the issue." Cardinal Silva opened the discussion by lamenting that Chile had a military government for the first time in 150 years. The cardinal perhaps surprised Kissinger when he answered in the affirmative to the secretary's question on whether "these military people have a Nazi mentality." Kissinger thereafter lied to Cardinal Silva, telling him that he "made it very clear" to Pinochet that "we support the return of democracy in Chile."[87] Two days later, Kissinger erupted to Rogers when he heard that Robert White, deputy permanent representative to the OAS and the future ambassador to Paraguay, defended a critical OAS Commission on Human Rights report on Chile. Kissinger demanded that White be replaced. Kissinger declared, "I have not become a super liberal" and the OAS "is not an institution that is going to humiliate the Chileans."[88] General Pinochet proved even more devious than Kissinger. The embassy reported that Chilean security forces were now "disappearing" people as a way of reducing the number of political prisoners in Chile. In a speech on 11 September 1976, celebrating the third anniversary of the military *golpe*, Pinochet reaffirmed the "hard-line" approach on human rights and set a tone "for continued and even increasing authoritarianism." The dictator did tell his audience that he enjoyed meeting Kissinger in Santiago.[89]

Left unspoken in Pinochet's speech was the determination of the regime to annihilate its critics wherever they lived. The U.S. Congress had passed legislation that continued to prohibit the transfer or sale of U.S. military equipment to Chile, and it cut economic aid to Chile for fiscal 1977 to $25 million. Orlando Letelier was an obvious target for the regime. The foreign minister had been the first high-ranking member of the Allende government to be incarcerated. During his time in jail, which included several months on frigid Dawson Island in the Tierra del Fuego archipelago, Letelier was tortured. After he was released with the help of international pressure, Letelier went into exile. He became a member of the Institute for Policy Studies, a politically liberal organization in Washington, DC. He lobbied the U.S. Congress and Western European governments to oppose economic assistance to Pinochet's Chile. Colonel Manuel Contreras, the head of DINA, the secret Chilean police organization, directed the assassination of Letelier. Assistant Secretary Rogers had once characterized Contreras as "the most notorious symbol of repression in Chile."[90] Colonel Contreras reported directly to Pinochet. The CIA would eventually determine that General Pinochet ordered the car-bomb attack on Letelier. The attack took place in a section of Washington known as "Embassy Row" near the Irish and Romanian embassies.

The attack on Foreign Minister Letelier and Ronni and Michael Moffitt came under the aegis of Operation Condor. In November 1975, Colonel Contreras met in Santiago with security chiefs from Argentina, Bolivia, Paraguay, and Uruguay to exchange information on political leftists and to collaborate in assassinating them. Brazil would also participate in the exchange of information, although it did not engage in international assassination plots. The project earned the name "Operation Condor" after the national bird of Chile. Information sharing, cooperation, and international assassination predated the November 1975 meeting. The assassination of Chilean General Carlos Prats and his wife in Buenos Aires in 1974 involved the acquiescence of Argentine security forces. In October 1975, Bernardo Leighton, a Chilean Christian Democratic leader, was shot in the back of the head in Rome. Leighton's wife was left paralyzed by a bullet that hit her in the spine. Michael Vernon Townley, who was born in Iowa, masterminded the attacks on Prats, Leighton, and Letelier for Colonel Contreras and DINA.[91] Townley had lived in Chile and had dual citizenship. His father had been president of Ford Motor Company in Chile. Townley had worked with Chilean extremist groups, such as Patria y Libertad, and had extensive contacts with right-wing, anti-Castro Cubans.

By mid-1976, Washington had received numerous reports about cooperation between the military dictatorships and the international assassination project. The ubiquitous General Vernon Walters of the CIA had twice hosted Colonel Contreras in Washington. On 7 January 1975, Walters informed Kissinger that Pinochet and President Isabel Perón had good relations and that their respective security services were exchanging information. On 9 July, Walters informed Kissinger that Chileans have "excellent liaison relationships with both the Argentine and Brazilian Services with broad exchange of information."[92] The U.S. ambassadors in Argentina, Chile, and Uruguay had also raised the alarm in their dispatches. The ambassadors and their staffs, which included CIA agents, had independent sources of information. Ambassador Ernest Siracusa, for example, had learned of the Uruguayan plot to assassinate Representative Ed Koch of New York. Ambassador George Landau discovered that Michael Townley traveled to the United States on a Paraguayan passport. The embassies knew, of course, that the corpses of foreign nationals were appearing on the streets of Buenos Aires, Santiago, and Montevideo. Prosecutors would ultimately determine that there were 169 victims of Condor operations in Argentina alone.[93]

On 3 August 1976, Assistant Secretary Shlaudeman brought the issue directly to Kissinger with a lengthy, detailed memorandum, "The 'Third World

War' and South America." Shlaudeman could not have been more explicit. He opened with the assertion that the military regimes of the Southern Cone had "established *Operation Condor* to find and kill terrorists of the 'Revolutionary Coordinating Committee' in their own countries and in Europe." He added, "Brazil is cooperating short of murder operations." Shlaudeman then explained his finding. Uruguayan Foreign Minister Juan Carlos Blanco was the intellectual exponent of the "Third World War" concept. South America's dictators were taking the lead in waging war against international communism, because the West had gone soft and failed to comprehend the threat. The South Americans considered themselves "the last bastion of Christian civilization." "Subversives," which presumably included the "Revolutionary Coordinating Committee," included anyone who opposed government policy. Shlaudeman recommended to the secretary of state that the United States bring the South American dictators "back to our cognitive universe." The Third World War idea, Shlaudeman warned, "leads to dangerous consequences."[94] Shlaudeman's deputy, Hewson Ryan, added that the international assassination project "was a violation of the very basic fundamentals of a civilized society."[95]

By 23 August, Shlaudeman had drafted a démarche to be presented by the ambassadors to the military dictatorships of the key Condor countries—Argentina, Chile, and Uruguay. The ambassadors would be directed to approach the governments delicately by raising the issue of "rumors" that interstate cooperation included "plans for the assassination of subversives, politicians, and prominent figures both within the national borders of certain Southern Cone countries and abroad." The ambassadors were to add that if "these rumors were to have any shred of truth, they would create a most serious moral and political problem." Kissinger signed off on the démarche after being informed by Shlaudeman, "What we are trying to head off is a series of international murders that could do serious damage to the international status and reputation of the countries involved."[96] The ambassadors had various reactions to the draft. Ambassador Hill, who had already demonstrated courage in confronting the Argentine admirals and generals, raised no objection. Ambassador Popper did not want to approach Pinochet, who had a reputation for intimidating foreign diplomats in his office. Popper explained that the general "might well take as an insult any inference that he was connected with such assassination plots." He suggested that an approach be made to Colonel Contreras. Ambassador Siracusa wanted no part of the démarche. He worried about his personal safety, delicately noting that raising the issue of rumors of international assassinations "will have a bad effect on the integrity of my acceptance here." He recommended that the State Department raise the issue with the Uruguayan ambassador in Washington.[97]

On 30 August, Assistant Secretary Shlaudeman discussed Siracusa's fears in a memorandum to Kissinger. Shlaudeman had consulted with the CIA. Shlaudeman did not believe the ambassador would be endangered if he delivered the démarche to the Uruguayan government, for the CIA knew that security services throughout the Southern Cone were fully aware of Operation Condor. Shlaudeman now suggested a parallel approach be made both to the government in Montevideo and to the Uruguayan ambassador in Washington. But on 16 September, while traveling in Africa, Kissinger canceled the presentation of the démarche and instructed that "no further action be taken on this matter."[98] Kissinger has never explained this decision. A charitable explanation would be that he feared for the "integrity" of Ambassadors Popper and Siracusa. On the hand, he never expressed concern for the health of Ambassador Hill, who faced threats from right-wing death squads in Argentina. The secretary had also repeatedly opposed pushing human rights issues onto the agendas of the military dictatorships. His decision came five days before the attack on Orlando Letelier. As Deputy Assistant Secretary Ryan recalled, "We were extremely reticent about taking a strong forward public posture, and even a private posture in certain cases, as was this case in the Chilean assassination." Ryan wondered if the démarche would have saved Letelier's life.[99] The issue was revived in 2004 when former Assistant Secretary Rogers, now a member of the Kissinger Associates lobbying firm, defended his boss in the august journal *Foreign Affairs*. Rogers claimed that the démarche on Operation Condor and international assassinations had been delivered to the military dictatorships.[100] But Kissinger's 16 September telegram from Lusaka, Zambia, which was declassified in 2010, undercut Rogers and confirmed that Kissinger had quashed the démarche. This was further settled by a 20 September missive from Shlaudeman to the ambassadors "to take no further action" in regard to the démarche.[101]

Officials in Washington and Santiago reacted in different ways to the car-bomb attack. NSC staff members thought it *"too* obvious" that right-wing Chileans had carried out the attack. Why would rightists create a "martyr for the Chilean Left"? Ambassador Popper noted that it was difficult to believe DINA's "rather fanatical leaders would expose themselves to the consequences of being implicated in a terrorist attack in Washington." On 23 September, the CIA informed President Ford that the culprits had not been identified, although it would be hard for the Chilean government to escape responsibility for the crime.[102] Henry Kissinger responded by instructing Assistant Secretary Shlaudeman to have a CIA officer meet with DINA Chief Contreras. Contreras predictably denied that Operation Condor had an assassination component. On 8 October, Shlaudeman told Kissinger, "The approach to Contreras seems to me sufficient action for the time being."[103] The Department of Justice, however, took seriously a terrorist act in the nation's capital. On 9 October 1976, Attorney General Edward Levi wrote to CIA Director George H. W. Bush. Levi informed Bush that his investigators believed "that the responsible parties may be outside the United States, and that the assassination may be part of a program of violent activities directed by foreign powers." Levi requested that the CIA adhere to U.S. laws and support the Department of Justice's criminal investigation.[104]

Ambassador George Landau had retained a critical piece of information. He had a copy of Michael Townley's visa application to the United States, using a Paraguayan passport. (The Carter administration subsequently appointed him as ambassador to Chile.) The Carter administration successfully pressured Chile to extradite Townley to the United States in 1978 for crimes committed in the United States. Townley plead guilty, identified the anti-Castro Cuban-Americans who assisted him, and implicated Contreras and General Pinochet. As part of a plea deal, Townley received a ten-year sentence and a pledge that he would not be extradited to Argentina or Italy to stand trial for the 1974 murder of General Prats and his wife in Buenos Aires and the 1975 attack on Bernardo Leighton and his wife in Rome. After serving sixty-two months in a federal penitentiary, Townley was placed in the federal witness protection program. Townley, who was born in 1942, may still be alive. An Italian court would subsequently convict Townley in absentia for the attack on the Leightons and sentence him to fifteen years in jail. Pinochet refused to extradite Colonel Contreras to the United States. But jurists in democratic Chile convicted him in 1993 for his role in the assassination of Letelier and imposed a seven-year sentence. In the twenty-first century, Chilean courts repeatedly convicted Contreras of his innumerable crimes against Chileans and sentenced him to hundreds of years in prison. He died in prison in 2015.

General Pinochet, who relinquished power in 1990, never faced justice for perpetrating terrorism in Washington or for the horrors he inflicted on Chileans. From 1998 until his death in December 2006, international and domestic jurists harassed him, but his lawyers successfully argued that he was too old and infirm to stand trial. Chileans were especially outraged when they discovered that Pinochet, who always presented himself as a model of rectitude who lived on his modest military salary, had stashed away $28 million in international banks. In 1987, "convincing evidence" surfaced that tied Pinochet to the 21 September 1976 attack. A guilt-ridden Armando Fernández Larios, an officer in DINA, who had accompanied Townley to the United States under a Paraguayan passport, made his way back to the United States and confessed to Justice Department authorities. On 6 October 1987, Secretary of State

George P. Shultz informed President Ronald Reagan and asked "whether we can or would want to consider indicting Pinochet." This was "a blatant example of a chief of state's direct involvement in an act of state terrorism." Shultz concluded, "What we now know about Pinochet's role in these assassinations is of the greatest seriousness and adds further impetus to the need to work toward complete democratization of Chile."[105] In 2003, Secretary of State Colin Powell apologized to the people of democratic Chile for the U.S. role in the overthrow of Salvador Allende. Both Republican secretaries of state were implicitly condemning the policies of Henry Kissinger.

An assessment of Henry Kissinger's policies toward the six nations of southern South America will always play a major role in the historical judgment on his career as a foreign-policy maker. It will not do, as some of his apologists have suggested, to overlook his unseemly embrace of the murderous military dictatorships of Argentina, Bolivia, Brazil, Chile, Paraguay, and Uruguay. The amount of time and effort he devoted to the six nations underscored the significance he attached to relations with them. But the industrious Kissinger did not limit his attention to South America. He engaged with the military governments of Central America. And he played a historically significant role in transforming the status of the Canal Zone in the Central American nation of Panama.

CHAPTER 5

Kissinger and Central America

Guatemala, Nicaragua, and Panama

In his diplomacy toward the key Central American nations of Guatemala, Nicaragua, and Panama, Henry Kissinger revealed essential elements of his approach to Latin America and to the world. He supported policies that aided and abetted the murderous military regimes that controlled Guatemala. He looked on the military dictators of Guatemala in the same way that he related to the military dictators of Argentina, Brazil, Chile, and Uruguay. He also had no problem embracing the long-standing U.S. client in Nicaragua, the Somoza family. Since the onset of the Cold War, the Somoza dynasty had been the CIA's most reliable ally in Latin America. Although ever the inveterate cold warrior, Kissinger displayed sensitivity to nationalism and international economic injustice. As national security adviser and secretary of state, he pushed his presidents and U.S. public opinion to envision the day when Panama would exert full sovereignty over the Canal Zone.

Guatemala in Blood

The scholar Piero Gleijeses labeled the U.S.-sponsored overthrow of the government of Jacobo Arbenz Guzmán (1950–1954) as "wanton criminal negligence," adding that the Eisenhower administration had acted with "supreme indifference toward the fate of the Guatemalan people." Richard H. Immerman, author of the pathbreaking study *The CIA in Guatemala* (1988), simply, but tellingly, concluded that the "CIA's 1954 coup made moderation impossible."[1] Both distinguished historians were pointing to what took place in Guatemala after 1954. By the time an international commission negotiated a peace agreement in 1996 between warring factions, a minimum of 200,000 Guatemalans had died in political violence. Most victims were indigenous people, descendants of the ancient Maya. More than 500,000 refugees had been created in the decades-long civil war. But to characterize what happened in Guatemala as civil war can be misleading. Casualties did not mount because of pitched battles between government forces and leftist guerrillas, with citizens caught in the crossfire. Guatemalans died with bullets to the head from right-wing death squads or when soldiers entered the villages of indigenous people and perpetrated wholesale massacres. Massacres took place in 626 Mayan villages. The Guatemalan Commission for Historical Clarification (1999), an international "truth commission," determined that government forces and their allied death squads were responsible for 93 percent of the deaths in Guatemala's "civil war." The commission held the armed left responsible for 3 percent of the casualties.[2]

This mayhem took place in an impoverished, unequal, and grossly unfair society. The Guatemalan Revolution (1944–1954), which was first led by Juan José Arévalo (1944–1950) and then President Arbenz, aimed to break the hold of elites and foreign companies on Guatemalans and bring the nation into the twentieth century. Labor and social legislation was enacted, and land was redistributed to 100,000 families, improving the lives of 500,000 people. This was a substantial reform for a country of 3.14 million people. The land program, which resembled the U.S. Homestead Act (1862), was, in the context of the Cold War, deemed "communism" both in Guatemala and in the United States. The military dictators who dominated Guatemala between 1954 and 1986 abolished progressive socioeconomic legislation and returned the land to wealthy owners, including the United Fruit Company of Boston. A report prepared for Governor Nelson Rockefeller prior to his one-day visit to Guatemala in 1969 documented Guatemala's unjust society. Life expectancy was forty-nine years of age. Gastrointestinal maladies were a primary cause of death. Eighty percent of the rural population was illiterate. Two percent of landowners possessed 70 percent of the land. Per capita income was $300 a year.[3] U.S. Ambassador John O. Bell (1962–1965) put into words what this meant for Guatemalans, especially the majority indigenous population: "[A] *finca* [i.e., large landed estate] in Guatemala is like an 1850 plantation in Mississippi with the social structure pretty similar." The American Federation of Labor agreed with Ambassador Bell, noting that agricultural workers were "in conditions of servitude if not actual slavery." They worked eighty-four hours a week and earned fifty cents a day. A U.S. diplomat was appalled when in the 1970s he witnessed plantation workers being exposed to toxic herbicides and insecticides.[4]

Like Confederate officers in the U.S. slave states, Guatemalan landowners and their military allies fought tenaciously to hold on to their privileges over dark-skinned people. Indeed, some of these elite landowners were descendants of U.S. slave owners who fled to Guatemala after 1865. Colonel Carlos Castillo Armas (1954–1957) and General Miguel Ydígoras Fuentes (1957–1963) directed the initial repression. In the months after the June 1954 *golpe de estado*, the Castillo Armas regime murdered several thousand supporters of President Arbenz. Thereafter, the regimes passed anticommunist laws that deemed activities such as union organizing to be subversive. The regimes also restricted voting to literate Guatemalans, effectively disenfranchising the indigenous majority. Guatemalan leaders understood that U.S. officials would overlook financial corruption and political repression as long as they trumpeted anticommunist views and respected U.S. investments. President Ydígoras permitted the CIA to train Cubans on Guatemalan soil in 1960–1961 in preparation for the Bay of Pigs invasion. Ydígoras committed an indiscretion, however, when he announced he would hold a free election in 1963. Former President Arévalo planned to run. President John F. Kennedy warned Ydígoras that Arévalo "would undoubtedly campaign as an anti-Communist moderate, but he would be dangerous if he won [the] election." When the Guatemalan president inexplicably resisted U.S. pressure, the Kennedy administration encouraged a military *golpe*. On 31 March 1963, Colonel Enrique Peralta Azurdia (1963–1966) seized power.[5] In 1966, the military scheduled an election, and a noncommunist liberal, Julio César Méndez Montenegro (1966–1970), won. Méndez Montenegro, who was the nation's last civilian president for sixteen years, was allowed to take office by the military only after he signed a statement relinquishing civilian oversight of the military and giving it carte blanche in internal security matters.

By the mid-1960s, Guatemala had descended into a hell of violence, torture, and death. Several hundred guerrillas operated in Guatemala under umbrella organizations such as the MR-13 Rebellion or the Fuerzas Armadas Rebeldes (Armed Rebel Forces) or FAR. Although inspired by the Cuban Revolution, the guerrillas were home-grown soldiers who fought against repression and social injustice. As Ambassador Bell remarked to a U.S. interviewer, "You'd be a revolutionary [if you experienced] the unfairness of life in Guatemala."[6] The Guatemalan rebels never posed a meaningful threat to the military dictators. And their tactics guaranteed that they would generate little international sympathy. They financed their rebellion by robbing banks and kidnapping wealthy Guatemalans and holding them for ransom. They also assassinated military officers and international diplomats, including U.S. Ambassador John Gordon Mein in 1968 and West German Ambassador Karl von Spreti in 1970. These kidnappings and murders provided the military governments with a rationale for unleashing death squads such as Mano Blanco ("White Hand") and Ojo por Ojo ("Eye for Eye"). Military units claimed that indigenous villagers aided and abetted guerillas and therefore everyone, including children, deserved death. Both international and domestic jurists would subsequently find that military rulers were engaged in genocide against indigenous people.

U.S. presidential administrations bolstered Guatemala's coercive forces. In September 1961, President Kennedy approved military assistance for Guatemala, accepting a finding that it was among the "prime targets" for communist subversion. Between 1961 and 1963, the administration sent $4.3 million in military aid, which was a large increase over the $950,000 in military aid that the Eisenhower administration delivered between 1956 and 1960. U.S. Army Special Forces visited Guatemala, and Guatemalan officers received counterinsurgency training in a center established in their country. Seven hundred twenty officers a year also took basic police courses and studied riot-control techniques under U.S. command. The Kennedy and Johnson administrations ultimately supplied the 6,500 Guatemalan police officers with all their handguns, 50 percent of their shoulder weapons, and more than 6,000 tear gas grenades.[7] As the Historical Clarification Commission noted, U.S. military assistance "was directed toward reinforcing the national intelligence apparatus and for training the officer corps in counterinsurgency techniques, key factors which had significant bearing on human rights violations during the armed confrontation." U.S. military aid and concomitant anticommunist policies culminated "in criminal counterinsurgency."[8]

The Guatemalan army and police made ferocious use of their new hardware and training. Under the rubric of Operación Limpieza ("Operation Cleanup"), Guatemalan forces, advised by U.S. police trainers, carried out eighty roundups and multiple assassinations in early 1966. In March 1966, they captured about thirty insurgents, including Víctor Manuel Gutiérrez, a leader of Guatemala's small Communist Party and a former ally of President Arbenz. Security forces interrogated, tortured, and executed the prisoners. They placed the bodies of Gutiérrez and the others in burlap bags and dumped them into the Pacific Ocean. The Guatemalans had set a precedent that would be followed by the military dictators of the Southern Cone in "disappearing" people. Guatemalan security forces also initiated the practice of "scorched earth" tactics, destroying villages to undermine popular support for insurgents. In

October 1966, military troops commanded by Colonel Carlos Arana Osorio murdered 8,000 peasants in Zacapa Department. U.S. Green Berets trained and guided the Guatemalan forces. The Zacapa operation set the stage for future atrocities in Guatemala and El Salvador, such as the massacre of 900 citizens of the village of El Mozote in December 1981 in El Salvador. Colonel Arana, the future president of Guatemala (1970–1974), earned the title "the Butcher of Zacapa."[9] The brutality of the forces of repression knew no bounds. In 1968, security forces murdered Rogelia Cruz Martínez, an architecture student, leftist, and former "Miss Guatemala" who had represented her nation at the Miss Universe contest in Long Beach, California in 1959. In this case, the murderers publicly displayed Cruz's mutilated and raped, naked corpse.[10]

U.S. officials in Guatemala had varying reactions to these horrors. In 1968, Viron P. Vaky, who was the U.S. embassy's deputy chief of mission, reported to Washington that his colleagues, including Ambassador Mein, reasoned that "murder, torture, and mutilation are all right if our side is doing it and the victims are Communists." Ambassador Mein had suggested to Guatemalan security forces that they bury the bodies of those that they summarily executed. The ambassador advised that leaving bodies to be found would leave a bad impression with the international press.[11] Vaky would of course go on to serve for two years on Henry Kissinger's NSC staff in the vain hope that the Nixon administration would not pursue mindless anticommunism. John Longan, a U.S. security trainer who organized Operación Limpieza, subsequently conceded that the Cold War was not the main issue in the armed confrontations in Guatemala. Longan observed that Guatemalan security forces "will continue to be used, as in the past, not as much as protectors of the nation against Communist enslavement, but as the oligarchy's oppressors of legitimate social change." Ambassador Bell added to Longan's observation: "We are so scared of violent change that we endorse anybody that has the power to maintain calm. And that normally turns out to be a military dictator."[12]

Henry Kissinger did not create the U.S. alliance with Guatemala's murderous criminals and racists, but he deepened and strengthened those ties. Embassy officers recalled that the CIA had thoroughly penetrated leftist groups. The CIA station in Guatemala City was unusually large and had unusual responsibilities for a nation of five million people in 1970. Ever since PBSUCCESS, the 1954 covert intervention against President Arbenz, the CIA had played a prominent role in relations with Guatemala. The CIA took over reporting on labor developments and union activity in Guatemala, and CIA agents prepared biographies of prominent political and civil leaders. These were tasks normally assigned to foreign service personnel. CIA officers had not penetrated, however, either the Guatemalan military officer corps or the right-wing death squads. This arrangement virtually guaranteed that the CIA station would exaggerate the threat of the left and be uninformed about the assassinations and mass murders carried out by military forces and death squads. As one U.S. diplomat recalled, "I was surprised to find that we knew almost nothing about what the right-wing terrorists were up to."[13] CIA officers identified insurgents and leftist leaders. Beginning in 1970, with the approval of Kissinger, the information was passed on to the Guatemalan military dictators. The leftist suspects would experience the predictable regimen—arrest, interrogation, torture, summary execution, and disappearance. In the embassy's euphemism, the suspects were "neutralized." Kissinger's approval of this collaboration was labeled in the NSC and 40 Committee as an "OBE," or "off-budget enterprise." But as Ambassador Nathaniel Davis (1968–1971) remarked, passing intelligence to Guatemala's security apparatus might "pull us closer in."[14]

The ascension of Colonel Arana to the Guatemalan presidency in mid-1970 further entangled the United States in Guatemala's madness. The Méndez Montenegro government had designated Arana its ambassador to Nicaragua in order to move him out of the country. From Managua, Arana announced his candidacy for president, vowing that if the guerrillas did not surrender, "we will not hesitate to do our duty." Ambassador Davis recommended to Washington that the United States stay neutral in the election, although he hoped a civilian member of the Méndez Montenegro's party would win and thereby retain at least the appearance of constitutionalism. But in the March 1970 election, Colonel Arana, running on "law and order" themes, won a plurality with 42 percent of the votes. During the campaign, he had threatened to overthrow the government. As CIA analysts in Washington quickly surmised, if the National Assembly did not choose Arana as president, the armed forces would.[15] The embassy proved naïve about an Arana regime, predicting that he "will not adopt extreme rightist positions." Perhaps more realistically, it added that his election was "fully compatible" with U.S. security interests. The Office of National Estimates at the CIA ridiculed Ambassador Davis's optimism about the Butcher of Zacapa. Too many Guatemalans, both insurgents and peaceful people, had suffered at his hands in the past. Political polarization and violence would likely intensify. Ambassador Davis thought it a good idea for the United States to develop new programs to train and equip Guatemalan police to maintain public safety. CIA analysts again warned that the Arana government would "indulge in counterterror." The ambassador reported that he was unsure whether Arana knew about the activities of death squads such as Ojo por Ojo. In June 1970, CIA analysts in Washington responded that Arana had unleashed death squads in the past and "condones the *Ojo* organization's actions as a necessary expedient."[16]

Bureaucratic divisions characterized analyses of violence in Guatemala. The embassy and the CIA station in Guatemala City blamed the left and offered excuses for the government. CIA analysts in Washington understood the homicidal nature of Guatemalan elites and their military allies. The Nixon administration and Henry Kissinger settled the dispute by embracing the Butcher of Zacapa. Vice President Spiro Agnew met with President-elect Arana in July 1970. Agnew and Kissinger joked over the phone about the idea of Agnew giving Arana a lecture on the new government "moving decisively to remove vigilante groups."[17] The administration responded positively to Guatemala's new request for $12 million in military aid. The administration rushed eight A-37B jet aircraft to Guatemala for use in counterinsurgency campaigns. It also sent public safety equipment on a "crash basis" to the Guatemalan police. The State Department instructed Ambassador Davis to request that Arana and his henchmen avoid murdering legitimate political opponents. But the request was not bolstered by any threat to reduce aid.[18]

In November 1970, a few months into his presidency, Arana declared a "state of siege" and launched a new campaign "unprecedented in terms of force and toughness" against Guatemalans who opposed him. One ludicrous part of the campaign was to blame the spirit of the 1960s for Guatemala's poverty, injustice, and violence. Soldiers and police boarded buses and shaved the heads of young Guatemalans on the premise that men with long hair were prone to be subversive. Exempted from the haircut campaign were "well dressed, long-haired youths." Security forces also abused young women in mini-skirts.[19] Whereas the students and young people were not routinely murdered for their appearances, thousands of Guatemalans died at the hands of Colonel Arana's government. The wheelchair-bound Alfredo Mijangos, a prominent Christian Democrat politician, was assassinated in front of his family on the steps of a church. U.S. diplomats recalled "bodies floating down rivers each morning." Another popular place to dump bodies was at Kilometer 13 of the Pan American Highway.[20] In August 1971, James E. Flannery of the CIA reported to State Department and NSC officers that the CIA station had tracked what had happened to thirty-two people who had been arrested since January. Twenty-five had been executed. Flannery also reported that President Arana had participated in the drawing up of death lists. Flannery's briefing was drawn from a paper on Guatemala developed by the CIA in Washington. Arana had appointed a relative of his wife, Major Elías Ramírez Cervantes, to head the Security Service. Major Ramírez was a brute and a thief. He pocketed $10,000 that was given to him by President Arana for antiguerrilla activities. He told CIA agents that "he never interrogated prisoners without killing them." He also admitted that Arana "personally prepared lists of persons for him to eliminate."[21]

The CIA briefing so unnerved Arnold Nachmanoff, the NSC staff member responsible for Latin America, that he wrote to his boss, Henry Kissinger, on 19 August 1971. The United States had rushed security aid to President Arana and now had a pending $2 million military assistance program. But Nachmanoff warned, "We have a major policy problem on our hands." The Guatemalans were using U.S. equipment and money for "punitive instruments for counter-terrorism and political assassination," and President Arana was drawing up death lists. Nachmanoff suggested that the United States needed to reconsider U.S. aid to Guatemala and asked the committee on covert activities, the 40 Committee, to discuss the issue. Kissinger initially agreed to submit the topic for discussion, but at the 16 September meeting, he curtly ended discussion, noting that the subject did not properly come under the subject of "covert action."[22] Thereafter, the State Department contented itself with sending emissaries to Guatemala City urging the government to take steps to improve its dreadful international image. The only critical U.S. voice came from congressional visitors to Guatemala, such as Pat Holt, a leading staff member of the Senate Foreign Relations Committee. Holt argued that the United States needed to disassociate itself from Guatemala's ongoing political violence. Peaceful Guatemalan politicians told him that the U.S. military and police equipment and training programs made the United States "complicit" in the decisions by security forces to torture and murder.[23]

The brutality and madness that Arnold Nachmanoff warned Kissinger about in August 1971 continued through the Arana years. The embassy kept "a barometer" of political violence in Guatemala, recording ninety incidents a month in 1971 and sixty incidents a month in 1972. As the embassy officer in charge of the death chart later confessed, "It was a pretty stupid exercise—the violence was endemic and horrific and was not changing over a month to month period."[24] The embassy's barometer largely measured only urban political violence. The embassy and the CIA station had little information on what was happening in the highland villages, where indigenous people lived. An especially gruesome incident occurred in Guatemala City in September 1972. CIA agents reported that Guatemalan security forces captured nine people, four of them associated with Guatemala's Communist Party. Colonel Arana met for four hours with his advisers to deliberate the fate of the captured personnel. Arana ordered that all be executed and their bodies be disappeared. The CIA agents added that the secret murders were "reportedly based on the conviction that any other course would have been seen as a sign of weakness and an acknowledgment of the Government's fear of retaliation by extreme left." William J. Jorden of the NSC staff relayed the CIA report to Kissinger. He initialed the report.[25]

Secretary of State Kissinger had another opportunity to think about Guatemala when, in March 1974, citizens went to the polls to choose a successor to President Arana. Arana picked his defense minister, General Kjell Laugerud García, the son of a Norwegian father and Guatemalan mother, to succeed him. The former army chief of staff, General Efraín Ríos Montt, broke ranks with his military colleagues and ran for the presidency on a populist and anti-corruption platform. As in 1970, the embassy advised that neither candidate posed a threat to U.S. national security interests. The embassy and the new ambassador, Francis J. Meloy Jr., a career foreign service officer, hoped for a free election but did not urge Arana to safeguard the electoral process. The embassy claimed that U.S. leverage in Guatemala was "approximately zero."[26] This was a dubious assessment in view of the past history of the United States in Guatemala in the 1950s and 1960s and the massive U.S. military and police aid programs and intelligence-gathering apparatus in the nation. The Arana regime prepared for the election by organizing "voting tombstones" in remote areas but was stunned when Ríos Montt won more than 50 percent of the vote. It took a few days for the regime to rearrange the results and declare General Laugerud the winner. The regime thereafter assassinated civilian politicians and student protestors to underscore to Guatemalans that the military still determined the fate of Guatemala.[27] When presented with an outline of electoral fraud in a client nation of the United States, Secretary Kissinger ruled, "We don't have to say anything." He added, "I would just say we will stay the hell out of it." For his part, the embittered Ríos Montt returned to military service, but he would subsequently seize power and serve as president (1982–1983).[28] He would prove even more bloodthirsty than the Butcher of Zacapa. Ríos Montt presided over the slaughter of tens of thousands of indigenous people during the eighteen months he held power.[29]

Human rights issues bedeviled U.S.-Guatemalan relations during the last years of Secretary Kissinger's service. U.S. legislators and international and domestic proponents of human rights now placed Guatemala within the context of the horror taking place in the Southern Cone countries. In mid-1974, Representative Henry Reuss (D-WI) proposed legislation that would bar U.S. military aid to "military dictators." Such legislation would have jeopardized granting Guatemala $2 million in credit for military purchases. State Department officers in Washington engaged in the sophistry that such restrictions could not be applied to Guatemala, because outgoing President Arana had received a plurality of the vote in 1970 and therefore, by definition, had not created a "military dictatorship."[30] The U.S. officials did not speculate, however, whether General Laugerud, who achieved a plurality in 1974 only after the vote tabulation was manipulated by President Arana, fulfilled the definition of a "military dictator." U.S. diplomats expressed confidence that the new president would "curtail government use of illegal violence" and pursue some modest socioeconomic reforms. By early 1975, that optimism had dissipated. The Guatemalan military feared that the growing insurgency in Nicaragua, led by the Sandinista movement, might inspire the downtrodden of Guatemala. Laugerud vowed to use "vigorous and brutal tactics" against guerillas and, like Arana, authorized summary executions. The embassy conceded that the "fundamental fact of life in Guatemala" was that "civilian politics were secondary to wishes of the army."[31] In February 1975, the embassy was required by congressional mandate to submit a report on the status of human rights in Guatemala in order to maintain U.S. economic and military aid. Ambassador Meloy signed off on a fallacious report that only a small number of violent, political extremists had suffered human rights abuses under the Laugerud dictatorship. Guatemala therefore remained eligible for U.S. aid, because it had not violated the Foreign Assistance Act of 1974 by engaging in a "consistent pattern of gross violations" of human rights. Meloy further offered that political violence had always been a part of Guatemalan politics and society.[32]

The level of government-sponsored violence intensified in 1976. In February 1976, a powerful earthquake, with a magnitude of 7.5 on the Richter Scale, shattered the nation, killing 23,000 and injuring another 76,000 citizens. The government and allied right-wing death squads took advantage of the confusion "to eliminate elements deemed undesirable." Bodies bearing evidence of torture and execution began showing up among the earthquake victims. The U.S. embassy's "barometer" of political violence began to rise precipitously. The Air Force, using the U.S-supplied A-37B jet fighters, were bombing rural areas, and "on the ground peasants were reportedly terrorized by groups of armed unknowns who hauled them out of their houses and took them away." The embassy presumed that the "armed unknowns" were government security forces.[33] This graphic reporting came as the new ambassador, Davis Eugene Boster (1976–1979), a career foreign service officer, was about to arrive in Guatemala City. Boster came to embrace the idea that promoting human rights should be central feature of U.S. foreign policy. The embassy now rejected the thesis of Boster's predecessor, Francis Meloy, that violence was ingrained in Guatemalan history and culture. The embassy opined that the origins of violence "lie in the tension produced by attempting to maintain a government that neither taxes nor spends, an electoral system which permits dissent but rarely rewards it, and an economic and social system designed to preserve the comfort and ease of a tiny majority."[34] Boster's deputy chief of mission, John T. Bennett, agreed with that analysis and with Boster's belief that the government exaggerated the threat of guerrillas in order to justify its repression of the poor. Bennett repeatedly heard "cock-and-bull" stories from government officials of communist plots to take over Guatemala.[35]

Secretary of State Kissinger obviously did not agree with Ambassador Boster's promotion of human rights. In 1975–1976, his only role in U.S.-Guatemalan relations was to urge moderation on the military dictatorship on the issue of independence for neighboring British Honduras (Belize). The Guatemalan military opposed independence until the United Kingdom granted territorial concessions to Guatemala. Kissinger permitted the suspension of the shipment of C-47 aircraft to Guatemala, because U.S. officials feared Guatemala would use the transport planes in an invasion of British Honduras. But he ordered his subordinates to take no reprisals against Guatemala. He remarked that Guatemala could be counted on "to vote with us" at the United Nations. When they met with Kissinger, Guatemalan officials always assured Kissinger that they were anticommunists and sworn enemies of Fidel Castro.[36]

The Somozas

As in Guatemala, social injustice and repression characterized daily life in the Nicaragua of the Somoza dynasty. In 1970, the population of one of Latin America's smallest nations was 2.4 million, although the population had grown by 600,000 in the 1960s. Despite the population growth, life expectancy at birth was fifty-four years of age. Seventy percent of Nicaraguans were illiterate. Nicaragua was an agricultural nation, producing bananas, sugar, cotton, and beef. A mere 1.4 percent of landowners owned 41 percent of the land. Fifteen to twenty percent of Nicaraguan campesinos were landless. Per capita income was less than $500 in current dollars. The Somoza clan had dominated political and economic life since the mid-1930s. The latest and greediest of the clan was Anastasio Somoza Debayle (1967–1979). "Tacho" Somoza, a graduate of West Point, probably wished that he had been born a wealthy, powerful citizen of the United States. He spoke impeccable English, traveled extensively in the United States, and referred to himself as a "Latin from Manhattan." He married Hope Portocarrero, an accomplished, educated woman of Nicaraguan descent and a native of Miami. Doña Hope, who was often listed on international "best dressed" lists, gave birth to five children. President Somoza openly consorted, however, with his mistress, the "voluptuous" Dinorah Sampson.[37] Somoza and his family perceived Nicaragua as their personal estate. The family amassed a wealth of perhaps $300 million. One relative was locally known as "Tío Luz" ("Uncle Light"), because he controlled the national power and light company. The Somozas also owned a plasma bank that exported the blood of poor Nicaraguans who gave their blood in return for money. The family sold the blood of its own people! President Somoza demanded that Nicaraguan businesses give him a share of their profits, and he required citizens to join his party if they wanted work in the government or the professions. President Somoza could be counted on to siphon off 25 percent of foreign aid for his personal use.[38]

The United States was intimately involved in Nicaragua's history during the twentieth century. During the first third of the century, U.S. interest in the Central American nation revolved around an inter-oceanic canal. Nicaragua has long been judged by engineers as a place where the two oceans could be connected. The Bryan-Chamorro Treaty (1916) gave the United States the option of constructing a passageway through Nicaragua. Once it began building a canal through Panama, the United States wanted political and financial stability throughout the region. U.S. Marines almost continually occupied Nicaragua from 1909 to 1933. U.S. military forces helped create what one U.S. diplomat labeled the "two monsters" of Nicaraguan life—the Guardia Nacional (National Guard) and the Somoza dynasty.[39] The Marines trained and equipped a military constabulary to strengthen the authority of the central government and promoted Anastasio Somoza García (1935–1956) to lead the Guardia Nacional. Somoza used his control of the guard to establish a dictatorship and family control over the nation. Subsequent U.S. presidents appreciated the stability that the Somoza dynasty maintained in Nicaragua. In 1939, President Franklin Roosevelt hosted President Somoza in a grand ceremony in Washington. The two presidents were attired in top hats and morning coats. In turn, Nicaragua backed U.S. initiatives during World War II and the Cold War. President Eisenhower denounced the September 1956 shooting of Somoza by a young Nicaraguan poet and dispatched an airplane to Nicaragua to carry Somoza to a U.S. hospital in the Canal Zone.[40] Eisenhower's action was an ironic comment on the state of medical facilities in Somoza's Nicaragua. During President Kennedy's tenure, officers of the 6,000-man Guardia Nacional studied counterinsurgency tactics at the School of the Americas in the Canal Zone. President Kennedy was impressed with President Luis Somoza (1956–1963) and did not press democracy, a central premise of the Alliance for Progress, upon the dictator.[41]

Although the origins of *Somocismo* were rooted in the military occupation years, the Somozas proved adept at ingratiating themselves with the United States. The family turned the nation over to the CIA. Colonel Castillo Armas of Guatemala organized his forces in Nicaragua before launching his 1954 attack on the Arbenz government. Airplanes stationed in Nicaragua bombed Cuba during the Bay of Pigs operation in 1961. Luis Somoza won President

Kennedy's gratitude by permitting Cuban exiles to use Nicaragua as a base for attacking Castro's Cuba. Ambassador Guillermo Sevilla-Sacasa (1943–1979), a Somoza family member, became dean of the diplomatic corps and an effective spokesman for his nation in Washington. Anastasio Somoza Debayle focused on cultivating U.S. legislators. Representative John M. Murphy (D-NY), who had attended West Point with Somoza, was a frequent visitor to Nicaragua and a stalwart defender of the regime in Washington. (Murphy would be convicted in 1980 in the Abscam bribery scandal and serve eighteen months in a federal penitentiary.) Representative Charles N. Wilson (D-TX) also journeyed to Managua. A stout anticommunist who became famous for organizing resistance to the Soviet invasion of Afghanistan, Wilson defended Somoza as an anticommunist friend of the United States. (Wilson, who was popularly known as "Good Time Charlie," boasted of keeping a hot tub with handcuffs in his bedroom.) U.S. diplomats in Managua assumed that when influential men such as Murphy and Wilson came to Nicaragua, President Somoza's welcome included more than an abrazo. The Nicaraguan dictator was also known to tape his conversations with U.S. diplomats.[42]

The Nixon administration was not disposed to change U.S. policy toward the Somoza dynasty. President Nixon first met the Somozas in 1955 during his infamous tour of Central America, when he also called on Fulgencio Batista and Rafael Trujillo. Nixon believed, of course, that "Latin" countries required "strong leadership." The president reacted negatively when he heard that the State Department believed Somoza needed to liberalize his regime in order to avoid the fate of his assassinated father. Nixon responded, "Well, then frankly, I don't want him to liberalize his regime; I hope he keeps it like it is."[43] Nixon and Kissinger rejected the advice of the State Department that the president not host Somoza when he came to the United States in 1971 to attend his twenty-fifth graduation reunion from West Point. The State Department observed that "Somoza is considered by many Americans, both liberals and conservatives, to be a dictator who runs his nation as a feudal estate." The department further worried that Somoza would use the visit to argue in Nicaragua that President Nixon and the United States favored his continuation in power.[44] On 2 June 1971, Nixon hosted President Somoza in the Treaty Room of the White House. Nixon fondly recalled his visit to Nicaragua in 1955 and "the many years of friendship that have existed between Nicaragua and the United States and more particularly, his own warm personal relationships with President Somoza and his father." Both presidents thought that the United States should continue to assist the Latin American military. They further agreed that the military regime in Brazil had performed well. Somoza noted that "the patriotism and responsibility of the Latin American military was evident" in

Brazil. Nixon assured Somoza that the warm feelings that had characterized U.S.-Nicaraguan relations would "grow stronger under his Administration."[45] Henry Kissinger followed the boss's lead. In late June 1971, he responded to an inquiry from the Defense Department about whether $100,000 found in a residual fund should be transferred to Nicaragua with a rhetorical question: "Why shouldn't it be considered—because it's a dictatorship?"[46]

President Nixon had already taken a meaningful step to strengthen his ties with the Somoza dictatorship in appointing Turner B. Shelton (1970–1975) to represent him in Managua. Shelton disgraced himself and sullied the reputation of the United States during his time in Nicaragua. Shelton had an unusual reputation for a diplomat, having started out in Hollywood producing "B-grade" or "blue" movies. President Eisenhower appointed Shelton, a donor to the Republican Party, consul general in the Bahamas and then arranged for him to become a career foreign service officer. While in the Bahamas, he met Charles "Bebe" Rebozo, Nixon's closest friend. Shelton met Nixon and spent significant time with him in Budapest in the 1960s, when Nixon called on the U.S. embassy, where Shelton served as deputy chief of mission. Ambassador Shelton presided over an embassy in revolt in Managua.

President Anastasio Somoza Debayle, President Nixon, and spouses Hope Somoza and Patricia Nixon, at the White House in June 1971. Nixon and Kissinger stood by the Nicaraguan dictator even as he squashed the population's democratic aspirations and looted the country. Nixon Library.

The resident diplomats were "appalled" by Shelton's behavior, calling him "the worst ambassador we've ever sent to Latin America."[47] The ambassador refused to sign any report that raised questions—repression, corruption, disappearances—about the Somoza dictatorship. James R. Cheek, a political counselor, spoke for many when he charged that Shelton "literally worshiped Somoza and almost embarrassingly so." Cheek would later win an award, the Rivkin Foreign Service Award, for finding ways to disseminate "dissent" reports about the reality of Somoza's Nicaragua. Somoza reciprocated Shelton's devotion by commissioning a new currency, a twenty-peso note that had the images of Somoza and Shelton on it. The State Department, including Secretary of State William P. Rogers, wanted to remove Shelton from Nicaragua. Diplomats speculated that Shelton "had to have some dirt" on Nixon or Rebozo.[48]

Aggrieved U.S. diplomats and informed Nicaraguans understood that Shelton and the Nixon administration were ignoring a looming crisis in Nicaragua. When Governor Nelson Rockefeller made a one-day stop in Managua during his 1969 tour of Latin America, anti-Somoza elites complained to him that the Somoza-Debayle families had turned the nation into their private hacienda and controlled political life. Rockefeller recorded in his notes "tremendous dissatisfaction, bitterness, frustration, and hatred which exists in an important segment of the population under present circumstances." After his visit, Rockefeller received a letter from Pedro Joaquín Chamorro, publisher of the opposition newspaper *La Prensa*. President Somoza permitted a modicum of free expression in newspapers because he understood most Nicaraguans could not read. Chamorro wrote that Nicaragua's problem "centered around an annihilated, rotten, and obsolete political system." Nicaragua's expanding population of young people blamed the United States for Somoza because of the historic and continued U.S. relationship with the Guardia Nacional. Chamorro worried that frustrated young people were listening to extreme leftist voices. He explained, "The situation in our country is tense and I fear that it is nearing collapse more rapidly than some people suspect."[49] The U.S. embassy concurred with that analysis in the period before Ambassador Shelton arrived in Managua. Guerrilla activity had begun to increase in the northern mountains of Nicaragua.

In a momentous development, the inspirational leader of the Catholic Church in Nicaragua, Archbishop Miguel Obando y Bravo (1970–2005), turned against the Somoza regime. The archbishop was a moderate in both his political and liturgical views. He did not embrace liberation theology or all ideas inherent in the Medellín conclave of 1968. But Archbishop Obando y Bravo believed in democracy. Somoza was supposed to leave office in 1972, but he concocted a scheme to postpone presidential elections until 1974. In late November 1971, the archbishop announced that he would no longer participate in fraudulent elections. Ambassador Shelton predictably criticized the archbishop for not trusting in his idol.[50] But the archbishop persisted. In May 1972 he issued a pastoral letter criticizing the government, and in July he addressed university students, telling them that "a situation of violence is crushing the masses." He recommended that the students resist by adopting the peaceful tactics of Mohandas Gandhi and the U.S. civil rights movement. In October 1972, he explained his views to political officer Cheek, noting that the Church must stand up for the "little man" and that "the Church must fight injustice and other evils besetting mankind by peaceful means."[51]

The beginning of the end of the Somoza dynasty began on 23 December 1972. A powerful earthquake destroyed Managua, which had been built on a fault line. Ten thousand Nicaraguans died, 70 percent of structures collapsed, and over 300,000 people were left homeless. The U.S. embassy collapsed, falling into a pit created by the earthquake. A staff member died at the embassy, but James Cheek would win an award for heroism from the State Department for frantically burrowing through the rubble, amid the aftershocks, to rescue an injured staff member. The aftermath of the natural calamity would reveal to the international community the depravity of the Somoza regime. International aid agencies rushed to help Nicaragua. Schoolchildren in the United States donated money. The great baseball player Roberto Clemente of the Pittsburgh Pirates died helping Nicaraguans. His plane, overloaded with relief supplies, crashed off the coast of his native Puerto Rico. Clemente had wanted to supervise the distribution of the aid, because he had learned that the supplies he had sent on three previous flights had not reached earthquake survivors. The supplies had been stolen. Nicaragua received $32 million in emergency aid; the Somoza clan stole half of it. The officers and soldiers of the Guardia Nacional looted Managua. They also sold donated aid supplies to desperate Nicaraguans.[52]

Ambassador Shelton and his imperious spouse, Leslie Shelton, also acted badly during the crisis. The magnificent embassy residence, with its eight bedrooms, survived the earthquake. It had been built on solid rock and overlooked Managua. Leslie Shelton refused to allow the injured to enter her palace or use one of the many bathrooms. Cheek and others had carried the injured female staff member to the embassy residence, using a door as a pallet. She had to wait on the residence's grounds before a helicopter arrived to rescue her. The U.S. Marines, who served as the embassy's guard, decided to build latrines near the residence. Leslie Shelton arranged for her beautician to make regular calls at her residence.[53] Cheek's cable about the behavior of the ambassador and his wife reached the secretary of state's office and was "leaked" to the press. Jack Anderson, a columnist for the *Washington Post*, published a series of exposés on the situation in Nicaragua. In mid-May 1973, Secretary of State Rogers visited Managua, becoming the first secretary of state to come to Managua since Philander Knox in 1912. Rogers was appalled by what he learned and saw during his five-hour visit. The State Department's Agency for International Development launched a home-building program for Nicaragua but took care to limit official Nicaraguan participation in the project.[54]

President Somoza's and Ambassador Shelton's deplorable conduct did not motivate President Nixon to change his Nicaraguan policy. Always, as a U.S. diplomat recalled, "the Nixon White House felt very close to Somoza."[55] In a discussion with U.S. diplomat Maurice Williams, who headed the U.S. relief effort in Nicaragua, Nixon affirmed that Ambassador Shelton had done "a heroic job." Latin Americans, Nixon opined, lacked managerial talent. If the press asked Williams, "How can we support a dictator?" Nixon instructed him to respond, "You don't comment on politics but just how it is a humanitarian matter." One gesture Nixon made was to suggest over the telephone to Henry Kissinger that he donate part of his 1973 Nobel Prize winnings to disaster relief in Pakistan, Africa, and Nicaragua. It would, the unctuous Nixon opined, be a "good gesture" and would show "interest in Africa, our Pakistani friends and Nicaraguans. Would hit three areas."[56] Kissinger deflected the unsolicited advice, ultimately choosing to donate the money to the children of veterans who died in Vietnam. Once Nixon was out of office, President Gerald Ford and Secretary of State Kissinger removed Shelton from Nicaragua in mid-1975. Shelton actually took steps to delay his departure and spent the embassy's money on lavish parties for Somoza. In one of his last dispatches, Shelton assessed the issue of human rights in Nicaragua with the happy judgment that there had been "a distinct absence of widespread, assiduous and severe repression of ordinary rights and liberties for the last two decades."[57] Kissinger resisted entreaties from Shelton's congressional friends to give him an important new diplomatic assignment.[58] Shelton became the U.S. ambassador to the Naval War College in Newport, Rhode Island. Leslie Shelton presumably enjoyed the elegant social scene of Newport. But Kissinger did not change the U.S. approach to Somoza, sending another political appointee to Managua. Ambassador James D. Theberge, a conservative Republican, acted professionally, but, like Shelton, remained, if not blindly loyal, uncritical of the Somoza regime. He recommended that Kissinger visit Nicaragua in 1976. As Theberge noted, it was "impossible to exaggerate the psychological and political importance" to Somoza "of symbolic signs of friendship and acceptance by the United States."[59]

Whereas Secretary Kissinger left Managua off of his travel schedule, he took no steps to alter the long-standing U.S. support for its Nicaraguan client. In the aftermath of the earthquake, Somoza exercised "emergency" powers, further restricting political activity. In November 1973, political counselor James Cheek secretly informed Washington that "no opposition political party worthy of the name presently exists in Nicaragua."[60] As Archbishop Obando y Bravo had feared, Somoza stole the 1974 presidential election, claiming to have won 91.7 percent of the vote for a seven-year term. But 60 percent of Nicaraguans, including the archbishop, had abstained from the electoral farce. Kissinger issued no objection to the continuation of the dictatorship. The U.S. training and equipping of the Guardia Nacional continued apace. The United States spent $600,000 a year in training expenses and $5 million a year on military aid to Nicaragua. It also offered Nicaragua $2.5 million a year in credits to purchase U.S. military equipment. And the Ford administration supported Nicaragua's applications for loans from the Inter-American Development Bank.[61] Both of Kissinger's assistant secretaries, William D. Rogers and Harry Shlaudeman, journeyed to Managua in 1976. Rogers listened to Somoza's objections to press criticism of him in the United States. Somoza complained to Shlaudeman that there was an "anti-Somoza faction" in the State Department. Shlaudeman raised the issue of human rights but hastily added that "U.S. policy was to avoid involvement in attempts to change internal political structures." Both Rogers and Shlaudeman reaffirmed the traditional U.S. backing for Nicaragua and, by implication, the Somoza dynasty. Vice President Nelson Rockefeller reiterated that support when Somoza came to Washington in April 1976. Rockefeller's talking points noted, "We have neither any reason nor the intention to make any fundamental change in our relations with Nicaragua."[62]

In the "dissent" cable that he sent to Washington in mid-1974, Cheek warned that Somoza would have to change or he would be swept out of power in five to ten years. "Revolutionary change" was in the offing for Nicaragua. Speaking about his famous cable in 2010, Cheek judged Somoza an intelligent person who knew what needed to be done to rebuild Managua, "but, morally, he was so corrupt and so addicted to absolute power that he couldn't change."[63] Cheek had been, of course, prophetic about the future of Somoza's Nicaragua. Public disgust with Somoza's response to the natural disaster, his electoral machinations, and his ceaseless greed accrued to groups working to overthrow him. Since the early 1960s, insurgents had fought, with little success, against the Somozas. The Guardia Nacional easily routed them. The principal rebel group was the Frente Sandinista de Liberación Nacional (FSLN), or Sandinista National Liberation Front. The Sandinistas were inspired by the courage and idealism of the Nicaraguan hero Augusto César Sandino (1895–1934) and by the Cuban Revolution. In the 1970s, other insurgent groups allied with the Sandinistas. The Sandinistas gained international attention when they staged a daring raid in late December 1974 at a holiday party attended by government officials and relatives of Somoza, including Ambassador Sevilla-Sacasa. Ambassador Shelton had left the party prior to the raid. In a move the CIA dubbed "unusual for him," President Somoza acceded to the demands of the Sandinistas to secure the release of the hostages.[64] He paid a ransom, released Sandinistas held in jail, and gave them safe passage to Cuba.

In the aftermath of the events of December 1974, Somoza declared a "state of siege" and unleashed the Guardia Nacional on the insurgents. The repression seemed initially successful. On 27 December 1976, the CIA declared, "The FSLN has all been destroyed." The national leader, Carlos Fonseca Amador, had been killed.[65] But the violence and corruption perpetrated by Somoza and the Guardia Nacional transformed increasing numbers of Nicaraguans into rebels. In January 1978, Somoza's henchmen assassinated Pedro Chamorro of *La Prensa*, shredding his body with shotgun blasts. His widow, Violeta Barrios de Chamorro, joined the insurgency. Between 1977 and 1979, the Guardia Nacional tore the country apart, killing over 40,000 Nicaraguans. In mid-1979, Somoza fled the country, heading to dictator Alfredo Stroessner's Paraguay. The next year Somoza was assassinated in Asunción by a commando team of political leftists. They shot a rocket-propelled grenade into Somoza's unarmored Mercedes, killing him instantly. Somoza's incinerated body was buried in Miami.

Henry Kissinger praised James Cheek at the Rivkin Award ceremony in Washington. But he ignored the warnings in Cheek's dissent cable. And he ignored the looming crises in Guatemala and El Salvador. In August 1975, the deputy chief of mission in El Salvador, Sam Moskowitz, foretold of "an eventual prospect of revolutionary upheaval." As in Guatemala and Nicaragua, military dictatorship, death squads, population growth, and social injustice had created a combustible mixture. And the leaders of El Salvador's Catholic Church would no longer stay silent. The only response Secretary of State Kissinger apparently had to such warnings was to make jokes about the "Soccer War," El Salvador's 1969 confrontation with Honduras.[66] Central American nations lacked the vital strategic and economic interests that would interest Kissinger. The Southern Cone nations, Mexico, and oil-producing Venezuela were essential to the United States and garnered the secretary's attention. But in an ironic twist, President Ronald Reagan would name Kissinger to chair a committee to review the exploding violence in Central America in the 1980s and make recommendations.[67] Revolution in Central America now mattered.

A Treaty for Panama

The one Central American nation that Henry Kissinger focused on was Panama. U.S. relations predictably revolved around the Panama Canal and the Canal Zone that the United States occupied within Panama. Frustrated by Colombia's recalcitrance on negotiating an inter-oceanic canal, President Theodore Roosevelt had aided Panamanian nationalists in detaching Panama from Colombia in November 1903. The Roosevelt administration thereafter negotiated the Hay-Bunau-Varilla Treaty (1903) with a French diplomat and businessperson, Philippe-Jean Bunau-Varilla, who represented both Panama and the French company that had begun work on a canal in the 1880s. The United States purchased the French assets for $40 million. The treaty gave the United States the right to build, operate, and defend a canal in perpetuity. U.S. laws would govern life in the Canal Zone. In turn, Panama received a one-time payment of $10 million and an annual fee of $250,000. U.S. engineers and foreign laborers completed the canal in 1914. The canal became a strategic and economic asset to the United States and a source of pride for U.S. citizens. The United States gradually increased the fees it paid to Panama. But as late as 1970, the annual fee remained a paltry $1.93 million.

The United States made good use of the 553 square miles that constituted the Canal Zone that bisected Panama. It established military bases and training facilities, including the School of the Americas. The U.S. personnel who lived there, "the Zonians," enjoyed a subsidized country club–style life. U.S. diplomats in Panama sarcastically dubbed life in the Canal Zone as "a complete socialist operation literally from cradle to grave," with the federal government providing excellent housing, schools, and health care. As a member of Congress in the 1950s, Gerald Ford was astounded to discover that Zonians payed $15 a month rent to live in government-owned housing.[68] Major Dwight D. Eisenhower and his wife lived in the Canal Zone between 1922 and 1924 and were offended by the haughty attitudes of U.S. citizens and the injustices that Panamanians suffered in work and pay.[69] Zonians kept themselves apart from Panamanians and discriminated against people of color. Richard C. Barkley, who joined in 1974 the U.S. negotiating team for a new canal treaty, characterized the Canal Zone as "a lily-white community." Barkley added, "The Zone was not only a *de facto* colony of the United States, but it was a privileged colony, and it had some of the qualities of the old south." In 1970, approximately 50,000 U.S. citizens basked in the good life in the Canal Zone. Some were second- or third-generation Zonians. So disdainful were the Zonians of Panamanians that they required Panamanians to acquire driver's licenses issued by

Zonian authorities if they wished to travel across the Canal Zone to visit the other part of their country.[70]

Beyond the historical and everyday wrongs that Panamanians endured over the canal and the Canal Zone, other issues troubled them. Since independence, political life had been controlled by a small, light-skinned elite, which maintained close ties with U.S. officials. The minuscule population of 1.5 million had a higher per capita income and longer life expectancy than Guatemalans or Nicaraguans. Panamanians earned money by providing services to the Zonians. The Nixon administration claimed that the U.S. presence in Panama generated $160 million a year in additional revenue. But the distribution of income in Panama was among the most unequal in Latin America. And Panamanian poverty was accentuated by having in the middle of the country a separate, wealthy nation of foreigners who despised them. In October 1968, officers in the National Guard overthrew the recently elected president. Omar Torrijos Herrera emerged as the leading figure among the military conspirators and would dominate the country until his death in an airplane crash in 1981. General Torrijos challenged the traditional way of doing things in Panama. As one of eleven children, Torrijos grew up in modest circumstances. His parents were teachers. Panama's economic elites came from the coastal cities of Panama City and Colón; Torrijos grew up in the interior. Torrijos enrolled in a military academy as a teenager and made his way up the ranks of the Guardia Nacional. He embodied the aspirations of Panama's small middle class that was racially mixed, spoke Spanish, and resented foreign influence in Panama, although Torrijos took pride in graduating from the School of the Americas. Torrijos, a populist dictator, addressed his nation's socioeconomic inequities, focusing on urban housing and land reform. He also showed sympathy toward indigenous people, and his sister established preschool programs. One U.S. diplomat recalled that Torrijos "ran an authoritarian but not despotic regime."[71] His reforms did not unduly alarm U.S. officials, because Torrijos was an anticommunist who maintained Panama's ban on the Communist Party.[72] Torrijos would prove, however, more aggressive and effective than Panama's traditional ruling class in undoing the Hay-Bunau-Varilla Treaty.

U.S. officials accepted the validity of many of the issues that Panamanians raised about the Canal and the Canal Zone. In Henry Kissinger's words, the United States had established a "semi-colonial" relationship with Panama.[73] As part of the Good Neighbor Policy, President Franklin Roosevelt renounced in 1936 the U.S. self-proclaimed right to intervene in Panama's internal affairs. In 1959, in a response to a melee precipitated by Panamanian students, President Eisenhower agreed that Panamanians could fly their flag alongside the U.S. flag in the Canal Zone. Panamanians would also be permitted to apply for skilled jobs in the Canal Zone. Zonians resisted such changes.[74] Both the students and Eisenhower administration officials were aware, of course, that Egypt had established its authority over the Suez Canal in 1956. In line with his desire to improve inter-American relations through the Alliance for Progress, President Kennedy wanted to do something for Panama. As characterized by Assistant Secretary of State for Latin America Edward Martin, Kennedy had a "guilt complex" about Panama. The president hoped to erase a "black mark" in history and wished to make Panama "happy." But the president did not want a domestic debate about a new treaty to mar his reelection prospects. As Kennedy explained in mid-1962 to Panamanian President Roberto Francisco Chiari (1960–1964), "1964, 1965, 1966 would be a better time to go about a basic document." Kennedy tried to placate Panama by providing "a very active" economic assistance program of $78 million between 1961 and 1964. In July 1963, using a special assistance fund, Kennedy transferred $3 million to Panama to supplement the annual payment of $1.93 million. Kennedy informed Ambassador to Panama Joseph Farland, "We do not want an explosion in Panama, we must keep the lid on the next couple of years the best we can." Kennedy conceded to aides, however, "We would probably be forced to renegotiate the treaty in the not too distant future regardless of any delaying actions we might conduct."[75]

The explosion that Kennedy feared erupted less than two months after his death. On 9 January 1964, a confrontation between university students and Zonians led to four days of fighting, resulting in over 300 casualties, with twenty-one Panamanians and four U.S. soldiers dying in the melee. In December 1964, after being elected with a powerful mandate, Johnson announced that the United States would negotiate "an entirely new treaty" with Panama.[76] Johnson appointed Robert B. Anderson, the former secretary of the treasury and a good friend of Eisenhower, to be the U.S. negotiator. Both Eisenhower and Harry Truman backed Johnson's initiative. In mid-1967, the United States and Panama reached agreements on three treaties that established Panamanian sovereignty over the canal, returned the canal to Panama in 1999, arranged for the United States to operate a projected sea-level canal until 2067, and gave the United States the exclusive right to defend both canals. Neither U.S. nor Panamanian legislators voted to ratify the treaties. Johnson, now weakened by political fury over the war in Vietnam, chose to defer ratification until after the 1968 election. Panamanians found much to like in the treaty, but they objected to several provisions, including treaty articles that gave the U.S. effective control over the Canal Zone until 1999 and retained U.S. military bases in Panama. As a future Panamanian negotiator would observe, "It is difficult, if not impossible, to be an independent state with such an overwhelming presence in the middle of the national territory."[77]

Panama and the United States made no progress on a treaty during President Nixon's first term in office. General Torrijos focused on consolidating his political power and blunting efforts to overthrow him. He was also disinclined to support a treaty negotiated by representatives of elite Panamanian families. In any case, President Nixon, who always questioned the abilities of Latin Americans, saw no reason to push for a treaty that would cost him politically among U.S. nationalists and political conservatives. As Nixon lamented in reference to Panama, "God-damn the small countries that don't do what we want."[78] And the Zonians had powerful friends in the U.S. Congress who made their case that only U.S. citizens could operate the canal's intricate lock system. Any president who wanted to change the colonial relationship with Panama and remove what one U.S. diplomat called "a bone in the throat of U.S. foreign policy in Latin America" knew they would have to overcome the inflated value that the U.S. public put on the canal.[79] By 1970, the canal was no longer strategically or economically vital to the United States. U.S. naval strength was in aircraft carriers and nuclear submarines, not the battleships of World War II. Aircraft carriers were too wide to go through the canal, and nuclear submarines, for operational reasons, did not go through the canal. The Joint Chiefs of Staff now quietly labeled the canal an "important" but not "vital" asset. The canal was significant to countries such as Bolivia, Chile, Ecuador, and Peru that shipped their goods to the East Coast of the United States. But U.S. manufacturers now had multiple ways, such as Eisenhower's interstate highway system, to send their products across the nation.[80]

The 1967 treaties seemingly solved the obsolescence of the canal by proposing a sea-level canal that the United States would control for one hundred years. But digging an enormous ditch to connect the Pacific Ocean with the Caribbean Sea, an idea that had been studied intensively since the Eisenhower years, posed insurmountable difficulties. To achieve cost feasibility, engineers proposed using nuclear depth charges for excavation. That proposal was certain to petrify Central Americans and most of humanity. In any case, the Limited Test Ban Treaty (1963) between the United States and the Soviet Union prohibited nuclear cratering technology. The lock system had been designed to overcome the problem of sea-level differences between the Pacific and Caribbean. A sea-level canal would therefore become a tidal canal, with ships able to go one way for only twelve hours before the tides reversed. Directly connecting the two bodies of water meant that sea creatures from the Pacific would enter the Caribbean, with the potential for ecological catastrophes. Nonetheless, the Nixon administration clung to the sea-level canal scheme through 1972.[81]

President Nixon kept Robert Anderson as his chief negotiator in Panama. This decision reflected not confidence in Anderson but rather Nixon's unwillingness to negotiate seriously with Panama. The president disdained Anderson, because President Eisenhower had once proposed that Anderson, not Nixon, be the Republican vice-presidential candidate in 1956. Nixon flatly refused to meet Anderson between 1969 and 1972. Anderson also discredited himself by mixing his business interests with public affairs. In 1987, he would be sentenced to prison for financial improprieties. As Kissinger observed, "Anderson is a pain in the neck," who turned everything "into personal advantage."[82] That Nixon's man in Panama was the unloved and unreliable Anderson pleased the Defense Department and especially the Army Department, which oversaw the canal and the Canal Zone. Defense officials judged they could keep Panamanians calm by negotiating into perpetuity. They opposed basic changes in the treaty of 1903, although they believed Panamanians could be bought off with a higher annual fee of perhaps $25 million.[83] Secretary of Defense Melvin Laird vigorously argued the Defense Department case aided by his liaison on Panama Canal issues, Colonel John P. Sheffey. State Department officials characterized Colonel Sheffey as an "ardent, loud-voiced defender of Defense Department views."[84]

Henry Kissinger's views on Panama and the canal evolved, and he would exert leadership once he became secretary of state. When it came to Latin America, Kissinger would prove that he was prepared to accommodate legitimate nationalist concerns, provided that Latin American calls for change did not involve perceived Cold War issues. On 1 June 1970, he advised Nixon that the United States "cannot realistically refuse" to reopen talks with Panama. To refuse to negotiate would open the United States to charges of bad faith and would exacerbate Panamanian nationalism. He added, "[The] 1903 arrangement is increasingly considered offensive by Panama and is an incongruity in the pattern of our present-day relationship in the hemisphere and the world." Kissinger initially favored a new treaty that continued to maintain U.S. control over the canal for an "open-ended" period and a gradual diminution of U.S. authority in the Canal Zone over a twenty-year period. By late 1971, however, he accepted the reasoning of the State Department and Ambassador Anderson that Panama would only sign a treaty that fixed a date for the end of U.S. control over the canal. Kissinger hoped that a new treaty would give the United States control of the canal for at least another fifty years.[85] To be sure, in the period between 1969 and 1972, Kissinger did not closely follow Panamanian issues. In early 1973, he confessed to U.N. Ambassador John Scali that he did not have "very clear views" on Panama.[86] But once Panama forced the issue on the global stage in March 1973, Kissinger acted effectively and decisively.

By 1972, Omar Torrijos was in a political position to end the U.S. charade of perpetual, inconclusive negotiations. He had created a fervent following at home by promising Panamanian ownership of the canal. In October 1972, he warned presidential emissary Edward R. Finch Jr., the uncle of President Nixon's son-in-law, Edward Cox, that he was "sitting on a powder keg as far as the Panama Canal is concerned." General Torrijos promised to keep his nation calm until after the U.S. presidential elections. But Torrijos rejected Nixon's request that Panama cease introducing the canal issue into international fora such as the OAS and the United Nations.[87] Although he lacked the strong formal education of traditional Panamanian elites, Torrijos displayed a shrewd understanding of power. By bringing international partners into the bilateral negotiations, he would tilt the balance of power.[88] Panama gained Latin American support for one of the rotating seats on the U.N. Security Council and persuaded the Security Council to hold a session in Panama in March 1973. At that session, the United States suffered an embarrassing defeat. Torrijos addressed the Security Council, equating Panama's aspirations with the anticolonial struggle. Ambassador Scali vetoed a resolution sponsored by Panama and Peru that called for an abrogation of the 1903 treaty and the affirmation of Panama's sovereignty and jurisdiction over the Canal Zone. It was only the third time that the United States had exercised its veto power in the history of the United Nations. Thirteen of the fifteen members of the Security Council voted for the resolution. The United Kingdom abstained on the resolution, but it implied that it accepted the justice of Panama's cause. As Panamanian Foreign Minister Juan Antonio Tack concluded, "The United States has vetoed Panama's resolution, but the world has vetoed the United States."[89]

Within a year after the Security Council meeting in Panama, Secretary of State Kissinger was in Panama City attending a splendid ceremony. He joined Foreign Minister Tack in agreeing to a list of eight principles that would guide future negotiations. The Tack-Kissinger agreement of February 1974 called for the abrogation of the 1903 treaty and the negotiation of a new treaty with a fixed termination date for U.S. control of the canal. The Canal Zone would be gradually transferred to Panama. U.S. military installations and bases would disappear. Panama would receive enhanced revenues and would share in the defense of the canal. Kissinger had already underscored his commitment to a new relationship by urging President Nixon to appoint Ambassador Ellsworth Bunker, the nation's most distinguished diplomat, to be the new U.S. negotiator.[90] Bunker had previously served as ambassador to the OAS and ambassador to five disparate countries—Argentina, Italy, India, Nepal, and South Vietnam. Bunker would meet regularly with his Panamanian counterparts on the island of Contadora, off Panama's Pacific coast. Kissinger gave Bunker broad latitude, assuring him, "If you get into trouble with Defense or the president, come to me."[91] On his return from Panama, Kissinger gushed to his friend

David Rockefeller, "We did very well—had a tremendous public reception—you wouldn't be able to tell that from the press—but nevertheless it is true."[92]

Various interpretations have been offered to explain Kissinger's seemingly sudden engagement with Panama. Political scientist Tom Long has argued that General Torrijos forced Kissinger's hand by effectively transforming the canal into a global issue.[93] In fact, Torrijos told Edward Finch that he needed Kissinger to be directly involved with Panama.[94] Ambassador to Panama William J. Jorden agreed that the Security Council veto had hurt U.S. prestige. An ensuing outbreak of protest and confrontation in the Canal Zone "would have done for us about what an outburst of violence and general strike in Eastern Europe would have done for [Soviet Premier Leonid] Brezhnev." Jorden and others have argued that Kissinger loved the "limelight" and "relished the intricacies of any major negotiation." Kissinger also always fell under the sway of Latin American hospitality whenever he visited a Latin American country. At the signing ceremony in Panama, the secretary, in Jorden's words, "beamed with pleasure and waved to his new admirers. They clapped louder still."[95] And his power waxed as Nixon's declined over Watergate. Such explanations are plausible and not mutually exclusive. But Kissinger had a sense of history. He understood the 1903 treaty was a vestige of a discredited past. As a hardworking diplomat, he was always eager to find solutions that improved bilateral and multilateral relations and preserved U.S. national security. It was how he defined his responsibility as national security adviser and secretary of state on non-East-West challenges.

Henry Kissinger was not able to transform the Tack-Kissinger set of principles into a new treaty. It was not for lack of effort. Between February 1974 and January 1977, Kissinger addressed Panama Canal issues more than a hundred times in meetings with President Ford, at NSC sessions, in conversations with Ambassador Bunker, in meetings with State and Defense Department officers, in talks with Panamanian officials and Latin American presidents, in discussions with U.S. legislators, in telephone conversations, and in public addresses. Kissinger had assets he could count on in his quest for a treaty. He operated from the conviction that his stewardship of foreign policy required him to change the historic U.S. relationship with Panama. As he patiently explained to Senator Strom Thurmond (R-SC), a treaty opponent, it took "a basic minimum of consent and cooperation" from Panama to operate the canal. Given the Panamanian sense of injustice, Kissinger reasoned that it was "impossible for the United States to maintain the position it has seen since 1903."[96] Kissinger knew that Latin America and the rest of the world stood with Panama. He warned President Ford, "If these negotiations fail, we will be beaten to death in every international forum and there will be riots all over Latin America."

He told the NSC that the United States did not want to be in a position of defending what "looks like pure colonialism." The canal's lock system was also vulnerable to sabotage. By May 1975, the U.S. military debacle in Vietnam had ended with the collapse of the Saigon regime. Two months later, Kissinger predicted to Ford, "We will have a Vietnam in the Western Hemisphere." The U.S. Army could again be engaged in guerrilla warfare. He theatrically asked U.S. senators if they envisioned the permanent stationing of the 82nd Airborne Division in Panama.[97] As for the Zonians, his sympathy for them was "zero." The Canal Zone was "nothing more than a vestige of colonialism."[98] Kissinger's debating approach in his discussions with U.S. officials and citizens about the canal was to deflect questions about negotiating positions and emphasize that the United States had a "problem" in its relationship with Panama and Latin America.[99] Responsible officials and citizens needed to address the problem.

Domestic and international figures aided Kissinger in his treaty campaign. Panamanian officials agreed with Kissinger that Ambassador Ellsworth Bunker was "a man of towering integrity."[100] Bunker shared Kissinger's view that the price of forcibly holding the canal would be too costly for the United States. He and Kissinger constantly pressed President Ford to give Bunker flexibility in his Contadora Island negotiations. Bunker's legendary diplomatic skills were

President Ford and Kissinger met with Latin American ambassadors shortly after Ford assumed office in August 1974. Ford assured the ambassadors that negotiations over a new canal treaty with Panama would continue. Ford Library.

most evident in his meetings with Defense Department officials. He observed to them that "the United States should not wish to be the only country in the world exercising extra-territoriality."[101] The eighty-year-old Bunker sat silently as he was verbally abused by the able but bombastic Secretary of Defense, James R. Schlesinger. Schlesinger professed the extremist position that the United States had the legal right to hold the canal in perpetuity.[102] Seeking to curry favor with the Defense Department, Bunker added Richard R. Wyrough, a career military officer, to his negotiating team.[103]

Omar Torrijos continued to play a critical role in the canal saga. Kissinger would ultimately applaud the Panamanian strongman for having done "a superhuman job."[104] Torrijos bet his political credibility on his solemn pledge to the Panamanian people that he would undo the injustices of 1903. But the Panamanian general and his foreign ministers, Juan Tack and then Aquilino Edgardo Boyd de la Guardia, understood that the canal issue had become embroiled in the vicissitudes of U.S. domestic politics. They accepted that a treaty might not be concluded until after the 1976 presidential election. Torrijos "appealed for patience and calm" from the Panamanian people.[105] Kissinger wrote to him, assuring him that the United States was operating in good faith. Torrijos continued to present Panama's case internationally, established relations with Cuba in 1974, and visited Havana in January 1976. But Torrijos took care not to provoke the United States and publicly accepted Fidel Castro's advice "to be patient and peaceful" in negotiating with the United States.[106] To be sure, Torrijos allowed Panamanians to vent. In 1975, demonstrators stoned the U.S. embassy in Panama City in 1975, and in 1976 several U.S. vehicles were blown up in the Canal Zone. Lieutenant Colonel Manuel Antonio Noriega of the Guardia Nacional authorized the bombings, which created no casualties.[107] Kissinger and Bunker had a good grasp of Panamanian moderation, as well as frustration, because the CIA had sources within the Panamanian negotiating team and within the Guardia Nacional.[108]

Secretary Kissinger appreciated the backing that Latin American leaders gave to Panama's cause. Indeed, he told Foreign Minister Tack that he wanted Latin American heads of state to proclaim that it was "urgent that a new treaty be worked out."[109] In 1975, the popularly elected presidents of Colombia, Costa Rica, and Venezuela wrote to President Ford and called for a new treaty that would transfer to Panama control over the canal and sovereignty over the Canal Zone by the end of 1994. Further delay would not be "in agreement with the trends of the times." The presidents, who noted that they led countries that were traditionally friendly toward the United States, also pointed out that the continued U.S. military presence gave Panama "the character of a colonial outpost."[110] In September 1975, Colombian President Alfonso López

Michelsen came to the Oval Office and warned President Ford that "without a treaty Panama could be another Vietnam." Kissinger responded that he hoped that López Michelsen would inform U.S. legislators of the depth of feeling in Latin America over the canal issue. Kissinger had previously told the NSC that the officials he admired the most in Latin America, the military dictators of Brazil, would not support the United States on canal issues.[111]

Despite this international support, Kissinger failed to achieve a treaty because he met determined resistance from the Defense Department, U.S. legislators, and the U.S. public. Most important, he failed because President Ford declined to exercise leadership. By the end of 1974, Ambassador Bunker was telling Washington that "a treaty was in sight" but that he needed to offer Panama reasonable terms. His original negotiating instructions had been to seek a fifty-year treaty, with an additional thirty to fifty years if the canal was expanded. These terms were "unrealistic." Panama demanded control of the canal by the year 2000. Panamanian control of the canal by 2000 had been an essential part of the 1967 treaty negotiated by Robert Anderson. Bunker speculated that the Panamanians might accept a U.S. defense responsibility of a longer duration. Bunker judged that treaty ratification prospects were good, because liberal Democrats had made significant electoral gains in Congress in the 1974 elections.[112] Several months previously, Kissinger had predicted to the Panamanians, "I rather think that more liberals than conservatives will be elected. So these elections will place your treaty in a much better position."[113]

Through the first eight months of 1975, President Ford vacillated over Ambassador Bunker's request. He presided over two comprehensive NSC meetings on Panama. He received numerous papers and studies on canal issues. Secretary Kissinger repeatedly badgered him to make a decision. Kissinger admitted to aides, however, that the president could not decide "without being knifed in the back by the Defense Department."[114] Finally, on 18 August 1975, Ford issued NSDM 302, which gave Bunker the authority to negotiate terms that would cede control of the canal to Panama on 31 December 1999. To appease the Defense Department, Bunker would also need to secure a defense arrangement for the canal for forty to fifty years in duration and a future U.S. role in an expanded canal, with either the construction of a third lane of locks or a sea-level canal.[115] Ford had let valuable time pass, because he was in a weak political position. He feared that if he alienated political conservatives he would not secure the Republican nomination for the presidency. Thirty-four senators, mainly conservative Republicans such as Strom Thurmond, had vowed to defeat a treaty. House members had passed a resolution deploring the Contadora negotiations. Kissinger conceded, "My mail is 100 percent against a treaty."[116] Governor Ronald Reagan of California challenged Ford for the Republican nomination. Reagan's popular line was "When it comes to the Canal, we built it, we paid for it, it's ours, and we should tell Torrijos and company that we are going to keep it."[117]

Although Ford faced political storms, he still bore responsibility for his indecisiveness. Principled conservatives, such as Senator Barry Goldwater (R-AZ), changed their views when they heard from Latin American officials about the necessity of a new canal treaty.[118] In April 1976, Senator Jacob Javits (R-NY), a Ford supporter, advised his friend "to be very presidential," because "this is an important issue for the U.S., Panama, and Latin America." Ford agreed that he would "take the offensive," in order "to avoid losing all of Latin America, including Mexico with whom we have 6,000 miles of border." In the end, Javits's injunction to "Be the President" went unheeded by Ford.[119] During the presidential campaign, Ford gave a series of conflicting statements about how he would handle canal negotiations in the future. His opponent, Governor Jimmy Carter of Georgia, made similarly ambivalent comments, suggesting that he would "never" give up practical control of the canal but would continue to negotiate with the Panamanians.[120] Panama was not a decisive issue in the presidential contest. President Ford's knowledge of international affairs was, however, a key concern for U.S. voters. Ford's bumbling assertion during the second presidential debate that the Soviet Union did not dominate Poland was no more accurate than his idea that the U.S.-Mexican border stretched for 6,000 miles.

Gerald Ford acted presidential in defeat, announcing in August 1977 his support for treaties negotiated by the Carter administration. Kissinger agreed that the proposed treaties were "in the national interests of the United States."[121] During the presidential transition, Kissinger had spoken about Panama with President-elect Carter and Secretary of State–designate Cyrus Vance. He assured Panamanian Foreign Minister Boyd that he would urge the new administration to give the treaty negotiations "a high priority." He also vowed that "he would do all he could to keep the matter from becoming a partisan one in the United States." Kissinger added that "optimism is in order" and that 1977 was the "opportune" time for concluding a new treaty. He praised the Panamanians for having shown "great wisdom and patience" during the difficult year of 1976. Kissinger also dispatched Ambassador Bunker back to Contadora "to symbolize in a positive way the continuity of the United States commitment to the negotiation."[122]

Omar Torrijos, Jimmy Carter, and Sol Linowitz, the president's special envoy, justifiably have earned plaudits for negotiating and achieving the ratification of the Panama Canal Treaties (1978). Panama took control of its canal at the end of the century and established jurisdiction over the Canal Zone. The two countries found ways to finesse the nettlesome issue of safeguarding the canal. Carter wisely retained Ambassador Ellsworth Bunker on the negotiating team. Linowitz admired and respected the senior diplomat and worked harmoniously with Bunker in achieving a treaty. In his memoirs, Henry Kissinger was modest about his role in the historic transformation in U.S.-Panamanian relations.[123] But Kissinger can claim substantial credit for keeping the negotiations going between 1973 and 1976, persuading the Panamanians to ignore irresponsible political rhetoric in the United States, and assuring them that the United States would terminate a "colonial" situation.

Henry Kissinger's overall approach to inter-American affairs was evident in his diplomacy toward Central American nations. He embraced the murderous military tyrants who terrorized Guatemala and slaughtered indigenous people in the name of anticommunism. He overlooked the brutality, criminality, and larceny that characterized daily life in Nicaragua. The Somoza regime's saving grace was that it aped U.S. foreign policy and made a home for the CIA in Nicaragua. Secretary Kissinger responded positively, however, to the nationalist concerns of Panamanians. It did not matter to him that Panama was led by an authoritarian. What mattered was that the status of the canal and the Canal Zone did not raise East-West concerns, for the Torrijos government accepted U.S. leadership in the Western Hemisphere. Other Latin American nations—Mexico, Ecuador, Peru, and Venezuela—similarly cooperated with the United States in international fora and the global arena. Kissinger worked hard to resolve their respective bilateral issues with the United States.

CHAPTER 6

Diplomatic Solutions

Mexico, Peru, Ecuador, and Venezuela

When they recalled the history of inter-American relations between 1969 and 1976, State Department officials who worked in Washington and foreign service officers assigned to posts in Latin America habitually lamented that Henry Kissinger did not prioritize relations with Latin America. They further noted that he launched no grand initiatives for the region, such as the Good Neighbor Policy or the Alliance for Progress. Their assessments were accurate. Nonetheless, the energetic Kissinger devoted more of his time to Latin America than did the prominent Cold War leaders that he succeeded: George Marshall, Dean Acheson, John Foster Dulles, and Dean Rusk at the State Department, and Robert Cutler, McGeorge Bundy, and Walt Rostow at NSC. When he left public service in January 1977, Kissinger could point to solid achievements in inter-American affairs. He took the lead in resolving both old and new issues that marred relations with Mexico, Peru, Ecuador, and Venezuela.

Mexico and the Colorado River

U.S. relations with neighboring Mexico have historically been important and complicated. As Jack B. Kubisch, who served as both deputy chief of mission in the embassy in Mexico City and as one of Kissinger's assistant secretaries of state for Latin America, noted, "There is no country in the world, I suppose, with which we have a broader range of interaction, negotiations and discussions than with the government of Mexico."[1] Beyond the traditional foreign-policy matters of international and regional security, relations with Mexico involved issues of natural resources, immigration, trade, tourism, and cross-border crime. For both citizens of Mexico and the United States, bilateral relations inevitably became enmeshed in domestic politics. The International Boundary and Water Commission (1889), which had offices both in El Paso, Texas, and in the neighboring Mexican city of Ciudad Juárez, Chihuahua, had long addressed bilateral issues that had domestic ramifications. The commission was administered jointly by the State Department and the Mexican Ministry of Foreign Relations. For example, the Rio Grande (known as *Rio Bravo* in Mexico) frequently wandered from its banks, moving part of Mexico into the United States. The commission played a key role in returning the Chamizal region to Mexico in 1964.

In 1970, Mexico was at a crossroads in its history. Between 1910 and 1940, life had been tumultuous in the aftermath of the Mexican Revolution (1910–1920), confrontations in the 1920s over the authority of the Catholic Church in Mexican life, and the Mexican government's epic showdown in the 1930s over the role of British and U.S. oil companies in Mexico. President Lázaro Cárdenas (1934–1940) established a framework for rapid economic growth. Cárdenas emphasized economic nationalism and social justice, expropriating foreign-owned properties, redistributing land, and safeguarding the rights of laborers. In essence, President Cárdenas implemented the socioeconomic components of the Constitution of 1917. He also created political stability, solidifying the political appeal of the Partido Revolucionario Institucional (Institutional Revolutionary Party), or "PRI." Mexican leaders thereafter focused on economic growth and industrialization, instead of redistribution, as the way to conquer poverty. The government spent money on transportation and communication systems, invested in higher education, and welcomed foreign investment and trade back into the country. The government also invested in tourism, building seaside resorts such as Acapulco and promoting archaeological research and preservation. Between 1946 and 1958, the country's economy doubled in size. In the 1960s, economic growth often hit an impressive 6 percent a year.

By the end of the 1960s, Mexico's economic progress was tangible. Mexico City had been transformed into a global city. The city's subway system, which opened in 1969, was a technological marvel. The architecture and artistry at the National University of Mexico dazzled Mexicans and tourists. The nation became self-sufficient in the production of iron, steel, and petroleum. The middle class grew substantially. Economic growth had not, however, resolved all problems. Perhaps 50 percent of the population, especially those living in rural areas, still lived in poverty. The problems of poverty and economic inequality were compounded by Mexico's astounding population growth. The population grew from 22 million in 1945 to 52 million in 1970 and would reach 87 million by 1990. The country also had looming balance of trade and balance of payment problems, because Mexico's manufacturers, which had been protected by governmental subsidies and tariffs, were not globally competitive. By 1976, Mexico would be forced to devalue its currency, the peso, twice. The devaluation would especially hit middle-class consumers who preferred products made in the United States.

During the postwar period of economic growth, ties between the United States and Mexico thickened. Trade amounted to nearly $3 billion in 1970, as compared to $350 million in 1945. U.S. direct investments grew from the wartime amount of $286 million to $1.8 billion in 1970. In 1964, President-elect Gustavo Díaz Ordaz (1964–1970) suggested to President Lyndon Johnson that the two countries sign a bilateral trade agreement that would guarantee a market in the United States for Mexico's agricultural and mineral exports. The new Mexican leader was advocating what would become the North American Free Trade Agreement, or NAFTA (1994).[2]

The movement of people across the 2,000 miles of border deepened ties between the two neighbors. Between 1924 and 1965, the United States sharply restricted immigration from Latin America. Residents of Puerto Rico were the only "Hispanics" or "Latinos" who could readily move to the continental United States. In 1942, as a wartime measure, the United States and Mexico signed a guest worker agreement, known as the *bracero* program, to allow Mexican nationals to work in U.S. agriculture and at other manual labor jobs. Between 1942 and 1964, when the *bracero* program lapsed, approximately 4.5 million people were registered as entering the United States to work. Some guest workers obtained long-term work permits or visas, whereas some decided to stay in the United States without documentation. In 1965, President Johnson signed the Hart-Celler Act, which sharply raised the total number of people who would be permitted to immigrate legally and abolished the restrictions on immigration from Latin America. Ambitious Mexicans from impoverished, overpopulated rural areas began to cross the border to participate in the booming U.S. economy of the 1960s and early 1970s. The U.S. Census Bureau would report that the Hispanic population, which was less than 1 percent of the general population in 1900, amounted to 6 percent of the population by 1980. Mexicans and Mexican-Americans comprised about 65 percent of Hispanics.[3]

What seemingly marred U.S.-Mexican relations was Mexico's refusal to succumb to U.S. pressure and break relations with communist Cuba. Mexico was the only Latin American country that continuously preserved diplomatic relations with Cuba after 1959. The Mexican Foreign Ministry held that in the spirit of the Mexican Revolution, Mexico could not condemn another nation that sought change and progress through the revolutionary process. But U.S.-Mexican differences over Cuba were more apparent than real. In October 1962, Mexico denounced the Soviet Union during the Cuban Missile Crisis. Moreover, having a Mexican embassy in Havana proved beneficial to the United States. The Mexican embassy routinely shared intelligence information with the United States about developments in Cuba. In the late 1960s, Mexico helped a CIA agent infiltrate its embassy in Havana. The agent, Humberto Carrillo Colón, operated under Mexican diplomatic cover until Cuban security services identified him in 1969 as a CIA spy.[4]

At home, Mexican officials promoted anticommunism. The government had embraced industrial capitalism and was on the path to joining the international capitalist world. It persecuted radicals, such as the famed muralist David Alfaro Siqueiros. President Díaz Ordaz advised President Johnson that he favored cultural exchanges but that he "would exclude painters, since in Mexico, because of a certain snobbish approach, many painters were Communists, and he would not want to send them to the U.S."[5] In a horrific incident, on 2 October 1968, police and soldiers opened fire on about 5,000 student demonstrators who had assembled in the Plaza de las Tres Culturas in the District of Tlatelolco in Mexican City. Minister of the Interior and future president Luis Echeverría Alvarez (1970–1976) supervised the action. As he prepared to assume the presidency, Echeverría assured Washington that "he would continue vigorous anticommunist line he had followed as Interior secretary and would not permit radical activism." When he called on Nixon and Kissinger in Washington in June 1972, President Echeverría further pledged to back the United States in its dealings with the Soviet Union and China and stated his opposition to another Cuba in Latin America.[6] U.S. diplomats who served in Mexico in the 1960s and 1970s uniformly recalled that the CIA moved freely throughout Mexico. The agency had intimate ties with the Ministry of the Interior and was granted permission to keep a close watch on the activities of the Cuban and Soviet embassies in Mexico City. CIA agents also surveilled Mexicans and reported their intelligence to the Interior Ministry. Henry Dearborn, who served as the U.S. embassy's deputy chief of mission from 1967 to 1969, noted that the CIA station chief, Win Scott, "was the one man who could go in and see the President [Díaz Ordaz] whenever he wanted to."[7]

Henry Kissinger became a fan of Mexico. His first encounter with the country came in mid-1970 when he traveled to Mexico City to meet with President Díaz Ordaz. He found Mexico "very interesting." He was also impressed with the sincerity of the Mexican professors and students that he had met. Thereafter, he looked forward to spending time there, especially in Acapulco, explaining that the sun was "unique" there.[8] He enjoyed his honeymoon in 1974 in Acapulco with his bride, Nancy Maginnes. (His boss had also taken his honeymoon in Acapulco with Patricia Ryan.) Kissinger became good friends with Mexican Foreign Minister Emilio Óscar Rabasa (1970–1975), who had a home in Acapulco. They frequently spoke on the telephone, with Kissinger asking Rabasa to advise him on inter-American relations. Rabasa invited Kissinger to attend his twenty-fifth wedding anniversary in Mexico. Rabasa offered to open his home to Kissinger's parents. Kissinger dismissed accounts that Mexico was a leftist or "Communist" country.[9]

During his eight years in public service, Kissinger studiously avoided the nettlesome issues of illegal immigration and the international trafficking of narcotics. Mexico took an ambivalent view about the migration of Mexicans into the United States. Foreign Minister Rabasa confessed to Kissinger that "as a Mexican it hurt him deeply to have to face the fact that so many people wanted to leave Mexico to work in the United States."[10] Mexico initially pushed for a new guest-worker program but eventually advocated that the United States grant legal status to undocumented workers. Mexican leaders also belatedly came to the conclusion that the country could not sustain its explosive population growth and began in the 1970s to promote the idea of family planning. In October 1973, Secretary of State Kissinger responded to Rabasa that he did not understand the problem of illegal immigration. The two countries would establish a joint commission to study the problem. But three years later, Kissinger again admitted a lack of knowledge about immigration when he held a lengthy discussion with the new foreign minister, Alfonso García Robles. The secretary expressed sympathy for immigrants and vaguely offered to be useful in resolving problems.[11] His humanity toward Mexican immigrants was most evident when he reacted to Foreign Minister Rabasa's worry that the U.S. House of Representatives might allocate funds to build a wall between the United States and Mexico. Kissinger labeled the idea "utterly ridiculous" and "absurd" and vowed that "it will never happen." He authorized Rabasa to inform the Mexican press of his views. Ever the comedian, Kissinger added that if a wall was built it would have to run south of his beloved Acapulco.[12]

When President Nixon launched his "War on Drugs," Kissinger did not enlist in the campaign. Even before he formally declared war, Nixon fired the first salvo by interdicting border commerce with "Operation Intercept." In September 1969, the Department of Justice snarled border traffic looking for narcotics, especially marijuana. Both the Mexican government and press vigorously protested the unilateral action. Things became worse when U.S. agents "frisked" a Mexican consular officer. President Díaz Ordaz characterized Operation Intercept as a "brutal action."[13] The United States spent the next year apologizing to Mexico. In November 1969, Nixon wrote a letter to Díaz Ordaz expressing his "personal regret" for causing friction and dispatched Kissinger to Mexico City in 1970 to smooth relations.[14] As in the case of immigration, the two countries decided to establish a joint commission to study the issue. The countries engaged in the unproductive debate on whether international drug trafficking was a supply or demand issue. Whenever he met with Mexican officials, Kissinger did not push the issue; he simply expressed the hope that Mexico would cooperate with the United States. In October 1974, President Gerald Ford, Echeverría, Kissinger, and Rabasa met in the town of Magdalena de Kino, Sonora, for two and a half hours. Kissinger freely participated in the discussion, but when the issue of narcotics trafficking arose, he fell silent.[15] Kissinger showed a similar disinterest in narcotics trafficking when he met with Colombian officials.

The issue that Mexico considered paramount in bilateral relations was the salinity of the Colorado River. Seven states in the arid Southwest, including California and Arizona, drew on the waters of the Colorado River. Water from the Colorado was consumed in the city of Los Angeles. By treaty (1944), the United States guaranteed a million and a half acre feet of water from the Colorado to Mexico. Farmers in the Mexicali region of Baja California used the water to irrigate their crops. By 1969, the United States still delivered the requisite amount of water but with increasing difficulty. In the postwar period, the populations and economies of Southwestern states were growing, leading to increasing amounts of water use. Snowpacks from the surrounding mountains were also declining. A growing Mexicali region could never hope for additional water. The Colorado was so heavily used that it became the one major U.S. river that did not flow into the ocean. The river was dried up by the time it reached the Gulf of California, which Mexicans named the Sea of Cortez.[16]

The water that farmers received in Mexicali in the 1960s ruined their crops, because it had a high salt content. In the postwar period, the United States had developed a program for veterans to establish citrus orchards in the Yuma, Arizona, region. Citrus plants in this hot, dry climate required up to twelve to fifteen feet of water per year. Water from the Colorado was pumped into this Welton Mohawk Irrigation District. The drainage, which was salty, ended up in the Colorado and ultimately into the Mexicali Valley. The 1944 water treaty did not address the quality of water. But aides informed Kissinger that Mexico had a legitimate grievance and the United States could lose if Mexico took the case of Mexicali farmers to an international court.[17] The International Boundary and Water Commission would normally be tasked to find a solution to the dispute. But the governors of the seven states had created a Colorado River Basin committee, the Committee of Fourteen, and had staffed the committee with expert hydraulic engineers and skillful lawyers who countered solutions with technical objections and legal arguments. Carl Hayden (D-AZ), who had served in the Senate from 1927 to 1969, safeguarded the citrus growers of Yuma. The frustrated Mexican government had found no relief from either the Kennedy or Johnson administrations.[18]

Henry Kissinger educated himself about the Colorado River and developed a process that led to a solution. The staff of the NSC prepared for him in 1971–1972 detailed analyses of the technical issues surrounding the flow of water from the Colorado and further warned him about the powerful domestic opposition to conciliating Mexico.[19] President Nixon wanted to make further amends for the Operation Intercept debacle and directed Kissinger to resolve "irritants" in bilateral relations.[20] President Echeverría made the salinity issue a priority and discussed it with Nixon for over an hour on 15 June 1972 when the two presidents met at the White House. Kissinger had previously had lengthy exchanges with Foreign Minister Rabasa on finding ways forward. Kissinger advised Nixon to assure Echeverría, "We will present to the Mexican Government before the end of your term our proposals for solving this problem once and for all." In specific, he recommended that Nixon appoint a "well known and capable person" to study the issue and report back with definitive recommendations "in a reasonable period of time." The appointee would have access to the full resources of the U.S. government.[21] Kissinger asked Herbert Brownell, who had been attorney general during the Eisenhower administration, to head the study team. Kissinger would take the same approach two years later when he recommended that another older, distinguished public servant, Ellsworth Bunker, negotiate the future of the Panama Canal.

Brownell, under the guidance of Kissinger, proved an efficient negotiator. He took a bus tour of the Mexicali Valley, and the Mexican government arranged for tomato farmers to show him how their land had turned white from the salt from the drainage of the Welton Mohawk District in Arizona.[22] President Echeverría raised the stakes by assuring the Mexican public that the United States would make dramatic concessions on the salinity issue.[23] As Kissinger had recommended, the administration had already taken interim steps, arranging for additional pumping of water that achieved a 25 percent reduction in the salinity of water within a week. By the end of 1972, Brownell had submitted a report. In May 1973, Kissinger submitted Brownell's ideas to Nixon with the recommendation that Brownell be empowered to negotiate directly with Mexico. Before submitting the report to Nixon, Kissinger had battled the federal bureaucracy, especially the Department of Interior and the Office of Management and Budget. As Kissinger related his heroics to Foreign Minister Rabasa, "We overrule everyone and blood is still flowing."[24] On 28 May 1973, President Nixon issued NSDM 218, which authorized Brownell to negotiate with Mexico.[25]

Brownell struck an agreement with Mexico within a few months. The plan had two parts. Between 1973 and 1978, the United States would continue to take steps to reduce further the salinity by building canals and pumping stations. Kissinger estimated that this would cost $110 million to $130 million. By 1978, the United States would commence building a desalinization plant in Yuma that would use a new technology of "reverse osmosis" to ensure that the water Mexico received from the Colorado would be of high quality.[26] The plant became operational in the 1980s and cost $285 million to construct.[27] The United States bore the entire cost of both the temporary and permanent solutions to the salinity issue. In turn, Mexico agreed not to seek damages for the harm caused since 1961 to the farmers of the Mexicali Valley. Foreign Minister Rabasa understood Kissinger and knew that his friend appreciated flattery. Rabasa spoke accurately, however, when he credited Kissinger "with being the catalyst who solved the salinity problem after 12 years of impasse." Herbert Brownell had performed magnificently, but "the agreement would not have been possible without HAK's personal interest and involvement."[28] An obviously pleased Kissinger told Nixon on 27 August 1973 that the agreement on the Colorado River represented "a major breakthrough in our relations with Mexico." Kissinger had achieved the objective he presented to Nixon in 1972— "a definitive, equitable, and just solution."[29]

Peru and the International Petroleum Corporation

In mid-1974, in a telephone conversation that he held on international economic issues with State Department legal adviser Carlyle E. Maw, Secretary of State Kissinger exclaimed that "American businessmen are certified morons."[30] During his eight years of public service, Henry Kissinger talked endlessly with domestic and international officials and often in embellished terms. But he held consistent, firm views on the relationship between international business and the making of foreign policy. He professed that economic differences should never be allowed to affect fundamental relations between countries. Economic disputes should be settled on political, not economic grounds. And foreign-policy makers should never act as lawyers for private companies.[31] Kissinger's philosophy on foreign economic policy was especially evident in his approach to the International Petroleum Corporation (IPC). IPC, which was a wholly owned subsidiary of Standard Oil of New Jersey, had operated for decades like a sovereign entity within Peru. Kissinger maneuvered skillfully to reach a negotiated solution that addressed Peru's nationalist concerns about what Kissinger dubbed a "lousy" company.[32]

Peru, a nation of 13 million people in 1970, had many of the socioeconomic problems that characterized life in several other Latin American nations. Life expectancy was fifty-three years of age. The population was expanding rapidly at 3.1 percent a year. Annual per capita income was less than $400. The indigenous population, about one-third of all Peruvians, lived largely outside of a cash economy, and many did not speak Spanish. Only about 60 percent of the population was literate. A substantial part of the population had no access to piped water. Peru was, however, a happy place for U.S. investors. President Augusto B. Leguía (1919–1930), an authoritarian who ruled during the so-called Oncenio, wanted to "Americanize" his country and welcomed U.S. investment. By 1970, U.S. direct investment approached $700 million. The chief companies were Cerro de Pasco, which mined copper, the W. R. Grace Company, which had a variety of food-producing enterprises, and IPC. U.S. commercial enterprises, such as Sears Roebuck, Goodyear, and Coca-Cola, were also prominent in Peru.[33]

Peru had proven to be a reliable Cold War ally of the United States. So pleased was the Eisenhower administration with Manuel Odría's (1948–1956) anticommunist policies that it awarded the dictator the Legion of Merit, the nation's highest award for personages. In the aftermath of the Odría regime, Peruvians expressed their displeasure with the U.S. embrace of dictatorship. University students in Lima threw stones at Richard Nixon during the vice president's momentous 1958 tour of South America.[34] The Kennedy administration planned to devote significant resources from the Alliance for Progress to Peru to improve Peruvian life and undercut the appeal of communism. Administration officials worried that Peru's dreadful inequities "provided one of the best illustrations of a 'potential for social revolution' in Latin America."[35] The administration reacted strongly when the Peruvian military annulled the results of the mid-1962 presidential election and seized power. The United States broke diplomatic relations with Peru and suspended economic and military aid. The veteran Peruvian politician and populist Víctor Haya de la Torre had garnered the most votes. The administration thought that Haya de la Torre would pursue the goals of moderate, evolutionary reform and anticommunism. Under U.S. pressure, the military agreed to schedule a new election in mid-1963. This time the politically moderate Fernando Belaúnde Terry (1963–1968) won a plurality of votes. Belaúnde believed in the Alliance for Progress and had visions of developing a trans-Andean highway along the lower eastern slopes of the Andes Mountains.[36]

In his inaugural address, President Belaúnde stunned the United States when he pledged to resolve the contentious issue of the legal validity of the land titles held by IPC within ninety days. Numerous legal tomes and doctoral dissertations have been written analyzing this legally complex issue. Under traditional Spanish legal codes, subsoil rights (oil in the ground) are the possession of the government or nation. The revolutionary Mexican Constitution of 1917 asserted that doctrine. Indigenous people knew of pits that oozed black pitch or tar in the northwestern region of Peru near what would become the city of Talara and the oilfields of La Brea y Pariñas. In 1826, the new Peruvian government and its liberator, Simón Bolívar, granted to Don José de Quintana an enormous parcel of land of 41,000 *pertenencias* (approximately 410,000 acres) in gratitude for his help in the independence movement. The deed seemingly included subsoil rights, although there was no thought of petroleum production in the early nineteenth century. The deed was repeatedly sold, with British interests and then IPC acquiring it in 1913. Various Peruvian courts challenged whether the deed conferred subsoil rights. The Leguía regime, always solicitous of foreign investors, agreed to submit deed questions to an international arbitral board consisting of Peruvians and British representatives and headed by an official from the Federal Court of Switzerland. In 1922, the arbitral board confirmed the validity of the deed and ruled that IPC was liable for only minuscule taxes on the land. The company would pay only $15 a year in taxes on a *pertenencia* it exploited and fifty cents a year on an unexploited *pertenencia*. The arbitral board did not unequivocally rule on the subsoil issue.[37]

IPC exploited the region, and by 1930 oil accounted for 30 percent of Peruvian exports, and the company supplied Peru with 80 percent of its petroleum needs. But the company acted, as one historian noted, like a "state within a state." The parent company, Standard Oil, had far more financial resources than did the Peruvian government. It provided loans to friendly politicians, and it bribed officials. It also treated its workers badly, although it would improve working and living conditions for IPC employees in the 1950s and 1960s.[38] IPC acted like Creole Petroleum acted in Venezuela during the regime of dictator Juan Vicente Gómez (1908–1935). Creole was also a wholly owned subsidiary of Standard Oil. It would take massive intervention by the State Department during World War II, when Venezuelan oil was vital to Allied victory, to force

Creole to share Venezuela's bounty with Venezuelans.[39] In the postwar period, IPC stood on what it considered its contractual rights. Peruvian nationalists charged that the company owed the nation hundreds of millions of dollars in unpaid taxes on the five-decade-long exploitation of the nation's nonrenewable natural resource.

For five years, the Belaúnde government negotiated with IPC. Other U.S. companies in Peru became frustrated with IPC's reluctance to strike a deal, fearing that Peruvian nationalism would turn against them. The U.S. government did not perceive the issue in the same way. Despite its stated commitment to alleviating poverty in Peru, the Kennedy and then Johnson administrations defended the contractual rights of IPC. Assistant Secretary of State Thomas Mann labeled the issue a "legal question that ought to be submitted either to the World Court or to arbitration."[40] Mann and other U.S. officials backed this up by restricting Alliance funds for Peru. The country may have lost as much as $150 million in economic aid. As one scholar concluded, President Belaúnde was the perfect candidate to carry out the Alliance for Progress. He was cut from the same cloth as President Eduardo Frei in Chile. But "Washington seemed more concerned with defending the interests of the International Petroleum Corporation than in supporting Belaúnde's reform agenda." Belaúnde managed to redistribute land to only 9,000 families.[41]

The Peruvian military, led by General Juan Velasco Alvarado (1968–1975), overthrew President Belaúnde on 3 October 1968. The *golpe de estado* came shortly after Belaúnde announced a settlement of the IPC issue. The government would regain control over the La Brea y Pariñas oilfields. But the agreement seemed to leave the company in a favorable position in terms of the refining and marketing of oil, and the agreement absolved IPC of back taxes. On 9 October, General Velasco announced to the nation that he had ordered troops to take control of the La Brea y Pariñas oilfields. On 6 February 1969, Velasco expropriated all of IPC's properties and presented the company with a bill for $690,524,283 in back taxes. A private company could never own the subsoil rights of Peru. The tax bill amounted to far more than the value of the expropriated properties. Peru, Velasco proclaimed, had "taken the final step to close this ignominious chapter in its history." The general assured international investors that Peru still welcomed foreign investment. IPC was a "special and unique" case. General Velasco also noted that Peru had historically had close relations with the United States. He hoped that economic sanctions, especially the Hickenlooper Amendment, would not be imposed on his nation.[42]

By 1976, military dictators commanded Argentina, Bolivia, Brazil, Chile, Paraguay, Peru, and Uruguay. Peru's era of military rule (1968–1980), however, seemed unique. The military rulers declared that they were seeking a "third way" between capitalism and communism. They pledged to restore the communal ideals of the pre-Columbian past, ensuring that workers had a voice in management decisions in private companies. They promised land reform and measures to rectify Peru's income inequalities. The state would play a larger role in the economy. The government nationalized major industries, including those owned by foreigners. Academic scholars initially waxed eloquent about the "Peruvian Experiment," thinking the military dictators would usher in social justice, if not "socialism," to Peru.[43] In fact, Peru's military dictators acted like their South American military counterparts. They mismanaged the economy, piled up international debt, and wasted money on military hardware. Military officers used their control of major sectors of the economy to enrich themselves. And the generals proved authoritarian and repressive, not fulfilling promises to give Peruvian civilians a meaningful role in their government.[44] What perhaps differentiated the Peruvian military dictators from their South American counterparts was that they did not inflict wholesale murder and torture on their people. General and President Francisco Morales Bermúdez (1975–1980) participated, however, in Operation Condor. Disillusioned Peruvians returned Fernando Belaúnde Terry (1980–1985) to the presidency in 1980.

General Velasco and his minions also seemingly wanted to challenge U.S. hegemony in the Western Hemisphere. The government established relations with Cuba and the Soviet Union and sided with Third World nations in their demand for justice on international economic issues. The military also purchased arms, including tanks and jet aircraft, from the Soviet Union. U.S. intelligence analysts concluded, however, that Peruvian ties with the Soviet Union were economic rather than political. Peru paid near market prices for Soviet military equipment. Peru also worried about the military might of its southern neighbor, Chile.[45] The War of the Pacific (La Guerra del Pacífico; 1879–1884) had been disastrous for Peru, with Chile seizing resource-rich territory in southern Peru. In any case, Peruvian military rulers assured U.S. officials of their commitment to anticommunism. In 1972, for example, President Velasco informed Ambassador Taylor Belcher of the "importance of increasing cooperation between Peru and the US in the face of our common foe, communism, and expressed particular interest in re-establishing collaboration in the intelligence field."[46] Kissinger happily relayed the ambassador's report to President Nixon. CIA analysts judged President Morales Bermúdez a political moderate who "was inclined to use a more cooperative approach in relations with Washington."[47] U.S. officials, especially Kissinger, also judged Peru within the context of U.S. hostility to Salvador Allende's Chile. In 1971, Kissinger assured the Peruvian foreign minister that "we are interested in the success of the Peruvian revolution—both for its own sake and as a non-Marxist alternative to the Chilean experience in Latin America."[48]

During the opening months of his presidency, Richard Nixon demanded a powerful response to the expropriation of IPC, including the application of the Hickenlooper Amendment (1962). The amendment required the United States to cut off, within six months, economic aid to a nation that expropriated U.S. properties without "just, fair, and adequate" compensation. Peru would lose annually $35 million in economic aid and special access to the U.S. sugar market, which amounted to $65 million in sales for Peruvian sugar producers. Nixon always professed that Latin America's poverty was due to the lack of foreign investment. As he informed his Cabinet, the "wooly heads" in the State Department believed foreign aid and trade preferences would stimulate economic development. He exclaimed, "We could put ten times in and it wouldn't do it. The future of Latin America will be determined . . . by what private enterprise does."[49] Expropriation ruined the investment climate. Nixon wanted to be as "hard as hell" on Peru. As he told Kissinger over the telephone in April 1969, "The purpose is not to negotiate, but purpose is to fight. Line up the troops and go after them every which way we can."[50] When Kissinger suggested that the United States respond generously to the 31 May 1970 earthquake that devastated parts of Lima and surrounding areas by providing $100 million in aid, Nixon erupted. He wrote on the margin of the recommendation, "No. I want to give Velasco just as little as we can—in specifics—He is using the earthquake to build his socialist state."[51] Nixon once conceded that "it makes sense" when Kissinger told him that it would enhance national security if the United States worked with the anticommunist Velasco. But Nixon also listened to his friend and champion of U.S. foreign investment, Treasury Secretary John Connally, who wanted to confront Peru over the IPC expropriation.[52] It would take Kissinger years to waylay the Hickenlooper Amendment approach and arrive at a settlement that saved face for both Peru and the United States.

The Nixon administration initially considered a covert intervention in Peru. At Kissinger's request, in April 1969 CIA Director Richard Helms investigated potential remedies. Helms found, however, that "Velasco's overthrow and replacement by an element more amenable to meaningful negotiations does not appear possible." Helms broached the idea of bribing General Velasco.[53] Kissinger listened with greater interest, however, to the analyses of the Latin American experts on his NSC staff—Arnold Nachmanoff, William Jorden, and Viron Vaky—and Ambassador Belcher. They pointed out that the regime was neither anti-American nor opposed to international capitalism. Peruvians simply supported the expropriation of the reviled IPC. Any invocation of the

Hickenlooper Amendment would infuriate Peruvians and rally the rest of Latin America to the Peruvian cause. Moreover, IPC had a dubious reputation within the international business community. Peter M. Flanigan, a presidential assistant who focused on international trade, informed Kissinger that IPC had acted in an "intransigent manner" and that his friends in the business community told him that "IPC acted in a manner which led to its subsequent nationalization." Defending IPC risked jeopardizing other U.S. investments in Peru.[54] As early as May 1969, Kissinger had concluded that a policy of limiting the flow of U.S. aid and international loans to Peru would not save IPC. These realities did not stop Nixon from fulminating about the expropriation. Progress on U.S.-Peruvian relations would await the decline of Nixon's power in 1973–1974 and his replacement by Gerald Ford.

In February 1974, the United States and Peru resolved the expropriation issue. The Nixon administration had designated James Greene, a vice president of Manufacturers Hanover Trust of New York, to negotiate directly with Velasco and his aides. The complicated agreement called for the creation of a $150 million fund to compensate expropriated companies. The U.S. government would contribute money to the expropriation fund. Expropriated companies that would be compensated from the fund included Cerro Pasco, W. R. Grace, and Star-Kist, the tuna company. The agreement did not mention IPC, although the company would quietly receive $22 million in compensation.[55] Ambassador Belcher ventured that Peru signed the agreement because the generals feared that the United States would do to Peru what it had done in September 1973 to Allende's Chile.[56] But U.S. officials recognized that the agreement represented a victory for Peru. Peru had acquired properties worth far more than $150 million. Both IPC and Cerro claimed their respective properties were worth $100 million. Nonetheless, the Nixon administration celebrated the agreement, because Peru had tacitly accepted the compensation principle and had agreed to welcome future foreign investors.[57]

As in the case of the Colorado River salinity issue, Kissinger believed that he worked his diplomatic magic. He found legal ways to avoid invoking the Hickenlooper amendment, and he outmaneuvered adversaries, such as Treasury Secretary Connally, who tried to block international loans to Peru. He thereafter developed a sense of bonhomie with General Miguel Ángel de la Flor Valle, the Peruvian foreign minister. The jokes flowed between the two, with Kissinger claiming that it was more fun to negotiate with Latin Americans than with dour Arabs.[58] In February 1976, the secretary of state stopped in Lima to meet with President Morales Bermúdez. He confessed to the general, "It took me a while to understand the authentic national nature of the process in Peru." But after assessing Peru properly, he said, "I made a

Kissinger and Peru's foreign minister, General Miguel Ángel de la Flor Valle, enjoy each other's company in Lima in February 1976. The resolution of the IPC controversy was an unheralded diplomatic triumph for Kissinger. United States Information Services (USIS) photo.

great effort to avoid the application of the Hickenlooper amendment and to establish a better understanding." Kissinger and Morales Bermúdez toasted U.S.-Peruvian friendship with a glass of pure Pisco. Always wanting the last word, Kissinger remarked to the general, "After this I will agree to everything you ask."[59]

Kissinger Mediates the Great "Tuna War"

As the representative of the world's richest nation, Henry Kissinger sought to facilitate good relations with Western Hemisphere nations to promote their economic development and prosperity. As evidenced in his approach to the Colorado River salinity issue, he advocated spending U.S. public money to reach a diplomatic solution that would conciliate a friendly nation. During his eight years in public office, Kissinger also reliably backed grants, loans, and trade preferences to Latin American nations that he judged sufficiently anticommunist. He once remarked to a Latin American leader that when it came to international economic issues, he aligned himself with the Democratic Party.[60] Kissinger's belief that the United States should take the lead in preserving an open international economic system was again revealed in the unique solution he found to organizing a ceasefire in the great "tuna war" between the United States and Ecuador.

The United States has traditionally given scant attention to relations with the small South American nation of Ecuador. As the U.S. embassy candidly noted in 1969, "Ecuador's small size, less strategic geographic position, and lack of important raw materials (except petroleum) diminish its bilateral significance to the U.S."[61] During the 1960s and 1970s, Ecuador was a troubled country. It experienced explosive population growth, with the population rising from 4.6 million in 1962 to 7.1 million in 1975, despite having one of the highest infant mortality rates in Latin America. The country was poor and unfair. One percent of the population owned 45 percent of the land. Half of school children failed to finish elementary school because their parents could not afford school uniforms, textbooks, and school supplies.[62] The political system was chaotic, with generals and civilians passing through the presidential office. President Carlos Julio Arosemena Monroy (1961–1963) had a serious drinking problem. He was drunk when he met President Kennedy in the White House to discuss the Alliance for Progress.[63] From the 1950s through the 1970s, José María Velasco Ibarra was president five different times. But he managed to finish only one of his presidential terms. The military habitually removed Velasco Ibarra from office. Despite the problems, Ecuadorians have a reputation throughout Latin America for creating a charming society and having a rich indigenous culture. Quito, the capital, has an altitude of 9,000 feet and may be the loveliest city in Latin America.

A Pacific nation, Ecuador is situated near the Humboldt Current, one of the richest areas of marine life on the planet. Erosion from the nearby Andes Mountains fertilizes the Humboldt Current with nutrients such as nitrates and phosphates. Encouraged by the United States, the nations of Chile, Ecuador, and Peru began to develop a tuna fishing industry to supply U.S. markets during World War II. Ecuador took the lead in extending what it considered its "territorial waters." In 1951, Ecuador adopted a twelve-mile territorial sea. In 1952, Chile, Ecuador, and Peru signed the Declaration of Santiago calling for nations to exercise jurisdiction and sovereignty over the waters 200 miles from their coastlines. In 1966, Ecuador established the world's first 200-mile territorial sea and incorporated the principle into its constitution. Ecuador justified its unilateral action on the grounds that it needed to conserve marine life from excessive fishing. The nation also wanted to protect its famous Galapagos Islands. The United States traditionally held to a three-mile territorial sea, although, under pressure from domestic coastal and sport fishers, the United States adopted a twelve-mile territorial sea in 1966. In 1968, the United States delivered a diplomatic protest to Ecuador over the 200-mile declaration, asserting the traditional "freedom of the seas" principle. It also rejected the conservation argument, noting that yellowfin and skipjack tuna migrated vast distances.[64] Such disputes would prompt the United Nations to sponsor a Law of the Sea Conference (1973–1982).

U.S. tuna boats, primarily based in San Diego, began to fish the waters of the Humboldt Current in the 1950s. Over time, the boats became more sophisticated, with large refrigeration capacities. They also began to fish with nets. Incidents arose as early as 1954, with Ecuador seizing the *Santa Ana* and *Antarctic Maid* and forcing them to unload their cargo in the coastal city of Guayaquil and pay a fine. Nonetheless, in the 1960s and 1970s the U.S. tuna industry became a big business, because it also involved cannery employees, who worked for enterprises such as Star-Kist and Bumble Bee. The industry developed strong friends from among the senators and representatives from the Pacific states who served in Washington. In the 1960s, they attached amendments to foreign and military aid bills calling on the president to retaliate against nations that seized U.S. fishing boats. They additionally arranged for U.S. boats to be compensated with public funds for any fines they paid. The tuna industry also received stout support from the AFL-CIO, because one of the union's affiliates was the Cannery Workers and Fishermen's Union. The Department of Defense joined in the tuna boat cause, because it feared a 200-mile limit would hamper the U.S. navy operating in regions such as the Formosa Straits. With such backing, the tuna boats refused to purchase licenses to fish in the territorial waters of Ecuador.[65] Tuna boat captains were also arrogant, acting, in the words of one U.S. diplomat, like "cowboys." They would destroy fish rather than have the Ecuadorian navy distribute the seized fish to the impoverished population.[66]

The great tuna war erupted in 1971 when Ecuador seized fifty-one boats and imposed $2.4 million in fines. The Ecuadorian military used spotter airplanes and ships previously supplied to it by the United States. The Ecuadorian navy fired at tuna boats but fortunately missed. During the early 1970s, Ecuador seized one hundred boats and imposed $6 million in fines.[67] In the United States, the high-seas confrontation evoked a nationalistic reaction, with calls for military retaliation. (Public support ebbed, however, when citizens realized that the nets of tuna boats often snared and killed America's favorite sea mammal, the adorable dolphin.[68]) With his characteristic disdain for Latin Americans, President Nixon demanded a belligerent response to Ecuador's assertion of the 200-mile limit.[69] At the president's direction, Secretary of State

Rogers called in Ecuador's ambassador to the United States, and in the words of William P. Stedman Jr., who served in the Peru-Ecuador section of the State Department, "reamed out" the ambassador, who "was a very, very nice, decent man."[70] The United States also suspended military sales to Ecuador and threatened to impose economic and military sanctions.

National Security Adviser Kissinger was disgusted by the treatment of Ecuador. On 29 January 1971, shortly after Rogers demeaned the Ecuadorian ambassador, Kissinger observed to David Packard of the Defense Department, "State f—— that up. They shouldn't have thrown down the gauntlet unless they were prepared to pick it up."[71] Kissinger knew that Ecuador had dire economic problems and that the mercurial president Velasco Ibarra took strong measures against domestic leftists. Military sanctions would harm the U.S. relationship with the Ecuadorian military and diminish Washington's influence over the long term. Kissinger's friend Nelson Rockefeller had asked him to support Ecuador's economic development and suggested to him possible solutions to the tuna boat issue.[72] Kissinger promised Packard and aides that he would speak with Nixon. In early February 1971, Kissinger urged on Nixon "a negotiated practical settlement which does not prejudice the juridical position of either side" in regard to the law of the sea. Kissinger, the diplomat, advocated finding a "disguised way."[73] Over the next year, he would send additional memoranda to Nixon on the fisheries issue and would receive Nixon's approval to reach a negotiated solution. In his search for a ceasefire, Kissinger received help from the U.S. embassy in Quito, Under Secretary of State John N. Irwin II, and a young desk officer for Ecuador in Washington, Rozanne L. Ridgeway. Ridgeway would become a star within the department, serving as ambassador to Finland and East Germany and assistant secretary of state for European and Canadian affairs. She became an expert on the law of the sea.[74]

With the help of these diplomats, Kissinger found, by October 1972, a "scenario" to conciliate President Nixon, the Defense Department, and Ecuador. To improve the negotiating atmosphere, the United States released economic aid for Ecuador, and the president, at Kissinger's urging, quietly lifted the ban on military sales to Ecuador. U.S. diplomats also secretly met with the Ecuadorian military, which had overthrown Velasco Ibarra in early 1972. The United States would hereafter notify Ecuador of the names of U.S. tuna boats fishing in Ecuador's waters. In turn, Ecuador would issue licenses to the tuna boats. The United States would pay $150,000 a year to Ecuador for the licenses. The flat fee would be labeled a "conservation" fee, with the United States ostensibly joining an international effort to protect tuna from overfishing.[75] The deal was modeled on an agreement to resolve a dispute over U.S. commercial boats fishing for shrimp off the coast of Brazil. But the "conservation" agreement with Brazil had at least the patina of credibility, for shrimp do not migrate long distances, as do tuna.[76] Ecuador was pleased, because the United States was conceding that the foreign tuna boats needed licenses to fish within the 200-mile limit. But this "disguised way" appeased the Defense Department. By emphasizing "conservation," the United States was tacitly conceding that Ecuador had "jurisdiction" over the disputed waters but not "sovereignty." The U.S. Navy had preserved the principle of free navigation of the seas. The resolution of jurisdiction and sovereignty issues would await the Law of the Sea Conference, which commenced in 1973. Kissinger further recommended that no major public announcement accompany the agreement. The administration would notify, on a classified basis, congressional leaders and key legislators involved with fishing issues of the agreement.[77] Although there would be periodic confrontations over tuna fishing into the early 1980s, Kissinger had successfully negotiated a ceasefire.

Kissinger's tuna diplomacy pointed to his celebrated capacity for hard work and his obvious intellectual and analytic abilities. By the end of the process, he had become conversant on key maritime issues. He praised the Law of the Sea Conference and implicitly accepted Brazil, Chile, Ecuador, and Peru's argument for a 200-mile zone.[78] A 200-mile zone would mean that a fishing trawler from the Soviet Union, bristling with antennae, could not patrol twelve miles off the U.S. coast, fishing and spying.[79] The U.N. Convention on the Law of the Sea would establish a 188-mile "economic zone" between the twelve-mile and 200-mile limits. By the end of the 1980s, the United States had adopted that principle. Henry Kissinger, student of Klemens von Metternich and Otto von Bismarck, had added to his scholarly expertise a knowledge of the migratory habits of yellowfin tuna.

Venezuela, OPEC, and Nationalization

Critical developments in foreign economic policies took place between 1969 and 1977. In 1971, beset by domestic economic problems and low public approval ratings, President Nixon took the United States off the gold standard, ending the convertibility of the U.S. dollar to gold or other assets. Nixon also imposed a 10 percent surcharge on imports and a ninety-day freeze on domestic prices and wages. Two years later another momentous event disrupted international commerce. Oil-producing Arab nations, led by Saudi Arabia, imposed an embargo on exports of oil to the United States in the aftermath of the October 1973 confrontation between Israel and Egypt and Syria. The ensuing precipitous increase in the price of oil benefited Venezuela and prompted the South American nation to nationalize the massive investments held by U.S. oil and steel companies. Henry Kissinger successfully worked to maintain harmony between the United States and Venezuela during a tumultuous time.

Venezuela had an unusual economic history and a unique relationship with the United States. During the nineteenth century, the nation produced cacao and coffee for the international market. It had a small population and a series of authoritarian rulers. But the country had beneath its surface what would prove to be the largest reserves of petroleum in the world. During the 1920s, international oil companies such as the British-Dutch combine Royal Dutch Shell, Creole Petroleum (a subsidiary of Standard Oil of New Jersey), and Gulf Oil transformed the country into a major exporter of oil. Until 1970, Venezuela was the principal exporter of petroleum in the world and usually the third-largest global producer after the United States and the Soviet Union. With the oil bounty, Venezuela achieved by 1970 a per capita income of about $1,200 a year, making Venezuela, along with Argentina, the wealthiest nation in the region. Venezuela earned also relatively good marks on measures of socioeconomic health, such as literacy rates and life expectancy. Still, the population, which had reached 11.6 million, was growing too rapidly at 3 percent a year. Half of the population was under the age of fifteen. Economic development was uneven. The rural areas stagnated, and the country was spending too much of its oil income on imported food. Caracas was a raucous capital city, with flashy buildings and astounding traffic jams. Middle-class Venezuelans journeyed to Miami with empty suitcases and returned with them stuffed with U.S. consumer goods. Venezuelan sports enthusiasts loved *beisbol* not *fútbol*. Luis Aparicio, who played shortstop for three major league teams, was a national hero and future member of the Baseball Hall of Fame.

Since 1958, Venezuelans had maintained a competitive, two-party political system. Except for a brief period from 1945 to 1948, the *trienio*, Venezuelans had no previous experience with open, free elections. Citizens had endured two vicious military dictatorships under Juan Vicente Gómez (1908–1935) and Marcos Pérez Jiménez (1948–1958). After a mass uprising overthrew Pérez Jiménez, the Acción Democrática party, led by Rómulo Betancourt (1959–1964) and Raúl Leoni (1964–1969), ushered in an era of constitutional rule and free elections. A historical watershed transpired when Rafael Caldera (1969–1974), the leader of the Christian Democrats, captured the presidency and power was peacefully transferred. During the 1960s, leftist guerrillas inspired by the Cuban Revolution fomented urban and rural terrorist attacks on the government. By 1970, their day had past. President Caldera declared an amnesty, and former guerrillas joined the political process.

Relations between the United States and Venezuela had been cordial and strong since the U.S.-assisted overthrow of Cipriano Castro (1899–1908). Venezuela had been a hospitable place for U.S. investors. By 1970, U.S. direct investments amounted to $2.7 billion, the highest in Latin America. The bulk of the investments were in the extractive industries of oil and iron ore. Venezuela was the third-best market for U.S. exporters, trailing only the far more populous countries of Brazil and Mexico.[80] Venezuela was also a dependable ally of the United States. During World War II, the country expanded petroleum production to aid the Allied cause. President Betancourt loathed Fidel Castro and enlisted in President Kennedy's war on Cuba. Betancourt dispatched destroyers to assist the United States in the quarantine of Cuba during the 1962 Missile Crisis. Betancourt also made it clear that he would assist any U.S. efforts to assassinate Castro. In turn, the Kennedy and Johnson administrations supplied copious amounts of economic and military aid to the Betancourt and Leoni administrations to help the governments underwrite land and housing initiatives and defeat domestic guerrillas. President Kennedy perceived Betancourt, a stout anticommunist and progressive reformer, to be a model politician for the Alliance for Progress.[81]

Issues that marred the salubrious nature of U.S.-Venezuelan relations revolved around the production, sale, and price of oil. In the 1960s, the world was awash in oil, with countries such as Saudi Arabia, Libya, and Nigeria rapidly expanding production. The price of Venezuelan crude oil fell from $2.65 a barrel in 1957 to $1.81 in 1969. Gasoline prices, which were often less than 30 cents a gallon in the 1960s, fueled the remarkable economic growth that the United States enjoyed in the 1960s. Venezuela tried to address the problem by helping found a cartel, the Organization of Petroleum Exporting Countries (OPEC), with Saudi Arabia in 1960. Juan Pablo Pérez Alfonso, the famous oil minister of Venezuela, argued that low prices facilitated the depletion of a nonrenewable natural resource vital to industrial civilizations. But OPEC exercised little influence in the 1960s, because the United States still had the capacity to break any price-fixing scheme by expanding petroleum production. The low price of oil also ironically reduced Venezuela's oil exports. In 1959, responding to pressures from domestic oil producers, President Eisenhower imposed a mandatory quota on oil imports. But the president exempted from the quota both Canada and Mexico, reasoning that overland shipments of oil would be secure in wartime. Venezuela protested the discrimination, noting that it had been a reliable supplier in war and peace to the United States. For example, during the 1967 "Six-Day War" between Israel and the Arab world, Venezuela expanded its production to ensure there would not be global shortages of oil. Under the quota, Venezuela's share of U.S. imported oil fell from

67 percent in 1957 to 42 percent in 1969. Faced with declining revenues, Venezuela raised taxes on the foreign oil companies in the 1960s. The U.S. and British-Dutch companies responded by slowing down drilling exploration for new oil fields.[82]

Even before he was formally inaugurated, President Caldera pressed the United States to put Venezuela on an equal footing with Canada and Mexico, sending emissaries in early 1969 to meet with the new Nixon administration. President Caldera hoped that the United States did not judge Venezuela "a second-class friend." Caldera also raised the "terms of trade" issue, noting that the price of petroleum had declined by 25 percent during the 1960s, whereas the prices of the industrial wares that Venezuela imported had risen by 25 percent. These terms of trade, Caldera opined, "constituted one of the most accusing documents that might be written in the history of mankind." Kissinger and his NSC advisers wanted the administration to conciliate Venezuela and urged the president to meet with Caldera.[83] Nixon and Caldera had a pleasant meeting in Washington in June 1970. Thereafter, Nixon raised the U.S. quota on imports of Venezuelan home heating oil by 35,000 barrels a day. Although he had hoped for an increase of 100,000 barrels, Caldera left Washington pleased with Nixon's gesture. He apparently concluded that the harmonious discussion signified that President Nixon would place Venezuela on an equal footing with Canada and Mexico.[84] A year later, the goodwill had dissipated. The Nixon administration reacted harshly to new measures imposed on the oil companies operating in Venezuela. In April 1971, presidential aide Peter M. Flanigan, a former banker, informed the U.S. ambassador, Robert McClintock, that Venezuela would no longer be eligible for a hemispheric preference on oil imports.[85] Nixon groused about Venezuela "giving us a hard time." Nixon added, "God-damn the small countries who do not do as we want."[86] In September 1972, the Nixon administration declined to give Venezuela any share of the latest 600,000 barrels a day increase in the oil quota. The administration further rejected the judgment of Minister of Mines Hugo Pérez de la Salvia that it was "badly advised" on oil matters. The minister warned that the United States could not become self-sufficient in oil and would inevitably become dependent on Venezuela's natural resource.[87]

The United States declined to refashion its diplomacy toward Venezuela because U.S. officials failed to grasp the import of the rapidly changing world of oil. Two simultaneous developments—the failure of domestic oil producers to meet anticipated production goals and the unanticipated ability of OPEC to act cohesively—left the United States vulnerable to an energy crunch. Whereas the United States had been a net importer of oil since 1948, the nation had enjoyed a steady increase in output in the postwar period. Crude oil production was 3.52 billion barrels in 1970, 27 percent higher than in 1960. U.S. experts had predicted that domestic production would reach 3.94 billion barrels in 1975; however, it reached just 3.05 billion barrels. At the same time, demand for oil had escalated. In the days before the Arab oil embargo of 1973, the United States was consuming 17 million barrels a day. Five years previously, consumption had been 13 million barrels a day. Demand for oil was similarly rising in prosperous Western Europe and Japan.[88]

International developments also upended the prevailing economic theory that cartels like OPEC would be unable to control production and prices. Arab nations simmered over the humiliating military defeat the Arab world suffered at the hands of Israel in 1967 and vowed to use oil as a weapon. Shah Mohammed Reza Pahlevi of Iran, tired of his status as a client of the West, wanted the financial resources to play an expanded diplomatic and military role in the Middle East and southwestern Asia. And Colonel Muammar el-Qaddafi, the fiery pan-Arabist and virulently anti-Zionist leader of Libya, exposed the vulnerabilities of the international oil companies. In 1970, he forced the oil companies to revise their contracts and provide an additional 30 cents per barrel to Libya. Qaddafi seemed fanatical enough to fulfill his vow to shut down oil production in Libya unless the companies acceded to his demands. The Libyan's victory initiated three years of "Libyan leap-frog," as individual OPEC members pressed the international oil companies for price and profit concessions and a share in their operations. Between January and October 1973, Venezuela ordered the companies to raise prices four times, reaching $4.44 a barrel. OPEC had planned to meet in October 1973 to discuss fixing the price at $6 a barrel. The chaos generated in the West by the Arab oil embargo, which lasted from 18 October 1973 until 18 March 1974, enhanced OPEC's sense of power. On 22 December 1973, OPEC, led by Iran, set the price at $11.65 a barrel.[89]

Venezuelans initially reacted ungraciously to the sudden shift in the global balance of power. President Caldera gloated, "If the United States didn't have the intelligence to offer us a hemispheric preference . . . for so long, it now makes little difference to us." During the embargo, Venezuela faithfully exported oil to the United States, proving, as the embassy in Washington archly observed, "the reliability of Venezuela's oil in times of emergencies." The new president, Carlos Andrés Pérez (1974–1979) of Acción Democrática, intensified the rhetoric, launching a blistering attack on the industrial world in general and the United States in particular. In his inaugural address, he declared that Venezuela would "take up the defense of Latin American rights, trampled by the economic totalitarianism of the developed countries." The Venezuelan leader insisted that the United States must repeal economic sanctions against Cuba, relinquish the Panama Canal, and show more interest "in Venezuela and Latin America than in our raw materials."[90] President Pérez soon tempered his Third World rhetoric. During the 1960s, as Minister of Interior, he had directed the crushing of the armed Venezuelan left. He also opposed Cuba's adventures in Angola. The president further understood that Venezuelans were addicted to U.S. consumer goods.

With the support of Caldera, President Pérez announced in 1974 that Venezuela would nationalize the extractive oil and iron-ore industries. The government calculated the net book value of the foreigners' unamortized investments and paid the U.S. steel companies approximately $100,000 and the oil companies $1.028 billion in interest-bearing Venezuelan bonds. The nationalization process was complete by 1 January 1976. The government rejected the demand of political leftists in the Venezuelan legislature to expropriate without compensation. Although the international oil companies groused about the value of the compensation, they accepted the deal. Venezuela would need to purchase the technology of the international oil companies in order to exploit their natural bounty. The new oil laws also permitted mixed government-industry enterprises. Venezuela's greatest potential oil fields were in eastern Venezuela, the Orinoco Tar Belt. This region contained potentially 700 billion barrels of molasses-like petroleum, which was also laden with heavy metals and sulfur. Geologists and petroleum engineers predicted that with technological advances and massive infusions of capital the Tar Belt could be exploited.[91] Recalling the expropriation, Ambassador to Venezuela Harry W. Shlaudeman observed that "these big oil companies have plenty of money and in the end it [i.e., expropriation] didn't really affect them."[92]

Although irritated by President Pérez's bombastic rhetoric, Henry Kissinger worked to avoid a confrontation over the expropriation process and preserve good relations with "our old friend."[93] In 1974, the U.S. Congress passed legislation, the "Generalized System of Preferences," that granted developing nations special access to the U.S. market. Congress excluded, however, OPEC members from the new trade system. Kissinger testified against the exclusion, noting that Ecuador and Venezuela reliably sold oil to the United States. He also privately deplored the exclusion to Venezuelan officials.[94] As for the expropriation of the largest U.S. investment in Latin America, the secretary of state took a relaxed attitude. In a 16 July 1974 meeting with his staff, Kissinger observed, "I assume we don't care whether he [President Pérez] nationalizes as long as there's adequate compensation." In mid-1975, he assured Venezuelan Foreign Minister Ramón Escovar Salom, "I substantially agree with your position. We have no problem with you on this."[95] Kissinger adopted a policy developed by his NSC staff and an interdepartmental group on Latin America. The United States would support nationalization "to protect its vital interests."

An orderly nationalization process would preserve U.S. access to Venezuelan oil and promote a future service role for U.S. oil companies in Venezuela. An agreeable ending to Creole Petroleum and Gulf Oil's traditional presence in Venezuela also opened the door to new investments and sales.[96] Venezuela's oil revenues had soared from $2 billion to $9 billion. The U.S. embassy in Caracas was tasked with recycling the "petrodollars" back to the United States, or as economic officer Robert B. Morley put it, "to take advantage of Venezuela's new wealth to sell U.S. goods and services in that market."[97] The new policy succeeded. The value of U.S. sales to Venezuela rose from $924 million in 1972 to $2.62 billion in 1976. And U.S. capitalists directly invested almost $1 billion, mainly in manufacturing, in Venezuela between 1974 and 1976.[98]

In February 1976, a month after the formal nationalization ceremony, Secretary Kissinger journeyed to Caracas to mark the new era in U.S.-Venezuelan relations. The conversation was pleasant and respectful, although Kissinger implicitly criticized the Venezuelan for his rhetoric. He praised President Pérez for being "an authentic popular leader." The secretary noted, "I take Latin America seriously," but complained of "confrontational" styles of politics. He wanted the U.S. relationship with Latin America to be like the relationship with Europe. He elaborated: "In human terms, our relations with Latin America are in fact warmer than with Europe, but our relations with Europe have a constancy which doesn't exist in Latin America." As an example, Kissinger pointed to the style of President Echeverría of Mexico. Kissinger claimed that the Mexican leader "gives a blood curdling speech about the United States and then he'll send a private letter to me saying that we shouldn't pay too much attention to what he said publicly." Pérez told Kissinger that Venezuela opposed Cuba's intervention in Angola. In turn, Kissinger pledged to submit a new Panama Canal treaty to Congress by February 1977. In his report to President Ford, Kissinger characterized the Venezuelan leader as "a commanding figure, quick, energetic, tireless, proud of his country and its democracy and utterly in control of his government." With the nationalization of the oil industry, President Pérez "can now relate to us as an equal, without rancor or embarrassment."[99]

The U.S. recognition of Venezuela's new wealth and influence in Latin America was evident in Kissinger's discussion with Foreign Minister Escovar in Santiago in June 1976. The two men had become friends. They engaged in a review of the issue of human rights and the policies of Chile's General Pinochet. Escovar stated that it would be "useful" if the United States expressed a "clearer" position on democracy. Escovar added, "We believe there is a great tendency in the United States to favor authoritarianism to fight communism." Kissinger responded, "I agree completely the best defense against communism is democracy. Institutional processes are vital."[100] Kissinger's response to his friend was not sustained by the policies he pursued toward the military dictatorships of South America—Argentina, Bolivia, Brazil, Chile, Paraguay, and Uruguay.

In his memoirs, Kissinger boasted, "My visits to Latin America were warmly received" by the end of 1976. He favorably compared his receptions to the outbursts and protests that greeted Vice President Nixon in 1958 and Governor Rockefeller in 1969.[101] In fact, Kissinger could point to solid accomplishments in resolving bilateral issues with Mexico, Peru, Ecuador, and Venezuela. He had also prepared the way for a new treaty with Panama. He was a master diplomat when he tackled non–Cold War bilateral issues. But Kissinger also had significant failures in his approach to Latin America. As revealed in his conversation with President Pérez, his diplomacy broke down in multilateral fora. He also failed to broker a new relationship with Communist Cuba.

CHAPTER 7

Failed Initiatives

The New Dialogue, Cuba

Henry Kissinger proved to be an effective national security adviser and secretary of state. Working with President Richard Nixon, he helped destroy the Chilean government of Salvador Allende, facilitated a military *golpe* against the Bolivian government of Juan José Torres, and covertly intervened in the Uruguayan elections of 1972. Nixon and Kissinger relentlessly quashed perceived communist threats to U.S. hegemony in Latin America. Kissinger also promoted the regional and global aspirations of authoritarian Brazil. He further persuaded Nixon to resolve border grievances that Mexico had with the United States. As secretary of state, he found imaginative solutions to nettlesome bilateral issues with several South America nations. And he went a long way toward leading the United States to a new relationship with Panama, especially with regard to control over the canal and the Canal Zone. Secretary of State Kissinger had, however, two notable failures in his approach to Latin America. He failed to deliver on his promise of a new multilateral relationship with Latin America. He also failed to temper the hostility that had existed since 1959 between the United States and Fidel Castro's Cuba.

The New Dialogue

Within two weeks after being confirmed by the U.S. Senate, the new secretary of state announced a bold initiative for Latin America. On 5 October 1973, at an elegant luncheon on Park Avenue in New York City for members of the Center for Inter-American Relations, Kissinger proclaimed in a toast that he wanted a new approach to the region.[1] A few months previously, he had announced the "Year of Europe." Now, apparently, Latin America would also have its time in the sun. Dubbing his approach "the New Dialogue," Kissinger promised to negotiate on a multilateral basis and to focus on the pressing issues of investment and trade, development, technology transfers, and economic justice. Responding to the initiative, Latin American foreign ministers produced an eight-point agenda of economic issues for discussion at a meeting held in Bogotá in November 1973.[2]

Kissinger decided to announce the initiative for several reasons. Two days before the luncheon, former Secretary of State Dean Rusk telephoned Kissinger to offer congratulations to the new secretary. Rusk gently noted to Kissinger that Latin Americans felt "neglected" and urged him to rectify this through "flattery." Rusk suggested a cruise on the Potomac River for Latin American ambassadors to the United States and the OAS. Rusk believed the ambassadors would enjoy writing to their respective capitals about their experience sailing the Potomac with the celebrated Kissinger. Kissinger welcomed Rusk's idea but responded that he could accomplish the mission with his luncheon.[3] Kissinger had hardly neglected Latin America. Latin American citizens who cherished the principles of constitutionalism and democracy immediately suspected that the Nixon administration had played some role in the overthrow of Allende on 11 September 1973. The New Dialogue might show that the United States was not consumed by anticommunism. The luncheon also came one day before the outbreak of the Arab-Israeli War and subsequent oil embargo. The economic relationship between the prosperous, industrial "North" and the developing "South" became a contested global topic for a few years. The U.N. Commission on Latin America (ECLA), which had been founded by the prominent Argentine economist Raúl Prebisch, argued that the oil embargo exposed the weakness of the North and underscored the new strength of the global South.[4]

For a few months, Kissinger cheerfully engaged in the New Dialogue. He now acknowledged what he had often previously denied—that a "special relationship" existed between the United States and Latin America. He told U.S. legislators that he wanted a new, mature relationship with the southern neighbors, adding, "If we cannot do it with countries with whom we have similar cultures and more or less the same political heritage, we cannot do it anywhere." Kissinger initially had to overcome the resistance of his president, who preferred just to tell Latin Americans that "we love them." Nixon wanted that all discussion centered on the attraction of private capital and the treatment of U.S. corporations in Latin America. Anything else, in Nixon's words, was "pretty flimsy stuff."[5] Nonetheless, Kissinger enjoyed his three days in February 1974 in Tlatelolco (an area in Mexico City), swapping ideas with Latin America's foreign ministers. Kissinger, who disliked listening to speeches, appreciated the format of the conference, which sharply limited formal addresses. He proudly reported to U.S. ambassadors that "the most significant outcome of the meeting was the beginning of a new mood of confidence among the Latins in the sincerity of U.S. intentions and a sense of excitement regarding the future of U.S.-Latin American relations."[6] Although Kissinger reveled in the attention he garnered at Tlatelolco, he had not abandoned the traditional U.S. policy of preserving a sphere of influence. He explained to his staff, "What we're trying to do is prevent Latin America from sliding into the non-aligned bloc and compounding our problems all over the world." Kissinger could foresee larger Latin American nations acting like France and forming a bloc that was "defined by opposition to the United States." But "on the positive side," Kissinger asserted, "Latin Americans still are flattered to cooperate with us—or, at least flatter us when we show an interest in working with them."[7]

The good feelings engendered at the talkfest at Tlatelolco could only be sustained by concrete results. The foreign ministers established working groups to consider issues such as the identification of common fiscal and tax problems and "principles applicable to transnational enterprises."[8] Kissinger sponsored a dinner for Latin American ambassadors in Washington in mid-April. He told President Nixon, who attended and gave a brief speech, that the major point of the dinner was "to give them the sense that they've moved to the center of our attention, historic relationships." Nixon asked, "What you want is just a more friendly gesture, don't you?" Nixon had previously observed in the telephone conversation, "We don't like them that well." Kissinger responded, "What is most important is the warm gesture." Kissinger fussed over the seating arrangements and the size of the gathering, which amounted to over one hundred guests. At the president's suggestion, the First Lady, Kissinger's new bride, Nancy Maginnes, and the wives of the Latin Americans attended. In Nixon's view, extending an invitation to women made the dinner less significant.[9]

Exhilaration in inter-American relations lasted only a few more months. Constitutional governments, such as Mexico and Venezuela, wanted to repeal economic sanctions against Cuba and reincorporate Cuba into the inter-American community. The sanctions had been imposed by the OAS in 1964 in response to Cuba's alleged violation of Venezuela's sovereignty in November 1963. Kissinger was prepared to ask Nixon to avoid penalizing U.S. corporations that made goods in Argentina and sold them to Cuba.[10] But as he explained to his friend Emilio Rabasa, Mexico's foreign minister, "I have a massive problem with my President." For personal and political reasons, Nixon would not countenance any fundamental change in the U.S. isolation of Cuba. President Ford would eventually permit Kissinger to explore a new approach toward Cuba. At an inter-American conclave held in Quito in November 1974, a resolution calling for the lifting of sanctions against Cuba failed to attract the requisite two-thirds vote. Recriminations flowed, with Latin American delegates blaming the United States for not pressing the South American military dictatorships to favor the resolution. Anger also erupted over the Trade Act of 1974 and the exclusion of OPEC members Ecuador and Venezuela from the generalized system of trade preferences. From the Latin American perspective, the United States was violating the spirit of the New Dialogue by directing economic coercion against Ecuador and Venezuela. A conference to be held in Buenos Aires in early 1975 to implement concrete measures that would address Latin America's economic issues was shelved. On 1 March 1975, Kissinger implicitly buried multilateralism and the New Dialogue in a major speech he gave on inter-American relations in Houston. He had accepted the advice of aides to focus hereafter on bilateral issues.[11]

Kissinger lamented to his Houston audience that "Latin America is perennially tempted to define its independence and unity through opposition to the United States." In his memoirs, Kissinger quoted a State Department memorandum that asserted, "The dominant political fact is that the United States remains the one country in the hemisphere able to invoke regional unity— against itself."[12] Kissinger probably did not appreciate the irony inherent in such analyses. Scholars have pointed out that in the mid-nineteenth century, the citizens of the nation-states in Middle, Central, and South America began to use the term "Latin America" as a form of protest against U.S. interventionism. In particular, they called for regional unity to oppose William Walker's filibustering campaign (1855–1857) to create an English-speaking slave state in Nicaragua. "Latin Americans" erupted when President Franklin Pierce extended diplomatic recognition to Walker's Nicaragua.[13] Kissinger should have understood that Latin American constitutionalists and democrats would have judged his declaration that the relationship with Latin America was based on the "principles of non-intervention, the sovereign equality of nations, and mutual respect among partners" to be an ironic, if not hypocritical, statement. Kissinger had violated those principles in his efforts to destabilize Bolivia and Chile and influence electoral results in Uruguay. Irony also infused Kissinger's failure to grasp that the Latin Americans were practicing "realism" in foreign policy. As U.S. Ambassador to Mexico John Joseph Jova recalled, Kissinger had said, "What we want is the Latin Americans to get together and establish unified positions and then we can negotiate with them." Kissinger, the self-proclaimed practitioner of realism, did not like the results.[14] In developing unified positions on trade, investment, and prices, Latin Americans were deploying "balance of power" tactics against the hegemonic United States.

The collapse of the New Dialogue demonstrated that Kissinger did not trust multilateral initiatives in inter-American relations. In his innumerable meetings with Latin American officials—presidents, foreign ministers, ambassadors— Kissinger was unfailingly polite and upbeat. To be sure, he dominated conversations and made himself the focus of attention with his self-deprecating jokes. But he showed energy and skill in proposing solutions to both difficult and mundane bilateral issues. Secretary Kissinger ordered his staff, for example, to relieve the "Costa Ricans' anxiety for a minuscule increase in their meat quota."[15] He told aides and friends, "I like them [i.e., Latin Americans] personally."[16] Foreign Minister Rabasa was his *amigo*. He considered Colombian President Alfonso López Michelsen to be a philosopher-king. Kissinger also related well, of course, to authoritarians such as the murderous military generals who ruled Brazil. And he joined in ridiculing those who defended human rights in conversations with Uruguayan Foreign Minister Juan Carlos Blanco, the author of the preposterous doctrine of the Third World War against communist subversion. Nonetheless, the documentary record sustains Kissinger's observation in his memoirs that he enjoyed receiving the "warmth and affection I don't get anyplace else—including Europe." With Latin Americans, he wrote, "we have a sense of family."[17]

Exertions of regional independence, however, prompted Kissinger to take a patronizing, condescending tone toward the Latin American family. Whereas he liked individual officials, Kissinger thought that "efficiency was not their strong point." He confirmed Nixon's prejudices by informing the president that Latin American foreign ministers were "an ineffectual lot."[18] "Ineffectual" foreign ministers wanted the termination of economic sanctions against Cuba. Kissinger responded, "I don't mind changing our policy, but I do mind being pushed." Instead, he preferred manipulating family members. Flattery and his celebrity presence would produce results. He instructed President Ford that "the Latins and Arabs are two places [*sic*] where with flattery you can get more than you anticipated." Flattery included in engaging in sexist stereotypes. He remarked to Alejandro Orfilia, secretary general of the OAS, "The Latins understand men. They respect frankness. They respect men, not assistant professors of political science."[19] But the men of Latin America could fail to respect

Kissinger with a Latin American leader he admired, Colombian President Alfonso López Michelsen. Unusual for a secretary of state, Kissinger spent the night at the homes of Latin American officials. United States Information Services (USIS) photo.

U.S. power. In early 1975, when told the Buenos Aires conference would be postponed, Kissinger erupted: "What do we get from the new dialogue? It seems to me that the new dialogue consists of a list of things for us to do and there is not much interest in what Latin Americans can do for us."[20] In the aftermath of the postponement of the conference, Kissinger decided he would forego launching "any major U.S. initiatives for the hemisphere." The Latin American community had to learn not to feel "free, without serious penalty, to denounce the United States, even while looking to us for security and economic progress."[21]

Kissinger, Nixon, and Cuba

In his March 1975 speech in Houston, Secretary of State Kissinger noted, "We see no virtue in perpetual antagonism between the United States and Cuba."[22] Kissinger publicly announced what he had long believed. As he had remarked in September 1971 in a telephone conversation with Assistant Secretary of State for Inter-American Affairs Charles A. Meyer, "It isn't extraordinarily logical to say we want to talk to China but we wouldn't talk to Cuba." During the Nixon years, National Security Adviser Kissinger longed to open a dialogue with Cuba. But he was stymied by Nixon's obsessive hostility to Fidel Castro and the Cuban Revolution. As he further remarked to Meyer, "On this subject it is almost impossible to talk to the President." Discussing a new approach toward Castro's Cuba "hits the President's rawest nerve."[23] Only in the waning days of the Nixon presidency was Secretary of State Kissinger able to initiate an opening to Cuba. His secret efforts between 1974 and 1975 to normalize relations with Cuba would end in abject failure.

When President Nixon took office on 20 January 1969, the relationship between the United States and Cuba was antagonistic but stable. The bilateral relationship had moved a long way from what had transpired during what historian Michael Beschloss has labeled the "crisis years" (1960–1963) of the Cold War.[24] In March 1960, President Eisenhower had authorized a multifaceted "program" to overthrow the revolutionary government of Cuba. Part of Eisenhower's program included training, equipping, and supporting an army of exiled Cubans to invade the island of Cuba and foment a mass uprising against Castro.[25] President Kennedy put Eisenhower's program into action when he authorized the Bay of Pigs operation of April 1961. Fidel Castro and his military forces easily routed the invaders. Beginning in the Eisenhower years and continuing through the Kennedy presidency, the CIA launched a variety of bizarre efforts to assassinate Castro and other leaders of the revolution. In the aftermath of the Bay of Pigs disaster, President Kennedy authorized Operation Mongoose. Operating with a $50 million budget, four hundred CIA employees and thousands of Cuban exiles carried out raids against Cuba. The exiles used speedboats to make their way from Florida to Cuba to infiltrate the island. A Cuban official later cited "5,700 acts of terrorism, sabotage and murder" in 1962 alone. The Kennedy administration also continued to act like it intended to invade Cuba. In the spring of 1962, U.S. Marines trained for an amphibious assault by invading Vieques Island, Puerto Rico. The military exercise carried the codename "ORTSAC," or "Castro" spelled backward. Secretary of Defense Robert S. McNamara would later lament that the Kennedy administration was "hysterical" about Cuba.[26]

The U.S. war against Castro helped precipitate the momentous confrontation of the Cold War, the Cuban Missile Crisis of October 1962. In part, Cuban leaders accepted the offer of the Soviet Union to install nuclear missiles in Cuba because they feared the United States was preparing to invade the island. The thirteen-day crisis culminated with U.S. and Soviet leaders striking a deal over Cuba. The Soviets removed their nuclear-tipped missiles, and, in turn, the United States offered a "no-invasion pledge." But in the aftermath of the deal, the Kennedy administration conditioned its no-invasion pledge with the provisos that Cuba must cease being a source of communist aggression, that the United States reserved the right to halt subversion from Cuba, and that the United States intended for the Cuban people to gain their freedom one day. The administration did not believe that Cuba would ever conform to U.S. standards. President Kennedy consequently authorized the intensification of economic sanctions on Cuba. Assassination plots continued. In June and in November 1963, President Kennedy, dubbed "Higher Authority" in CIA parlance, approved new sabotage and terrorism attacks against Cuba. Kennedy's belligerence seemed justified when Venezuela announced in early November 1963 that it had discovered a cache of Cuban weapons on the Venezuelan coast. The weapons were allegedly left there for leftist radicals who wanted to disrupt the December 1963 Venezuelan presidential election.[27] In 1964, the United States used the arms cache issue to persuade two-thirds of the members of the OAS to support a resolution calling on member states to sever all political and economic ties with Cuba.

President Lyndon Johnson did not adopt his predecessor's approach to Cuba. He maintained economic sanctions against Cuba and tried to cajole European allies to sever political and economic ties with Cuba. In his characteristic salty language, Johnson wanted "to pinch their [i.e., Cuba's] nuts." More diplomatically, Johnson advised European governments that "economic sanctions against Cuba was the only weapon short of war that could make the support of Castro's Cuba more costly to the Soviet Union." The United States argued that an embargo of trade could create "conditions of economic stringency that might ultimately bring about the elimination of the Communist regime." Some friends succumbed to U.S. pressure. Belgium, for example, canceled a sale of locomotives to Cuba. But Prime Minister Sir Alec Douglas-Home of the United Kingdom rejected a personal appeal from President Johnson during the prime minister's visit to the White House in 1964. The United Kingdom continued to trade with Cuba, because it depended on international trade for its economic vitality.

Although he tried to strangle the Cuban economy, President Johnson proved less militaristic toward Cuba than President Kennedy had been. He seems to have been repelled by the nature of some U.S. actions, such as assassination plots. He told CIA Director John McCone that he no longer wanted his CIA chief to have the image of a "cloak and dagger role." After he left office, Johnson confessed in an interview, "We were running a damned Murder Incorporated in the Caribbean." Johnson also terminated the funding and support of Cuban exile groups that attacked Cuba. On 19 December 1963, at his first briefing on the covert war against Castro, CIA officials reviewed the sabotage and terrorism attacks that "Higher Authority" had approved in June and November 1963. Johnson asked the pointed question "whether there is any significant insurgency within Cuba." Desmond Fitzgerald, the CIA official who directed the covert campaign, admitted, "There is no national movement on which we can build." Johnson ordered the CIA to cancel its next attack on a major target—a power plant in Matanzas, Cuba. By June 1965, the United States no longer waged covert, violent war against Cuba. Johnson had accepted the uncomfortable truth that Castro retained widespread popular support and that exile attacks on the island were unlikely to inspire a massive uprising against the Castro regime. As Assistant Secretary for Latin America Thomas Mann calculated, "As long as that army is loyal to him [i.e., Castro], he is going to be there until he dies." Mann further observed in a memorandum to Secretary of State Dean Rusk that Cuban political figures in exile in Miami had little support within Cuba.[28]

The Johnson administration found it easier to accept the presence of a communist regime in the Western Hemisphere because it understood that the Soviet Union had accepted ground rules for its support of Castro. By 1969, the Soviet Union was providing Cuba with $1 million a day in economic and military aid. The aid blunted the U.S. effort to generate chaos on the island with trade embargoes and economic sanctions. But the price the Soviet Union exacted for the aid was the demand that the Cubans cease exporting revolution in Latin America. The Soviet Union did not want a repeat of the Cuban Missile Crisis. It was not in the interest of the Soviet Union to challenge the United States in its traditional sphere of influence. Castro had to learn to follow the Soviet Union's lead and remember that within the global socialist movement, Soviet security had the highest priority. When Castro visited the Soviet Union in May 1963, Premier Nikita Khrushchev informed the Cuban that Moscow would not support armed insurrection in Latin America. A Cuban official would later say that Castro believed that Khrushchev wanted nothing to do with Latin America and "would never send a single revolver to the region." The next Soviet leader, Leonid Brezhnev (1964–1982), erupted when he found out in 1966 that the Argentine revolutionary Ernesto "Che" Guevara was in Bolivia with Castro's blessing, albeit not his material support. Brezhnev's colleague Alexei Kosygin delivered a rebuke to Castro in mid-1967, demanding that Cuba cease meddling in Latin America. Kosygin had just concluded the Glassboro Summit with President Johnson and implied to the president that he would deliver such a message to Castro. Bolivian troops caught and executed the emaciated and bedraggled Guevara in October 1967. Guevara and his small band of mainly Cuban-born guerrillas had generated little support among the peasants of southeastern Bolivia. The Bolivians, many of whom were of indigenous heritage and did not speak Spanish, did not like foreigners in their country. They informed Bolivian troops of Guevara's guerrillas. The death of Guevara symbolized the collapse of 1960s revolutionary movements. A State Department officer summarized in 1967 that "the confident predictions of sweeping Communist victories which have often emanated from Havana have not been borne out." A year later, an NIE entitled "The Potential for Revolution for Latin America" confirmed that finding. The intelligence community found that "in no case do insurgencies pose a serious short-run threat to take over a government."[29]

During the Nixon presidency, intelligence analysts continued to conclude that Castro no longer embraced revolution. On 28 August 1971, in his daily brief, President Nixon was informed that, following the Che Guevara fiasco, Castro had reassessed his policy of supporting rebel groups. Havana had "sharply reduced its aid to guerrilla-oriented revolutionary movements in Latin America." Castro now wanted to end his isolation in the hemisphere and build normal ties with Cuba's Latin American and Caribbean neighbors. The CIA followed that report with a study in September 1971 that reported, "Havana's involvement in this activity [i.e., violent subversion] is at its lowest level since Fidel Castro assumed power." In January 1972, another PDB asserted that Castro had changed his "aggressive tactics" over the past four years and was "now engaged in a more conventional pursuit of economic and political ties with selected countries in the region." Soviet authorities had pressured Castro to give up his revolutionary adventures, "which Moscow saw as both unrealistic and damaging to its own strategy for increasing Communist influence in the area." In June 1973, a PDB recounted that Castro had stayed on course and that his new strategy was "bearing fruit." Argentina, Chile, Barbados, Guyana, Jamaica, Peru, and Trinidad-Tobago had reestablished relations with Cuba.[30] To be sure, Castro could not always contain himself. He peppered Salvador Allende with unsolicited and unwanted advice. Allende demanded that Castro abandon his plans to supply arms to extreme leftists in Chile.[31]

Castro's decision to seek regular diplomatic relations with his neighbors caught the attention of the new national security adviser. Moreover, the NSC received reports in early 1969, through Switzerland's ambassador in Havana, that Castro was interested in a dialogue with the United States.[32] Cuba further wanted to resolve the issue of the hijacking of planes and reach an accord with the United States. Between 1968 and 1972, there were 325 global hijackings. Of these, 173 of the planes were diverted to Cuba. Pushing Kissinger to think about an examination of U.S. policy toward to Cuba was his NSC staffer Viron Vaky, the veteran diplomat to Latin America. Kissinger expressed confidence in Vaky and relied on him for advice on inter-American affairs.[33] Vaky prepared a memorandum for Kissinger that was sent to the president.

Vaky penned that Cuba was not presently "a neuralgic problem." But the question was "whether we are missing opportunities to affect the future and whether we should study changing circumstances and likely future developments to determine that."[34] For his own reasons, President Nixon favored a review of policy.

Kissinger presided over an examination of Cuban policy in 1969. At Kissinger's request, the CIA produced several studies on past U.S. policies toward Cuba and the potential for renewed attacks on Cuba, including paramilitary missions, economic warfare, and recognizing a Cuban government in exile. The CIA retained its pessimism about the feasibility of U.S. actions that had caused President Johnson and Assistant Secretary Mann to conclude that Castro would rule Cuba until he died. Reviewing the past, the CIA noted that between 1961 and 1967 the United States had conducted over 400 maritime infiltration missions into Cuba. What successes the raids achieved were outweighed by the negative reaction they engendered both in Cuba and throughout the world. As the CIA noted, "It can be argued that the raids consolidated internal support of Fidel Castro to a degree far surpassing the damage done to the Cuban physical plant." The CIA found it "not feasible" to believe that the United States could impose a global trade embargo on Cuba or engage in "the utilization of incendiary devices against Cuban ships." The CIA also judged that Castro remained in control and secure at home.[35] Under Secretary of State Elliot Richardson warned Kissinger that to recognize a provisional Cuban government in exile "would be universally viewed as tantamount to a declaration of war against Castro's Cuba." Richardson added that such a move would alienate most Latin American nations.[36] Thomas L. Hughes, the director of the State Department's Bureau of Intelligence and Research, advised that the Soviet Union, Castro's patron, favored a relaxation in U.S.-Cuban tensions. Soviet leaders reasoned that such a rapprochement might help lessen their Cuban economic burden, moderate Castro's behavior, and improve Soviet-American relations.[37]

Analytic studies demonstrating the bankruptcy of U.S. policy toward Cuba made no impression on President Nixon. In September 1969, when he read about a Cuban official speculating that there could be an improvement in relations, Nixon instructed an aide to deliver a two-word message to Kissinger and the State Department: "Absolutely not."[38] Whereas the president could imagine a new relationship with the Soviet Union and the People's Republic of China, he would not contemplate shaking Fidel Castro's hand. Nixon had persuaded himself that the issue of communism in Cuba had led to his defeat at the hands of Senator Kennedy in the 1960 presidential election. In 1959, the Cubans had traded a right-wing dictator for a left-wing dictator. Fulgencio Batista had been friendly toward the United States, whereas Castro turned out to be "an implacable and dangerous enemy."[39] Nixon especially blamed the State Department and officials such as Assistant Secretary of State for Latin America R. Richard Rubottom and William A. Wieland, the director of the Office of Caribbean Affairs, for misleading him. Within weeks after taking office, Nixon warned Kissinger that the State Department "careerists are pro-Castro for the most part."[40] Nixon also commiserated with his bitterly anti-Castro, Cuban-American *amigo* in Florida, Charles "Bebe" Rebozo. Kissinger once lamented to Secretary of State William P. Rogers that "as long as the President is in Florida, he will do anything" when it came to Cuba.[41] If he needed a realpolitik rationale for his policy, CIA Director Richard Helms provided it at a 25 March 1970 meeting in the Oval Office. Nixon asked Helms for advice. Helms recommended no change in the policy of isolating Cuba. Helms observed that Cuba was costing the Soviet Union a million dollars a day and causing financial "headaches" for the Soviet authorities. Nixon responded, "You have convinced me." Kissinger was present at the meeting with Helms.[42] President Nixon had delivered a message to his national security adviser.

During the Nixon years, Cuban exile groups such as Alpha-66 continually launched paramilitary attacks on Cuba. Cuban armed forces regularly crushed the invaders. Viron Vaky recommended to Kissinger that the Department of Justice be brought in to prosecute Cuban exiles who violated U.S. law when they attacked Cuba from U.S. soil. Both CIA Director Helms and General Alexander M. Haig, a presidential assistant, responded to Vaky's recommendation by noting that Nixon favored the anti-Castro activity of Alpha-66.[43] State Department officer Ronald D. Goddard, who oversaw Cuban affairs from Miami and then Washington, recalled that the United States did not enforce its neutrality laws. There were no prosecutions of Cubans "unless they really went beyond the pale," as when a Cuban exile fired a round from a bazooka at a visiting Soviet vessel docked in Miami Harbor.[44] President Nixon became apoplectic in mid-December 1971 when he learned that Cubans had seized the *Johnny Express* and its Cuban-American captain and crew off the coast of the Bahamas. The ship carried a Panamanian flag and was seized in British territorial waters. In a series of telephone calls from Key Biscayne, Florida, to Kissinger, Secretary of State Rogers, and Secretary of Defense Melvin R. Laird, Nixon became unhinged. He had just met with the wife of the captain. Nixon was "god-damned mad." In the president's words, it "was a case of piracy on the high seas by an international outlaw," and he demanded "a plan to go in and shoot them up." Kissinger, Rogers, and Laird tried to calm Nixon by pointing out that under international law this was a case for Panama and the United Kingdom. Neither nation perceived the ship seizure as an attack on its sovereignty. At the outset of the faux crisis, Kissinger suggested to Nixon that the *Johnny Express* could have been on a raid against Cuba.[45] Indeed, in August 1972,

William Jorden of the NSC confirmed Kissinger's suspicions. The *Johnny Express* had been used as a "mother ship" for infiltration raids into Cuba.[46]

The election of Salvador Allende in Chile in late 1970 strengthened Nixon's vow: "I'm not changing the policy towards Castro as long as I'm alive."[47] Allende resumed relations with Cuba in early 1971. Nixon thought that a relaxation of his policy toward Cuba would signal to Allende and other Latin American leftists that he would accept Latin American leaders that he judged threats to U.S. national security. In the midst of the *Johnny Express* incident, Nixon told Kissinger, "Probably only you know how I feel about the Cuban business." He promised Kissinger to write "a memorandum on this and on Allende which is for your eyes only so you will know in the future how far I am willing to go."[48] Significant progress in bilateral relations did not deter Nixon on Cuba. Through the good offices of the government of Switzerland, the United States and Cuba struck a deal in early 1973 on air piracy. The United States and Cuba agreed to punish or extradite hijackers of airplanes.[49] The State Department informed its diplomatic posts throughout Latin America of the good news, hoping the agreement would "serve as an effective deterrent to this serious crime." But at Nixon's request, the State Department informed its diplomats that they could inform their host governments that the United States "firmly supports OAS sanctions respecting Cuba and intends to continue doing so until Cuba alters its policies toward the hemisphere."[50]

According to a study team commissioned to review Cuban policy, the United States had two fundamental issues with communist Cuba. Cuba had served as a base for Soviet military power, and it had exported "revolutionary doctrine and violence" to Latin America. The "double-barreled" problems had seemingly disappeared.[51] The Soviet Union had agreed in October 1962 not to deploy offensive weapon systems to Cuba, and Cuba had gradually accepted the Soviet Union's injunction that it should not meddle in Latin America. Castro was promoting normal diplomatic relations with Caribbean and Latin American nations. But in September 1970, the specter of the Soviet Union using Cuba to project military power in the Western Hemisphere briefly returned. U.S. surveillance planes photographed evidence of the Soviets constructing facilities on Alcatraz Island, a tiny dot of land in Cienfuegos Bay in southern Cuba, that could service, or "tender," Soviet submarines. This would presumably permit Soviet submarines armed with nuclear missiles to patrol for longer periods of time in waters close to the United States. Both Richard Nixon and Henry Kissinger have celebrated the resolution of the issue in their respective memoirs. They chose to hide the development from the public, approach the Soviets quietly, and permit the Soviets "to back away from the crisis by denying it ever existed." Kissinger effectively used his back channel with Soviet

Ambassador Anatoli Dobrynin to communicate the resolve of the United States. The dismantling of the facilities on Alcatraz Island further confirmed the validity of the 1962 deal that ended the missile crisis. Nixon and Kissinger favorably compared their performance to President Kennedy's chancy issuing of a public ultimatum to the Soviet Union on 22 October 1962. As Nixon pointedly instructed in his memoirs, "Through strong but quiet diplomacy we had averted what would have been known as the Cuban Nuclear Submarine Crisis of 1970 and which, like its predecessor, might have taken us to the brink of nuclear confrontation with the Soviet Union."[52]

Nixon and Kissinger addressed the submarine tender issue solely within the context of Soviet-American relations. They assumed that Cuba had become dependent on Soviet largesse and went along with Soviet military planning. They further judged that the Soviets would sacrifice Cuba if it came to a Soviet-American confrontation. In the president's words, "Even though the strategic balance has changed drastically since 1962 the Soviets would never trade Russia for Havana." Minutes of discussions about the Soviet submarines demonstrate that other key officials, such as Admiral Thomas H. Moorer, chairman of the Joint Chiefs of Staff, agreed with Nixon and Kissinger's analyses.[53] To be sure, Nixon thought that the crisis presented an opportunity to damage the hated Castro. Responding to a Kissinger report on 18 September 1970 about activities in Cienfuegos Bay, Nixon demanded on a "crash basis" a recommendation for "what CIA can do to support *any* kind of action which will irritate Castro."[54] Only Viron Vaky, with his sensitivity to the Latin American viewpoint, tied the submarine issue to Cuba's national security concerns. On 5 October 1970, he forwarded a report to Kissinger from the Canadian embassy in Havana. The Canadians believed that Castro was preoccupied with exile activity and feared an exile invasion, perhaps from Central America. Although Cuban forces had "rolled up" the recent forays by Alpha-66 invaders, the exiles had carried with them sophisticated weapons and clandestine equipment. Vaky purposely remarked that the Department of Defense had "the capacity for clandestine support of such activity." Vaky also warned Alexander Haig in the White House that Cuban exiles had plotted to assassinate Cuban diplomats at the United Nations. In Vaky's reasoning, these attacks on Cuba suggested an answer to the question of "what the Cubans got out of agreeing to Soviet construction at Cienfuegos." Perhaps the Cubans received increased military aid from the Soviets to repel the exile attacks. From Vaky's perspective, the exile raids were "unguided missiles" that sent the wrong signals to the Soviets and the Cubans.[55]

Henry Kissinger agreed with Viron Vaky that the exile attacks damaged U.S. foreign policy. By the end of 1971, he had an ally in General Haig, who carried the title of deputy assistant to the president for national security affairs. Haig wanted Kissinger to make an oral approach to Nixon on the exile raids "so that the President [would] not have to treat this as a test of his manhood." Haig noted that the U.S. government had been inhibiting exile activity "and thus in conflict with the President's handwritten directive." Kissinger and Haig agreed that exile attacks risked retaliatory actions by the Soviets. The Soviets might resume naval activity in the Caribbean and increase military aid to Cuba. They also accepted the findings of intelligence analysts that "the exile groups have *virtually no capability to mount meaningful operations* against Cuba."[56] Neither man was able, however, to persuade Nixon to issue an explicit directive putting the full force of the government into upholding U.S. neutrality laws. Moreover, some elements of Nixon's national security team dissented from Kissinger and Haig's judgment. CIA Director Helms protested when, in early 1972, the State Department issued a public warning to Cuban exiles not to attack Cuba from U.S. soil. Helms grumbled, "It seems to me we go out of our way to make things tough for that tiny number of individuals who are prepared to do something active, if not always useful."[57] Sporadic exile raids against Cuba continued, and the U.S. continued to sponsor hostile actions within Cuba. In January 1974, Kissinger asked General Brent Scowcroft of the NSC to make sure that no clandestine activities occurred in Cuba between 26 and 28 January. Soviet Premier Brezhnev would be visiting the island on those days.[58]

Kissinger, Ford, and Cuba

After he became secretary of state in September 1973 and through the rest of the Nixon presidency, Henry Kissinger made small but significant gestures to signal to Castro's Cuba that the United States was interested in opening a dialogue. He persuaded President Nixon to grant an exemption to permit subsidiaries of U.S. businesses in Argentina to trade with Cuba. Nixon grudgingly perceived the exemption as a way to conciliate Argentina and protect U.S. businesses in Argentina from retaliation. But he would not change policy. For example, in March 1974, Nixon disapproved a license to permit a U.S. firm in Canada to sell locomotives to Cuba.[59] But as Nixon's power waned over the Watergate scandal, Kissinger acted without informing the president. He agreed to speak confidentially with U.S. business executives who wanted to make business contacts in Cuba. The amount of U.S. radio broadcast hours aimed at Cuba, such as on Voice of America, was reduced in mid-1974.[60] Most important, in April 1974, Kissinger asked Frank Mankiewicz to carry an unsigned, handwritten note to Castro. Mankiewicz, who directed the Peace Corps in Latin

America and had worked in the presidential campaigns of Senator Robert Kennedy and Senator George McGovern, was now a political journalist and would later become the president of National Public Radio. Nixon considered Mankiewicz a "political enemy." Mankiewicz, however, told Kissinger that he was a "great admirer" of Kissinger's diplomacy. Mankiewicz traveled to Havana in July 1974 to film an interview with Castro. In the note, Kissinger suggested that the United States and Cuba should discuss bilateral issues discreetly and through intermediaries. Castro responded positively and gave Mankiewicz a box of cigars to present to Kissinger. A U.S. Customs officer tried to seize the cigars as contraband. Mankiewicz responded by warning, "Son, this box of cigars is a personal gift for Secretary of State Henry Kissinger. Are you sure you want to take them away?" Kissinger received his present from Cuba. The secretary did not, however, smoke.[61]

Kissinger informed President Ford about his initiatives toward Cuba on 15 August 1974, a week after Ford assumed the presidency. Ford had received an extensive briefing paper on Cuba prepared in the State Department. Kissinger told Ford that Castro wanted to meet with the secretary of state. Kissinger opposed a "high visibility" meeting, but he observed to Ford, "We have to loosen up or we isolate ourselves." The strategy he recommended on Cuba was to move slowly, even diffidently, and "to treat Cuba low-key as just another country." Kissinger ended the conversation by stating the obvious when he observed, "Nixon had strong personal views on Cuba. This would be a change of his policy."[62]

Secretary of State Kissinger called for a fresh approach toward Cuba for several reasons. As indicated in his diplomacy toward the Soviet Union and the People's Republic of China, Kissinger accepted the value of speaking with communist adversaries. As he explained to Argentine Foreign Minister Alberto Vignes, "From the foreign policy standpoint it would help to remove anomalies in our relations with other countries."[63] And Cuba posed no threat to the United States or hemispheric security. Intelligence analysts continued to report that Cuban efforts to overthrow Latin American governments were "at a low ebb." "Tangible support" for revolutionary movements was "negligible."[64] The U.S.-aided destruction of Chilean constitutionalism made certain that Nixon's fatuous fear that Castro's Cuba and Allende's Chile would envelop the rest of Latin America in a "red sandwich" would never take place. Kissinger also grasped that Latin Americans judged U.S. policy toward Cuba an anachronistic remnant of the Cold War past. A majority of Latin American countries had concluded that the cost of maintaining sanctions against Cuba outweighed the benefits. In particular, the democratic stalwarts of northern South America— Colombia and Venezuela—now saw "the policy as a relic overtaken by détente" and "a bar to greater Latin American unity."[65] Colombia and Venezuela had led the movement in the early 1960s to exclude Cuba from the inter-American community. Only the anticommunist military dictatorships in southern South America continued to oppose an opening to Cuba. A détente with Cuba would also represent a major diplomatic triumph and burnish Secretary Kissinger's eminent international reputation.

From August 1974 through 1975, Kissinger moved cautiously and quietly in regard to Cuba. He advised President Ford that diplomatic relations should not be restored until after the 1976 presidential elections.[66] Kissinger assumed that he would be secretary of state in 1977 and afterward. On 30 August 1974, Kissinger authorized a study to consider what the United States wanted from Cuba as the price for the resumption of diplomatic relations. He allowed Senator Jacob Javits (R-NY) and former Senator Charles Goodsell (R-NY) to travel to Cuba. He wanted limited publicity for the trips, advising them to travel to Cuba through Mexico and reminding them that they could not be official emissaries. As he told Goodsell, "We are in contact and they [i.e., the contacts] have to be kept to one channel." Kissinger approved greater travel opportunities for Cubans to the United States, although he opposed Cuban delegates attending a high visibility World Energy Conference held in Detroit in September 1974. And in early 1975, he rejected the idea of having a Major League Baseball team play exhibition games in Cuba.[67] He also opposed permitting Cuba to send a delegate to an inter-American foreign minister's meeting scheduled for Buenos Aires in early 1975. The Buenos Aires conclave was subsequently canceled. But Kissinger worked out a formula at the OAS meeting held in San José, Costa Rica, in July 1975 that gave OAS members the right to resume political and economic relations with Cuba. Sixteen nations, including the United States, voted for the "Freedom of Action" resolution. Five nations, all right-wing military dictatorships, either opposed or abstained on the resolution.[68] Kissinger thereafter recommended to President Ford that the United States terminate its obligatory sanctions on Latin American countries that traded with Cuba and modify its restrictions on subsidiaries of U.S. companies in Latin America that wanted to export to Cuba. He advised the president, "These steps will be recognized as constructive ones by Castro and will put the onus on him to take the next conciliatory gestures towards us." On 15 September 1975, Kissinger, on behalf of the president, issued NSDM 305: "Termination of U.S. Restrictions on Third Countries Trading with Cuba."[69]

In a freewheeling discussion on 9 June 1975 with trusted aides Deputy Under Secretary Lawrence S. Eagleburger and Assistant Secretary for Latin America William D. Rogers, Secretary of State Kissinger laid out his game plan for normalizing relations with Cuba. As he often did, Kissinger used Rogers as his foil, pushing against the idea that the United States should put much thought or effort into relations with Cuba. Given his portfolio, Rogers was naturally enthusiastic about achieving a diplomatic breakthrough. He also observed that the United States had "few cards" to play with Cuba. Kissinger protested that Cuba was "not a popular issue," that Cuba was "not important," and that "Cuba can do nothing for us except to embarrass us in Latin America." Kissinger further asserted that it was "not my style of work" to establish diplomatic relations before achieving an agreement that Cuba would compensate the United States for properties expropriated after the revolution of 1959. Rogers, who was never intimidated by Kissinger, shot back that "this was the way it was done with China." The United States established a relationship with China before compensation was agreed upon. After more banter, Kissinger agreed with Rogers's recommendation that a message be sent to Fidel Castro. He concluded, "It is better to deal straight with Castro. Behave chivalrously; do it like a big guy, not like a shyster." In particular, Castro could be told that the United States was "moving in a new direction" and that Kissinger would consider meeting a Cuban official, albeit not Castro, at the United Nations. The United States would take steps to improve relations but "reciprocity [would be] necessary." Without good faith gestures from Cuba, Kissinger insisted, "we shall stop."[70]

The mid-1975 discussion between Kissinger, Eagleburger, and Rogers on how to proceed with Cuba was in the context of initial exploratory talks that had taken place on 11 January 1975. Facilitated by the good offices of Frank Mankiewicz, Eagleburger and Rogers had met with two Cuban diplomats for coffee at a cafeteria at LaGuardia Airport in Queens, New York. The meeting was cordial but lacked substance. The Cubans were not empowered to negotiate, although they noted that progress would be difficult as long as the United States maintained its economic blockade against Cuba. Eagleburger handed the Cubans a two-page document that Kissinger had approved. The document stated that the United States was interested in exploring "a more normal relationship between our two countries."[71] The document notably did not ask Cuba to undermine its revolution or transform its political system. Over the next several months, the United States would send four messages to Cuba but would receive no reply.

A substantial exchange of views took place on 9 July 1975, however, when Eagleburger and Rogers met again with the Cuban diplomats, Ramón Sánchez Parodi and Nestor García. The meeting was formal, with a banquet-style lunch in a suite at the Pierre Hotel in New York City. The meeting lasted more than four hours. Rogers opened the discussion by announcing the good news that Kissinger would be prepared to meet with a senior Cuban official at the United Nations. Rogers further informed the Cubans that the United States would support the "Freedom of Action" resolution at a forthcoming OAS meeting.

The United States, Rogers promised, would dismantle its economic blockade against Cuba, if Cuba addressed issues of concern to the United States. Among the nine issues Rogers raised were compensation, political prisoners, travel, family visits, press access, and Cuban respect for U.S. sovereignty over Puerto Rico. Eagleburger, serving as the voice of Kissinger, then added, "We are engaged in a process of mutual accommodation but . . . Cuba was not the single most important issue on our foreign relations agenda." The Cubans had anticipated the issues the United States would raise and gave detailed responses, although they continued to underscore that the blockade was a substantial barrier to substantive negotiations. They made the rhetorical point that Cuba could not reciprocate on the blockade issue, because their nation had not imposed an economic blockade on the United States. Rogers assessed the meeting positively. The meeting had been free of polemics. The Cubans had agreed to "discuss" the blockade issue but not "negotiate" the blockade. Rogers judged this a "verbal breakthrough."[72] A month later, a pleased Kissinger informed Ford about the meeting and received permission to meet with a Cuban official at the United Nations. Kissinger also added, "The next move is up to them."[73]

Cuba's next moves destroyed Kissinger's conception of a Cuban-American détente. Cuba first irritated U.S. officials by introducing in August 1975 a resolution at the United Nations to give special status to the Puerto Rican independence movement. Cuba had long pronounced the status of Puerto Rico a "colonial" issue. The reality was that the overwhelming majority of Puerto Ricans favored either the retention of commonwealth status or statehood but not independence. Kissinger authorized the State Department to send a "tough" note to the Cubans. As Eagleburger remarked, the Cuban action was "anything but a 'positive step' in keeping with the relationship we have been trying to develop."[74] Despite the Cuban interference, intelligence analysts predicted that the rapprochement in Cuban-American relations would continue. The CIA concluded that Castro desired to negotiate an improvement in relations "but did not want to appear anxious for reconciliation." A NIE on Cuba's changing international role, which was issued on 16 October 1975, predicted that Castro would engage in protracted discussions with the United States. The NIE guessed that "there is a better than even chance" that Castro would engage in substantive negotiations if the United States partially reduced the scope of its economic sanctions on Cuba. If substantive negotiations took place, Castro might pay a small percentage of the claims for expropriated U.S. properties and curtail Cuba's activities in support of independence for Puerto Rico. Castro would never, however, renounce his relationship with the Soviet Union or relinquish his self-perception as the leader of developing nations throughout the world, the so-called Third World.[75]

What closed the Cuban-American opening of 1974–1975 was indeed Castro's belief that he had the duty to play a prominent role on the global stage. In late 1975, Cuba rushed 30,000 troops to Angola to rescue a Marxist-led liberation movement that was fighting to gain control over the former Portuguese colony. The intervention shocked U.S. leaders, including Henry Kissinger, for the United States was working with the apartheid regime in South Africa to support purported anticommunist Angolans such as Jonas Savimbi. The Cubans routed the South African troops and their Angolan allies. Although the Angolan intervention of the mid-1970s surprised international observers, it represented the continuation of Cuba's African policy. Since 1962, Cuban volunteers, soldiers and doctors, had fought and worked in Africa. In response to Algerian requests, Castro dispatched arms and troops to assist Prime Minister Ahmen Ben Bella in securing his nation's independence. In late 1964, Che Guevara toured the continent to assess revolutionary possibilities. A year later, Guevara was in the African bush leading a column of Cuban fighters in Zaire. Between 1964 and 1974, small groups of Cuban combat troops assisted Guinea-Bissau fighters in the independence struggle of the Portuguese colony. Prior to the intervention in Angola, about 2,000 Cubans served in Africa, suffering nine fatalities. By comparison, historian Piero Gleijeses has calculated that only forty Cubans fought in Latin America during the 1960s, including Guevara's pathetic mission to Bolivia in 1967.[76] Kennedy and Johnson administration officials habitually exaggerated Cuban activities in the Western Hemisphere and barely noticed the Cuban intervention in Africa.

On 24 November 1975, Henry Kissinger declared to an audience in Detroit that his attempt to reconcile with Cuba would not survive "armed intervention in the affairs of other nations."[77] His declaration reflected both a realistic appraisal of the domestic and international milieu and the emotional outrage of a spurned suitor. With presidential campaign season approaching, President Ford could not countenance a détente with communist Cuba. He would be attacked repeatedly by Governor Ronald Reagan for negotiating a new arrangement for the Panama Canal with the friendly, noncommunist country of Panama. On 20 December, Ford announced that he had ended efforts to improve relations with Cuba in light of Cuban interference in Puerto Rico and Angola.[78] The intervention also seemingly threatened détente with the Soviet Union on the assumption that the Soviets had directed the intervention. In a conversation with Foreign Secretary James Callahan of the United Kingdom, Kissinger asserted that permitting 12,000 Cuban troops to march around Angola is simply incompatible with détente. Callahan agreed that officials of the Soviet Union needed to understand that détente was not limited to Europe.[79] In fact, Castro took the initiative and entangled the Soviets in the intervention. Kissinger also could legitimately point out that the intervention alarmed Latin American nations and not just the fanatically anticommunist military dictators. In February 1976, Kissinger visited Lima, Caracas, and Bogotá. Cuba was "much on the mind" of the leftist military rulers in Peru. President Carlos Andrés Pérez denounced the intervention in Angola when he hosted Kissinger at the presidential palace, Miraflores. Pérez worried that Cubans might send troops to neighboring Guyana, a country with which Venezuela had longstanding border disputes. Colombian President Alfonso López Michelsen fretted that Castro would ignite a race war in the Caribbean. The Colombian foresaw Castro "emerging from Angola as a successful fighter against white imperialism and with extraordinary credentials as the savior of the blacks everywhere."[80] Colombia and Venezuela had notably been the two democratic countries that had lobbied for the suspension of OAS sanctions against Cuba.

The last attempt at reconciliation occurred on 7 February 1976 when Deputy Under Secretary Eagleburger met with Nestor García in New York to discuss U.S. residents visiting their families in Cuba. The meeting was unproductive.[81] Intelligence analysts now abandoned their previous year's optimism about the future of Cuban-American relations. Cuban forces had triumphed militarily in Angola and enhanced Castro's international prestige. The Cuban Revolution was secure and successful, albeit still dependent on massive amounts of Soviet aid. In the aftermath of Vietnam, Watergate, and the Church Committee revelations about U.S. covert activities in Chile, Castro had concluded that "imperialism" was in eclipse and that "Communist and Third World forces [had] gained the upper hand." The CIA foresaw Cuban intervention throughout Africa—Rhodesia, Mozambique, Namibia, and Zaire. Cubans could be "expected to perform in Africa in a manner somewhat reminiscent of the European colonial powers of the last century."[82] The CIA proved ironically prescient. Between 1975 and 1991, over 43,000 Cuban civilians—health workers and educators—served in Angola. The teachers declined to learn Portuguese, reasoning that their Angolan students should be able to understand their Caribbean version of Spanish. The Cuban advisers also tried to impose "civilizatory" habits on Angolans in terms of personal conduct, hygiene, and sexual attitudes and practices. Angolan citizens grew to resent the imperial attitudes of Cubans as much as they despised the nostrums of their Portuguese colonial masters.[83]

Secretary Kissinger had badly misjudged Cuba's readiness to normalize relations with the United States. Castro would not compromise his independent foreign policy. As the CIA had put it, Cuba would "not sacrifice its revolutionary bona fides for the sake of détente."[84] Securing the end of U.S. economic sanctions would be helpful, but Castro reasoned that he could always count on the Soviets. And the economic blockade continued to provide Castro with a ready excuse in explaining the multiple economic failures of the Cuban Revolution. Kissinger reacted to Castro's rejection of his advances in petty and grandiose ways. In March 1976, he responded to suggestions that the United States lift passport restrictions on travel to Cuba: "Absolutely not. Out of the question." In 1975, he had no objection to Coca-Cola establishing a subsidiary in Cuba. When told in June 1976 by Joseph Califano, the former Secretary of Health, Education, and Welfare (who represented Coca-Cola), that Cuba was still interested in having the popular soft drink available in Cuba, Kissinger retorted, "We would be violently against it."[85]

Kissinger indeed thought violence should be aimed at Castro and the Cubans. On 15 March 1976, he vented his feelings in a meeting with President Ford. Kissinger advised the president, "Sooner or later we have to crack the Cubans." If the Cubans expanded their adventurism into Namibia or Rhodesia, Kissinger allowed, "I would be in favor of clobbering them." The secretary had previously talked tough about the Cubans in discussions with Iranian, Saudi, and Pakistani officials. He stated to Saudi Petroleum Minister Ahmad Zaki Yamani, "[The] next time Cuba attempts something like Angola, they will get into massive trouble. The War Powers Act gives us 60 days to do something, and I think we could take care of Cuba in that period." Kissinger told Pakistani Prime Minister Zulfikar Ali Bhutto that he believed "the Cubans have to be taught a lesson." President Ford responded by giving Kissinger permission to task the Washington Special Actions Group (WSAG) and the NSC to develop potential U.S. responses to Cuban interventionism.[86]

Talk of war filled the WSAG meeting of 24 March 1976. Representatives from the Departments of State and Defense, the Joint Chiefs of Staff, the CIA, and the NSC attended the meeting, which was chaired by Kissinger and held in the White House Situation Room. Secretary of Defense Donald Rumsfeld, perhaps surprised by the substance of the meeting, inquired, "Are you talking in terms of military planning?" He warned that action against Cuba could affect relations with the Soviet Union. Kissinger responded that a number of things could be looked at, including an invasion or blockade of Cuba. Kissinger conceded that a blockade could lead to a confrontation with the Soviet Union. Representing the CIA, General Vernon Walters promised a new proposal for a covert campaign against Cuba. Acting as the voice of moderation, Rumsfeld suggested a study of the U.S. political goals for Cuba and Africa before developing a plan for hostile actions against Cuba. Deputy Secretary of Defense William P. Clements disputed his boss, noting he was "appalled" by Cuban actions and wondering, "Are we just going to sit here and do nothing?" Clements later assured Kissinger that U.S. citizens were "mad" about Cuba and wanted action. Kissinger instructed General George S. Brown to develop plans for military operations and not to think of "halfway" measures. Kissinger added, "If we decide on a blockade it must be ruthless and rapid and efficient." Brown implicitly questioned Clements's thesis that the U.S. public favored war against Cuba and possibly the Soviet Union. Noting "the congressional angle," the general offered, "There is no sense in taking a course of action unless it can achieve its objectives quickly." National Security Adviser Brent Scowcroft observed that there were international and domestic constraints on U.S. actions. General Scowcroft opined that an invasion of Cuba "could be ruled out." An increasingly frustrated Kissinger fell back on the hoary "credibility" argument. If the United States could not do something about a country of eight million people, he said, "then in three or four years we are going to have a real crisis." But Kissinger grasped the tenor of the WSAG meeting. Key members of the national security bureaucracy did not want to go to war over Cubans in Angola. On 21 April 1976, the secretary of state lamented to President Ford, "[The] contingency plans aren't doing well and . . . no one but you and I are in favor of cracking the Cubans."[87]

Although Henry Kissinger did not fulfill his wish to "crack," "humiliate," or "clobber" the Cubans, violent actions against Cuba did ensue from Cubans based in the United States and in Latin America. Whether by circumstance, happenstance, or official design, Cuban exile attacks on Cuba mounted in 1976. A CIA paper developed in the spring of 1976 raised the possibility of "signaling interest in economic or military targets to clandestine sources in Cuba and to exiles in Florida."[88] On 19 April 1976, Coordinator of Cuban Affairs Culver Gleysteen reported to Assistant Secretary Rogers that militant exiles were operating again, with attacks on two Cuban fishing vessels and FBI reports of exile plans to attack Cuban embassy personnel, Soviet vessels, and Cubana de Aviación airplanes. Gleysteen recommended and Rogers approved issuing a statement that U.S. law enforcement agencies warn that that they would "vigorously enforce U.S. laws prohibiting the use of U.S. territory as a base for military actions against foreign countries."[89] On 24 May 1976, the State Department followed up by writing a letter to Attorney General Edward Levi asking him to condemn exile terrorism and to instruct FBI agents to redouble their efforts against militant exiles. On 31 April, a Cuban-American broadcaster, Emilio Milián, had lost his legs in a terrorist car bombing. The broadcaster, a fervent anticommunist, had publicly opposed exile terrorism. Other Cuban-Americans who called for reconciliation with Cuba had been assassinated. The Department of Justice rejected the State Department's request, however, arguing that a statement on exile terrorism could prejudice pending prosecutions of other Cubans accused of bombings.[90]

Cuban exile terrorism continued through 1976. Cuban exiles worked with Colonel Manuel Contreras of DINA and his assistant Michael Townley in the assassination of former Chilean Foreign Minister Orlando Letelier and Ronni Moffitt in Washington, DC, on 21 September 1976. Cuban exiles also perpetrated mass murder. On 6 October 1976, two bombs exploded on Cubana de Aviación Flight 455 eleven minutes after takeoff from Seawell Airport in Bridgetown, Barbados. The flight was bound for Jamaica. All seventy-three people aboard the Douglas DC-8 aircraft were killed. The passengers included the champion Cuban national fencing team and Guyanese intending to study at Cuban medical schools. Many of the fencing team members were teenagers. Two days later, the CIA denied to the State Department that it bore responsibility for the bombing, claiming, "The CIA has been out of the Cuban exile business for a long time."[91] Over the next two weeks, Assistant Secretary of State Henry Shlaudeman reported to Kissinger that "a small group of anti-Castro Cubans are the central actors in this and many other recent terrorist acts in the hemisphere." Shlaudeman linked the attack on Flight 455 to the assassinations of Letelier and Moffitt. Prime suspects in the bombing were Cuban exiles Orlando Bosch and Luis Posada Carriles. Both men, who were now in Venezuela, had extensive experience working with the CIA in the 1960s in attacking Cuba. CIA sources in Venezuela subsequently reported that Bosch bragged about his organization's assisting the assassination of Letelier and that Posada predicted the downing of a Cuban airplane. Shlaudeman reported to Kissinger that the evidence pointed to Posada planning the bombing.[92] Venezuelan authorities subsequently arrested Bosch and Posada, but the Venezuelan judicial system failed to convict them on grounds of lack of direct evidence.

Kissinger responded to the downing of Flight 455 slightly more forcefully than he had to the assassination of Letelier. On 16 September, five days before the bombing on Embassy Row in Washington, Kissinger had blocked sending a démarche to the South American military dictators who had enlisted in Operation Condor, warning them against international terrorism and assassination. In response to this latest outrage perpetrated by anticommunist zealots, Kissinger accepted Shlaudeman's recommendation that he sign a memorandum to Attorney General Levi expressing concern over Cuban exile activity and urging vigilance by the FBI. Kissinger opposed, however, issuing a public statement that went into detail about previous U.S. ties with the prime suspects in the bombing. In a speech on 15 October, a furious Fidel Castro had linked the bombers to the CIA. Castro alleged, "At the beginning we were uncertain whether the CIA had directly organized the sabotage or carefully prepared it through its covert organization formed by Cuban counterrevolutionaries. Now we decidedly believe the first assumption is correct." No evidence has ever surfaced to sustain Castro's extreme charges. But Cuba's intelligence agencies knew much about the relationship between the CIA and militant Cuban exiles. As Shlaudeman admitted to Kissinger, "The FBI and CIA probably have more information on these groups than all of the other interested governments, except Cuba itself." The task for the United States was to contain the "embarrassment" by calling for Barbados to assume jurisdiction over the bombing case. A worried Shlaudeman warned Kissinger that "should Cuba take jurisdiction by default the trial would be a propaganda feast for Fidel." The U.S strategy became a public relations exercise, shifting attention away from allegations of U.S. complicity in the bombing and stimulating cooperative efforts against terrorism in the Caribbean.[93]

Secretary of State Kissinger's détente policy toward Cuba proved a colossal failure. Cuban-American relations had not been normalized. Kissinger now insisted that the prerequisites for normalization included the withdrawal of Cuban combat troops from Angola and the end of Cuban support for Puerto Rican independence. Castro responded to the renewed hostility by suspending the 1973 airplane hijacking agreement.[94] The last months of Kissinger's tenure as secretary of state had been marked by two acts of international terrorism that were linked to U.S. Cold War policy toward Cuba. Kissinger had rejected action that might have stopped the assassinations of Orlando Letelier and Ronni Moffitt on U.S. soil. He and his aides also declined to act decisively to share evidence about what the United States knew about the prime suspects in the downing of Cubana de Aviación Flight 455. One of the prime suspects, Luis Posada Carriles, would allegedly be involved in future terrorist activities.[95]

Henry Kissinger could point to solid achievements in bilateral relations in the Western Hemisphere. He helped resolve, for example, the Colorado River salinity issue that had bedeviled U.S. relations with Mexico. He also could claim credit for hastening the historical transfer of the Panama Canal and the Canal Zone back to Panama. Latin Americans applauded his work on the canal issue. He lacked, however, the patience and persistence to develop a new, multilateral relationship with Latin America. The New Dialogue came to nothing. He also failed to reduce tensions between the United States and communist Cuba. Cuba bore equal responsibility for the failure of Kissinger's détente initiative. Kissinger would not, however, be primarily remembered in Latin America for his bilateral achievements and failures. He would be tied to U.S. interventions in Bolivia, Chile, and Uruguay and held accountable for his disregard for human rights in Latin America and his reluctance to oppose mass murder by right-wing tyrants in countries as disparate as Argentina and Guatemala.

Conclusion

The Judgment on Henry Kissinger in Latin America

This book has demonstrated that Henry Kissinger pursued ambitious and energetic policies toward Latin America during a critical period of the Cold War. Latin American citizens judge the overthrow of President Salvador Allende of Chile to be one of the most momentous events in the history of modern Latin America, and Kissinger has long been identified with the Chilean tragedy of 11 September 1973. But the war against Allende was not an isolated incident in Kissinger's approach toward the region. Militarism, murder, and mayhem characterized life in Central and South America during the 1970s. In the second decade of the twenty-first century, Latin Americans continue to investigate and prosecute those responsible for grotesque violations of human rights. Henry Kissinger aided and abetted the savage despots of the 1970s. On the other hand, Kissinger deployed his formidable diplomatic and negotiating skills to resolve a variety of long-standing bilateral economic disputes, and he worked tirelessly to transform the status of the Panama Canal. This conclusion offers a judgment of Kissinger's stewardship of U.S. policies toward Latin America by assessing his public defense of his policies, his place within the history of inter-American relations, and his responsibility for what befell much of the region in the 1970s.

Kissinger and His Memoirs

Some interpretative questions about Henry Kissinger can be readily evaluated. The commonplace assumption about Kissinger and Latin America is correct. Kissinger did not assign priority to relations with Latin America. His memoirs provide an accurate assessment of his judgment of the significance of Latin America in international affairs. Other than repeated attempts to absolve himself of participation in the campaign to destabilize the Chilean government, he scarcely mentioned Latin America in the first two volumes of his extensive memoirs. He devoted only one section of the third volume to recounting his approach toward Latin America. And he again returned to defending himself on charges that he bore responsibility for the demise of President Salvador Allende. Although he ultimately made an extensive tour of South America and visited Mexico, Central America, and the Caribbean, Kissinger often postponed his trips to Latin America, because he wanted to tend to other global issues in Southeast Asia or the Middle East that he judged more significant to U.S. national security. His bosses, Presidents Nixon and Ford, similarly discounted relations with Latin American nations. Except for brief visits to neighboring Mexico, neither president traveled to Latin America during his years in the White House.

This is not to say that critical developments in inter-American affairs did not happen between 1969 and 1977. The U.S.-aided overthrow of the constitutional government in Chile remains one of the most momentous episodes in the history of postindependence Latin America. The covert interventions in Bolivia and Uruguay had significant ramifications for the condition of human rights in both nations. Kissinger did not address either intervention in his memoirs. Mass murder, summary executions, and grotesque corruption characterized daily life in countries as different as Argentina, Brazil, Guatemala, and Nicaragua. The silence of Kissinger's memoirs on these outrages indicates that leading U.S. officials, including Kissinger, overlooked or dismissed concerns about them. International terrorists also struck within the Western Hemisphere. Orlando Letelier, the former Chilean foreign minister, and Ronni Moffitt, Letelier's twenty-five-year-old assistant and a U.S. citizen, were assassinated in Washington, DC. A Cuban commercial airliner was blown out of the sky by a bomb placed by Cuban exiles who had previously worked for the CIA. Kissinger chose not to denounce these terrorist incidents or explain what actions he might have taken to prevent them. On the other hand, his memoirs address certifiably positive developments in inter-American relations, such as his role in hastening the transfer of the Panama Canal and the Canal Zone to Panama. He also found it surprising that he enjoyed his time with Latin

Americans. His telephone conversations and detailed, lengthy memoranda of conversations with Latin American officials sustain those points. His good feelings about Mexico undoubtedly motivated him to find a solution to the Colorado River salinity issue.

The paradox of Kissinger and Latin America is that he devoted more time and effort to the region than his predecessors. George Marshall, Dean Acheson, John Foster Dulles, and Dean Rusk did not devote two hours to a meeting with a Latin American foreign minister. Secretaries of state traditionally relied on their assistant secretaries of state to conduct relations with hemispheric neighbors. For example, Assistant Secretary of State Thomas Mann was appropriately dubbed "Mr. Latin America" during the Lyndon Johnson administration. Kissinger, however, did it all. He journeyed to the country retreats of Hugo Banzer, the dictator of Bolivia, and Alfonso López Michelsen, the constitutional president of Colombia. Kissinger conversed about the differences between the migratory habits of shrimp off the coast of Brazil and tuna in the Humboldt Current. He attended approximately one hundred sessions on negotiations for a new treaty with Panama. He contributed ideas to the seating arrangements for a dinner in Washington for Latin American ambassadors. He chatted endlessly about Latin American issues, big and small, on the telephone. National security advisers such as McGeorge Bundy, Walt Rostow, and Kissinger's replacement, Brent Scowcroft, did not feel compelled to define their responsibilities in that way. The memoirs of Acheson and Rusk, which rarely touch on inter-American affairs, are modest efforts compared to the more than three thousand pages composed by Kissinger. To be sure, Acheson's entitling his memoir *Present at the Creation* indicated that he, like Kissinger, considered himself a historic figure.[1]

Kissinger's character and personality help explain why he devoted himself to inter-American relations. One scholar judged that Kissinger was "not a good person" and possessed "a fundamentally flawed personality" but conceded that he was "extraordinarily smart, hard-working, and charming."[2] Kissinger took his work seriously. His memoranda of conversation with Latin American officials demonstrate that he studied his briefing books. He educated himself on complex issues, whether they were hydraulic engineering, the law of the sea, or the title and deed history of the International Petroleum Corporation of Peru. As indicated in his remarks after being selected in mid-1973 to be secretary of state by President Nixon, Kissinger felt obligated to perform as a way of validating his immigrant background. He had come to the United States with his family in 1938 "as a refugee from persecution." As a young man, he wrote, he "had worked in a shaving-brush factory, joined the U.S. Army as a private, and became a naturalized citizen." His immediate response to Nixon—"I hope to be worthy of your trust"—was an honest revelation of his emotions and convictions.[3]

Both as national security adviser and secretary of state, Kissinger dominated the making of policy toward Latin America, because he declined to delegate authority. He seems to have trusted only two advisers, Viron Vaky of the NSC and Assistant Secretary William D. Rogers. Vaky, who had broad experience as a diplomat in Latin America, tried to explain developments in countries such as Chile and Cuba within the context of their respective histories rather than within the context of the Cold War. Kissinger listened to Vaky but never followed his advice. Like President Nixon, Kissinger gave primacy to the Soviet-American confrontation when analyzing the domestic and international policies of individual Latin American nations. As secretary of state, Kissinger judged the diplomats who focused on Latin America, such as Assistant Secretary Jack B. Kubisch, to be competent but soft. He gleefully pointed out that the State Department's Latin Americanists should have pursued religious vocations as ministers, priests, or rabbis. Those diplomats have responded to Kissinger's insults by pointing out Kissinger's lack of respect for democracy, constitutionalism, and human rights. Rogers, a Democrat, agreed to serve as Kissinger's assistant secretary after Nixon resigned. Kissinger enjoyed Rogers and later became a business partner with him. He quietly agreed with Rogers, who had worked on the Alliance for Progress, that the United States should help underwrite Latin America's economic development. Rogers favored the normalization of relations with Cuba but negotiated with the Cubans from a script developed by Kissinger. Kissinger rewarded Harry W. Shlaudeman, who had been his man in Allende's Chile, with an appointment in 1976 as assistant secretary. But when Shlaudeman, who was appalled by the murderous behavior of the regimes in Argentina and Uruguay and the international assassination schemes associated with Operation Condor, tried to raise the alarm, he was rebuked by Kissinger.

Jussi Hanhimäki, the astute scholar of Kissinger's foreign policies, once suggested that Kissinger's memoirs be read as novels.[4] "Fiction" would be too elevated of a word to characterize what Kissinger wrote about Allende's Chile and his efforts to promote democracy in Latin America. His Chile thesis presented over and over in the three volumes was that Allende was a communist who was determined to destroy democracy and constitutionalism in Chile and turn his nation over to the communist camp. Allende's treachery and economic incompetence led patriotic Chileans to rise in rebellion and overthrow the perverse, despicable Allende. In any case, Kissinger alleges that he was not well informed about what was happening in Chile between 1970 and 1973.[5] Kissinger's credibility problem is that the last volume of his memoirs appeared in 1999. In that year, the Chile Declassification Process, authorized by President

Bill Clinton, led to the release of 20,000 documents on Chile. Inveterate scholars such as Peter Kornbluh and Tanya Harmer used those documents to undermine Kissinger's narrative.[6] The Historical Office of the State Department
assembled the key documents in chronological order that revealed the sustained
U.S. campaign to undermine Allende. Kissinger was centrally involved in the
plotting. Kissinger had an aide listen in to his telephone conversations and transcribe them. The conversations, some of which Kissinger tried to block from
declassification, present Kissinger and Nixon boasting about their role in the
overthrow of President Allende. Nixon had previously vowed in a telephone
conversation with Kissinger to destroy Allende or, in Nixon's words, "so you
will know in the future how far I am willing to go."[7]

Historians of Latin America would respond to Kissinger's lies about Chile
by emphasizing that Allende was a constitutional president who practiced peaceful, parliamentary politics. He had less than 50 percent of the Chilean electorate behind him, but the political strength of his Unidad Popular coalition
was growing. The political violence that marred his presidency was perpetrated
by the extreme right, which had access to CIA money. Allende admired Fidel
Castro but rejected the Cuban's advice and warned him not to meddle in Chilean domestic affairs. The Soviet Union declined to assist Chile, because it found
Allende's economic policies to be bizarre and unworkable. The Soviets were
also adhering to the rules of détente by not challenging the United States in
its traditional sphere of influence. Allende twice tried to assure U.S. officials
that Chile would never serve as a Soviet military base in the Western Hemisphere. An argument can be made that Chile on its own was heading for a political and economic cataclysm. But it is a counterfactual thesis, for the United
States promoted political violence in the country and tried to "strangle" the
Chilean economy. Jonathan Haslam has used the smart term "assisted suicide"
to incorporate the international and domestic dimensions in the death of *la
vía Chilena*.[8]

Kissinger has continued to abjure responsibility for the tragedy that became
Chile, with over 3,000 deaths, 100,000 tortured, and 200,000 exiled during seventeen years of military dictatorship under General Augusto Pinochet. Pinochet also stole public funds and authorized international terrorism in the United
States. In the aftermath of the release of documentary evidence, Kissinger has
resorted to claiming that his memory is dim of such long ago events. Memory loss is a normal process of aging, but in the second decade of the twenty-
first century Kissinger displayed the cognitive sharpness to publish thoughtful
books and comment publicly on contemporary international affairs. In his
memoirs, H. R. Haldeman, Nixon's chief of staff, charged Kissinger with being a hypocrite, alleging that he wanted to stay in the good graces of political

liberals who socialized in the Georgetown neighborhood of Washington.[9] Kissinger presumably did not want academic colleagues and social acquaintances to know that he had waged war against a democratically elected leader. Indeed, at a talk that he gave at Georgetown University in April 1971, the notes for which are deposited at the Nixon Library, Kissinger conceded to a graduate student that the 1970 election of Salvador Allende was not a Cold War event but rather a reflection of Chilean domestic politics. Kissinger may have also chosen not to speak about Chile because his actions belied his faith in the "realist" approach to foreign policy.[10] The central tenet of "realism" is that policymakers judge a country by how it acts in the international arena and not by the course and content of its domestic politics. Allende's Chile posed no threat to U.S. national security. President Allende went out of his way to assure U.S. officials that Chile would never be the Cuba of the 1962 missile crisis. Kissinger had been accurate when he jibed that "Chile was a dagger pointed at the heart of Antarctica."

Perhaps the most misleading assertion that Kissinger made in his memoirs was his professed dedication to democracy promotion. He explained, "Cold War reality impelled us to maintain a constructive relationship with authoritarian regimes of South America," but then claimed, "We did make the fostering of democratic institutions a significant element in our Latin American policy . . . [and] we exercised our influence to advance the cause of democratic institutions."[11] The documentary record does not support Kissinger's claims. In his congressional testimony and public addresses, Kissinger commended the virtues of democracy, constitutionalism, and respect for fundamental human rights. But in private conversations with Latin American officials, he ignored those subjects. In one case, he agreed with Venezuelan Foreign Minister Román Escovar Salam that "the best defense against communism is democracy." That conversation took place in June 1976 in Santiago, Chile, with Escovar urging Kissinger to pressure the Pinochet regime to change its ways.[12] But as historian Peter Kornbluh revealed after he gained access to the 8 June 1976 memorandum of conversation between Kissinger and Pinochet, the secretary of state declined to recommend democracy in that conversation. Kissinger had provided a disingenuous account of his conversation with Pinochet in his memoirs.[13]

What the documentary record does sustain is that Kissinger either directly or through subordinates chastised, rebuked, and even shouted at diplomats who promoted democracy and human rights in Latin America. Ambassadors Robert C. Hill in Argentina, John H. Crimmins in Brazil, David Popper in Chile, George Landau in Paraguay, and Deputy Chief of Mission in Uruguay Frank V. Ortiz were subjected to Kissinger's wrath. The classic Kissinger put down— "Cut out the political science lectures"—was directed at Ambassador Popper.

He ridiculed the "missionary instinct" of U.S. diplomats in conversations with representatives of murderous regimes. Kissinger vowed to replace Robert White, a U.S. representative to the OAS and a future ambassador, when White defended a report exposing the gross abuses of human rights in Chile. He threatened Assistant Secretary Harry Shlaudeman with "You better be careful" when he learned that the State Department had delivered a démarche calling on Argentina to respect the rule of law and basic human rights. Shlaudeman took the tirade as if he were a private in the U.S. Marine Corps in front of a drill sergeant, responding only with "Yes, sir." Only Assistant Secretary Rogers had the confidence to answer back to Kissinger, when he repudiated Kissinger's contention that human rights had not been imperiled by the Pinochet regime. A constant in Kissinger's philosophy on human rights issues was that public denunciations of authoritarian regimes would prove counterproductive. "Engagement" and "quiet diplomacy" with anticommunist authoritarians would improve the lives of persecuted people. Scholars will search in vain through Kissinger's copious memoranda of conversation and thousands of transcripts of telephone conversations to find Kissinger putting into practice his philosophy of how to improve human rights in Latin America. Indeed, CIA Director William Colby informed Kissinger that the presidents of Brazil directly participated in summary executions. Arnold Nachmanoff of the NSC similarly warned Kissinger that the president of Guatemala authorized summary executions. Kissinger chose not to approach either the Brazilians or the Guatemalans about their murderous ways.

Continuity and Change

Henry Kissinger waged Cold War in Latin America. In the name of anticommunism, he directed the overthrow of a leftist general in Bolivia, worked to destabilize a popularly elected socialist government in Chile, and interfered in a free, open election in Uruguay. He was excited and joyful whenever he met with the military dictators of Brazil. He became loquacious in conversations with the Uruguayan foreign minister and in their ruminations about the inevitable death of democracy in Latin America and probably Europe. He pushed the bureaucracy to expedite military and economic aid to the military thugs that ran Argentina and Guatemala and to Alfredo Stroessner, the longtime strongman of Paraguay. He expressed appreciation to tyrants of small countries, such as Anastasio Somoza Debayle of Nicaragua and Joaquín Balaguer of the Dominican Republic (1966–1978), for loyally following the U.S. lead at the United Nations. Kissinger, who made a courtesy call to Santo

Secretary of State Kissinger with President Joaquín Balaguer in Santo Domingo in June 1976. Kissinger gushed over Balaguer's authoritarian, repressive regime. United States Information Services (USIS) photo.

Domingo in early June 1976, happily reported to President Ford that the Dominican Republic was "an island of sanity in an otherwise turbulent area." Kissinger added that the Dominican Republic's "political stability is assured as long as Balaguer is around."[14]

Sympathetic analysts of Kissinger's career, such as Niall Ferguson, and those that are mildly critical, such as Jussi Hanhimäki, make the unimpeachable point that Kissinger's anticommunist policies toward Latin America were not especially unique. Since the late nineteenth century and the pronouncement of Secretary of State Richard Olney (1895–1897) that "our fiat is practically law" in the Western Hemisphere, the United States has perceived Latin America as a sphere of influence. Thomas H. Karamessines of the CIA carried on Olney's bombastic tradition when he informed Kissinger that it would be unnecessary to interfere in the 1973 Argentine presidential election. During the Cold War, U.S. policymakers believed that any gain for communism in the Western Hemisphere would accrue to the Soviet Union and inevitably weaken the United States. Secretary of State Dean Rusk once told Argentine officials that if Argentina failed to support the anti-Castro policies of the United States, it would embolden the Red Army to attack West Berlin.[15] Being an impeccable scholar, Hanhimäki added that U.S. policymakers were often unable "to grasp the intrinsic significance of local and regional circumstances to the unfolding of the Cold War."[16] President Dwight Eisenhower, Secretary of State John Foster Dulles, and CIA Director Allan Dulles initiated the practice of covert interventions in Latin America when the United States fomented the overthrow in June 1954 of President Jacobo Arbenz Guzmán of Guatemala. Leading U.S. officials had decided that President Arbenz had become dependent on the Guatemalan Communist Party, which by definition was subservient to the Soviet Union. Secretary of State Dulles was especially shocked and disappointed when U.S. investigators dispatched to Guatemala City could find no evidence of a Soviet-Guatemalan connection in the Guatemalan archives. The CIA intervention precipitated endless rounds of political violence in Guatemala. Kissinger's dealings with Colonel Carlos Arana, "the butcher of Zacapa," were rooted in the nation's violent history that followed the overthrow of President Arbenz.

An analog can be found for every Kissinger misdeed in Latin America. President John Kennedy initiated the destabilization of constitutional governments in Brazil and British Guiana (Guyana). President Lyndon Johnson finished the job, leading to decades of repressive rule in Brazil and Guyana. Both presidents authorized a massive, covert U.S. intervention in the Chilean election of 1964 to ensure the defeat of Salvador Allende and the election of Eduardo Frei of the Christian Democratic Party. President Johnson ordered the invasion of the Dominican Republic in 1965 to forestall an alleged communist takeover of the island nation. Johnson later privately admitted that he had overreacted. Nonetheless, President Johnson personally directed CIA Director Richard Helms to take measures to ensure that Joaquín Balaguer won the 1966 election that the United States supervised. This intervention also forestalled the election of Juan Bosch, the former president of the Dominican Republic and a committed democrat. Secretary of State Kissinger had noxious conversations with Foreign Minister César Guzzetti of Argentina, Foreign Minister Patricio Carvajal of Chile, and Foreign Minister Juan Carlos Blanco of Uruguay. But there was a U.S. tradition of cozying up to Latin American tyrants. In a toast in Havana, Vice President Nixon compared Fulgencio Batista, the sleazy Cuban dictator, to Abraham Lincoln. President Eisenhower awarded the Legion of Merit, the nation's highest award for foreign personages, to Marcos Pérez Jiménez of Venezuela. The award's citation noted the dictator's anticommunism and his solicitous treatment of U.S. oil companies. And it would be impossible to top the always uninformed Ronald Reagan rubbing shoulders with Efraín Ríos Montt of Guatemala at a conference in Honduras in December 1982. President

Reagan told the U.S. press that Ríos Montt was a good anticommunist and a misunderstood guy. In May 2013, a Guatemalan court convicted the dictator of genocide and crimes against humanity. During his brief time in office between 23 March 1982 and 8 August 1983, Ríos Montt supervised the slaughter of 40,000 Mayan people.[17]

Whereas Kissinger emulated the Cold War policies of his predecessors, it would be an exaggeration to conclude that he did not make a distinctive mark in the history of inter-American relations. In the aftermath of the assassination on 30 May 1961 of the malevolent Rafael Trujillo (1930–1961), President Kennedy speculated on what U.S. policy should be toward the Dominican Republic. Both the Eisenhower and Kennedy administrations had belatedly decided that Trujillo was a Cold War liability. The dictator was so dastardly that he might force desperate Dominicans into the hands of "Castro-Communists." Both administrations pressured Trujillo to go into exile. When the aged dictator resisted, the CIA passed arms to dissidents who assassinated Trujillo. The dictator's son, known as "Ramfis," seized power, capturing and torturing his father's enemies. Ramfis was aided by his father's two brothers, known locally as the "wicked uncles." Like the Somoza family in Nicaragua, the Trujillo family had turned the country into the family *hacienda*. The restoration of the family tyranny posed a dilemma for President Kennedy. According to presidential aide Arthur M. Schlesinger Jr., Kennedy listed his policy choices: "There are three possibilities in descending order of preference: a decent, democratic regime, a continuation of the Trujillo regime, or a Castro regime. We ought to aim at the first, but we really can't renounce the second until we are sure we can avoid the third."[18] Kennedy's memorable remark about the descending order of possibilities proved to be a reliable guide for what choices his and other Cold War presidential administrations would make throughout Latin America. In the case of the Dominican Republic, Kennedy chose the first option. The United States used extreme pressure, including shows of U.S. naval and air force, to drive the Trujillo family out of the country. The United States thereafter arranged for a transition government and supervised a fair presidential election in late 1962.

During the Cold War, the United States often chose the option of promoting a "decent, democratic regime" if policymakers judged that leaders and parties were anticommunists and allies in the Cold War struggle. In 1945, the Truman administration embraced the Larreta Doctrine, named after Uruguay's foreign minister, Eduardo Rodríguez Larreta. Foreign Minister Larreta proposed that Latin American nations consider multilateral action against any hemispheric nation violating elementary human rights. In 1952, Secretary of State Acheson quashed talk of destabilizing the Arbenz government. Acheson ridiculed the idea that any Latin American nation could ever pose a threat to the vital interests of the United States. Acheson sharply criticized President Kennedy for ordering the Bay of Pigs invasion in 1961. President Eisenhower authorized the overthrow of President Arbenz and did not question Secretary of State Dulles's embrace of purported anticommunist dictators, but at an NSC meeting in February 1955, Eisenhower sharply rebuked Treasury Secretary George Humphrey, who observed that "whenever a dictator was replaced, Communists gained." Eisenhower pointed out to the NSC that "the United States must back democracies," for he "firmly believed that if power lies with the people, then there will be no aggressive war."[19] After Vice President Nixon's stormy trip to South America in 1958, Eisenhower and his new secretary of state, Christian Herter, took steps to promote democrats, such as Rómulo Betancourt of Venezuela. The Eisenhower administration also severed diplomatic relations with Trujillo and abandoned Cuba's Batista in 1958.

Ambivalence continued to characterize the U.S. approach to Latin America in the 1960s. President Kennedy, Attorney General Robert Kennedy, and Secretary of State Rusk were, in Secretary of Defense Robert McNamara's view, "hysterical" about Castro's Cuba. The administration demanded that Latin American nations sever ties with Cuba. But democracy promotion and economic development were the central goals of the Alliance for Progress. The United States vowed to pursue "enlightened anticommunism." The administration funneled aid to the popularly elected governments of Chile, Colombia, Costa Rica, and Venezuela. In 1962, President Kennedy suspended relations with Peru when the Peruvian military nullified a democratic election. The Kennedy and Johnson administrations made the momentous decision to destabilize the constitutional government of João Goulart. Military dictatorship in Brazil created a "domino" effect throughout the region. By 1976, ruthless military dictators dominated South America. The Brazilian generals assisted the United States in destabilizing governments in Bolivia and Uruguay. But the Johnson administration was dismayed when the Brazilian generals issued Institutional Act No. 5, which outlawed political activity. As it left office, the Johnson administration was contemplating sanctions against Brazil.

Second thoughts never troubled Henry Kissinger when it came to the choice between democracy and dictatorship. His foreign-policy philosophy led him to "deal realistically with governments in the inter-American system as they are," as President Nixon emphasized in his 1969 Pan American Day speech. Of course, Kissinger violated his philosophy in his approach toward Chile and Uruguay, the stalwart democracies of South America. Recognizing that Cold

War administrations gave primacy to anticommunism over democracy and respect for human rights, as indicated in President Kennedy's descending list of preferences, it is nonetheless difficult to imagine any of Kissinger's national security adviser or secretary of state predecessors engaging in the behaviors that characterized Kissinger's eight years in power. Secretary of State Marshall would not have traveled to the country home of a Bolivian dictator. McGeorge Bundy would not likely have engaged in joke fests with foreign ministers of dictatorial governments. Secretary Rusk would probably not report his excitement to President Johnson that the Brazilian military dictators really liked him. Dean Acheson would not have discussed the dim prospects for the survival of democracy in Western Europe with the Uruguayan foreign minister. Perhaps only Secretary of State Alexander M. Haig Jr. (1981–1982) would have ignored intelligence that a U.S. client in Central America was authorizing "death squads" and summary executions. Haig explained away atrocities in El Salvador, whereas Kissinger chose not to discuss the murderous behavior of President Arana of Guatemala.

As national security adviser, Kissinger ridiculed U.S. diplomats who spoke up for human decency. As secretary of state, he repeatedly threatened to ruin the careers of U.S. officials who defended democracy and human rights. Henry Kissinger was not just a typical cold warrior but an unscrupulous one who backed murderous dictatorships, even when veteran State Department officers recoiled at such excesses. Kissinger's practice of mocking and condemning U.S. diplomats who were appalled by wholesale murder was largely unprecedented in the history of U.S. diplomacy in Latin America. In 1947, Secretary Marshall replaced Assistant Secretary Spruille Braden, who had previously been ambassador to Argentina. Braden had launched a less than subtle campaign in 1945–1946 to persuade Argentine voters not to elect Juan Perón, whom Braden judged a fascist. Marshall acted not, however, against democracy promotion but because Latin Americans considered Braden to be an interventionist. Assistant Secretary of State for Human Rights Patricia Derian (1977–1981) often met resistance from her superiors in the State Department for relentlessly denouncing Latin American dictators. Derian stayed in office and saved the lives of Latin Americans. A U.S. diplomat in the embassy in Buenos Aires, F. Allen "Tex" Harris, faced opposition in Washington for tracking the fate of the disappeared in Argentina during *la guerra sucia*. An award in his name was subsequently created for creative dissent in the U.S. foreign service. James Cheek won the Rivkin Foreign Service Award for his "dissent" cable about the looming revolutionary situation in Somoza's Nicaragua. Secretary Kissinger praised Cheek at the awards ceremony but ignored the diplomat's warning.

As scholar Gary Bass has pointed out, Kissinger ruined the career of diplomat Archer Blood, who penned a "dissent" cable about Nixon and Kissinger's policy in East Pakistan (Bangladesh).[20]

Any fair assessment of Kissinger's place in the history of inter-American relations must note also that he had real achievements. Presidents Truman, Eisenhower, Kennedy, and Johnson understood that the United States had an unsustainable colonial relationship with Panama. Eisenhower and Kennedy pursued reforms with Panama but lacked the political courage to negotiate a new treaty with Panama over the canal and the Canal Zone. With the backing of Truman and Eisenhower, Johnson initiated negotiations with Panama, and his negotiating team arrived at an agreement with Panama. Bedeviled by Vietnam and his declining political fortunes, Johnson declined to present a treaty to the U.S. Senate. Kissinger had a strong sense of history and, after the political demise of Nixon, Secretary of State Kissinger worked diligently for a new treaty. In this case, his realism paid dividends. He was unmoved by critics of a new treaty, such as Governor Ronald Reagan, who decried negotiating with an authoritarian like Omar Torrijos. President Ford also lacked political courage and delayed reaching a final settlement with Panama. But Kissinger had established the framework for a treaty and subsequently supported the ratification of the Panama Canal Treaties (1978).

Kissinger's strong belief that economic issues should not divide countries and that he did not serve as an attorney for international corporations also served his diplomacy well. Kissinger understood that U.S. corporations, especially those that focused on the extraction of natural minerals, had violated the sovereignty of Latin American nations. He also did not particularly respect executives involved in international business. As such, he resolved nettlesome bilateral issues with Ecuador, Mexico, and Peru and analyzed the desires of Brazil, Ecuador, and Peru for a 200-mile economic zone, under a new Law of the Sea, with an open mind. This was a distinctive approach to inter-American relations that Latin Americans appreciated. Excepting perhaps for President Kennedy, who was not enamored by the conduct of U.S. businesses in Latin America, U.S. presidential administrations since Theodore Roosevelt had reflexively backed U.S. corporations in Latin America. In 1964, "Mr. Latin America," Thomas Mann, informed U.S. diplomats in Latin America that the protection of U.S. investments was to be given the highest priority. Kissinger also privately confessed that he was a Democrat when it came to foreign economic policy and supported generous grants of economic aid to Latin America. And the aged Kissinger would presumably continue to ridicule the idea that the United States should separate itself from Mexico with a Berlin-style "Wall."

The Question of Responsibility

Well into the second decade of the twenty-first century, Latin Americans are investigating what happened to their countries during the time that Henry Kissinger exercised power. In August 2018, the Grandmothers (*abuelas*) of the Plaza de Mayo of Argentina announced they had reunited the 128th "appropriated" child with relatives. In 1976, the man, now forty-two, had been stolen at the age of five months from his mother, Rosario del Carmen Ramos of the northwestern province of Tucumán. Former police and military officers kidnapped the mother and took the infant. Ramos's body has never been found. The Grandmothers have established a DNA bank to help in the search for the approximately 500 children who were stolen during *la guerra sucia*.[21] Since 1977, the Grandmothers and Mothers have marched every Thursday afternoon at 3:30 p.m. in the Plaza de Mayo in downtown Buenos Aires to demand an accounting of their missing children and grandchildren. Argentina, Brazil, Chile, Guatemala, El Salvador, and Uruguay have established truth commissions to establish what happened in their countries. Argentina and Chile have been especially vigorous in prosecuting war criminals. Manuel Contreras, the head of DINA and a central player in Operation Condor, received jail sentences that amounted to 526 years. The Argentine generals received life sentences. The head of the military junta, General Jorge Videla, died in prison. Kissinger had been General Videla's guest of honor at the World Cup in 1978. Latin Americans have established memorials at torture centers such as the Naval Mechanical School (ESMA) and Automotores Orletti in Buenos Aires and Villa Grimaldi on the outskirts of Santiago. Museos de la memoria (museums of memory) that detail the descent into darkness have been established in Montevideo and other cities. Pope Francis (2013–), the first Latin American pontiff, has taken steps to sanctify Roman Catholic clergy who resisted the terror in Central and South America.

The good Pope Francis would undoubtedly forgive the United States and Henry Kissinger for the past. But Latin Americans with a sense of history would probably be less forgiving. During a tour of ESMA or the Museo de la Memoria in Montevideo, Kissinger's name will be raised or his photograph will appear. Latin Americans responded to the past when they elected to the presidency Michelle Bachelet of Chile, José Mujica of Uruguay, and Dilma Rousseff of Brazil. The three presidents were incarcerated and tortured in the early 1970s. In the twenty-first century, jurists in southern South America and Guatemala have considered Kissinger a person of interest. These views have been bolstered by the apologies that leading U.S. figures have issued. In 1999, President Bill Clinton apologized for the U.S. role in Guatemala since 1954. That year he launched the Chile Declassification Project. In 2003, Secretary of State Colin Powell expressed his disapproval of the U.S. intervention in Allende's Chile. In March 2016, President Barack Obama was in Argentina during the fortieth anniversary of the military's seizure of power. Obama had already announced the Argentina Declassification Project. He attended a ceremony at the stunning Parque de la Memoria (Memorial Park), which is located in Buenos Aires along the Río de la Plata. The president scattered flowers in the river as a tribute to Argentines who were tossed alive out of airplanes and helicopters into the river. Whereas Obama did not directly apologize, he pointedly noted, "There's been controversy about the policies of the United States early in those dark days." He elaborated: "Democracies have to have the courage to acknowledge when we don't live up to the ideals that we stand for; when we've been slow to speak out for human rights. And that was the case here."[22] President Obama chose to be diplomatic, but he was condemning Secretary of State Kissinger's interactions in 1976 with Argentine Foreign Minister Guzzetti.

As in the case of the veracity of his memoirs, some issues on Kissinger's historical responsibility can be readily assessed, whereas other issues require

This statue in the Río de la Plata near the Parque de la Memoria in Buenos Aires represents the Argentines who were dropped alive into the river from aircraft during the period of military rule from 1976 to 1983. President Barack Obama attended a ceremony at the memorial park in 2016 to mark the fortieth anniversary of the military's seizure of power and indirectly criticized Henry Kissinger. Author's photo.

more complex analyses. In his fine biography, Walter Isaacson argues that Kiss-inger fell under the "dark tutelage" of Richard Nixon.[23] This argument proj-ects that Kissinger would act differently under the genial Gerald Ford. Kissinger waited until after Nixon left office to push negotiations with Panama and ini-tiate a process to normalize relations with Cuba. He also agreed with diplo-mats in the embassy in Managua that Nixon's friend, Ambassador Turner Shelton, was an abomination and replaced him. Whereas Kissinger had more freedom under Ford than under Nixon, he did not change his approach to Latin America. He was as solicitous to General Pinochet as he was hostile to Presi-dent Allende. He continued to revel in his conversations and meetings with representatives of Latin America's thugs and assassins. His wild reaction to Cu-ba's intervention in Angola would have made Nixon proud.

Another thesis that can be readily discounted is the "theory of the two de-mons." As the thesis goes, Latin America became politically polarized. Left-wing radicals, inspired by the Cuban Revolution, carried out violent bombings, and the right-wing death squads overreacted. Innocent Latin Americans were cut down in the crossfire.[24] The thesis is chronologically inaccurate. Leftist up-heaval followed repression, as in Brazil when political activity was outlawed in 1968. Moreover, the various national and international truth commissions have established that the military, police, and allied death squads bore over-whelming responsibility for the mayhem. These were the groups that received U.S. security assistance. Salvador Allende did not authorize murder. In Guate-mala, the Historical Clarification Commission blamed the political right for 93 percent of the more than 200,000 murders. Maya were killed because they were indigenous people. Argentine Jews suffered unspeakable atrocities because of their religious identity.

A sophisticated issue is the scholarly problem known in the historical lexi-con as "agency." Historian Max Paul Friedman warned scholars of inter-American relations not to overemphasize U.S. influence in the region. Latin Americans had "agency." It was the light-skinned elites and mixed-blood *ladi-nos* of Guatemala who decided to murder Maya. Alfredo Stroessner was a cun-ning, ruthless dictator who manipulated and mocked his own people for thirty-five years. General Pinochet and his henchmen organized Operation Condor. The Uruguayan military decided it was a good idea to assassinate Rep-resentative Ed Koch of New York City. Latin American rightists developed strange national security doctrines that held that they were waging World War III. Friedman's article could be helpful to those who would like to absolve the United States of responsibility for Latin America's Cold War problems. A skeptic might point out, however, that most of the region's military dictators had trained in U.S. war colleges. A military attaché in the embassy in Santiago identified U.S. citizens who would subsequently be executed by Pinochet's forces. Dan Mitrione was not innocently plying his trade in Brazil and Uruguay. But Friedman did not let his enthusiasm for agency overwhelm his good historical sense. As he noted in his seminal article, "Agency and independence are not the same things."[25] Stroessner secured economic and military aid from the United States by dutifully following the U.S. lead in the international arena. But he miscalculated when he harbored an international drug trafficker during the time of President Nixon's War on Drugs. Within forty-eight hours after receiving an emissary from Nixon, Stroessner extradited the drug trafficker to the United States.

Henry Kissinger declined to pressure dictators who violated elementary human rights. In fact, he made support for Latin American dictators a central feature of his policy. But Kissinger had the power to defend the rule of law, for Latin Americans perceived that they lived in the U.S. sphere of influence. As reported by the U.S. embassy in Buenos Aires, Foreign Minister Guzzetti returned from his encounters with Kissinger in 1976 in a "state of jubilation." He had received the tacit approval from the most powerful person in international affairs for the "dirty war." In 1975, Foreign Minister Carvajal asked Kissinger what Chile should do with released political prisoners. Kissinger responded, "You will know what to do. We cannot go beyond what we have already said. What other problems do we have to discuss?" This response followed Kissinger disparaging his State Department for being "made up of people who have a vocation for the ministry" and labeling criticism of Chile's human rights record a "total injustice."[26] By contrast, Patricia Derian and Tex Harris saved the lives of Argentines, including publisher Jacobo Timerman, an Argentine Jew. In 1983, Argentina restored democracy, and Derian and President Jimmy Carter were guests of honor at the inauguration of President Raúl Alfonsín (1983–1989). Argentina would later award Derian its highest award for foreign personages. The Carter administration's pressure on Paraguay and Uruguay led to a sharp reduction in political prisoners in both countries. General Pinochet's regime murdered or disappeared fewer Chileans between 1977 and 1980 than in any other four-year period between 1973 and 1990.[27] Kissinger objected to Senator Edward Kennedy's tying human rights provisos to foreign aid packages. In 2008, President Bachelet of Chile traveled to Hyannis Port and personally presented an award to the dying senator for his defense of human rights during the Pinochet years.

Latin American nations also demonstrated agency through Operation Condor, the international assassination scheme. Operation Condor operatives kidnapped and murdered at least 377 opponents of the dictatorships of southern South America. The kidnappers and assassins struck in Western Europe, the

United States, and throughout Latin America.[28] Henry Kissinger had received intelligence briefings about Operation Condor. Foreign Minister Guzzetti created a diplomatic gaffe when he informed Kissinger about the scheme in their discussion on 10 June 1976. When details emerged in the early twenty-first century of official knowledge about Operation Condor in relationship to the car bombing that killed Orlando Letelier and Ronni Moffitt, embarrassed friends of Kissinger, such as William D. Rogers, claimed that the secretary of state had unequivocally warned the dictatorships not to perpetrate violence abroad. But once again the documentary record undermined claims of innocence and responsible behavior. Kissinger blocked the transmission of the démarche that warned against violence. Cuban exiles also showed agency when they accelerated their attacks on Cuba in 1976, culminating in the terrorist act of the downing of Cubana de Aviación Flight 455 in October 1976, killing seventy-three passengers and crew. These attacks followed Kissinger's frustration in failing to persuade the national security bureaucracy to "clobber" Cuba for its imperial adventure in Angola.

When a scholar begins to add up the interventions in Bolivia, Chile, and Uruguay, the preference shown for dictatorship over constitutionalism and democracy, the tolerance of mass murder, the ridiculing of human rights concerns, the failure to move effectively on threats of international terrorism and warnings that Argentine Jews were subjected to extreme repression, it would seem too gentle to characterize Kissinger's policies as "short-sighted."[29] It also remains a mystery how a scholar would conclude that Kissinger's approach toward Latin America contributed to Cold War victory over the Soviet Union.[30] The overthrow of Salvador Allende did not hasten the collapse of the communist system. The attack on Chile had symbolic elements. It served, in one scholar's view, "the larger purpose of sustaining Washington's international primacy."[31] Nonetheless, Secretary of State Acheson's insight that Latin America weighed little in the Cold War balance of power remains credible three decades after the breaching of the Berlin Wall. Historians need not engage Christopher Hitchens's polemical screed on war criminality to accept the judgment of Jon Lee Anderson, a distinguished author and journalist, that "the latest revelations compound a portrait of Kissinger as the ruthless, if not active co-conspirator of Latin American military regimes engaged in war crimes."[32] Historian Mark Lawrence predicted a historiographical irony would ensue once a comprehensive study of inter-American relations between 1969 and 1976 appeared. As Lawrence noted, Latin America, the part of the world Nixon and Kissinger "consistently regarded at least important to U.S. interests, would mar their reputation at least as much as any other region or issue."[33] Kissinger's diplomatic achievements in Latin America alter but do not undermine Lawrence's prediction.

Finally, this study agrees with scholars as disparate as Roham Alvani, Walter Isaacson, Barbara Keys, and Jeremi Suri that Kissinger had a peculiar need to be perceived as tough, powerful, and manly. Powerful political leaders, not democratic politics, best preserved peace and liberty in a pitiless and brutal world. Weakness was synonymous with death.[34] As demonstrated in the paper trail of memoranda of conversation and transcripts of telephone conversations, Kissinger reveled in the company of authoritarians such as Joaquín Balaguer of the Dominican Republic and military dictators such as the Brazilian generals and the Bolivian general Hugo Banzer. He engaged Uruguayan Foreign Minister Blanco in a conversation about the unsuitability of democratic processes in the contemporary world. Kissinger finished the conversation by congratulating Blanco for his "strength" and "courage." Blanco would be subsequently indicted by Uruguayan jurists for orchestrating the murder of legislators who practiced democratic politics. Kissinger thought Latin Americans estimable, because they respected "frankness" and understood "men" and did not show the self-control and doubt of "an assistant professor of political science." Men of action—authoritarians, military dictators, and Henry A. Kissinger—did not need the constraints of constitutional norms and democratic habits. History was on their side. Kissinger explained this in a colloquy he had in mid-1976 in Mexico City with Héctor Cuadra, a human rights activist. Kissinger agreed with Cuadra that human rights had intrinsic moral value. But he rejected the idea that the defense of human rights promoted stability and international peace. As he pointed out to the professor, "The Roman Empire lasted a thousand years. It had no human rights."[35]

Notes

Introduction

1. Richard M. Nixon, *RN: The Memoirs of Richard Nixon* (New York: Grosset & Dunlap, 1978), 185–93, 485–90; Gerald R. Ford, *A Time to Heal: The Autobiography of Gerald R. Ford* (New York: Harper & Row, 1979).

2. Henry Kissinger, *White House Years* (New York: Simon & Schuster, 1979), 653–83; Kissinger, *Years of Upheaval* (New York: Simon & Schuster, 1982), 374–413; Kissinger, *Years of Renewal* (New York: Simon & Schuster, 1999), 314–15, 749–61.

3. Telephone conversation between Nixon and Kissinger, 16 September 1973, document 357, *FRUS, 1969–1976* 21: *Chile, 1969–1973* (Washington, DC: GPO, 2014).

4. Kissinger, *Years of Renewal*, 740.

5. Memorandum from Director of CIA William Colby to Kissinger, 11 April 1974, *FRUS, 1969–1976* E-11, Part 2: *Documents on South America, 1973–1976* (Washington, DC: GPO, 2015), 278–79.

6. Kissinger, *Years of Renewal*, 732.

7. Memorandum from NSC Adviser Brent Scowcroft to President Ford on Kissinger visit to Bogotá, 23 February 1976, *FRUS, 1969–1976* E-11, Part 2: *Documents on South America, 1973–1976*, 735–37; Kissinger, *Years of Renewal*, 748.

8. CIA memorandum for the record, 16 August 1971, document 355, *FRUS, 1969–1976* E-10: *Documents on American Republics, 1969–1972* (Washington, DC: GPO, 2009); memorandum for the record of meeting of 40 Committee, 16 September 1971, document 358, ibid.

9. Ariel Dorfman, foreword to *The Trial of Henry Kissinger*, by Christopher Hitchens (New York: Twelve Edition, 2012), ix–xxxv.

10. Quoted in briefing memorandum from Winston Lord, Director of Policy Planning Staff, to Kissinger, 1 September 1976, document 47, *FRUS, 1969–1976* E-11, Part 2: *Documents on South America, 1973–1976*. See also DoS to embassy in Argentina, 15 September 1976, document 53, ibid.

11. Memorandum of conversation between Kissinger and President Francisco Morales Bermúdez, 18 February 1976, document 316, ibid.

12. Jussi M. Hanhimäki, "'Dr. Kissinger' or 'Mr. Henry'? Kissingerology, Thirty Years and Counting," *DH* 27 (November 2003): 637–76; Hanhimäki, ed., "Roundtable Review," *H-DIPLO* 18, no. 3 (2016), http://www.tiny.cc/Roundtable-XVIII-3.

13. Barbara Keys, "The Kissinger Wars," *American Historian* 10 (November 2016): 16–22.

14. Jussi M. Hanhimäki, *The Flawed Architect: Henry Kissinger and American Foreign Policy* (New York: Oxford University Press, 2004), xviii, 485–92.

15. Mario Del Pero, *The Eccentric Realist: Henry Kissinger and the Shaping of American Foreign Policy* (Ithaca, NY: Cornell University Press, 2010), 4–10, 148–49.

16. Walter Isaacson, *Kissinger: A Biography*, with a new introduction (New York: Simon & Schuster, 2005), 9–10, 209, 655–59.

17. Memorandum of discussions between Nixon and Brazilian president, 9 December 1971, document 143, *FRUS, 1969–1976* E-10: *Documents on American Republics, 1969–1972*.

18. Jeremi Suri, *Henry Kissinger and the American Century* (Cambridge, MA: Belknap Press of Harvard University Press, 2007), 1–15, 239–42.

19. Niall Ferguson, *Kissinger, 1923–1968: The Idealist* (New York: Penguin Press, 2015), 11, 24, 27–32, 876.

20. Daniel Feierstein, "Political Violence in Argentina and Its Genocidal Characteristics," in *State Violence and Genocide in Latin America: The Cold War Years*, ed. Marcia Esparza, Henry R. Huttenbach, and Daniel Feierstein (New York: Routledge, 2010), 44–63.

21. Hitchens, *Trial of Henry Kissinger*, 82–117. See also Jon Lee Anderson, "Does Henry Kissinger Have a Conscience?," *New Yorker*, 20 August 2016, https://www.newyorker.com/news/news-desk/does-henry-kissinger-have-a-conscience.

22. Gary J. Bass, *The Blood Telegram: Nixon, Kissinger, and a Forgotten Genocide* (New York: Alfred A. Knopf, 2013), xii–xxiv, 5–9, 79–82, 255, 319. See also Robert K. Brigham, *Reckless: Henry Kissinger and the Tragedy of Vietnam* (New York: Public Affairs, 2018).

23. Greg Grandin, *Kissinger's Shadow: The Long Reach of America's Most Controversial Statesman* (New York: Metropolitan Books, 2015), 27–40, 97, 142–53.

24. Keys, "Kissinger Wars," 16.

25. Jeremi Suri, "Henry Kissinger in Historical Context: War, Democracy, and Jewish Identity," *Passport* 39 (September 2008): 6.

26. Douglas Brinkley and Luke Nichter, *The Nixon Tapes, 1971–1972* (Boston: Houghton Mifflin Harcourt, 2015), ix–xv; idem, *The Nixon Tapes, 1973* (Boston: Houghton Mifflin Harcourt, 2015).

27. John A. Farrell, *Richard Nixon: The Life* (New York: Doubleday, 2017); Tim Weiner, *One Man against the World: The Tragedy of Richard Nixon* (New York: Henry Holt, 2015).

28. Suri, *Kissinger and the American Century*, 10–12; idem, "Kissinger in Historical Context," 4–9.

29. Robert Dallek, *Nixon and Kissinger: Partners in Power* (New York: HarperCollins, 2007), ix–x, 614–15.

30. Tom Blanton, "Kissinger, Dallek, and Suri in the Gangster Den," *Diplomatic History* 33 (September 2009): 769–74.

31. Robert D. Schulzinger, "Nixon and Kissinger," in *A Companion to Richard M. Nixon*, ed. Melvin Small (Malden, MA: Wiley-Blackwell, 2011), 362–79.

32. Nixon, *RN*, 433; Brinkley and Nichter, *Nixon Tapes, 1971–1972*, 16–19, 584; Kissinger telephone conversation with Rogers, 17 December 1971, *KTC*, ProQuest; Kissinger telephone conversation with Laird, 23 December 1971, ibid.; Kissinger, *White House Years*, 671, 674; Kissinger telephone conversation with Nixon, 16 December 1971, *KTC*, ProQuest.

33. John Robert Greene, *The Presidency of Gerald R. Ford* (Lawrence: University Press of Kansas, 1995), 16, 29, 120, 161; Ingo Trauschweizer, "Ford and the Armed Forces," in *A Companion to Gerald R. Ford and Jimmy Carter*, ed. Scott Kaufman (Malden, MA: Wiley-Blackwell, 2016), 158–59; Jason Friedman, "Just a Caretaker?," ibid., 200.

34. Kissinger, *Years of Renewal*, 188–91, 1064–68; Sisco, quoted in Greene, *Presidency of Gerald R. Ford*, 119.

35. Ford to Venezuelan President Pérez, 9 November 1976, document 403, *FRUS, 1969–1976* E-11, Part 2: *Documents on South America, 1973–1976*.

36. Mark Atwood Lawrence, "Latin America and the Quest for Stability," in Small, *Companion to Nixon*, 460–77.

37. Michael J. Francis, "United States Policy toward Latin America during the Kissinger Years," in *United States Policy in Latin America: A Quarter Century of Crisis and Challenge, 1961–1986*, ed. John D. Martz (Lincoln: University of Nebraska Press, 1988), 28–60.

38. Mark Atwood Lawrence, "History from Below: The United States and Latin America in the Nixon Years," in *Nixon in the World: American Foreign Relations, 1969–1977*, ed. Fredrik Logevall and Andrew Preston (New York: Oxford University Press, 2008), 269–88.

39. Tanya Harmer, *Allende's Chile and the Inter-American Cold War* (Chapel Hill: University of North Carolina Press, 2011); Jonathan Haslam, *The Nixon Administration and the Death of Allende's Chile: A Case of Assisted Suicide* (London: Verso, 2005); Peter Kornbluh, *The Pinochet File: A Declassified Dossier of Atrocity and Accountability* (New York: New Press, 2003).

40. William Michael Schmidli, *The Fate of Freedom Elsewhere: Human Rights and U.S. Cold War Policy toward Argentina* (Ithaca, NY: Cornell University Press, 2013); Matias Spektor, *Kissinger e o Brasil* (Rio de Janeiro: Jorge Zahar Editora, 2009); William M. LeoGrande and Peter Kornbluh, *Back Channel to Cuba: The Hidden History of Negotiations between Washington and Havana* (Chapel Hill: University of North Carolina Press, 2014).

41. Lawrence, "Latin America and the Quest," 461, 466.

42. Armando Uribe, *The Black Book of American Intervention in Chile*, trans. Jonathan Casart (Boston: Beacon Press, 1975), 30–34; Seymour Hersh, *The Price of Power: Kissinger in the Nixon White House* (New York: Summit Books, 1983), 262–65.

43. Nelson A. Rockefeller, *The Rockefeller Report on the Americas: The Official Report of a United States Presidential Mission for the Western Hemisphere* (Chicago: Quadrangle Books, 1969).

1. Getting Started

1. James G. Blight and Philip Brenner, *Sad and Luminous Days: Cuba's Struggle with the Superpowers after the Missile Crisis* (Lanham, MD: Rowman & Littlefield, 2007), 73–145.

2. Stephen G. Rabe, *The Road to OPEC: United States Relations with Venezuela, 1919–1976* (Austin: University of Texas Press, 1982), 193–95.

3. Ibid., 157, 165, 171.

4. For statistical evidence, see Celso Furtado, *Economic Development of Latin America: A Survey from Colonial Times to the Cuban Revolution* (London: Cambridge University Press, 1970); John H. Coatsworth and Alan M. Taylor, eds., *Latin America and the World Economy since 1800* (Cambridge, MA: Harvard University Press, 1998); Robert H. Holder and Rina Villars, *Contemporary Latin America: 1970 to the Present* (Malden, MA: Wiley-Blackwell, 2013).

5. Stephen G. Rabe, *The Most Dangerous Area in the World: John F. Kennedy Confronts Communist Revolution in Latin America* (Chapel Hill: University of North Carolina Press, 1999), 9–33.

6. Eduardo Frei Montalva, "The Alliance That Lost Its Way," *Foreign Affairs* 45 (April 1967): 437–48.

7. Rabe, *Most Dangerous Area*, 2, 148–50, 162, 171–72, 196–99.

8. Ibid., 152–55.

9. Ibid., 19, 149–52.

10. Stephen G. Rabe, *Eisenhower and Latin America: The Foreign Policy of Anticommunism* (Chapel Hill: University of North Carolina Press, 1988), 85–86.

11. Nick Cullather, *Secret History: The CIA's Classified Account of Its Operations in Guatemala, 1952–1954* (Stanford, CA: Stanford University Press, 1999).

12. Tad Szulc, *Twilight of the Tyrants* (New York: Henry Holt, 1959).

13. Rabe, *Eisenhower and Latin America*, 87–88, 104–5, 153–68.

14. Ibid., 127–33, 162–73; Rabe, *Most Dangerous Area*, 34–39.

15. Ibid., 24, 196.

16. Rabe, *Road to OPEC*, 142–46; Jeffrey F. Taffet, *Foreign Aid as Foreign Policy: The Alliance for Progress in Latin America* (New York: Routledge, 2007), 67–94, 149–74.

17. Stephen G. Rabe, *The Killing Zone: The United States Wages Cold War in Latin America*, 2nd ed. (New York: Oxford University Press, 2016), 70–80.

18. Rabe, *Most Dangerous Area*, 59–60.

19. Ibid., 71–77; Stephen G. Rabe, *U.S. Intervention in British Guiana: A Cold War Story* (Chapel Hill: University of North Carolina Press, 2005).

20. Taffet, *Foreign Aid*, 95–122.

21. Rabe, *Eisenhower and Latin America*, 108.

22. Rabe, *Most Dangerous Area*, 125–47; Martha K. Huggins, *Political Policing: The United States and Latin America* (Durham, NC: Duke University Press, 1998), 99–186.

23. Editorial note, *FRUS, 1952–1954: Guatemala* (Washington, DC: GPO, 2003), 447; Cullather, *Secret History*, 106–7; Rabe, *Killing Zone*, 45.

24. Nixon, *RN*, 185–93.

25. Ibid., 203.

26. Kent M. Beck, "Necessary Lies, Hidden Truths: Cuba in the 1960 Campaign," *DH* 8 (Winter 1984): 37–59.

27. Jeffrey J. Safford, "The Nixon-Castro Meeting of 19 April 1959," *DH* 4 (Fall 1980): 425–31.

28. Nixon, *RN*, 235.

29. Ibid., 485–89.

30. File 1621, folder 1, box 12, Itineraries, Wilderness Years, Series II: Trip Files: 1963–1967, PPS 347, Latin America 5/67, RMNL; file 1638, folder 5, ibid; Brazil Clippings folder, ibid.; memorandum of conversation between Nixon and Secretary of Foreign Relations Antonio Carillo Flores, 29 May 1967, file 1648, Mexico Correspondence folder, ibid.

31. File 1631, folder 1, box 12, article by Silvio Ferraz of *O Globoa*, "World's Problems and Nixon's Opinions," 16 May 1967, ibid.

32. File 1627, folder 1, box 12, article by Danton Jobis, "The Good Tyrant," 14 May 1967, ibid.

33. File 1642, Brazil Clippings folder, UPI Dispatch, 11 May 1967, box 12, ibid.; file 1646, Nixon statements in *Brazil Herald*, [undated], ibid.

34. Nixon, *RN*, 185. See also Irwin F. Gellman, *The President and the Apprentice: Eisenhower and Nixon, 1952–1961* (New Haven, CT: Yale University Press, 2015).

35. Stephen G. Rabe, "Eisenhower Revisionism: A Decade of Scholarship," *DH* 17 (Winter 1993): 97–115.

36. Bass, *Blood Telegram*, 251.

37. Memorandum from Nixon to Kissinger, 19 July 1971, document 147, *FRUS, 1969–1976*, XVII: *China, 1969–1972* (Washington, DC: GPO, 2006).

38. Iwan W. Morgan, "Nixon Biographies," in Small, *Companion to Richard M. Nixon*, 7–26.

39. Memoranda of conversations between Nixon and Lleras, 12 and 13 June 1969, documents 151–154, *FRUS, 1969–1976* E-10: *Documents on American Republics, 1969–1972*.

40. Conversation between Nixon, Kissinger, Chief of Staff H. R. Haldeman, General Alexander Haig, and CIA Director Richard Helms, 5 March 1971, document 36, ibid.

41. Ibid.

42. Memorandum from Senior Department of Defense Attaché in France, General Vernon Walters, to Kissinger, [undated but December 1971], document 144, ibid.

43. John A. Farrell, *Richard Nixon: The Life* (New York: Doubleday, 2017), 342–44, 350; Niall Ferguson, *Kissinger, 1923–1968: The Idealist* (New York: Penguin Press, 2015), 793, 833.

44. Ibid., 516–18.

45. Walter Isaacson, *Kissinger: A Biography*, with a new introduction (New York: Simon & Schuster, 2005), 203–5.

46. Nixon quoted on tape, 11 August 1971, in Douglas Brinkley and Luke Nichter, *The Nixon Tapes, 1971–1972* (Boston: Houghton Mifflin Harcourt, 2015), 229; Henry Kissinger, *White House Years* (New York: Simon & Schuster, 1979), 31, 349, 589, 887, 1127–28.

47. Memorandum of conversation between Kissinger and Foreign Minister of Venezuela Ramón Escovar Salom, 10 May 1975, document 390, *FRUS, 1969–1976* E-11, Part 2: *Documents on South America, 1973–1976*; memorandum of conversation between Kissinger and Peruvian Foreign Minister Ángel de la Flor, 20 February 1974, document 295, ibid.; memorandum of conversation between Kissinger and de la Flor, 24 September 1975, document 312, ibid.; memorandum of conversation between Kissinger and Mexican Foreign Secretary Emilio Rabasa, 4 October 1973, document 61, *FRUS, 1969–1976* E-11, Part 1: *Documents on Mexico, Central America, and the Caribbean, 1969–1976* (Washington: GPO, 2015).

48. Memorandum of conversation between Kissinger and Argentine Foreign Minister Alberto Vignes, 5 October 1973, document 8, *FRUS, 1969–1976* E-11, Part 2: *Documents on South America, 1973–1976*.

49. Conversation among Nixon, MacArthur, and Haig, 8 April 1971, document 122, *FRUS, 1969–1976* E-4: *Documents on Iran and Iraq, 1969–1972* (Washington: GPO, 2006). I thank Professor Douglas Little of Clark University for pointing me to this document.

50. Kissinger to Brent Scowcroft of NSC for Nixon, 21 February 1974, #1881, HAK trip to Mexico (2 of 5) folder, box 48, NSC: Kissinger Office Files: HAK Administrative

and Staff Files, RMNL; Kissinger to Scowcroft for Nixon, 23 February 1974, HAK trip to Mexico (3 of 5) folder, box 48, ibid.; memorandum of conversation between Kissinger and U.S. legislators on airplane trip to Panama, 7 February 1974, #1932, Memcons, 1/1/74–1/28/74, folder (2), box 1028, NSC: President/HAK Memorandums, RMNL.

51. Telephone conversation between Kissinger and Rogers, 17 January 1975, *KTC*, ProQuest.

52. Memorandum of conversation between Kissinger and Ford, 21 September 1974, document 23, *FRUS, 1969–1976* E-11, Part 1: *Documents on Mexico; Central America; and the Caribbean, 1973–1976.*

53. Telephone conversation between Kissinger and Rabasa, 13 July 1973, *KTC*, ProQuest; memorandum by U.N. Ambassador John Scali to Kissinger on Kissinger conversation with Foreign Minister Rabasa, 24 August 1973, document 59, *FRUS, 1969–1976* E-11, Part 1: *Documents on Mexico; Central America; and the Caribbean, 1973–1976.*

54. NSSM 15, 3 February 1969, document 1, *FRUS, 1969–1976* E-10: *Documents on American Republics, 1969–1972*; study prepared in response to NSSM 15, 5 July 1969, document 4, ibid.; handwritten notes of Nixon on Kissinger to Nixon, 7 May 1969, document 2, ibid.; Taffet, *Foreign Aid*, 185–94.

55. Minutes of NSC Review Group meeting, 3 July 1969, document 3, *FRUS, 1969–1976* E-10: *Documents on American Republics, 1969–1972*; Kennedy quoted in Rabe, *Most Dangerous Area*, 151.

56. Editorial note on NSC meeting, 9 July 1969, document 6, *FRUS, 1969–1976* E-10: *Documents on American Republics, 1969–1972*; NSSM 68, 12 July 1969, document 7, ibid.; Intelligence Memorandum 2609/69 on Roman Catholic Church by CIA, 9 October 1969, document 13, ibid.; embassy in Asunción to DoS, 20 August 1969, Church in Latin America folder, box H-159, NSSM 68 file, NSC: Institutional Files, RMNL.

57. Handwritten notes of Nixon on Kissinger to Nixon, 22 July 1969, document 7, *FRUS, 1969–1976* E-10: *Documents on American Republics, 1969–1972.*

58. Editorial note on NSC meeting, 7 July 1969, document 6, *FRUS, 1969–1976* E-10: *Documents on American Republics, 1969–1972.*

59. NSC Inter-Agency Review Group on Inter-American Affairs, "Review of U.S. Military Presence in Latin America," [undated but 1971], folder 1481, NSSM 108: Latin America, box H-178, NSC: Institutional Files, RMNL.

60. Assistant Secretary of State Charles A. Meyer to Kissinger, 12 January 1971, NSSM 68 folder, Church in Latin America, box H-159, NSC: Institutional Files, RMNL.

61. Minutes of NSC meeting, 15 October 1969, document 14, *FRUS, 1969–1976* E-10: *Documents on American Republics, 1969–1972*; Kissinger to Nixon, "Talking Points for NSC Meeting," 15 October 1969, folder 1753, box H-024, NSC Institutional Files: Meetings File, RMNL; Rear Admiral M. Staser Holcomb of Defense Department to Brent Scowcroft of NSC, 27 April 1976, IADB folder, box 12, WHCF: Subject Files, GRFL.

62. Study prepared in response to NSSM 15, 5 July 1969, document 4, *FRUS, 1969–1976* E-10: *Documents on American Republics, 1969–1972*; analytical summary prepared by NSC Interdepartmental Group for Latin America, [undated], document 5, ibid.

63. Vaky to Kissinger, 1 January 1970, document 21, *FRUS, 1969–1976* E-10: *Documents on American Republics, 1969–1972.*

64. Ernesto Capello, "Latin America Encounters Nelson Rockefeller: Imagining the *Gringo Patrón* in 1969," in *Human Rights and Transnational Solidarity in Cold War Latin*

America, ed. Jessica Stites Mor (Madison: University of Wisconsin Press, 2013), 48–73; Elizabeth A. Cobbs, *The Rich Neighbor Policy: Rockefeller and Kaiser in Brazil* (New Haven, CT: Yale University Press, 1992); Antonio Pecho Tota, *O amigo Americano: Nelson Rockefeller and Brazil* (São Paulo: Comphania dos Letras, 2014); Darlene Rivas, *Missionary Capitalist: Nelson Rockefeller in Venezuela* (Chapel Hill: University of North Carolina Press, 2002).

65. Nelson A. Rockefeller, *The Rockefeller Report on the Americas: The Official Report of a United States Presidential Mission for the Western Hemisphere* (Chicago: Quadrangle Books, 1969), 17.

66. Nixon to Kissinger, 14 February 1969, #1015, Nixon to Kissinger folder, box 341, NSC Files: Subject Files, RMNL; Robert Osgood of Planning Staff to Kissinger, 14 October 1969, #1399, NSSM 15 folder, box H-134, NSC Files: Institutional Files (H-Files), RMNL.

67. Rockefeller to Nixon, "Conversations with Leaders of 20 American Republics," [undated but summer 1969], folder 995-NAR Notes, box 121, RG 4, Series 0.8, RAC.

68. Capello, "Latin America Encounters Nelson Rockefeller," 58–59.

69. Rockefeller to Nixon on conversation with President Lleras of Colombia, [undated], folder 802 (Personal and Confidential-Colombia #7.008), box 103, RG 4, Series 0.8, RAC; Rockefeller quoted in notes on advisers breakfast meeting in Haiti, 2 July 1969, folder 1004, box 122, RG 4, Series 0.8, RAC.

70. Rockefeller to Nixon on meeting with General Onganía, [undated], folder 47, box 5, James Cannon Files, RG III 15-7, Subseries 2, RAC; Rockefeller account of meeting with General Onganía, [undated], folder 768 (Personal and Confidential, Argentina), box 98, RG 4, Series 0.8, RAC; Rockefeller to Nixon on meeting with General Costa e Silva, [undated], folder 790 (Personal and Confidential-Brazil), box 101, RG 4, Series 0.8, RAC.

71. Pedro Joaquín Chamorro to George Beebe of *Miami Herald* and a member of Rockefeller team, 20 May 1969, box 9, folder 78, Cannon Files, RG III 15-7, subseries 2, RAC.

72. Background briefing with Kissinger, 31 October 1969, folder 999, box 122, RG 4, Series 0.8, RAC.

73. Rockefeller, *Rockefeller Report*, 32–33.

74. Briefing Book on Brazil, #4.026, [undated], folder 59, box 6, Cannon Files, RG III, Subseries 2, RAC.

75. General Porter's presentation at discussion between Rockefeller and advisers in Asunción, 20 June 1969, folder 1152, box 146, RG 4, Series 0.8, RAC.

76. Rockefeller address to Center for Inter-American Affairs, 21 July 1969, folder 997, box 122, Record Group 4, Series 0.8, RAC; transcript of Rockefeller radio interview with Donaldson, 23 November 1969, folder 1196, box 148, Record Group 4, Series 0.8, RAC.

77. John J. Johnson, *The Military and Society in Latin America* (Stanford, CA: Stanford University Press, 1964).

78. Thomas C. Field Jr., *From Development to Dictatorship: Bolivia and the Alliance for Progress in the Kennedy Era* (Ithaca, NY: Cornell University Press, 2014).

79. Thomas E. Skidmore, *Brazil: Five Centuries of Change* (New York: Oxford University Press, 1999), 177–83.

80. Brent Friele to Rockefeller on views of Bronheim and Bronheim's testimony to U.S. Senate, Subcommittee on Latin American Affairs, 19 September 1969, folder 1201, box 148, RG 4, Series 0.8, RAC.

81. Embassy in Montevideo to DoS, "Role of Military in Latin America," 22 August 1969, #1435, NSSM 68 folder (Church in Latin America), box H-159, NSC: Institutional Files, RMNL.

82. Rockefeller quoted in editorial, *NYT*, 21 May 1969, 46.

83. Nixon quoted in editorial note on NSC meeting, 9 July 1969, document 6, *FRUS, 1969–1976* E-10: *Documents on American Republics, 1969–1972.*

84. Nixon to Haldeman, 26 October 1969, #1706, Presidential Memorandums-1970 folder, box 229, H. R. Haldeman Presidential Memorandums, 1969–1970, WH Special Files: Staff Member and Office Files, RMNL; memorandum of conversation between Kissinger and Galo Plaza, 13 October 1969, #1922, folder 19, box 1026 (Memorandums of Conversation 6-12/69), NSC: President/HAK Memorandums, RMNL.

85. Minutes of NSC meeting, 15 October 1969, document 14, *FRUS, 1969–1976* E-10: *Documents on American Republics, 1969–1972.*

86. Nixon speech in *DSB*, 17 November 1969, 409–14.

87. James Cannon to Rockefeller on reaction to Nixon speech, 5 November 1969, folder 1201, box 148, RG 4, Series 0.8, RAC; Mark Atwood Lawrence, "History from Below: The United States and Latin America in the Nixon Years," in *Nixon in the World: American Foreign Relations, 1969–1977*, ed. Fredrik Logevall and Andrew Preston (New York: Oxford University Press, 2008), 274.

88. Vaky to Kissinger, 1 January 1970, document 21, *FRUS, 1969–1976* E-10: *Documents on American Republics, 1969–1972.*

89. Rockefeller to Kissinger, 24 November 1969, #10.016, folder 1201, box 148, RG 4, Series 0.8, RAC.

90. Kissinger to Nixon, 17 February 1969, document 25, *FRUS, 1969–1976* E-10: *Documents on American Republics, 1969–1972*; NSDM 46, 5 March 1970, document 26, ibid.; NSDM 83, 7 September 1970, document 29, ibid.

91. Nixon to Kissinger, Haldeman, and Ehrlichman, 2 March 1970, #1708, Presidential Memorandums-1970 folder, box 229, H. R. Haldeman Presidential Memorandums, 1969–1970, WH Special Files: Staff Member and Office Files, RMNL. See also Nixon's dismissal of the importance of other developing nations, the "Third World," in an observation to Kissinger. Roham Alvandi, *Nixon, Kissinger and the Shah: The United States and Iran in the Cold War* (New York: Oxford University Press, 2014), 38.

2. Overthrowing Governments

1. Dwight Chapin of White House to Haldeman on conversation with Kissinger, 4 November 1970, #1787, NSC meeting of 19 November 1970 folder, box H-049, NSC Institutional Files: Meetings File, RMNL.

2. Edwin McCammon Martin, *Kennedy and Latin America* (Lanham, MD: University Press of America, 1994), 313–21; Stephen G. Rabe, *The Most Dangerous Area in the World: John F. Kennedy Confronts Communist Revolution in Latin America* (Chapel Hill: University of North Carolina Press, 1999), 112–13.

3. Jeffrey F. Taffet, *Foreign Aid as Foreign Policy: The Alliance for Progress in Latin America* (New York: Routledge, 2007), 81–93.

4. Cole quoted in Rabe, *Most Dangerous Area*, 114–15.

5. Henry Kissinger, *White House Years* (New York: Simon & Schuster, 1979), 655.

6. Editorial note on memorandum by Peter Jessup of 303 Committee to NSC, 23 July 1964, *FRUS, 1964–1968* 31: *South and Central America; Mexico* (Washington, DC: GPO, 2004), 582–83; Jonathan Haslam, *The Nixon Administration and the Death of Allende's Chile: A Case of Assisted Suicide* (London: Verso, 2005), 13–14. See also comments of political counselor in Chile Robert A. Stevenson on the lack of hard evidence of Soviet involvement in the election. Robert A. Stevenson OH, FAOHC (Arlington, VA: Association for Diplomatic Studies and Training, 2000), CD-ROM.

7. Kissinger, *White House Years*, 659; Joseph John Jova, U.S. embassy in Santiago, to Assistant Secretary of State Thomas Mann on conversation with Frei, 5 May 1964, *FRUS, 1964–1968* 31: *South and Central America; Mexico*, 568–70; Jova OH, FAOHC.

8. Embassy in Santiago to DoS, 25 March 1969, document 3, *FRUS, 1969–1976* E-16: *Documents on Chile, 1969–1973* (Washington: GPO, 2015).

9. Memorandum for the 303 Committee, 14 March 1969, document 3, *FRUS, 1969–1976* 21: *Chile, 1969–1973*.

10. Taffet, *Foreign Aid*, 67–75.

11. Armando Uribe, *The Black Book of American Intervention in Chile*, trans. Jonathan Casart (Boston: Beacon Press, 1975), 30–33.

12. Memorandum from Vaky to Kissinger, 22 October 1969, document 21, *FRUS, 1969–1976* 21: *Chile, 1969–1973*.

13. Kissinger quoted in Michael Grow, *U.S. Presidents and Latin American Interventions: Pursuing Regime Change in the Cold War* (Lawrence: University Press of Kansas, 2008), 98.

14. Korry quoted in discussion at DoS on upcoming Chilean election, 19 January 1970, document 28, *FRUS, 1969–1976* E-16: *Documents on Chile, 1969–1973*.

15. NIE 94-70, "The Outlook for Chile," 30 July 1970, document 47, *FRUS, 1969–1976* 21: *Chile, 1969–1973*; embassy in Chile to DoS, 4 September 1970, document 61, ibid.

16. Memorandum for the record, "Minutes of the Meeting of the 40 Committee," 25 March 1970, document 31, *FRUS, 1969–1976* 21: *Chile, 1969–1973*; memorandum for the 40 Committee, 22 June 1970 (approved 27 June 1970), document 38, ibid.; Kristian Gustafson, *Hostile Intent: U.S. Covert Operations in Chile, 1964–1974* (Washington: Potomac Books, 2007), 88–105.

17. Special NIE, "The Outlook for Chile under Allende," 4 August 1971, document 78, *FRUS, 1969–1976* E-16: *Documents on Chile, 1969–1973*.

18. Vaky to Kissinger, "Prospects for Chilean Presidential Election," 22 June 1970, #1884, Chile Wrap-Up and Post-Mortem, March 1971 folder (1 of 3), box 128, NSC: Kissinger Office Files: HAK Administrative and Staff Files, RMNL.

19. Kissinger, *White House Years*, 663.

20. Memorandum of conversation in DoS, "Anaconda Requests U.S. Government Financial Assistance for the Alessandri Election Campaign," 10 April 1970, document 32, *FRUS, 1969–1976* 21: *Chile, 1969–1973*; embassy in Chile to DoS on Anaconda Copper, 22 April 1970, document 33, ibid.

21. Kissinger, *White House Years*, 669; Richard M. Nixon, *RN: The Memoirs of Richard Nixon* (New York: Grosset & Dunlap, 1978), 489–90.

22. Kissinger talk at Georgetown University, 20 April 1971, #1924, Memcons, 1-04/71 folder, box 1026, NSC: President/HAK Memorandums, RMNL.

23. U.S. Congress, Senate, Select Committee to Study Governmental Operations with Respect to Intelligence Activities, *Alleged Assassination Plots Involving Foreign Leaders*, Senate Report No. 465, 94th Cong., 1st sess. (Washington, DC: GPO, 1975); idem, *Covert Action in Chile, 1963–1973*, 94th Cong., 1st sess. (Washington, DC: GPO, 1975).

24. John Hugh Crimmins OH, FAOHC; annotated news summary, 7 September 1970, box 32, POF, RMNL; telephone conversation between Nixon and Kissinger, 12 September 1970, document 82, *FRUS, 1969–1976* 21: *Chile, 1969–1973*.

25. Nixon quoted in Grow, *U.S. Presidents and Latin American Interventions*, 93.

26. Memorandum for the record, "Minutes of 40 Committee Meeting," 8 September 1970, document 70, *FRUS, 1969–1976* 21: *Chile, 1969–1973*.

27. Editorial note on meeting between Nixon and Helms, 15 September 1970, document 93, ibid.

28. Kissinger, *White House Years*, 674.

29. Helms testified in Senate Select Committee, *Alleged Assassination Plots*, 225–29.

30. Quoted in Gustafson, *Hostile Intent*, 102.

31. Vaky to Kissinger, 7 September 1970, document 66, *FRUS, 1969–1976* 21: *Chile, 1969–1973*; Vaky to Kissinger, 14 September 1970, document 86, ibid.; Vaky to Kissinger, 16 September, 1970, document 95, ibid.

32. Jack B. Kubisch OH, FAOHC.

33. Jova OH, ibid.; Samuel F. Hart OH, ibid.

34. Minutes of meeting of SRG, 14 October 1970, document, 150, *FRUS, 1969–1976* 21: *Chile, 1969–1973*.

35. Conversation between Nixon and Helms, 5 March 1971, document 36, *FRUS, 1969–1976* E-10: *Documents on American Republics, 1969–1972*.

36. Phillips quoted in Tim Weiner, *One Man against the World: The Tragedy of Richard Nixon* (New York: Henry Holt, 2015), 106.

37. Memorandum for the record, minutes of 40 Committee meeting, 6 October 1970, document 138, *FRUS, 1969–1976* 21: *Chile, 1969–1973*; paper prepared in CIA, 17 October 1970, document 157, ibid.

38. Memorandum for the record, "Minutes of 40 Committee Meeting," 6 October 1970, document 138, ibid.

39. Editorial note on message received by Army attaché Lieutenant Colonel Paul Wimert, 14 October 1970, document 151, ibid.

40. Minutes of meeting of SRG, 14 October 1970, document 150, ibid.

41. CIA intelligence information cable, 8 September 1970, document 67, ibid.

42. Minutes of 40 Committee meeting, 14 October 1970, document 149, ibid.; memorandum of conversation between Kissinger and Karamessines, 15 October 1970, document 152, ibid.

43. Telephone conversation between Nixon and Kissinger, 15 October 1970, document 153, ibid.

44. CIA in Washington to station in Chile, 16 October 1970, document 154, ibid.

45. Briefing notes prepared in CIA, "Recent Developments—Track II," 28 October 1970, document 168, ibid.

46. Quoted in Robert Dallek, *Nixon and Kissinger: Partners in Power* (New York: Harper-Collins, 2007), 236–38.

47. Kissinger, *White House Years*, 676–77. See also Peter Kornbluh, *The Pinochet File: A Declassified Dossier of Atrocity and Accountability* (New York: New Press, 2003), 31–35.

48. NSDM 93, 9 November 1970, document 175, *FRUS, 1969–1976* 21: *Chile, 1969–1973*.

49. Memorandum of conversation at NSC meeting, 6 November, 1970, document 173, ibid.

50. Walters to Kissinger, 3 November 1970, document 170, ibid.

51. Kissinger quoted in Dallek, *Nixon and Kissinger*, 239; Mark Atwood Lawrence, "History from Below: The United States and Latin America in the Nixon Years," in *Nixon in the World: American Foreign Relations, 1969–1977*, ed. Fredrik Logevall and Andrew Preston (New York: Oxford University Press, 2008), 277; Henry Kissinger, *Years of Upheaval* (New York: Simon & Schuster, 1982), 383.

52. Conversation between Nixon and Kissinger, 23 April 1972, document 63, *FRUS, 1969–1976* E-16: *Documents on Chile, 1969–1973*.

53. Interview with Nathaniel Davis, NSA, "Cold War Interviews," http://nsarchive2.gwu.edu//coldwar/interviews/episode-18/davis1.html. See also Nathaniel Davis, *The Last Two Years of Salvador Allende* (Ithaca, NY: Cornell University Press, 1985).

54. Samuel F. Hart OH, FAOHC; James J. Halsema OH, ibid.; Harry W. Shlaudeman OH, ibid.

55. Kissinger to Nixon, "International Development Bank Loans to Chilean Universities," 28 December 1970, #1803; NSC Meeting, 23 December 1970 folder, box H-050, NSC Institutional Files: Meetings File, RMNL; Senate Select Committee, *Covert Action in Chile*, 33–35; Claudia Kedar, "The World Bank-United States-Latin American Triangle: The Negotiations with Socialist Chile, 1970–1973," *International History Review* 39, no. 4 (2017): 667–90; Kornbluh, *Pinochet File*, 84.

56. Conversation between Nixon and Kissinger, 6 April 1971, document 59, *FRUS, 1969–1976* E-16: *Documents on Chile, 1969–1973*; conversation among Nixon, Treasury Secretary John Connolly, and Kissinger, 11 June 1971, document 75, ibid.

57. NSA interview with Davis; Hart OH, FAOHC.

58. Peter Winn, "The Furies of the Andes: Violence and Terror in the Chilean Revolution and Counterrevolution," in *A Century of Revolution: Insurgent and Counterinsurgent Violence during Latin America's Long Cold War*, ed. Greg Grandin and Gilbert M. Joseph (Durham, NC: Duke University Press, 2010), 239–75.

59. Gustafson, *Hostile Intent*, 140.

60. CIA study, November 1972, document 58, *FRUS, 1969–1976*, E-10 *Documents on American Republics, 1969–1972*; conversation between Nixon and Helms, 5 March 1971, document 36, ibid.; Tanya Harmer, *Allende's Chile and the Inter-American Cold War* (Chapel Hill: University of North Carolina Press, 2011), 195–99, 233–39; Kristian Gustafson and Christopher Andrew, "The Other Hidden Hand: Soviet and Cuban Intelligence in Allende's Chile," *Intelligence and National Security* 33, no. 3 (2018): 407–21; Nicola Miller, *Soviet Relations with Latin America, 1959–1987* (Cambridge: Cambridge University Press, 1989), 127–47.

61. Special NIE, 4 August 1971, "The Outlook for Chile under Allende," #1823, 9 September 1971 Meeting, Chile folder, box H-059, NSC Institutional Files: SRH Meetings, RMNL.

62. Kenneth D. Lehman, *Bolivia and the United States: A Limited Partnership* (Athens: University of Georgia Press, 1999), 164.

63. Stephen G. Rabe, *Eisenhower and Latin America: The Foreign Policy of Anticommunism* (Chapel Hill: University of North Carolina Press, 1988), 77–83.

64. Lehman, *Bolivia and the United States*, 148–49.

65. Thomas C. Field Jr., *From Development to Dictatorship: Bolivia and the Alliance for Progress in the Kennedy Era* (Ithaca, NY: Cornell University Press, 2014), 3; James F. Siekmeier, *The Bolivian Revolution and the United States, 1952 to the Present* (University Park: Pennsylvania State University Press, 2011), 131.

66. Field, *From Development to Dictatorship*, 67–97.

67. Ibid., 189–94.

68. Stephen G. Rabe, *The Killing Zone: The United States Wages Cold War in Latin America*, 2nd ed. (New York: Oxford University Press, 2016), 80–84.

69. Sterfield quoted in Field, *From Development to Dictatorship*, 190.

70. Ambassador to Bolivia William P. Stedman Jr. OH, FAOHC.

71. Ambassador to Bolivia Ernest V. Siracusa OH, FAOHC. See also Siekmeier, *Bolivian Revolution*, 127.

72. Embassy in Bolivia to DoS, 27 December 1969, document 84, *FRUS, 1969–1976* E-10: *Documents on American Republics, 1969–1972*; embassy in Bolivia to DoS, 23 January 1970, ibid.; Siracusa OH, FAOHC.

73. Back channel message from Assistant Secretary of State for Inter-American Affairs Charles A. Meyer to Siracusa, 9 January 1970, document 85, *FRUS, 1969–1976* E-10: *Documents on American Republics, 1969–1972*; embassy in Bolivia to DoS, 5 September 1970, document 91, ibid.

74. Meyers quoted in memorandum for the record of 40 Committee meeting, 6 July 1971, document 105, ibid. See also Lehman, *Bolivia and the United States*, 160–62.

75. Kissinger to Nixon, 7 October 1970, document 93, *FRUS, 1969–1976* E-10: *Documents on American Republics, 1969–1972*.

76. Kissinger to Nixon, 15 October 1970, document 95, ibid.; editorial note on tin sales, document 99, ibid.

77. Memorandum from Deputy Assistant for National Security Affairs Alexander Haig to Nixon, with handwritten notes by Nixon, 6 May 1971, document 100, ibid.; Siracusa OH, FAOHC.

78. Transcript of telephone conversation between Kissinger and Packard, 18 June 1971, *KTC*, ProQuest; memorandum from Arnold Nachmanoff of the NSC to Kissinger, with handwritten notes by Kissinger, 17 June 1971, document 102, *FRUS, 1969–1976* E-10: *Documents on American Republics, 1969–1972*; NSDM 114, 23 June 1971, document 103, ibid.

79. Memorandum for the record of 40 Committee meeting, 6 July 1971, document 105, ibid.; editorial note on covert actions in Bolivia, document 76a, ibid.; Siracusa OH, FAOHC.

80. CIA assessment, "Soviet Involvement in Bolivia," 11 June 1971, #1805, 17 June 1971, Bolivia folder (2), box H-055, NSC Institutional Files: SRG Meetings, RMNL; CIA intelligence memorandum, 16 June 1971, #1810, ibid.

81. Siracusa OH, FAOHC.

82. *PDB*, 23 August 1971, https://www.cia.gov/library/readingroom/collection/presidents-daily-brief-1969–1977. See also editorial note on covert actions in Bolivia, document 76a, *FRUS, 1969–1976* E-10: *Documents on American Republics, 1969–1972*.

83. "U.S. Denies Bolivia Role," *NYT*, 30 August 1970, 3.

84. *PDB*, 20 August 1971, https://www.cia.gov/library/readingroom/docs/DOC_0005992815.pdf; memorandum from Nachmanoff to Kissinger, with handwritten notes, 19 August 1971, document 107, *FRUS, 1969–1976* E-10: *Documents on American Republics, 1969–1972*.

85. Lehman, *Bolivia and the United States*, 165; Tanya Harmer, "Brazil's Cold War in the Southern Cone, 1970–1975," *Cold War History* 12 (November 2012): 660, 669–71.

86. Rabe, *Killing Zone*, 126–27; Harmer, "Brazil's Cold War," 659–81.

87. Memorandum from Ashley Hewitt of NSC staff to Kissinger, with Kissinger's handwritten notes, 4 March 1972, document 110, *FRUS, 1969–1976* E-10: *Documents on American Republics, 1969–1972*; Siracusa OH, FAOHC.

88. Embassy in Bolivia to DoS, 6 December 1972, document 115, ibid.; embassy in Bolivia to DoS, 2 February 1973, document 59, *FRUS, 1969–1976* E-11, Part 2: *Documents on South America, 1973–1976*; Deputy Chief of Mission in Bolivia Roger C. Brewin OH, FAOHC.

89. Memorandum of conversation between Kissinger and Banzer, 7 June 1976, document 79, *FRUS, 1969–1976* E-11, Part 2: *Documents on South America, 1973–1976*.

90. Embassy in Bolivia to DoS, 2 February 1973, document 59, *FRUS, 1969–1976* E-11, Part 2: *Documents on South America, 1973–1976*.

91. Andres Schipani of *BBC News*, La Paz, "Hidden Cells Reveal Bolivia's Dark Past," 5 March 2009, http://news.bbc.co.uk/2/hi/americas/7925694.stm. See also OH of Scott E. Smith, U.S. diplomat in Bolivia, FAOHC.

92. Siracusa OH, FAOHC.

93. Kissinger telephone conversation with Nixon, 26 August 1971, *KTC*, ProQuest.

94. Haslam, *Nixon Administration and the Death of Allende's Chile*, 79–157.

95. NSC memorandum for approval of spending money on Chilean elections, 11 January 1973, document 317, *FRUS, 1969–1976* 21: *Chile, 1969–1973*; memorandum from Acting Assistant Secretary of State John H. Crimmins to Undersecretary of State William Porter, "Additional Funds for Chilean Opposition for March Elections," 9 February 1973, document 319, ibid.

96. Memorandum from Crimmins to Porter, "Chilean Congressional Elections," 4 May 1973, document 325, ibid.

97. DoS to embassy in Chile, "Secretary's Meeting with President Allende," 29 May 1973, document 327, ibid.

98. Memorandum from Director of Operations Policy, Bureau of Intelligence and Research James R. Gardner to the Deputy Director for Coordination, Bureau of Intelligence and Research William McAfee, "ARA/CIA Meeting, 11 June 1973," 14 June 1973, document 229, ibid.; William J. Jorden of NSC Staff to Kissinger, "NIE on Chile," 10 July 1973, document 336, ibid.; Kubisch OH, FAOHC.

99. Editorial note on funding truckers' strike, document 339, *FRUS, 1969–1976* 21: *Chile, 1969–1973*.

100. Telephone conversation between Nixon and Kissinger, 4 July 1973, document 335, ibid. On failed coup, see CIA Information Report, 25 July 1973, document 338, ibid.

101. CIA reports on Pinochet, 6 August 1971 and 27 September 1972, both in Kornbluh, *Pinochet File*, 134–37; Senate Select Committee, *Covert Action in Chile*, 34; Lesley Gill, *The School of the Americas: Military Training and Violence in the Americas* (Durham, NC: Duke University Press, 2004), 79–80.

102. Memorandum from Phillips to Karamessines, 13 August 1973, document 341, *FRUS, 1969–1976* 21: *Chile, 1969–1973*; Executive Secretary of State Thomas R. Pickering to General Brent Scowcroft of NSC, "Chilean Contingency Paper: Possible Chilean Military Intervention," 8 September 1973, #1860, 12 September 1973 Meeting on Chile folder, box H-094, NSC Institutional Files: WSAG Meetings, RMNL; DoS to Scowcroft, "Chilean Contingency Paper: Possible Chilean Military Intervention," 8 September 1973, #1465, NSMM 78, Chile folder, box H-172, NSC Institutional Files, RMNL; Hart OH, FAOHC.

103. Nixon, *RN*, 490; Kissinger, *Years of Upheaval*, 374–413.

104. NSA interview with Davis; OH of William Lowenthal, U.S. embassy in Santiago, FAOHC; OH of James J. Halsema, Public Affairs Officer in U.S. embassy in Santiago, FAOHC.

105. Gustafson, *Hostile Intent*, 1.

106. Ariel Dorfman, "Now America, You Know How Chileans Felt," *NYT*, 17 December 2016, A21; Louis Nelson, "Nikki Haley on Russian Meddling: Election Interference Is 'Warfare,'" *Politico*, 19 October 2017, http://www.politico.com/story/2017/10/19/nikki-haley-russia-meddling-warfare-243942.

107. Shlaudeman OH, FAOHC; Colby to Kissinger and Kubisch, 25 August 1973, document 342, *FRUS, 1969–1976* 21: *Chile, 1969–1973*.

108. Telephone conversation between Nixon and Kissinger, 16 September 1973, document 357, ibid.

109. Memorandum from Kissinger to Nixon, 11 September 1973, document 347, ibid.; minutes of WSAG meeting, 12 September 1973, document 348, ibid.; minutes of WSAG meeting, 14 September 1973, document 353, ibid.

110. Kornbluh, *Pinochet File*, 201–3.

111. Memorandum from William J. Jorden of NSC staff to Kissinger, "Brazilian Views on Chile," 13 September 1973, document 90, *FRUS, 1969–1976* E-11, Part 2: *Documents on South America, 1973–1976*; John Hugh Crimmins of American Republic Affairs OH, FAOHC; Harmer, "Brazil's Cold War," 672–75; Davis, *Last Two Years*, 331–32.

112. Rose Styron, "Terror in Chile II: The Amnesty Report," *New York Review of Books* 21 (30 May 1974); Martha K. Huggins, *Political Policing: The United States and Latin America* (Durham, NC: Duke University Press, 1998), 99–115, 134–36; A. J. Langguth, *Hidden Terrors: The Truth about U.S. Police Operations in Latin America* (New York: Pantheon Books, 1978), 117–42.

113. Christopher Dietrich, "'Our Hand Doesn't Show': The United States and the Consolidation of the Pinochet Regime in Chile (1973–1977)," in *Dirty Hands and Vicious Deeds: The US Government's Complicity in Crimes against Humanity and Genocide*, ed. Samuel Totten (Toronto: University of Toronto Press, 2018), 134–218; Kornbluh, *Pinochet File*, 203–6; Gill, *School of the Americas*, 79–80.

114. "Terror in Chile I: Chicago Commission of Inquiry into the Status of Human Rights in Chile," *New York Review of Books* 21 (30 May 1974); memorandum from the Director of the Office of Bolivian-Chilean Affairs Rudy V. Fimbres and the Officer-in-

Charge of Chilean Political Affairs Robert S. Driscoll to Assistant Secretary of State for Inter-American Affairs Shlaudeman, "Charles Horman Case," 25 August 1976, document 243, *FRUS, 1969–1976*, E-11, Part 2 *Documents on South America, 1973–1976*; Hart OH, FAOHC; Pascale Bonnefoy, "Chilean Court Rules U.S. Role in Murders," *NYT*, 1 July 2014, A6; Pascale Bonnefoy, "Florida Jury Finds Former Chilean Officer Liable in '73 Killing," *NYT*, 27 June 2016, A6.

115. Thomas C. Wright, *State Terrorism in Latin America: Chile, Argentina, and International Human Rights* (Lanham, MD: Rowman & Littlefield, 2007), 65–66, 213; Sergio Bitar, *Prisoner of Pinochet: My Year in a Chilean Concentration Camp*, trans. Eric Goodman (Madison: University of Wisconsin Press, 2017), 18–119; Luz Arce, *The Inferno: A Story of Terror and Survival in Chile*, trans. Stacey Alba Skar (Madison: University of Wisconsin Press, 2004), 38–40; Mary Ellen Spooner, *Soldiers in a Narrow Land: The Pinochet Regime in Chile* (Berkeley: University of California Press, 1999), 49–82.

116. Pascale Bonnefoy, "Doubts Are Raised over Neruda's Death," *NYT*, 23 October 2017, C3; Alexei Barrionuevo, "Judge Accuses Three Tied to Pinochet of Fatally Poisoning a Chilean Ex-Leader in 1981," *NYT*, 8 December 2009, A6; "Chile: Six Charged in Murder of Former President Eduardo Frei Montalva," *DW*, 12 August 2017, http://www.dw.com/en/chile-six-charged-in-murder-of-former-president-eduardo-frei-montalva/a-40064034.

117. Brian Loveman and Elizabeth Lira, "Truth, Justice, Reconciliation, and Impunity as Historical Themes: Chile, 1814–2006," *Radical History* 97 (Winter 2007): 61–70; Steve J. Stern, *Remembering Pinochet's Chile: On the Eve of London, 1998* (Durham, NC: Duke University Press, 2004), xxi, 158–61; Styron, "Terror in Chile II: The Amnesty Report."

118. Steve J. Stern, *Reckoning with Pinochet: The Memory Question in Democratic Chile, 1989–2006* (Durham, NC: Duke University Press, 2010), 136–37; Thomas C. Wright, *Impunity, Human Rights, and Democracy: Chile and Argentina, 1990–2005* (Austin: University of Texas Press, 2014), 112; Naomi Roht-Arriaza, *The Pinochet Effect: Transnational Justice in the Age of Human Rights* (Philadelphia: University of Pennsylvania Press, 2005), 67–96.

119. Wright, *State Terrorism in Latin America*, 59–61; embassy in Chile to DoS, "Conversation with Pinochet," 12 October 1973, document 146, *FRUS, 1969–1976*, E-11, Part 2 *Documents on South America, 1973–1976*.

120. Transcript of Kissinger's staff meeting, 1 October 1973, document 142, ibid.; memorandum of conversation between Kissinger and Chilean Foreign Minister Admiral Ismael Huerta, 11 October 1973, document 145, ibid.; transcript of Kissinger's staff meeting, 31 January 1974, document 157, ibid.

121. Seymour M. Hersh, "Kissinger Said to Rebuke U.S. Ambassador to Chile," 27 September 1974, *NYT*, 18. The report that provoked Kissinger is in embassy in Santiago to DoS, 23 July 1974, document 170, *FRUS, 1969–1976*, E-11, Part 2 *Documents on South America, 1973–1976*.

122. Memorandum 1030/74 prepared in CIA, "Aspects of the Situation in Chile," 21 March 1974, document 161, ibid.; embassy in Santiago to DoS, 11 September 1974, "One Year of the Chilean Junta," document 173, ibid.

123. John Dinges and Saul Landau, *Assassination on Embassy Row* (New York: Pantheon Books, 1980), 207–27. For a multimedia presentation marking the fortieth

anniversary of the assassination, see "This Was Not an Accident. This Was a Bomb," *Washington Post*, 20 September 2016, http://www.washingtonpost.com/sf/national /2016/09/20/this-was-not-an-accident-this-was-a-bomb/?utm_term=.e8b7fc0c0683.

124. Memorandum from Executive Secretary of 40 Committee, Rob Roy Ratliff, to Kissinger, "Termination of the Chile Account," 11 June 1974, document 168, *FRUS, 1969–1976*, E-11, Part 2 *Documents on South America, 1973–1976*; Wright, *State Terrorism in Latin America*, 71–72.

3. Kissinger and Friends

1. Quoted in Frank O. Mora and Jerry W. Cooney, *Paraguay and the United States: Distant Allies* (Athens: University of Georgia Press, 2007), 183.

2. Quoted in Economic Counselor James J. Gormley OH, FAOHC.

3. Ambassador George Landau OH, FAOHC.

4. Mora and Cooney, *Paraguay and the United States*, 125–33.

5. Deputy Chief of Mission Roger M. Brewin OH, FAOHC.

6. Ambassador Robert E. White OH, FAOHC.

7. For a study of Trujillo's tactics, see Eric Paul Roorda, *The Dictator Next Door: The Good Neighbor Policy and the Trujillo Regime in the Dominican Republic, 1930–1945* (Durham, NC: Duke University Press, 1998).

8. Memorandum of conversation between Eisenhower and Stroessner in Panama City, 23 July 1956, *FRUS, 1955–1957* VII: *American Republics: Central and South America* (Washington, DC: GPO, 1987), 1010–11.

9. Mora and Cooney, *Paraguay and the United States*, 140, 165, 182.

10. Ibid., 178.

11. *PDB*, 28 July 1975, https://www.cia.gov/library/readingroom/docs/DOC _0006014860.pdf.

12. Foreign Aid Officer Peter M. Cody OH, FAOHC; Mora and Cooney, *Paraguay and the United States*, 133–80; Kirk Tyvela, *The Dictator Dilemma: The United States and Paraguay in the Cold War* (Pittsburgh: University of Pittsburgh Press, 2019), 48–73.

13. Country analysis for Paraguay, 7 February 1969, document 564, *FRUS, 1969–1976* E-10: *Documents on American Republics, 1969–1972*; country analysis for Paraguay, 13 February 1970, document 566, ibid.

14. *PDB*, 17 November 1969, https://www.cia.gov/library/readingroom/document /0006146467; *PDB*, CIA memorandum, "Stability in Paraguay," 9 April 1970, https:// www.cia.gov/library/readingroom/document/cia-rdp85t00875r001100090017-9.

15. Stroessner to Nixon, 20 July 1970, document 569, *FRUS, 1969–1976* E-10: *Documents on American Republics, 1969–1972*.

16. Kissinger's handwritten notes on memorandum from Vaky of NSC to Kissinger, 15 August 1970, document 570, ibid.

17. Embassy in Paraguay to DoS, 27 April 1971, document 573, ibid.

18. Memorandum from Secretary of State Rogers to Nixon, 28 July 1972, document 574, ibid.; embassy in Paraguay to DoS on mission of Gross, 19 August 1972, document 575, ibid.; Mora and Cooney, *Paraguay and the United States*, 187–91; Tyvela, *Dictator Dilemma*, 101–21.

19. Mora and Cooney, *Paraguay and the United States*, 187–91, 192–96.

20. Landau OH, FAOHC; Lars Schoultz, *Human Rights and United States Policy toward Latin America* (Princeton, NJ: Princeton University Press, 1981), 194–95.

21. Quoted material in Gormley OH, FAOHC. See also White OH, FAOHC.

22. Landau OH, FAOHC; Tanya Harmer, "Brazil's Cold War in the Southern Cone, 1970–1975," *Cold War History* 12 (November 2012): 675. For the investigation into the assassination, see Taylor Branch and Eugene M. Propper, *Labyrinth: How a Stubborn Prosecutor Penetrated a Shadowland of Covert Operations on Three Continents to Find the Assassins of Orlando Letelier* (New York: Viking, 1982).

23. Stephen G. Rabe, *The Killing Zone: The United States Wages Cold War in Latin America*, 2nd ed. (New York: Oxford University Press, 2016), 108–9.

24. Jeffrey F. Taffet, *Foreign Aid as Foreign Policy: The Alliance for Progress in Latin America* (New York: Routledge, 2007), 95–121.

25. Ambassador John Tuthill OH, FAOHC.

26. Embassy in Brazil to DoS, 14 December 1968, *FRUS, 1964–1968* 31: *South and Central America; Mexico*, 523–25; DoS to embassy in Brazil, 17 December 1968, ibid., 525–27.

27. Political Counselor Richard E. Johnson OH, FAOHC.

28. Quoted in Jeffrey L. Gould, "Solidarity under Siege: The Latin American Left, 1968," *American Historical Review* 114 (April 2009): 357–58. See also Virginia Langland, "Birth Control Pills and Molotov Cocktails: Reading Sex and Revolution in 1968 Brazil," in *In from the Cold: Latin America's New Encounter with the Cold War*, ed. Gilbert M. Joseph and Daniela Spenser (Durham, NC: Duke University Press, 2008), 308–49.

29. Analytic Summary of NSC 67, 8 December 1970, #1792, Brazil Program Analysis folder (1), box H-049, NSC Institutional Files: Meeting Files, RMNL.

30. Consul Curtis C. Cutter OH, FAOHC.

31. Gould, "Solidarity under Siege," 348–75.

32. Martha K. Huggins, *Political Policing: The United States and Latin America* (Durham, NC: Duke University Press, 1998), 99–204; Jeremy Kuzmarov, *Modernizing Repression: Police Training and Nation-Building in the American Century* (Amherst: University of Massachusetts Press, 2012), 208–31; Gould, "Solidarity under Siege," 372.

33. Huggins, *Political Policing*, 134–36, 151–52; A. J. Langguth, *Hidden Terrors: The Truth about U.S. Police Operations in Latin America* (New York: Pantheon Books, 1978), 40–44, 72–77, 117–39, 198–200.

34. Huggins, *Political Policing*, 166–67; Simon Romero, "Leader's Torture in '70s Stirs Ghosts in Brazil," *NYT*, 5 August 2012, A1.

35. Joan Dassin, ed., *Torture in Brazil: A Report by the Archdiocese of São Paulo*, trans. Jamie Wright (New York: Vintage Books, 1986), xxv–xxvi. See also Richard Sandomir, "Cardinal Paulo Evaristo Arns Dies at 95: Fought Torture in Brazil," *NYT*, 20 December 2016, A20.

36. The forty-three documents can be found at the NSA website: https://unredacted.com/2014/07/03/declassified-documents-given-by-biden-to-rousseff-detail-secret-dictatorship-era-executions-psychophysical-torture-in-brazil/.

37. Crimmins OH, FAOHC; Cutter OH, FAOHC.

38. Dassin, *Torture in Brazil*.

39. An analysis of Brazil's National Truth Commission can be found at the NSA website: https://nsarchive2.gwu.edu/NSAEBB/NSAEBB496/. The report can be found

at http://cnv.memoriasreveladas.gov.br/. See also Simon Romero, "Brazil Releases Report on Past Right Abuses," *NYT*, 11 December 2014, A16.

40. Walters to Kissinger, 31 December 1960, document 116, *FRUS, 1969–1976* E10: *Documents on American Republics, 1969–1972*.

41. Viron Vaky of NSC quoted in covering memorandum in Kissinger to Nixon, 15 April 1970, document 127, ibid.

42. Memorandum of meeting between Nixon and Rountree, 14 December 1970, document 134, ibid.

43. Telephone conversation between Kissinger and Secretary of State Rogers, 12 March 1971, *KTC*, ProQuest.

44. Telephone conversation between Kissinger and Nixon, 8 December 1971, ibid.

45. On Nixon's comments to Prime Minister Heath, see editorial notes to memorandum from CIA Acting Director Robert E. Cushman Jr. to Kissinger, 29 December 1971, document 145, *FRUS, 1969–1976* E10: *Documents on American Republics, 1969–1972*.

46. Walters quoted in conversation with Figueiredo in memorandum from Walters to Brent Scowcroft of NSC on conversation with Figueiredo, 25 July 1974, document 104, *FRUS, 1969–1976* E-11, Part 2: *Documents on South America, 1973–1976*; Nixon quoted in conversation with Rogers, 7 December 1971, document 11, NSA, *Electronic Briefing Book No 71*, https://nsarchive2.gwu.edu/NSAEBB/NSAEBB71/#docs.

47. Embassy in Brazil to DoS, 30 May 1973, document 88, *FRUS, 1969–1976* E-11, Part 2: *Documents on South America, 1973–1976*; memorandum of conversation between Kissinger and Foreign Minister Gibson Barboza, 26 September 1973, 26 September 1973, document 92, ibid.

48. Kissinger telephone conversation with Simon with accompanying footnote, 21 June 1976, document 103, ibid.; DoS embassy to Brazil, with letter from Kissinger to Silveira, 8 May 1976, document 133, ibid.

49. Embassy in Brazil to DoS, "Effects on U.S./Brazilian Relations of the German Agreement," 27 June 1975, document 117, ibid.; Crimmins OH, FAOHC. For Brazil's relations with Argentina, see Christopher Darnton, *Rivalry and Alliance Politics in Cold War Latin America* (Baltimore: Johns Hopkins University Press, 2014), 80–106.

50. DoS to embassy in Brazil, with personal message from Kissinger to Silveira, 20 June 1975, document 116, *FRUS, 1969–1976* E-11, Part 2: *Documents on South America, 1973–1976*.

51. Embassy in Brazil to DoS, "Effects on U.S./Brazilian Relations of the German Agreement," 27 June 1975, document 117, ibid.; Harmer, "Brazil's Cold War," 664, 676–77.

52. DoS to Kissinger, with letter from Silveira, 25 August 1975, document 121, *FRUS, 1969–1976* E-11, Part 2: *Documents on South America, 1973–1976*; Kissinger to embassy in Brazil, with letter from Silveira, 30 August 1975, document 122, ibid.

53. Telephone conversation between Kissinger and Assistant Secretary Rogers, 14 November 1975, *KTC*, ProQuest; telephone conversation between Kissinger and Silveira, 22 April 1975, ibid.

54. Memorandum from Walters to Scowcroft on conversation with Figuerido, 25 July 1974, document 104, *FRUS, 1969–1976* E-11, Part 2: *Documents on South America, 1973–1976*. See also NIE 93-1-75, "The Outlook for Brazil," 11 July 1975, document 119, ibid.

55. Embassy in Brazil to DoS, 26 January 1976, document 126, ibid.

56. Colby to Kissinger, 11 April 1974, document 99, ibid.

57. James N. Green, *We Cannot Remain Silent: Opposition to the Brazilian Military Dictatorship in the United States* (Durham, NC: Duke University Press, 2010), 115–18, 168–75.

58. DoS to embassy in Brazil, 3 March 1975, *FRUS, 1969–1976* E-11, Part 2: *Documents on South America, 1973–1976.*

59. Memorandum of conversation between Kissinger and President Geisel, 20 February 1976, document 128, ibid.

60. Scowcroft to President Ford, with report from Kissinger to Ford, 22 February 1976, document 129, ibid.

61. Green, *We Cannot Remain Silent,* 345–47; Richard Johnson OH, FAOHC.

62. Deputy Chief of Mission George B. High OH, FAOHC.

63. Political Officer James L. Tull OH, https://www.adst.org/OH%20TOCs/Tull,%20James%20L.toc.pdf.

64. Gould, "Solidarity under Siege," 354–57.

65. Langguth, *Hidden Terrors,* 260–84.

66. Ambassador Lawrence Pezzullo OH, FAOHC. See also Tull OH, https://www.adst.org/OH%20TOCs/Tull,%20James%20L.toc.pdf.

67. Schoultz, *Human Rights,* 14–15, 84–85.

68. Letter from Assistant Secretary of State for Inter-American Affairs Thomas Mann to Ambassador to Uruguay Wymberly Coerr, 23 June 1964, *FRUS, 1964–1968* 31: *South and Central America; Mexico,* 968–69; Mann to Secretary of State Dean Rusk, 1 December 1964, ibid., 974–76; information memorandum from Assistant Secretary of State for Inter-American Affairs Covey Oliver to Rusk, 18 August 1967, ibid., 984–85.

69. Briefing Book for Uruguay, Spring 1969, #5.035, folder 85, box 10, James Cannon Files, RG III, Subseries 2, RAC; Rockefeller conversation with Pacheco, not dated, #7.066, folder 904 (Personal and Confidential-Uruguay), box 116, Rockefeller Family Collection, RG 4, Series 0.8, RAC.

70. Rockefeller conversation with Costa e Silva, not dated, #6.043, folder 790 (Personal and Confidential), box 101, Rockefeller Family Collection, RG 4, Series 0.8, RAC.

71. Telephone conversations between Kissinger and Rockefeller, 26 June 1969 and 9 July 1969, *KTC,* ProQuest.

72. USAID, *U.S. Overseas Loans and Grants: Obligations and Loan Authorizations, July 1, 1945–September 30, 2015,* https://pdf.usaid.gov/pdf_docs/pbaah600.pdf.

73. USIA Officer Horace V. (Tex) Edwards OH, FAOHC.

74. Nixon to Pacheco, 6 August 1970, NSA, *Electronic Briefing Book No. 324,* https://nsarchive2.gwu.edu/NSAEBB/NSAEBB324/index.htm.

75. Rogers to Adair, 9 August 1970, ibid.; Adair to DoS, 9 August 1970, ibid.

76. DoS to Kissinger, 27 November 1971, document 8, NSA, *Electronic Briefing Book No. 71,* https://nsarchive2.gwu.edu/NSAEBB/NSAEBB71/doc8.pdf.

77. Gallup poll in ibid.

78. Lodge to DoS, 27 August 1971, document 4, ibid., https://nsarchive2.gwu.edu/NSAEBB/NSAEBB71/doc4.pdf.

79. Embassy in Montevideo to DoS, "Preliminary Analysis and Strategy Paper," 25 August 1971, document 2, ibid., https://nsarchive2.gwu.edu/NSAEBB/NSAEBB71/doc2.pdf.

80. Adair to DoS, 9 November 1971, document 6, https://nsarchive2.gwu.edu/NSAEBB/NSAEBB71/doc6.pdf; Adair to DoS, 7 December 1971, document 10, https://nsarchive2.gwu.edu/NSAEBB/NSAEBB71/doc10.pdf.

81. Nick Cullather, *Secret History: The CIA's Classified Account of Its Operations in Guatemala, 1952–1954* (Stanford, CA: Stanford University Press, 1999).

82. Conversation between Nixon and Rogers, 7 December 1971, document 11, NSA, *Electronic Briefing Book No. 71*, https://nsarchive2.gwu.edu/NSAEBB/NSAEBB71/doc11.pdf; memorandum by Arnold Nachmanoff of NSC to Kissinger on meeting with Médici, 8 December 1971, document 142, *FRUS, 1969–1976* E-10: *Documents on American Republics, 1969–1972.*

83. Memorandum of conversation by Kissinger on meeting between Nixon and Heath, 20 December 1971, document 15, NSA, *Electronic Briefing Book No. 71*, https://nsarchive2.gwu.edu/NSAEBB/NSAEBB71/doc11.pdf.

84. *PDB*, "Uruguay: The Military in a Crumbling Utopia," 15 November 1972, https://www.cia.gov/library/readingroom/docs/DOC_0005993627.pdf; *PDB*, 7 September 1971, https://www.cia.gov/library/readingroom/docs/DOC_0005992849.pdf.

85. *PDB*, "Cuba's Changing Relations with Latin America," 28 January 1972, https://www.cia.gov/library/readingroom/docs/DOC_0005993107.pdf.

86. *PDB*, 22 March 1973, https://www.cia.gov/library/readingroom/docs/DOC_0005993777.pdf.

87. *PDB*, 24 March 1973, https://www.cia.gov/library/readingroom/docs/DOC_0005993779.pdf; footnote on telegram 3341 from embassy in Montevideo to DoS, 12 November 1973, in embassy in Montevideo to DoS, 26 December 1973, document 339, *FRUS, 1969–1976* E-11, Part 2: *Documents on South America, 1973–1976.*

88. Siracusa OH, FAOHC.

89. Memorandum from Executive Secretary of DoS Theodore L. Eliot, Jr. to Kissinger, 9 February 1973, document 328, *FRUS, 1969–1976* E-11, Part 2: *Documents on South America, 1973–1976.*

90. Ortiz to DoS, 2 July 1973, document 335, ibid.; Rush to embassy in Montevideo, 3 July 1973, document 336, ibid.

91. Tull OH, https://www.adst.org/OH%20TOCs/Tull,%20James%20L.toc.pdf.

92. Memorandum of conversation between Kissinger and Blanco, 10 May 1975, document 341, *FRUS, 1969–1976* E-11, Part 2: *Documents on South America, 1973–1976.*

93. Amnesty International, *Political Imprisonment in Uruguay* (London: Amnesty International, 1979). The report can also be found at https://www.amnesty.org/download/Documents/204000/amr520131979en.pdf.

94. Letter from Russell E. Olson, political officer of embassy in Uruguay, to Aurelia A. Brazeal, country officer for Uruguay and Paraguay, 8 August 1973, document 342, *FRUS, 1969–1976* E-11, Part 2: *Documents on South America, 1973–1976*; memorandum of conversation between Siracusa and Blanco, 27 January 1976, document 347, ibid.; DoS to embassy in Montevideo on meeting with Ferreira, with accompanying footnote, 16 December 1975, document 343, ibid.; DoS to embassy in Montevideo on meeting with Ferreira, with accompanying footnote, 22 June 1976, document 353, ibid.

95. Siracusa OH, FAOHC.

96. Letter from Ryan to Koch, 11 June 1976, document 354, *FRUS, 1969–1976* E-11, Part 2: *Documents on South America, 1973–1976.*

97. *PDB*, 16 June 1976, https://www.cia.gov/library/readingroom/docs/DOC _0006015137.pdf.

98. Telegram from delegation with secretary of state in Mexico to DoS, "Secretary's Bilateral Meeting with Foreign Minister Blanco," 11 June 1976, document 350, *FRUS, 1969–1976* E-11, Part 2: *Documents on South America, 1973–1976.*

99. Siracusa to DoS, 7 June 1976, document 349, ibid.

100. Memorandum for the record of meeting between Joseph Grunwald of CIA and Assistant Secretary of State Shlaudeman, "Uruguay: Threat against Congressman Koch," 10 December 1976, document 366, ibid.

101. Shlaudeman to Kissinger, with accompanying footnote on Kissinger's 16 September 1976 response, 30 August 1976, document 359, ibid.

102. Siracusa to DoS, 2 December 1976, document 365, ibid.; Shlaudeman to Habib, "Uruguayan Personnel to the US," 31 December 1976, document 369, ibid.

103. Pezzullo OH, FAOHC.

104. Memorandum of conversation between Foreign Minister Blanco and Acting Secretary of State Charles W. Robinson, Shlaudeman, and Siracusa, 8 October 1976, document 363, *FRUS, 1969–1976* E-11, Part 2: *Documents on South America, 1973–1976.*

4. Mass Murder and International Assassination

1. Study by NSC Interdepartmental Group for Inter-American Affairs, 9 October 1969, document 59, *FRUS, 1969–1976* E10: *Documents on American Republics, 1969–1972.*

2. Roger R. Trask," Spruille Braden versus George Messersmith: World War II, the Cold War, and Argentine Policy, 1945–1947," *Journal of Inter-American Studies and World Affairs* 26 (February 1984), 69–95.

3. Stephen G. Rabe, *Eisenhower and Latin America: The Foreign Policy of Anticommunism* (Chapel Hill: University of North Carolina Press, 1988), 36–38.

4. Stephen G. Rabe, *The Most Dangerous Area in the World: John F. Kennedy Confronts Communist Revolution in Latin America* (Chapel Hill: University of North Carolina Press, 1999), 56–63. For data on trade and investment, see Rabe, *The Road to OPEC: United States Relations with Venezuela, 1919–1976* (Austin: University of Texas Press, 1982), 193–95.

5. Rockefeller conversation with Onganía, not dated, but 1969, #6.001, folder 768, box 98, Rockefeller Family Collection, Record Group 4, Series 0.8, RAC.

6. Kissinger telephone conversation with H. R. Haldeman, 18 March 1969, *KTC*, ProQuest; Kissinger telephone conversation with Secretary of State Rogers, 14 April 1969, ibid.

7. Labor attaché John T. Doherty OH, FAOHC; political officer Dan W. Figgins OH, FAOHC.

8. Nixon quoted in conversation between presidential adviser Peter M. Flanigan to Kissinger, 7 February 1972 in footnote to memorandum from Ashley Hewitt of NSC to Kissinger, 29 November 1971, document 73, *FRUS, 1969–1976* E10: *Documents on American Republics, 1969–1972.*

9. Memorandum from Kissinger to Nixon on letters from Ambassador Lodge, 16 October 1970, document 64, ibid.

10. Back-channel message from Ambassador Lodge to Assistant Secretary of State for Inter-American Affairs Charles A. Meyer, 30 June 1971, document 67, ibid.; back-channel message from Deputy Chief of Mission Milton Barall to Meyer, 2 July 1971, document 68, ibid.; memorandum from Alexander Haig of NSC to Nixon, 14 July 1971, document 69, ibid.

11. Kissinger to Nixon, 23 March 1971, document 65, ibid.; back-channel message from Lodge to Executive Secretary of DoS Eliot on visit of John Petty, 31 August 1971, document 72, ibid.; footnote on Kissinger meeting with Argentine Ambassador Ismael Bruno Quijano, 7 February 1972, document 75, ibid.

12. Memorandum from Karamessines to Kissinger, 2 February 1973, document 1, *FRUS, 1969–1976* E-11, Part 2: *Documents on South America, 1973–1976*.

13. DoS to embassy in Argentina on meeting between Rogers and Cámpora, 4 June 1973, document 3, ibid.

14. Memorandum of conversation between Kissinger and Vignes, 5 October 1973, document 8, ibid.; embassy in Argentina to DoS, 11 November 1973, document 10, ibid.

15. Memorandum prepared by CIA's Office of Current Intelligence, "Perónism in Power," with covering note from Walters to Kissinger, 21 June 1973, document 5, ibid.

16. Embassy in Argentina to DoS, 6 June 1973, document 4, ibid.

17. NIE 91–74, "Prospects for Argentina," 31 January 1974, document 13, ibid.

18. Transcript of Kissinger meeting with DoS staff, 10 July 1974, document 19, ibid.

19. *PDB*, 7 January 1975, https://www.cia.gov/library/readingroom/docs/DOC_0006007911.pdf.

20. Embassy in Argentina to DoS, "Human Rights: The Argentine Situation," 9 March 1976, document 36, *FRUS, 1969–1976* E-11, Part 2: *Documents on South America, 1973–1976*.

21. Memorandum of conversation between Kissinger and Vignes, 8 May 1975, document 27, ibid.

22. Embassy in Argentina to DoS, "Argentine Perceptions of the US," 30 January 1976, document 32, ibid.

23. Telephone conversation between Kissinger and Nixon, 17 April 1974, document 15, ibid.; accompanying footnote to Under Secretary of State Joseph Sisco to Kissinger, 10 July 1974, document 20, ibid.; telephone conversation between Kissinger and Secretary of the Treasury William Simon, 21 June 1974, *KTC*, ProQuest.

24. *PDB*, 27 December 1975, https://www.cia.gov/library/readingroom/docs/DOC_0006014989.pdf.

25. Embassy in Argentina to DoS, 10 September 1975, document 28, *FRUS, 1969–1976* E-11, Part 2: *Documents on South America, 1973–1976*.

26. Labor attaché Herman Rebhan OH, FAOHC. See also Federico Finchelstein, *Ideological Origins of the Dirty War: Fascism, Populism, and Dictatorship in Twentieth Century Argentina* (New York: Oxford University Press, 2014), 147.

27. Embassy to DoS on conversation with General Agosti and accompanying footnote, 21 February 1976, document 34, *FRUS, 1969–1976* E-11, Part 2: *Documents on South America, 1973–1976*; embassy in Argentina to DoS, "Ambassador's Conversation with Admiral Massera," 6 March 1976, document 38, ibid; accompanying footnote to em-

bassy in Argentina to DoS, 28 February 1976, document 35, ibid; DoS to embassy in Argentina, 13 March 1976, document 37, ibid.

28. Embassy in Argentina to DoS, "Argentine Perceptions of the US," 30 January 1976, document 32, ibid.; Tanya Harmer, "Fractious Allies: Chile, the United States, and the Cold War, 1973–1976," *DH* 37 (January 2013): 109–43; Harmer, "Brazil's Cold War in the Southern Cone, 1970–1975," *Cold War History* 12 (November 2012): 670, 680–81.

29. Ariel C. Armony, *Argentina, the United States, and the Anti-Communist Crusade in Central America, 1977–1984* (Athens: Ohio University Press, 1997).

30. Argentine National Commission on the Disappeared, *Nunca Más*, with an introduction by Ronald Dworkin (New York: Farrar, Straus, and Giroux, 1986).

31. Stephen G. Rabe, *The Killing Zone: The United States Wages Cold War in Latin America*, 2nd ed. (New York: Oxford University Press, 2016), 187; Tina Rosenberg, *Children of Cain: Violence and the Violent in Latin America* (New York: William Morrow, 1991), 17–19, 112–17.

32. Marguerite Feitlowitz, *A Lexicon of Terror: Argentina and the Legacies of Terror* (New York: Oxford University Press, 1998), 79–81, 193–255; Thomas C. Wright, *State Terrorism in Latin America: Chile, Argentina, and International Human Rights* (Lanham, MD: Rowman & Littlefield, 2007), 160–61.

33. Videla quoted in William Michael Schmidli, *The Fate of Freedom Elsewhere: Human Rights and U.S. Cold War Policy toward Argentina* (Ithaca, NY: Cornell University Press, 2013), 80; Menéndez, Pascarelli, and Saint Jean quoted in Wright, *State Terrorism*, 107; Videla quoted in Elias E. Lopez, "Jorge Rafael Videla, Jailed Argentine Military Leader, Dies at 87," *NYT*, 18 May 2013, D8.

34. Francisco Goldman, "Children of the Dirty War," *New Yorker*, 19 March 2012, https://www.newyorker.com/magazine/2012/03/19/children-of-the-dirty-war; Rosenberg, *Children of Cain*, 17–19, 112–17.

35. Wright, *State Terrorism*, 160–61; Manú Actis et al., *That Inferno: Conversations of Five Women Survivors of an Argentine Torture Camp* (Nashville: Vanderbilt University Press, 2006); Miriam Lewin and Olga Wornat, *Putas y guerrilleras: Crímenes sexuales en los centros clandestinos de detención* (*Whores and Guerrilla Members: Sexual Crimes in Clandestine Detention Centers*) (Buenos Aires: Grupo Editorial Planeta, 2014); Cecilia Macón, *Sexual Violence in the Argentinean Crimes against Humanity Trials: Rethinking Victimhood* (Lanham, MD: Lexington Books, 2017).

36. Shlaudeman OH, FAOHC.

37. Hill quoted in embassy in Argentina to DoS, 29 March 1976, document 41, *FRUS, 1969–1976* E-11, Part 2: *Documents on South America, 1973–1976*. See also Schmidli, *Fate of Freedom*, 45–50, 141–55.

38. Embassy in Argentina to DoS, 16 April 1976, document 42, ibid.; embassy in Argentina to DoS, "Conversation with Undersecretary of the Presidency, 25 May 1976, document 44, ibid.; embassy in Argentina to DoS, "Request for Instructions," 25 May 1976, document 45, ibid.; embassy in Argentina to DoS, "Possible International Implications of Violent Deaths of Political Figures Abroad," 7 June 1976, document 47; Martin Edwin Andersen, "Kissinger and the 'Dirty War,'" *Nation* 245 (31 October 1987): 477–80.

39. *PDB*, 23 June 1976, https://www.cia.gov/library/readingroom/docs/DOC _0006015144.pdf; accompanying footnote to embassy in Argentina to DoS, "Human

Rights Situation in Argentina, 27 August 1976, document 52, *FRUS, 1969–1976* E-11, Part 2: *Documents on South America, 1973–1976*.

40. Schmidli, *Fate of Freedom*, 50–55; Gustavo Morello, *The Catholic Church and Argentina's Dirty War* (New York: Oxford University Press, 2015); Robert W. Zimmerman, Desk Officer of East Coast Affairs Division of State Department's Latin American Section, OH, FAOHC.

41. Embassy in Argentina to DoS, "Luncheon Conversation with Senior Members of Govt.," 27 April 1976, document 43, *FRUS, 1969–1976* E-11, Part 2: *Documents on South America, 1973–1976*; accompanying footnote on 27 March démarche in embassy to DoS, "Request for Instructions," 25 May 1976, document 43, ibid.; embassy in Argentina to DoS, "Possible International Implications of Violent Deaths of Political Figures Abroad," 7 June 1976, document, 47, ibid.; embassy in Argentina to DoS, "Human Rights Situation in Argentina," 27 August 1976, document 52, ibid.; embassy in Argentina to DoS, "Ambassador Discusses US-Argentine Relations with President Videla on 21 September," 24 September 1976, document 54, ibid.

42. Schmidli, *Fate of Freedom*, 137–38; James P. Brennan, *Argentina's Missing Bones: Revisiting the History of the Dirty War* (Oakland: University of California Press, 2018), 19–88; "La Perla trial delivers justice for Córdoba," *Buenos Aires Herald*, 26 August 2016, 1–3.

43. Schmidli, *Fate of Freedom*, 53.

44. Shlaudeman OH, FAOHC.

45. Memorandum of conversation between Kissinger and Argentine Foreign Minister Ángel Robledo, 28 September 1975, document 29, *FRUS, 1969–1976* E-11, Part 2: *Documents on South America, 1973–1976*. For Schmidli's analyses of Kissinger, see *Fate of Freedom*, 43, 53–54, 65–66, 93.

46. Transcript of secretary of state's staff meeting, 26 March 1976, document 40, ibid. See also Natasha Zaretsky, "The US Role in Argentina's 'Dirty War' (1976–1983)," in *Dirty Hands and Vicious Deeds: The US Government's Complicity in Crimes against Humanity and Genocide*, ed. Samuel Totten (Toronto: University of Toronto Press, 2018), 278–432.

47. NSA, "Obama Declassification Holds Promise of Uncovering New Evidence on Argentina's Dirty War," *Electronic Briefing Book No. 546*, document 2, https://nsarchive .gwu.edu/briefing-book/southern-cone/2016-03-23/obama-declassification-holds -promise-uncovering-new-evidence.

48. Memorandum of conversation between Kissinger and Guzzetti, 10 June 1976, document 48, *FRUS, 1969–1976* E-11, Part 2: *Documents on South America, 1973–1976*.

49. Kissinger telephone conversation with Shlaudeman, 30 June 1976, *KTC*, ProQuest.

50. Transcript of the secretary of state's staff meeting, 9 July 1976, document 49, *FRUS, 1969–1976* E-11, Part 2: *Documents on South America, 1973–1976*.

51. Accompanying footnote to DoS to embassy in Argentina, "Harkin Amendment," 15 September 1976, document 53, ibid.

52. Embassy to DoS, "Ambassador Discusses US-Argentine Relations with President Videla," 24 September 1976, document 54, with accompanying footnote, ibid.

53. Memorandum of conversation between U.S. officials and Guzzetti, 6 October 1976, document 55, ibid.

54. Memorandum of conversation between Kissinger and Guzzetti, 7 October 1976, document 56, ibid.

55. Embassy in Argentina to DoS, "Foreign Minister Guzzetti Euphoric over Visit to United States," 19 October 1976, document 57, with accompanying footnote, ibid.

56. DoS to embassy, "Guzzetti's Visit to US," 22 October 1976, document 58, with accompanying footnote, ibid.

57. Henry Kissinger, "Moral Promise and Practical Needs," *DSB* 75 (29 October 1976): 1–8.

58. Finchelstein, *Ideological Origins*, 122–53.

59. Winston Lord, director of Policy Planning Staff, to Kissinger, 1 September 1976, document 47, *FRUS, 1969–1976*, E-11, Part 1: *Documents on Mexico, Central America, and the Caribbean, 1973–1976*; DoS to embassy in Argentina, "Harkin Amendment," 15 September 1976, document 53, *FRUS, 1969–1976* E-11, Part 2: *Documents on South America, 1973–1976*; Scowcroft to Rockefeller, 10 September 1976, box 7, CO-9, WHCF, GRFL.

60. Memorandum of conversation between Kissinger and Guzzetti, 7 October 1976, document 56, *FRUS, 1969–1976* E-11, Part 2: *Documents on South America, 1973–1976*.

61. Kissinger quoted in Douglas Brinkley and Luke Nichter, *The Nixon Tapes, 1971–1972* (Boston: Houghton Mifflin Harcourt, 2015), 148; Gary J. Bass, *The Blood Telegram: Nixon, Kissinger, and a Forgotten Genocide* (New York: Alfred A. Knopf, 2013), 86, 339.

62. Niall Ferguson, *Kissinger, 1923–1968: The Idealist* (New York: Penguin Press, 2015), 162–68. Kissinger's tribute to Folek Sama is reprinted on pp. 167–68.

63. Wright Thompson, "While the World Watched," *ESPN, The Magazine & ESPNFC* .com, 9 June 2014, http://www.espn.com/espn/feature/story/_/id/11036214/while -world-watched-world-cup-brings-back-memories-argentina-dirty-war.

64. Embassy in Argentina to DoS, "Henry Kissinger Visit to Argentina," June 1978, Argentina Declassification Project, Argentina-Carter-Reagan, and Bush VP Part 1, https://foia.state.gov/Search/Results.aspx?collection=ARGENTINA&searchText=*.

65. Pastor to Brzezinski, "Kissinger on Human Rights in Argentina and Latin America," 11 July 1976, ibid.

66. Kathryn Sikkink, *Mixed Signals: U.S. Human Rights Policy and Latin America* (Ithaca, NY: Cornell University Press, 2004), 106–47.

67. Schmidli, *Fate of Freedom*, 117–18; Fernando E. Rondon, deputy director of East Coast Affairs of State Department's Latin American Affairs, OH, FAOHC. For a transcript of Derian's conversation with Massera, see Zaretsky, "US Role in Argentina's 'Dirty War,'" document 8, 334–38.

68. Ibid. See also OH of Philip W. Pillsbury, cultural affairs officer, FAOHC.

69. Kissinger quoted in Finchelstein, *Ideological Origins*, 137.

70. Schmidli, *Fate of Freedom*, 184; Shlaudeman OH, FAOHC.

71. Kissinger quoted in Victor S. Navasky, *A Matter of Opinion* (New York: Farrar, Straus, and Giroux, 2005), 298. See also Andersen, "Kissinger and the 'Dirty War,'" 477–80.

72. Associated Press (Detroit), "Kissinger Defends 1970s Latin America Policy," *Michigan Daily*, 5 October 2004, https://www.michigandaily.com/content/Kissinger-defends -1970s-latin-america-policy.

73. Jon Lee Anderson, "Does Henry Kissinger Have a Conscience?," *New Yorker*, 20 August 2016, http://newyoker.com/news/news-desk/does-henry-kisssinger-have-a -conscience.

74. Henry Kissinger, *Years of Renewal* (New York: Simon & Schuster, 1999), 754.

75. Embassy in Chile to DoS, "Meeting with President Pinochet on UNHRC Study Group," 10 July 1975, document 195, *FRUS, 1969–1976* E-11, Part 2: *Documents on South America, 1973–1976.*

76. Editorial note on Church Committee, 9 November 1975, document 208, ibid.; Kissinger telephone conversation with Mel Elfin of *Newsweek*, 24 November 1975, *KTC*, ProQuest.

77. Accompanying footnote to DoS to embassy in Italy, "Chile Arms Package and Human Rights," 5 November 1974, document 176, *FRUS, 1969–1976* E-11, Part 2: *Documents on South America, 1973–1976*; accompanying footnote to memorandum of conversation between Kissinger and Chilean Chargé d'Affaires Enrique Guzmán, 24 December 1974, document 179, ibid.

78. Transcript of secretary of state's regional staff meeting, 3 December 1974, document 177, ibid.; memorandum of conversation between Kissinger and Ambassador Popper, 18 July 1975, document 197, ibid.; transcript of secretary of state's staff meeting, 8 October 1975, document 205, ibid.; transcript of telephone conversation between Kissinger and Ambassador to U.N. Daniel P. Moynihan, 11 November 1975, document 209, ibid.

79. Transcript of secretary of state's staff meeting, 6 October 1975, document 203, ibid.

80. Transcript of secretary of state's regional staff meeting, 3 December 1974, document 177, ibid.; transcript of secretary of state's staff meeting, 6 October 1975, document 203, ibid.

81. Memorandum from Stephen Low of NSC to Brent Scowcroft of NSC, "Disarray in Chile Policy," and accompanying footnote, 1 July 1975, document 193, ibid.; embassy in Chile to DoS, 17 December 1975, document 212, ibid.

82. Memorandum of conversation between Kissinger and Carvajal, 9 May 1975, document 188, ibid.; memorandum of conversation between Kissinger and Carvajal, 29 September 1975, document 201, ibid.

83. Kissinger, *Years of Renewal*, 752–59. For Kissinger's speech to the OAS General Assembly, see *DSB* 75 (5 July 1976): 1–5.

84. Memorandum of conversation between Kissinger and DoS officers, "Secretary's Trip in June, 1976 to OASGA," 1 June 1976, document 44, *FRUS, 1969–1976*, E-11, Part 1: *Documents on Mexico, Central America, and the Caribbean, 1973–1976.*

85. Transcript of telephone conversation between Kissinger and Rogers, 3 June 1976, *KTC*, ProQuest.

86. Memorandum of conversation between Kissinger and Pinochet, 8 June 1976, document 228, *FRUS, 1969–1976* E-11, Part 2: *Documents on South America, 1973–1976.*

87. Memorandum of conversation between Kissinger and Cardinal Silva, with accompanying footnote, document 229, 14 June 1976, ibid.

88. Transcript of telephone conversation between Kissinger and Rogers, 16 June 1976, document 230, ibid.

89. Embassy in Chile to DoS, "Illegal Detentions and Disappearances: Chile," 9 August 1976, document 239, ibid.; embassy in Chile to DoS, "Chile: Little Comfort in Pinochet's Third Anniversary Speech," 13 September 1973, document 244, ibid.

90. Rogers quoted in accompanying footnote of CIA Deputy Director Vernon Walters to Kissinger on visit of Contreras, 9 July 1975, document 194, ibid.

91. Rabe, *Killing Zone*, 144–45.

92. Walters to Kissinger on conversation with Contreras, 7 January 1975, document 181, *FRUS, 1969–1976* E-11, Part 2: *Documents on South America, 1973–1976*; Walters to Kissinger on visit of Contreras, 9 July 1975, document 194, ibid.

93. NSA, "Operation Condor Verdict: GUILTY," *Electronic Briefing Book No. 551*, https://nsarchive.gwu.edu/briefing-book/southern-cone/2016-05-27/operation-condor-verdict-guilty.

94. Shlaudeman to Kissinger, "The 'Third World War' and South America," 3 August 1976, document 238, *FRUS, 1969–1976* E-11, Part 2: *Documents on South America, 1973–1976*.

95. Deputy Assistant Secretary Hewson Ryan OH, FAOHC.

96. DoS to embassies in Argentina, Uruguay, Chile, and Bolivia, with accompanying footnote, "Operation Condor," 23 August 1976, document 241, ibid.

97. Embassy in Chile to DoS, "Operation Condor," with accompanying footnote, 24 August 1976, document 242, ibid.; embassy in Uruguay to DoS, "Operation Condor, 24 August 1976, document 358, ibid.

98. Action memorandum from Shlaudeman to Kissinger, with accompanying footnote on decision by Kissinger on 16 September 1976, "Operation Condor," 30 August 1976, document 359, ibid.

99. Ryan OH, FAOHC.

100. William D. Rogers and Kenneth Maxwell, "Mythmaking and Foreign Policy," *Foreign Affairs* 83 (January-February 2004): 160–65.

101. Embassy in Costa Rica to DoS, with accompanying footnote, "Operation Condor," 20 September 1976, document 245, *FRUS, 1969–1976* E-11, Part 2: *Documents on South America, 1973–1976*.

102. Mary Brownell and Dan Mozeleski of NSC to Les Janka of NSC, "Bombing of Former Chilean Ambassador's Car," 21 September 1976, document 246, ibid.; embassy in Chile to DoS, "Assassination of Orlando Letelier," 21 September 1976, document 247, ibid.; *PDB*, 23 September 1976, https://www.cia.gov/library/readingroom/docs/DOC_0006466853.pdf.

103. Shlaudeman to Kissinger, with accompanying footnote, "Operation Condor," 8 October 1976, *FRUS, 1969–1976* E-11, Part 2: *Documents on South America, 1973–1976*.

104. Levi to Bush, 9 October 1976, document 250, ibid. See also Deputy Chief of Mission in Chile Charles Grover OH, FAOHC.

105. Shultz to Reagan, "Pinochet and the Letelier and Moffitt Murders: Implications for US Policy," 6 October 1987, in NSA, "CIA: 'Pinochet Personally Ordered' Letelier Bombing," *Electronic Briefing Book No. 532*, document 3, https://nsarchive2.gwu.edu//dc.html?doc=3212949-Document-03-DOS-Pinochet-and-the-Letelier. See also Alan McPherson, "Strange Bedfellows at the End of the Cold War: The Letelier Assassination, Human Rights, and State Sovereignty," *Cold War History* (2019), DOI: *10.1080/14682745.2019.1583212*.

5. Kissinger and Central America

1. Gelijeses quoted in Nick Cullather, *Secret History: The CIA's Classified Account of Its Operations in Guatemala, 1952–1954* (Stanford, CA: Stanford University Press, 1999), xxix; Richard H. Immerman, *The CIA in Guatemala: The Foreign Policy of Intervention* (Austin: University of Texas Press, 1982), 201.

2. Daniel Rothenberg, ed., *Memory of Silence: The Guatemalan Truth Commission Report* (New York: Palgrave Macmillan, 2012), 179, 235–38.

3. Country Report: Guatemala, #7.48, 1969, folder 834, box 106, Series 0.8, RG 4, Rockefeller Family Collection, RAC.

4. John O. Bell OH, FAOHC; AFL quoted in Serafino Romuladi, *Presidents and Peons: Recollections of a Labor Ambassador in Latin America* (New York: Funk & Wagnalls, 1967), 240–46. See also Jim Handy, *Revolution in the Countryside: Rural Conflict and Agrarian Reform in Guatemala, 1944–1954* (Chapel Hill: University of North Carolina Press, 1994), 192–207.

5. Stephen G. Rabe, *The Most Dangerous Area in the World: John F. Kennedy Confronts Communist Revolution in Latin America* (Chapel Hill: University of North Carolina Press, 1999), 71–77.

6. Bell OH, FAOHC. On the lack of Cuban or Soviet influence in Guatemala in the 1970s, see political counselor William T. Pryce OH, http://adst.org/wp-content/uploads/2012/09/Guatemala.pdf.

7. Rabe, *Most Dangerous Area*, 76.

8. Rothenberg, *Memory of Silence*, 182.

9. Greg Grandin, *The Last Colonial Massacre: Latin America in the Cold War* (Chicago: University of Chicago Press, 2004), 97–102.

10. Mary Jane Treacy, "Killing the Queen: The Display and Disappearance of Rogelia Cruz," *Latin American Literary Review* 29 (January-June 2001): 40–51.

11. Vaky to Assistant Secretary of State Covey Oliver, "Guatemala and Counterterror," 29 March 1968, *FRUS 1964–1968* 31: *South and Central America; Mexico*, 237–41; Ambassador Mein to Oliver, 27 February 1968, ibid, 227–34.

12. Longan quoted in Grandin, *Last Colonial Massacre*, 99; Bell OH, FAOHC.

13. Deputy Chief of Mission John T. Bennett OH, FAOHC; political officer George Jones OH, FAOHC.

14. Editorial note, document 319a, *FRUS, 1969–1976* E-10: *Documents on American Republics, 1969–1972*; embassy in Guatemala to DoS, 15 November 1970, document 342, ibid.; memorandum from Alexander Haig of NSC staff to Kissinger, "Guatemala Item for 40 Committee," 16 November 1970, document 343, ibid.; DoS to embassy in Guatemala, 17 November 1970, document 344, ibid.; embassy in Guatemala to DoS, "Internal Security: State of Siege," 20 November 1970, document 345, ibid.

15. Memorandum prepared in DoS on Guatemalan elections, undated, document 327, ibid.; CIA, "LA Staff Note No 1-70," 6 March 1970, document 329, ibid.; *PDB*, 26 February 1970, https://www.cia.gov/library/readingroom/docs/DOC_0005977319.pdf.

16. Embassy in Guatemala to DoS, "Prognosis of What to Expect from Arana," 4 March 1970, document 328, *FRUS, 1969–1976* E-10: *Documents on American Republics, 1969–1972*; CIA, "LA Staff Note No 1-70," 6 March 1970, document 329, ibid.; CIA Weekly Summary, Special Report No. 0375/70B, "Political Change in Guatemala: Order vs. Violence," 19 June 1970, document 339, ibid.

17. Telephone conversation between Kissinger and Agnew, *KTC*, ProQuest, 16 July 1970.

18. Embassy to DoS on meeting with President-elect Arana, 25 March 1970, document 333, *FRUS, 1969–1976* E-10: *Documents on American Republics, 1969–1972*; memorandum for record of DoS meeting with CIA in Guatemala, 8 May 1970, document

337, ibid.; embassy in Guatemala to DoS on meeting with Arana on internal security, 19 May 1970, document 338, ibid.

19. *PDB*, 14 November 1970, https://www.cia.gov/library/readingroom/docs /DOC_0005977798.pdf; embassy in Guatemala to DoS, "State of Siege," 20 November 1970, document 345, *FRUS, 1969–1976 E-10: Documents on American Republics, 1969–1972.*

20. Political officer Jeffrey Davidow OH, http://adst.org/wp-content/uploads/2012 /09/Guatemala.pdf; Ambassador Davis Eugene Boster OH, FAOHC.

21. Memorandum for record of DoS, NSC meeting with CIA on Guatemala, 16 August 1971, document 355, *FRUS, 1969–1976 E-10: Documents on American Republics, 1969–1972*; paper prepared by CIA on Guatemala, undated, document 356, ibid.

22. Nachmanoff to Kissinger, 19 August 1971, document 357, ibid.; memorandum for record on 40 Committee meeting, 16 September 1971, document 358, ibid.

23. Memorandum of conversation between Holt with DoS officers, 27 October 1971, document 359, ibid.

24. Davidow OH, http://adst.org/wp-content/uploads/2012/09/Guatemala.pdf; embassy in Guatemala to DoS, "Guatemala at Year End," 24 January 1973, document 165, *FRUS, 1969–1976 E-11: Documents on Mexico; Central America; and the Caribbean, 1973–1976.*

25. Jorden to Kissinger, 28 September 1972, document 364, *FRUS, 1969–1976 E-10: Documents on American Republics, 1969–1972.*

26. Embassy in Guatemala to DoS, "The Presidential Campaign: Assessment and Analysis," 18 January 1974, document 175, *FRUS, 1969–1976 E-11: Documents on Mexico; Central America; and the Caribbean, 1973–1976*; embassy in Guatemala to DoS, "Guatemalan Election Crisis," 5 March 1974, document 178, ibid.

27. Embassy in Guatemala to DoS, "Presidential Electoral Campaign—Two and a Half Weeks to Go," 14 February 1974, document 176, ibid.; *PDB*, 5 March 1974, https:// www.cia.gov/library/readingroom/docs/DOC_0006007690.pdf; *PDB*, 6 March 1974, https://www.cia.gov/library/readingroom/docs/DOC_0005993176.pdf; *PDB*, 13 March 1974, https://www.cia.gov/library/readingroom/docs/DOC_0006007696.pdf.

28. Transcript of Kissinger's regional staff meeting, 7 March 1974, document 179, *FRUS, 1969–1976 E-11: Documents on Mexico; Central America; and the Caribbean, 1973–1976.* See also Pryce OH, http://adst.org/wp-content/uploads/2012/09/Guatemala.pdf.

29. Virginia Garrard-Burnett, *Terror in the Land of the Holy Spirit: Guatemala under General Efraín Ríos Montt* (New York: Oxford University Press, 2010).

30. Memorandum from Deputy Assistant Secretary of State for Inter-American Affairs William G. Bowdler to the director of the Office of Security Assistance and Sales, Bureau of Politico-Military Affairs, Ladd, "Military Assistance to Guatemala," 6 May 1974, document 184, *FRUS, 1969–1976 E-11: Documents on Mexico; Central America; and the Caribbean, 1973–1976.*

31. Embassy to DoS, "President Laugerud Gets Set: Thoughts on the Future," 16 July 1974, document 187, ibid.; embassy in Guatemala to DoS, "Laugerud Government: The First Six Months," 3 January 1975, document 191, ibid.

32. Embassy in Guatemala to DoS, "Human Rights in Guatemala," 22 February 1975, document 192, ibid.

33. Embassy in Guatemala to DoS, with accompanying footnote, "Internal Security following the Earthquake," 11 March 1976, document 224, ibid.; embassy in Guatemala

to DoS, "Political Violence during Laugerud's Second Year," 12 July 1976, document 230, ibid.

34. Boster OH, FAOHC; embassy in Guatemala to DoS with accompanying footnote, "Political Violence during Laugerud's Second Year," 12 July 1976, document 230, *FRUS, 1969–1976 E-11: Documents on Mexico; Central America; and the Caribbean, 1973–1976.*

35. Bennett OH, FAOHC.

36. Transcript of Secretary of State Kissinger's staff meeting, 28 October 1975, document 211, ibid.

37. Ambassador Lawrence Pezzulo OH, FAOHC; political counselor James R. Cheek OH, http://adst.org/wp-content/uploads/2012/09/Nicaragua.pdf.

38. Deputy Chief of Mission Robert E. White OH, FAOHC; political officer Robert Goddard OH, http://adst.org/wp-content/uploads/2012/09/Nicaragua.pdf. See also John A. Booth, Christine J. Wade, and Thomas W. Walker, *Understanding Central America: Global Forces, Rebellion, and Change*, 5th ed. (Boulder, CO: Westview Press, 2010), 81–88; Thomas W. Walker and Christine J. Wade, *Nicaragua: Living in the Shadow of the Eagle*, 5th ed. (Boulder, CO: Westview Press, 2011), 25–34.

39. USAID officer Charles Anthony Gillespie OH, http://adst.org/wp-content/uploads/2012/09/Nicaragua.pdf. See also Lester D. Langley, *The Banana Wars: An Inner History of American Empire, 1900–1934* (Lexington: University Press of Kentucky, 1983); Alan McPherson, *The Invaded: How Latin Americans and Their Allies Fought and Ended U.S. Occupations* (New York: Oxford University Press, 2014).

40. Stephen G. Rabe, *Eisenhower and Latin America: The Foreign Policy of Anticommunism* (Chapel Hill: University of North Carolina Press, 1988), 86–87.

41. Rabe, *Most Dangerous Area*, 141, 157–59.

42. Cheek OH, http://adst.org/wp-content/uploads/2012/09/Nicaragua.pdf; political officer Ronald E. Godard OH, ibid.; Gillespie OH, ibid.; Pezzulo OH, FAOHC.

43. Memorandum of conversation between Nixon, Kissinger, and Treasury Secretary John Connally, 11 June 1971, document 43, *FRUS, 1969–1976, E-10: Documents on American Republics, 1969–1972.*

44. Executive Secretary of State Department Eliot to Kissinger, "Nicaraguan President's Desire to Receive a Presidential Invitation to Visit the United States," 9 June 1970, document 496, ibid.

45. Memorandum for the record on meeting between Nixon and Somoza, 2 June 1971, document 504, ibid.

46. Transcript of telephone conversation between Kissinger and David Packard of Defense Department, 30 June 1971, *KTC*, ProQuest.

47. White OH, FAOHC; Gillespie OH, http://adst.org/wp-content/uploads/2012/09/Nicaragua.pdf.

48. Cheek OH, ibid. See also Tim Weiner, *One Man against the World: The Tragedy of Richard Nixon* (New York: Henry Holt, 2015), 51–53.

49. Rockefeller's personal and confidential notes on Nicaragua, undated, #9.021, folder 874-NAR notes, box 112, series 0.8, RG 4, Rockefeller Family Collection, RAC; Chamorro to Rockefeller associate George Beebe, 20 May 1969, #5.022, folder 78, box 9, subseries 2, RG III 15–7, James Cannon files, RAC.

50. Embassy in Nicaragua to DoS, "Cathedral Seizure," 28 September 1970, document 497, *FRUS, 1969–1976, E-10: Documents on American Republics, 1969–1972*; embassy

in Nicaragua to DoS, "Archbishop Upsets Political Situation," 20 November 1971, document 510, ibid.

51. Memorandum of conversation between Cheek and Archbishop Obando y Bravo, with accompanying footnote, 25 October 1972, document 516, ibid.

52. Cheek OH, http://adst.org/wp-content/uploads/2012/09/Nicaragua.pdf; Stephen G. Rabe, *The Killing Zone: The United States Wages Cold War in Latin America*, 2nd ed. (New York: Oxford University Press, 2016), 158.

53. Cheek OH, http://adst.org/wp-content/uploads/2012/09/Nicaragua.pdf.

54. Memorandum from Director of Office of Central American Affairs David Lazar to Assistant Secretary Kubisch, with accompanying footnotes, "Secretary's Proposed Visit to Nicaragua," 19 April 1973, document 239, *FRUS, 1969–1976* E-11: *Documents on Mexico; Central America; and the Caribbean, 1973–1976*; USAID officer Aaron Benjamin OH, http://adst.org/wp-content/uploads/2012/09/Nicaragua.pdf.

55. White OH, FAOHC.

56. Memorandum of conversation between Nixon and Williams, 9 January 1973, #1929, folder, Memcons, 1-3/73, folder (23), box 1026, NSC: President/HAK Memorandums, RMNL; telephone conversation between Nixon and Kissinger, 16 October 1973, *KTC*, ProQuest.

57. Embassy in Nicaragua to DoS, with accompanying footnote, "Human Rights Reporting," 8 February 1975, document 250, *FRUS, 1969–1976* E-11: *Documents on Mexico; Central America; and the Caribbean, 1973–1976*; chief of political section in embassy in Nicaragua Gerald M. Sutton to country officer for Nicaragua George A. Gowen III on Ambassador Shelton's behavior, 9 July 1975, document 253, ibid.

58. Telephone conversation between Kissinger and Senator Carl Curtis (R-NE), 17 June 1975, *KTC*, ProQuest.

59. Embassy in Nicaragua to DoS, "Secretary Kissinger's Trip to Latin America," 21 January 1976, document 258, *FRUS, 1969–1976* E-11: *Documents on Mexico; Central America; and the Caribbean, 1973–1976*.

60. Embassy in Nicaragua to DoS, "Elections in 1974: The Conservative Opposition," 9 November 1973, document 241, ibid.

61. Embassy to DoS, "Military Security Assistance Program for Nicaragua," 23 February 1976, document 260, ibid.; DoS to embassy in Nicaragua, "IDB Loan," 24 November 1976, document 269, ibid.

62. Embassy to DoS, "Assistant Secretary Rogers Meeting with Somoza," 3 February 1976, document 259, ibid.; embassy in Nicaragua to DoS, "Secretary Shlaudeman's Meeting with Somoza," 20 September 1976, document 268, ibid.; DoS to Rockefeller, "Your Meeting with Nicaraguan President Somoza," 19 April 1976, box 37, CO 111, WHCF, GRFL.

63. Cheek OH, http://adst.org/wp-content/uploads/2012/09/Nicaragua.pdf.

64. *PDB*, 30 December 1974, https://www.cia.gov/library/readingroom/docs/DOC_0006007905.pdf.

65. Staff notes prepared in CIA, "Nicaragua: State of Siege to End," 27 December 1976, document 270, *FRUS, 1969–1976* E-11: *Documents on Mexico; Central America; and the Caribbean, 1973–1976*.

66. Embassy in El Salvador to DoS, "The Coming Political Difficulties in El Salvador and U.S. Response," 5 August 1975, document 160, ibid.; memorandum of

conversation between Kissinger and Minister of Foreign Relations of El Salvador Mauricio Borgonovo Pohl, 24 February 1976, document 161, ibid.

67. *The Report of the President's National Bipartisan Commission on Central America*, with foreword by Henry A. Kissinger (New York: Macmillan, 1984).

68. Political officer William T. Pryce OH, http://adst.org/wp-content/uploads/2018/02/Panama.pdf; President Ford's observations in minutes of NSC meeting, 15 May 1975, document 77, *FRUS, 1969–1976, 22: Panama, 1973–1976* (Washington, DC: GPO, 2015). See also watch officer/intelligence analyst Clarke McCurdy Britnall OH, http://adst.org/wp-content/uploads/2018/02/Panama.pdf; Deputy Chief of Mission Herbert Thompson OH, ibid.; Walter B. Deering of Navy Oceanographic Office OH, ibid.

69. Rabe, *Eisenhower and Latin America*, 27.

70. Richard C. Barkley OH, http://adst.org/wp-content/uploads/2018/02/Panama.pdf; political officer J. Philip McClean OH, ibid.

71. Pryce OH, ibid. See also USAID Director David Lazar OH, ibid.; Director of Office of Panamanian Affairs Brandon Grove OH, ibid.

72. Kissinger to Dwight Chapin, "Request by Ex-President Arnulfo Arías of Panama to See the President, 7 October 1969, CF, CO 117, GRFL; DoS study, "Nature of the Torrijos Government," 17 April 1976, Panama Canal Treaty folder, box 6, WHCF: Special Files, GRFL.

73. Telephone conversation between Kissinger and Treasury Secretary William Simon, 18 April 1976, *KTC*, ProQuest.

74. Rabe, *Eisenhower and Latin America*, 138.

75. Rabe, *Most Dangerous Area*, 187–91.

76. Alan McPherson, "Courts of World Opinion: Trying the Panama Flag Riots of 1964," *DH* 28 (January 2004): 83–112.

77. Adolfo Ahumada quoted in Tom Long, "Putting the Canal on the Map: Panama Agenda-Setting and the 1973 Security Council Meeting," *Diplomatic History* 38 (April 2014): 431–55.

78. Nixon quoted by Kissinger in telephone conversation with U.N. Ambassador George H. W. Bush, 11 October 1971, *KTC*, ProQuest.

79. Quoted in rotational officer Ronald D. Goddard OH, http://adst.org/wp-content/uploads/2018/02/Panama.pdf.

80. Political officer J. Philip McLean OH, ibid.; Deputy Director of Panamanian Affairs Richard R. Wyrough OH, ibid.

81. Ambassador Robert M. Sayre OH, ibid.; Wyrough OH, ibid. See also John P. Walsh, acting executive secretary of DoS, to Kissinger, "The Actions and Decisions of the Department of State in the Panama Crisis of October-November 1968," 24 March 1969, CF, CO 117, GRFL.

82. Telephone conversation between Kissinger and Peter M. Flanigan of White House, 7 January 1971, *KTC*, ProQuest.

83. Memorandum from Secretary of Defense Melvin Laird to Nixon, 3 September 1971, document 553, *FRUS, 1969–1976* E-11: *Documents on Mexico; Central America; and the Caribbean, 1973–1976*.

84. Grove OH, http://adst.org/wp-content/uploads/2018/02/Panama.pdf.

85. Memorandum from Kissinger to Nixon, 1 June 1970, document 535, *FRUS, 1969–1976* E-11: *Documents on Mexico; Central America; and the Caribbean, 1973–1976*; memorandum from Kissinger to Nixon, 10 September 1971, document 554, ibid.

86. Telephone conversation between Kissinger and Scali, 22 February 1973, *KTC*, ProQuest.

87. Memorandum from Finch to Deputy Secretary of State John Irwin, 16 October 1972, document 560, *FRUS, 1969–1976* E-11: *Documents on Mexico; Central America; and the Caribbean, 1973–1976.*

88. Directorate of Intelligence, Intelligence Memorandum 2438/72, "Panama: 1973—The Year of the Treaty?," 28 November 1972, document 563, ibid.

89. Quoted in Tom Long, *Latin America Confronts the United States: Asymmetry and Influence* (New York: Cambridge University Press, 2015), 90.

90. Walter LaFeber, *The Panama Canal: The Crisis in Historical Perspective*, updated ed. (New York: Oxford University Press, 1989), 144. See also editorial note on Kissinger trip to Panama, document 32, *FRUS, 1969–1976, 22: Panama, 1973–1976.*

91. Kissinger quoted in William J. Jorden, *Panama Odyssey* (Austin: University of Texas Press, 1984), 215–16.

92. Telephone conversation between Kissinger and Rockefeller, 8 February 1974, *KTC*, ProQuest.

93. Long, "Putting the Canal on the Map," 454.

94. Finch to Irwin, 16 October 1972, document 560, *FRUS, 1969–1976* E-11: *Documents on Mexico; Central America; and the Caribbean, 1973–1976.*

95. Jorden, *Panama Odyssey*, 198–99, 218, 221; Grove OH, http://adst.org/wp-content/uploads/2018/02/Panama.pdf.

96. Kissinger to Nixon on letter from Senator Thurmond, 22 April 1974, document 38, *FRUS, 1969–1976, 22: Panama, 1973–1976*; Nixon to Thurmond, 22 April, 1974, document 39, ibid.

97. Kissinger quoted in footnote #3 of memorandum from Deputy Negotiator Morey S. Bell to Ambassador Bunker, 12 May 1975, document 76, ibid.; minutes of NSC meeting, 15 May 1975, document 77, ibid.; Long, *Latin America Confronts the United States,* 105; memorandum of conversation between Kissinger and six U.S. senators, 1 April 1976, document 116, *FRUS, 1969–1976, 22: Panama, 1973–1976.*

98. Minutes of SRG meeting, 22 April 1975, document 73, ibid.

99. Minutes of Kissinger's meeting with State Department staff, 15 April 1976, document 120, ibid.

100. Memorandum of conversation between Kissinger and Foreign Minister Tack, 24 February 1976, document 113, ibid.

101. Memorandum of conversation between Bunker and State and Defense Department officials, with accompanying footnote #6, 9 July 1974, document 49, ibid.

102. Jorden, *Panama Odyssey*, 251–52. See also transcript of Kissinger telephone conversation with Schlesinger, 27 June 1975, *KTC*, ProQuest.

103. Wyrough OH, http://adst.org/wp-content/uploads/2018/02/Panama.pdf.

104. Memorandum of conversation between Kissinger and Foreign Minister Boyd, 11 June 1976, document 126, *FRUS, 1969–1976, 22: Panama, 1973–1976.*

105. DoS to embassy in Panama, with accompanying footnote #3, 10 November 1975, document 103, ibid.; minutes of Kissinger's meeting with his staff, 12 October 1976, document 135, ibid.

106. DoS to Kissinger and embassy in Panama, "Torrijos's Adventure in Cuba," 20 January 1976, document 110, ibid.

107. Memorandum from Raymond A. Warren, CIA chief of the Latin American Division, Directorate of Operations, to director of CIA, "Panamanian National Guard G-2 Responsibility for Panama Canal Zone Bombings," 4 November 1976, document 140, ibid.

108. Memorandum from William W. Wells, CIA deputy director for operations, to multiple recipients including Ambassador Bunker, "Panamanian Efforts to Resolve Duration Issue in Canal Treaty Negotiations," undated, document 124, ibid.; memorandum from Wells to multiple recipients including Ambassador Bunker, "Preliminary Panamanian Drafts regarding a Canal Treaty Clause dealing with the Treaty Issues of Neutrality, Free Passage, and Defense," 24 December 1976, document 146, ibid.

109. Memorandum of conversation between Kissinger and Foreign Minister Tack, 24 February 1976, document 113, ibid.

110. Letter from Colombian President Alfonso López Michelsen, Costa Rican President Daniel Oduber, and Venezuelan President Carlos Andrés Pérez to President Ford, 24 March 1975, document 70, ibid.

111. Memorandum of conversation between Ford, Kissinger, and López Michelsen, 25 September 1975, document 100, ibid.

112. Memorandum from Bunker to Kissinger, 3 December 1974, document 59, ibid.

113. Memorandum of conversation between Kissinger and Foreign Minister Tack, 23 April 1974, document 40, ibid.

114. Minutes of Kissinger's meeting with staff, 14 April 1975, document 72, ibid.

115. NSDM 302, 18 August 1975, document 95, ibid.

116. Minutes of NSC meeting, 23 July 1975, document 90, ibid.

117. Reagan quoted in John Robert Greene, *The Presidency of Gerald R. Ford* (Lawrence: University Press of Kansas, 1995), 165.

118. Memorandum of conversation between Goldwater and William H. Itoh, Office of Congressional Relations, 9 December 1975, document 106, *FRUS, 1969–1976*, 22: *Panama, 1973–1976*. See also OH of Harry F. Nelson, Congressional Relations, Panama Canal Treaty, http://adst.org/wp-content/uploads/2018/02/Panama.pdf.

119. Memorandum of conversation between Ford and Javits, 14 April 1976, document 119, *FRUS, 1969–1976*, 22: *Panama, 1973–1976*.

120. Long, *Latin America Confronts the United States*, 108–10.

121. Jorden, *Panama Odyssey*, 442.

122. DoS to embassy in Panama, "Secretary's Bilateral with Foreign Minister Boyd on 12/3/76," 10 December 1976, document 144, *FRUS, 1969–1976*, 22: *Panama, 1973–1976*.

123. Henry Kissinger, *Years of Renewal* (New York: Simon & Schuster, 1999), 761.

6. Diplomatic Solutions

1. Jack B. Kubisch OH, https://adst.org/wp-content/uploads/2018/04/Mexico.pdf.

2. Stephen G. Rabe, *The Killing Zone: The United States Wages Cold War in Latin America*, 2nd ed. (New York: Oxford University Press, 2016), 114–15.

3. Ibid., 115–16.

4. Renata Keller, "A Foreign Policy for Domestic Consumption: Mexico's Lukewarm Defense of Castro, 1959–1969," *Latin American Research Review* 47 no. 2 (2012): 100–19. See also letter of Ambassador Robert H. McBride to Secretary of State Rogers, 17

September 1969, document 439, *FRUS, 1969–1976* E-10: *Documents on American Republics, 1969–1972*.

5. Díaz Ordaz quoted in Rabe, *Killing Zone*, 116.

6. Embassy in Mexico City to DoS, 7 March 1970, document 450, *FRUS, 1969–1976* E-10: *Documents on American Republics, 1969–1972*; conversation among Nixon, Echeverría, and Kissinger, 15 June 1972, document 482, ibid.

7. Henry Dearborn OH, https://adst.org/wp-content/uploads/2018/04/Mexico.pdf. See also General Services Office Supervisor Charles Anthony Gillespie Jr. OH, ibid.; Ambassador Joseph J. Jova OH, ibid.

8. Telephone conversation between Kissinger and McGeorge Bundy, 22 June 1970, *KTC*, ProQuest; telephone conversation between Kissinger and Mrs. Javits, 31 March 1972, ibid.

9. Telephone conversation between Kissinger and Assistant Secretary of State for Latin America Rogers, 17 May 1976, ibid.

10. Memorandum of conversation between Kissinger and Rabasa, 4 October 1973, document 61, *FRUS, 1969–1976* E-11, Part 1: *Documents on Mexico; Central America; and the Caribbean, 1973–1976*.

11. Memorandum of conversation between Kissinger and García Robles, 10 June 1976, document 96, ibid.

12. Telephone conversation between Kissinger and Rabasa, 13 July, 1973, *KTC*, ProQuest.

13. Embassy in Mexico City to DoS on conversation between Ambassador McBride and President Díaz Ordaz, 3 April 1970, document 451, *FRUS, 1969–1976* E-10: *Documents on American Republics, 1969–1972*.

14. Letter from Nixon to Díaz Ordaz, 18 November 1969, document 445, ibid.; embassy in Mexico City to DoS on meeting between Kissinger and Díaz Ordaz, 21 June 1970, document 453, ibid.

15. Memorandum of conversation between President Ford and President Echeverría, 21 October 1974, document 70, *FRUS, 1969–1976* E-11, Part 1: *Documents on Mexico; Central America; and the Caribbean, 1973–1976*.

16. Frederick H. Sacksteder of International Boundary and Water Commission OH, https://adst.org/wp-content/uploads/2018/04/Mexico.pdf.

17. Memorandum from William J. Jorden of NSC to Kissinger, 11 April 1972, document 475, *FRUS, 1969–1976* E-10: *Documents on American Republics, 1969–1972*.

18. Samuel D. Eaton of Policy Planning Staff OH, https://adst.org/wp-content/uploads/2018/04/Mexico.pdf.

19. Memorandum from Arnold Nachmanoff of NSC to Kissinger, 14 April 1971, document 460, *FRUS, 1969–1976* E-10: *Documents on American Republics, 1969–1972*; Jorden to Kissinger, not dated, document 474, ibid.

20. Kissinger to Secretary of State William P. Rogers and Secretary of Interior Rogers Morton on Nixon's decision, 28 April 1971, document 461, ibid.; Kissinger to Nixon, 6 May 1972, document 477, ibid.

21. Memorandum from Kissinger to Nixon, 15 June 1972, document 481, ibid.; conversation between Nixon, Echeverría, and Kissinger, with accompanying footnotes, 15 June 1972, document 482, ibid.

22. Political counselor H. Freeman Matthews Jr. OH, https://adst.org/wp-content/uploads/2018/04/Mexico.pdf.

23. Embassy in Mexico City to DoS on conversation between Ambassador McBride and President Echeverría, 16 December 1972, document 485, *FRUS, 1969–1976* E-10: *Documents on American Republics, 1969–1972.*

24. Memorandum of conversation between Kissinger and Rabasa, 11 July 1973, document 58, *FRUS, 1969–1976* E-11, Part 1: *Documents on Mexico; Central America; and the Caribbean, 1973–1976.*

25. NSDM 218, 28 May 1973, document 55, ibid.

26. Memorandum from Kissinger to Nixon, 27 August 1973, document 60, ibid.

27. For information on the desalinization plant, see http://www.swhydro.arizona .edu/archive/V2_N3/feature5.pdf.

28. Memorandum by U.N. Ambassador John Scali to Kissinger on Kissinger conversation with Foreign Minister Rabasa, 24 August 1973, document 59, *FRUS, 1969–1976* E-11, Part 1: *Documents on Mexico; Central America; and the Caribbean, 1973–1976.*

29. Memorandum from Kissinger to Nixon, 27 August 1973, document 60, ibid.

30. Kissinger telephone conversation with Maw, 22 June 1974, *KTC*, ProQuest.

31. Memorandum of conversation between Kissinger and President Francisco Morales Bermúdez, 18 February 1976, document 316, *FRUS, 1969–1976* E-11, Part 2: *Documents on South America, 1973–1976.*

32. Transcript of telephone conversation between Kissinger and Nixon, 5 April 1969, document 589, *FRUS, 1969–1976* E-10: *Documents on American Republics, 1969–1972.*

33. Charles T. Goodsell, *American Corporations and Peruvian Politics* (Cambridge, MA: Harvard University Press, 1974), 29–30, 40, 46.

34. Stephen G. Rabe, *Eisenhower and Latin America: The Foreign Policy of Anticommunism* (Chapel Hill: University of North Carolina Press, 1988), 39, 192.

35. Stephen G. Rabe, *The Most Dangerous Area in the World: John F. Kennedy Confronts Communist Revolution in Latin America* (Chapel Hill: University of North Carolina Press, 1999), 117.

36. Ibid., 116–21.

37. Richard N. Goodwin, "Letter from Peru," *New Yorker*, 17 May 1969, 41–109.

38. Lawrence A. Clayton, *Peru and the United States: The Condor and the Eagle* (Athens: University of Georgia Press, 1999), 104–10.

39. Stephen G. Rabe, *The Road to OPEC: United States Relations with Venezuela, 1919–1976* (Austin: University of Texas Press, 1982), 66–93.

40. Thomas Mann OH, https://adst.org/wp-content/uploads/2018/02/Peru.pdf.

41. Richard J. Walter, *Peru and the United States, 1960–1975: How Their Ambassadors Managed Foreign Relations in a Turbulent Era* (University Park: Pennsylvania State University Press, 2010), 139. See also Clayton, *Peru and the United States*, 234–48; Rabe, *Most Dangerous Area*, 121.

42. Velasco quoted in Walter, *Peru and the United States, 1960–1975*, 172.

43. See, for example, the essays in Abraham Lowenthal, ed., *The Peruvian Experiment: Continuity and Change under Military Rule* (Princeton, NJ: Princeton University Press, 1975).

44. Political officer Fernando E. Rondon OH, https://adst.org/wp-content/uploads /2018/02/Peru.pdf; political officer James F. Creagan OH, ibid. For academic "second thoughts" on Peru's military dictators, see essays in Cynthia McClintock and Abraham F. Lowenthal, eds., *The Peruvian Experiment Reconsidered* (Princeton, NJ: Princeton University Press, 1983).

45. SNIE 97–69, "Peru and the U.S.: Implications of the IPC Controversy," 6 March 1969, document 580, *FRUS, 1969–1976* E-10: *Documents on American Republics, 1969–1972*; Vaky to Kissinger on CIA analysis of President Velasco's foreign policies, 13 November 1969, document 610, ibid.; consulate in the Netherlands Antilles to DoS on memorandum of conversation between Secretary of State Rogers and Prime Minister of Peru, 27 May 1973, document 285, *FRUS, 1969–1976* E-11, Part 2: *Documents on South America, 1973–1976*; embassy in Argentina to DoS, "Comments on Internal Peruvian Politics," 29 November 1974, document 302, ibid.; CIA memorandum, "Peruvian Arms Procurement Policy," 21 March 1973, CF, CO 119, GRFL.

46. Kissinger to Nixon, 8 February 1972, document 633, *FRUS, 1969–1976* E-10: *Documents on American Republics, 1969–1972*.

47. CIA memorandum, "Prospects for Change in Peru's Leadership," 25 March 1975, document 307, *FRUS, 1969–1976* E-11, Part 2: *Documents on South America, 1973–1976*.

48. Memorandum of conversation between Kissinger and Peruvian Foreign Minister Edgardo Mercado Jarrín, document 631, *FRUS, 1969–1976* E-10: *Documents on American Republics, 1969–1972*.

49. Minutes of Cabinet meeting, 21 February 1974, document 12, *FRUS, 1969–1976* E-11, Part 1: *Documents on Mexico; Central America; and the Caribbean, 1973–1976*.

50. Transcript of telephone conversation between Kissinger and Nixon, 5 April 1969, document 589, *FRUS, 1969–1976* E-10: *Documents on American Republics, 1969–1972*. See also transcript of Kissinger telephone conversation with Nixon, 3 April 1969, *KTC*, ProQuest; transcript of telephone conversation between Kissinger and presidential emissary John Irwin, 5 April 1969, ibid.

51. Memorandum from Kissinger to Nixon, with Nixon's handwritten notes, 12 October 1970, document 620, *FRUS, 1969–1976* E-10: *Documents on American Republics, 1969–1972*.

52. Minutes of SRG meeting on expropriation, #1716, folder 3, box H-112, NSC Institutional Files: SRG Minutes, RMNL; memorandum from Connally to Peter Peterson, assistant to president for international economic policy, 26 April 1971, document 624, *FRUS, 1969–1976* E-10: *Documents on American Republics, 1969–1972*.

53. Kissinger to Nixon, 11 April 1969, document 592, ibid.

54. Study memorandum on U.S.-Peruvian relations of NSC Interdepartmental Group for Inter-American Affairs, 7 March 1969, document 581, ibid.; Vaky to Kissinger, 13 November 1969, document 610, ibid.; Vaky to Kissinger, 29 December 1969, document 611, ibid.; embassy in Peru to DoS, 2 January 1970, document 612, ibid.; Jorden to Kissinger, 16 November 1972, "SRG Meeting on Peru," 16 November 1972, #1849, 17 November 1972 Meeting on Peru folder, box H-065, NSC Institutional Files: SRG Meetings, RMNL; Flanigan to Kissinger, 10 February 1970, box 7, CO 1–9, WHCF, RMNL; Deane R. Hinton, assistant director of Council of International Economic Policy of White House, to Flanigan, "Memorandum of Conversation with Representatives of Southern Peru Copper Company," CF, CO 119, GRFL.

55. Walter, *Peru and the United States, 1960–1975*, 281–84; John M. Hennessy of Treasury Department to Treasury Secretary George Shultz, "IDB Lending to Peru," 12 April 1973, CF, CO 119, GRFL; editorial note, document 294, *FRUS, 1969–1976* E-11, Part 2: *Documents on South America, 1973–1976*.

56. Embassy in Peru to DoS, 7 March 1974, document 296, ibid.

57. Ibid.; memorandum from Director of the Policy Planning Staff Winston Lord to Kissinger, 14 February 1976, document 315, ibid.

58. Memorandum of conversation between Kissinger and de la Flor, 20 February 1974, document 295, ibid.; memorandum of conversation between Kissinger and de la Flor, 22 August 1974, document 298, ibid.

59. Memorandum of conversation between Kissinger and Morales Bermúdez, 18 February 1976, document 316, ibid. See also Henry Kissinger, *Years of Renewal* (New York: Simon & Schuster, 1999), 747.

60. Memorandum of conversation between Kissinger and President Carlos Andrés Pérez of Venezuela, 17 February 1976, document 396, *FRUS, 1969–1976* E-11, Part 2: *Documents on South America, 1973–1976.*

61. Embassy in Ecuador to DoS, 8 February 1969, document 296, *FRUS, 1969–1976* E-10: *Documents on American Republics, 1969–1972.*

62. Ronn Pineo, *Ecuador and the United States: Useful Strangers* (Athens: University of Georgia Press, 2007), 173–74.

63. Rabe, *Most Dangerous Area*, 124; USAID Officer Peter M. Cody OH, https://adst .org/wp-content/uploads/2018/02/Ecuador.pdf.

64. David C. Loring, "The Fisheries Dispute," in *U.S. Foreign Policy and Peru*, ed. Daniel A. Sharp (Austin: University of Texas Press, 1972), 57–118.

65. Ibid., 83–104; Pineo, *Ecuador and the United States*, 174–77.

66. USAID Officer Bernard E. Dupuis OH, https://adst.org/wp-content/uploads /2018/02/Ecuador.pdf.

67. Pineo, *Ecuador and the United States*, 174–77.

68. Ambassador to Ecuador Findley Burns OH, https://adst.org/wp-content /uploads/2018/02/Ecuador.pdf.

69. Ashley Hewitt of NSC to Kissinger, 18 January 1971, with accompanying footnote, document 305, *FRUS, 1969–1976* E-10: *Documents on American Republics, 1969–1972.*

70. Foreign Service Officer William P. Stedman Jr. OH, FAOHC.

71. Telephone conversation between Kissinger and Packard, 29 January 1971, *KTC*, ProQuest.

72. Telephone conversation between Kissinger and Rockefeller, 3 June 1969, ibid.; Vaky of NSC to Kissinger on Rockefeller conversation with President Velasco Ibarra, 12 December 1969, document 300, *FRUS, 1969–1976* E-10: *Documents on American Republics, 1969–1972.*

73. Kissinger to Nixon, with accompanying footnote, 9 February 1971, document 306, ibid.; Kissinger to Nixon, 2 January 1971, #1687, box H-229, NSC Institutional Files: NSDM 139: Fisheries Dispute with Ecuador, Peru, Chile, RMNL.

74. Stedman OH, FAOHC; Burns OH, https://adst.org/wp-content/uploads/2018 /02/Ecuador.pdf.

75. Kissinger to Nixon, 24 October 1972, document 318, *FRUS, 1969–1976* E-10: *Documents on American Republics, 1969–1972*; NSDM 194, 27 October 1972, document 319, ibid.

76. Executive Secretary Theodore L. Eliot of DoS to Kissinger, 28 April 1972, #1682, box H-229, NSC Institutional Files: NSDM 139: Fisheries Dispute with Ecuador, Peru, Chile, RMNL.

77. Kissinger to Nixon, 24 October 1972, document 318, *FRUS, 1969–1976* E-10: *Documents on American Republics, 1969–1972.* See also Ambassador to Ecuador Richard Bloomfield OH, https://adst.org/wp-content/uploads/2018/02/Ecuador.pdf.

78. Telephone conversation between Kissinger and Maw, 8 August 1975, *KTC*, ProQuest; telephone conversation between Kissinger and Winston Lord of Policy Planning staff, 3 August 1976, ibid.

79. Ambassador Burns OH, https://adst.org/wp-content/uploads/2018/02/Ecuador.pdf.

80. Rabe, *Road to OPEC*, 193–98.

81. Aragon Storm Miller, *Precarious Paths to Freedom: The United States, Venezuela, and the Latin American Civil War* (Albuquerque: University of New Mexico Press, 2016), 65–212; Rabe, *Most Dangerous Area*, 99–108.

82. Rabe, *Road to OPEC*, 154–67, 172–78.

83. Memorandum of conversation between emissaries of President-elect Caldera and Secretary of State Rogers, 5 February 1969, document 654, *FRUS, 1969–1976* E-10: *Documents on American Republics, 1969–1972*; embassy in Venezuela to DoS, 2 December 1969, document 659, ibid.; Kissinger to Nixon on a visit by President Caldera, 26 January 1970, document 661, ibid.

84. Memorandum of meeting between Nixon and Caldera, 4 June 1970, document 666, ibid.; embassy in Venezuela to DoS on Ambassador Robert McClintock's conversation with President Caldera, 28 October 1970, document 672, ibid.

85. Memorandum of conversation between Flanigan and McClintock, 29 April 1971, document 675, ibid.

86. Nixon quoted by U.N. Ambassador George H. W. Bush in telephone conversation with Kissinger, 11 October 1971, *KTC*, ProQuest.

87. Oil Minister Pérez de la Salvia quoted in embassy in Venezuela to DoS, 9 February 1972, document 679, *FRUS, 1969–1976* E-10: *Documents on American Republics, 1969–1972*.

88. Rabe, *Road to OPEC*, 178–79.

89. Ibid., 180–81.

90. Caldera and Pérez quoted in ibid., 182–83.

91. Ibid., 177–78, 183–187; Miguel Tinker Salas, *The Enduring Legacy: Oil, Culture, and Society in Venezuela* (Durham, NC: Duke University Press, 2009), 228–29.

92. Ambassador Harry W. Shlaudeman OH, https://adst.org/wp-content/uploads/2018/02/Venezuela.pdf.

93. DoS to embassy in Venezuela, "Secretary's Meeting with Dr. Manuel Pérez Guerrero, Venezuela's Minister of State for International Economic Affairs," 21 January 1975, document 387, *FRUS, 1969–1976* E-11, Part 2: *Documents on South America, 1973–1976*.

94. Kissinger telephone conversation with Treasury Secretary George P. Shultz, 19 February 1974, *KTC*, ProQuest; Kissinger telephone conversation with Assistant Secretary Rogers, 6 January 1975, ibid.; Kissinger telephone conversation with Representative Thomas M. Rees (D-CA), 25 February 1976, ibid.

95. Transcript of Secretary Kissinger's staff meeting, 16 July 1974, document 383, *FRUS, 1969–1976* E-11, Part 2: *Documents on South America, 1973–1976*; memorandum of conversation between Kissinger and Escovar, 10 May 1975, document 390, ibid.

96. Stephen Low of NSC to Kissinger, 4 June 1974, #1600, Venezuela folder, box H-205, NSC: Institutional Files, NSSM 203, RMNL; Jack B. Kubisch, chair of Inter-Departmental Group for Inter-American Affairs to Kissinger, "Review of U.S. Policy toward Venezuela," 26 July 1974, #1607, ibid.

97. Economic officer Robert B. Morley OH, https://adst.org/wp-content/uploads/2018/02/Venezuela.pdf. See also principal officer in Maracaibo James C. Cason OH, ibid.

98. Rabe, *Road to OPEC*, 189–90.

99. Memorandum of conversation between Kissinger and Pérez, 17 February 1976, document 396, *FRUS, 1969–1976* E-11, Part 2: *Documents on South America, 1973–1976*; memorandum from NSC Adviser Brent Scowcroft to Ford on Kissinger trip to South America, 19 February 1976, document 42, *FRUS, 1969–1976* E-11, Part 1: *Documents on Mexico; Central America; and the Caribbean, 1973–1976*.

100. Memorandum of conversation between Kissinger and Escovar in Santiago, Chile, 9 June 1976, document 401, *FRUS, 1969–1976* E-11, Part 2: *Documents on South America, 1973–1976*. See also telephone conversation between Kissinger and Escovar, 16 November 1976, *KTC*, ProQuest.

101. Kissinger, *Years of Renewal*, 769.

7. Failed Initiatives

1. Tanya Harmer, "Dialogue or Détente: Henry Kissinger, Latin America, and the Prospects for a New Inter-American Understanding, 1973–1977," in *Foreign Policy at the Periphery: The Shifting Margins of US International Relations since World War II*, ed. Bevan Sewell and Maria Ryan (Lexington: University of Kentucky Press, 2017), 229–62.

2. Embassy in Colombia to DoS, "Bogotá Meeting of Latin American Foreign Ministers," 19 November 1973, document 8, *FRUS, 1969–1976*, E-11, Part 1: *Documents on Mexico, Central America, and the Caribbean, 1973–1976*.

3. Kissinger telephone conversation with Rusk, 3 October 1973, *KTC*, ProQuest.

4. Harmer, "Dialogue or Détente," 231. For a discussion of the agenda for the Mexico City meeting, see Assistant Secretary Kubisch to Hinton of White House's Council on International Economic Policy, "Secretary Kissinger's Meeting with the Latin American Foreign Ministers in Mexico—The Issues and Options," 9 January 1974, CF, CO1-9, GRFL.

5. Memorandum of Kissinger conversation with U.S. legislators and State Department officials on plane trip to Panama, 7 February 1974, #1932, folder 1/1/74–1/28/74 (2), box 1028, NSC Files: President/HAK Memorandums, RMNL; minutes of Cabinet meeting, 21 February, 1974, document 12, *FRUS, 1969–1976*, E-11, Part 1: *Documents on Mexico, Central America, and the Caribbean, 1973–1976*; Brent Scowcroft of NSC to Kissinger on Nixon reaction to Mexico City conference, 21 February 1974, document 13, ibid.

6. DoS to All American Republic Diplomatic Posts, "The Conference at Tlatelolco: An Appraisal," 9 March 1974, document 14, ibid.

7. Transcript of Kissinger's staff meeting, 14 February 1974, document 10, ibid.

8. NSDM 257, "Latin American Initiatives," 10 June 1974, document 16, ibid.

9. Telephone conversation between Kissinger and President Nixon, 16 April 1974, *KTC*, ProQuest; telephone conversation between Kissinger and Scowcroft, 16 April 1974, ibid.

10. Telephone conversation between Kissinger and Assistant Secretary of State for Latin America Jack Kubisch, 18 April 1974, ibid.

11. DoS (Assistant Secretary of State Rogers) to Kissinger at Consulate in Jerusalem, 11 February 1975, document 29, ibid.; briefing memorandum from Rogers to Kissinger, "Some Reflections on Latin America," 4 March 1975, document 30, ibid.; Harmer, "Dialogue or Détente," 244–51.

12. Henry Kissinger, "The United States and Latin America: The New Opportunity" (address), *DSB* 72 (24 March 1975): 361–69.

13. Michel Gobat, "The Invention of Latin America: The Transnational History of Anti-Imperialism," *American Historical Review* 118 (December 2013): 1345–75.

14. Ambassador John Joseph Jova OH, https://www.adst.org/Readers/US%20Mission%20Organization%20of%20American%20States.pdf.

15. DoS to All American Republic Posts, "Kissinger Meeting with Staff on 25 November," 1 December 1975, document 37, *FRUS, 1969–1976*, E-11, Part 1: *Documents on Mexico, Central America, and the Caribbean, 1973–1976*.

16. Memorandum of Kissinger conversation with U.S. legislators and State Department officials on plane trip to Panama, 7 February 1974, #1932, folder 1/1/74–1/28/74 (2), box 1028, NSC Files: President/HAK Memorandums, RMNL.

17. Henry Kissinger, *Years of Renewal* (New York: Simon & Schuster, 1999), 732.

18. Kissinger to Scowcroft for President Nixon, 21 February 1974, #1181, folder HAK Trip to Mexico (2), box 48, NSC Files: Kissinger Office Files: HAK Administrative and Staff Files, RMNL.

19. Transcript of Kissinger's staff meeting, 16 July 1974, document 19, *FRUS, 1969–1976*, E-11, Part 1: *Documents on Mexico, Central America, and the Caribbean, 1973–1976*; memorandum of conversation between Kissinger and President Ford, 21 September 1974, document 23, ibid.; memorandum of conversation between Kissinger and OAS General Secretary Orfila, 13 February 1976, document 41, ibid.

20. DoS to All American Republic Diplomatic Posts, with accompanying footnote, "Postponement of Buenos Aires MFM," 31 January 1975, document 28, ibid.

21. Kissinger, *Years of Renewal*, 749.

22. Kissinger, "United States and Latin America," 364.

23. Telephone conversation between Kissinger and Meyer, 10 September 1971, *KTC*, ProQuest.

24. Michael Beschloss, *The Crisis Years: Kennedy and Khrushchev, 1960–1963* (New York: HarperCollins, 1991).

25. Stephen G. Rabe, *Eisenhower and Latin America: The Foreign Policy of Anticommunism* (Chapel Hill: University of North Carolina Press, 1988), 162–73.

26. Stephen G. Rabe, *The Killing Zone: The United States Wages Cold War in Latin America*, 2nd ed. (New York: Oxford University Press, 2016), 68–75.

27. Stephen G. Rabe, "After the Missiles of October: John F. Kennedy and Cuba, November 1962 to November 1963," *Presidential Studies Quarterly* 30 (December 2000): 714–26.

28. Rabe, *Killing Zone*, 78–80.

29. Ibid., 64–68, 83–85.

30. *PDB*, 28 August 1971, https://www.cia.gov/library/readingroom/docs/DOC_0005992829.pdf; Intelligence Memorandum, OCI No. 1730/71, 1 September 1971, document 242, *FRUS, 1969–1976* E-10: *Documents on American Republics, 1969–1972*; *PDB*, 28 January 1972, https://www.cia.gov/library/readingroom/docs/DOC_0005993107.pdf;

PDB, 13 June 1973, https://www.cia.gov/library/readingroom/docs/DOC_0005993848 .pdf.

31. Tanya Harmer, *Allende's Chile and the Inter-American Cold War* (Chapel Hill: University of North Carolina Press, 2011), 139–44, 266.

32. Memorandum of conversation between Secretary of State Rogers and Ambassador from Switzerland Alfred Fischli, 11 March 1969, document 197, *FRUS, 1969–1976* E-10: *Documents on American Republics, 1969–1972*; Kissinger to Nixon on message from Castro, with accompanying footnote, 4 April 1969, document 198, ibid.

33. Transcript of Kissinger telephone conversation with Rockefeller about Vaky, 26 January 1970, *KTC*, ProQuest.

34. Vaky to Kissinger, 24 March 1969, #1403, NSSM 32 folder, box H-141, NSC Files: Institutional Files (H-Files), RMNL. See also Vaky to Kissinger, 9 June 1970, #1451, NSSM 70 Haiti folder, box H-161, ibid. This document was misfiled in the wrong folder and box.

35. Memorandum prepared for 303 Committee, 26 April 1969, document 200, *FRUS, 1969–1976* E-10: *Documents on American Republics, 1969–1972*; paper prepared by CIA, undated, document 203, ibid.; NIE 85-69, "Cuba, Castro, and the Course of the Revolution," 2 September 1969, document 207, ibid.; minutes of NSC Review Group, 23 September 1969, document 209, ibid.

36. Richardson to Kissinger, 16 June 1969, document 204, ibid.

37. Hughes to Secretary Rogers, "Abstract of Research Memorandum RES-39, 5 May 1969, document 202, ibid. See also Thomas L. Hughes OH, https://adst.org/wp-content/uploads/2018/02/Cuba.pdf.

38. Memorandum from presidential assistant Kenneth Cole to Kissinger, 25 September 1969, document 210, *FRUS, 1969–1976* E-10: *Documents on American Republics, 1969–1972*.

39. Richard M. Nixon, *RN: The Memoirs of Richard Nixon* (New York: Grosset & Dunlap, 1978), 203. A biographer challenges Nixon's conviction that Cuba was a decisive issue in the 1960 election. See John A. Farrell, *Richard Nixon: The Life* (New York: Doubleday, 2017), 303.

40. Kissinger to Nixon, with Nixon handwriting in accompanying footnote, 31 January 1969, document 195, *FRUS, 1969–1976* E-10: *Documents on American Republics, 1969–1972*.

41. Transcript of telephone conversation between Kissinger and Rogers, 17 December 1971, *KTC*, ProQuest.

42. Memorandum for the record by Helms, 25 March 1970, document 215, *FRUS, 1969–1976* E-10: *Documents on American Republics, 1969–1972*.

43. Memorandum from Vaky to Kissinger, with accompanying footnote and handwritten note by Haig, 18 May 1970, document 220, ibid.

44. Ronald D. Goddard OH, https://adst.org/wp-content/uploads/2018/02/Cuba.pdf.

45. Telephone conversations (2) between Kissinger and Nixon, 16 December 1971, *KTC*, ProQuest; telephone conversation between Nixon and Haig, 16 December 1971, ibid.; telephone conversation between Kissinger and Rogers, 17 December 1971, ibid.; telephone conversation between Kissinger and Laird, 23 December 1971, ibid.

46. Jorden to Kissinger, 22 August 1972, document 262, *FRUS, 1969–1976* E-10: *Documents on American Republics, 1969–1972*; Jorden to Kissinger, 14 October 1972, document 264, ibid.

47. Conversation between Nixon and Kissinger, 9 December 1971, document 247, ibid.

48. Transcript of telephone conversation between Kissinger and Nixon, 16 December 1971, *KTC*, ProQuest.

49. Lars Schoultz, *That Infernal Little Cuban Republic: The United States and the Cuban Revolution* (Chapel Hill: University of North Carolina Press, 2009), 256–60; William M. LeoGrande and Peter Kornbluh, *Back Channel to Cuba: The Hidden History of Negotiations between Washington and Havana* (Chapel Hill: University of North Carolina Press, 2014), 123–26; Teishan A. Latner, *Cuban Revolution in America: Havana and the Making of a United States Left, 1968–1992* (Chapel Hill: University of North Carolina Press, 2018), 123–51.

50. DoS to Certain Diplomatic Posts, 9 March 1973, document 273, *FRUS, 1969–1976, E-11, Part 1: Documents on Mexico, Central America, and the Caribbean, 1973–1976*.

51. Interdepartmental Group for Inter-American Affairs, "Study Prepared in Response to NSSM 32, 2 July 1969, document 205, *FRUS, 1969–1976 E-10: Documents on American Republics, 1969–1972*.

52. Nixon, *RN*, 485–89; Henry Kissinger, *White House Years* (New York: Simon & Schuster, 1979), 632–52.

53. Nixon quoted in minutes of NSC meeting, 23 September 1970, document 226, ibid.; Moorer's views in minutes of SRG meeting, "Military Activity in Cienfuegos," 19 September 1970, #1710, SRG minutes folder (3), box H-111, NSC Institutional Files: Minutes, RMNL.

54. Kissinger to Nixon, with accompanying handwritten note from Nixon [italics in original], 18 September 1970, document 224, *FRUS, 1969–1976 E-10: Documents on American Republics, 1969–1972*.

55. Vaky to Kissinger, with accompanying footnote, 5 October 1970, document 228, ibid.

56. Nachmanoff of NSC to Kissinger, "U.S. Policy Towards Cuban Exile Groups," 28 September 1971, #1906, Cuba Memos to Discuss with President, 10-11/71 folder, box 128, NSC: Kissinger Office Files: HAK Administrative and Staff Files, RMNL; Kissinger to Nixon, undated, [underlining in original], #1907, ibid.; Haig to Kissinger, 3 October 1971, #1909, ibid.

57. Helms quoted on 28 January 1972 in editorial note, document 255, *FRUS, 1969–1976 E-10: Documents on American Republics, 1969–1972*.

58. Telephone conversation between Kissinger and Scowcroft, 22 January 1974, *KTC*, ProQuest.

59. Kissinger telephone conversation with Scowcroft on trade exemption for Argentina, 17 April 1974, ibid.; Kissinger and Treasury Secretary George Shultz to Nixon, "Canadian Request for Foreign Assets Control Exemption," 14 March 1974, document 279, *FRUS, 1969–1976, E-11, Part 1: Documents on Mexico, Central America, and the Caribbean, 1973–1976*.

60. Stephen Low of NSC to Scowcroft, "Voice of America Broadcast to Cuba," 19 June 1974, document 281, ibid.; CIA to 40 Committee, "Radio Programs Targeted at Cuban and Other Latin American Youth," 6 July 1976, document 282, ibid.

61. Telephone conversation between Kissinger and Mankiewicz, 24 April 1974, *KTC*, ProQuest; LeoGrande and Kornbluh, *Back Channel to Cuba*, 119.

62. Memorandum of conversation between Ford and Kissinger, 15 August 1974, document 284, *FRUS, 1969–1976*, E-11, Part 1: *Documents on Mexico, Central America, and the Caribbean, 1973–1976*; paper prepared in State Department, "Cuba Policy," 15 August 1974, document 283, ibid.

63. Kissinger quoted in LeoGrande and Kornbluh, *Back Channel to Cuba*, 127–28.

64. *PDB*, 5 November 1974, https://www.cia.gov/library/readingroom/docs/DOC _0006007860.pdf.

65. Accompanying footnote to State Department circular, 9 March 1973, document 273, *FRUS, 1969–1976*, E-11, Part 1: *Documents on Mexico, Central America, and the Caribbean, 1973–1976*; William Jorden of NSC to Kissinger, with memorandum from Kissinger to Nixon, 22 August 1973, document 275, ibid.

66. Memorandum of conversation between Ford and Kissinger, 7 January 1975, document 292, ibid.

67. Kissinger telephone conversation with Senator Javits, 10 August 1974, *KTC*, ProQuest; telephone conversation with Senator Goodsell, 6 February 1975, ibid.; telephone conversation between Kissinger and Assistant Secretary Rogers on baseball, 21 January 1975, ibid.; Low of NSC to Kissinger, "Visas for Cuban Delegation to the Ninth World Energy Conference," 5 September 1974, document 286, *FRUS, 1969–1976*, E-11, Part 1: *Documents on Mexico, Central America, and the Caribbean, 1973–1976*; Rogers to Kissinger, "Cuban Travel," 2 December 1974, document 290, ibid.

68. Embassy in Costa Rica to DoS, "OAS Meeting," 30 July 1976, document 33, ibid.

69. Kissinger to Ford, "Third Country Sanctions against Cuba," 19 August 1975, document 301, ibid.; NSDM 305, 15 September 1975, document 303, ibid.

70. Memorandum of conversation, 9 June 1975, document 297, ibid.

71. LeoGrande and Kornbluh, *Back Channel to Cuba*, 130–33.

72. DoS to Kissinger in Bonn, "Meeting with Cubans," 1 July 1975, document 299, *FRUS, 1969–1976*, E-11, Part 1: *Documents on Mexico, Central America, and the Caribbean, 1973–1976*.

73. Memorandum of conversation, 7 August 1975, document 300, ibid.

74. DoS (Eagleburger) to Kissinger in Alexandria, Egypt, 25 August 1975, document 302, ibid.

75. NIE 85-1-75, 16 October 1975, document 304, ibid.

76. Piero Gleijeses, *Conflicting Missions: Havana, Washington, and Africa, 1959–1976* (Chapel Hill: University of North Carolina Press, 2002).

77. Kissinger's 24 November 1975 speech in Detroit, *DSB* 73 (15 December 1975): 844.

78. Kissinger, *Years of Renewal*, 784; DoS to Kissinger in Ocho Rios, Jamaica, with accompanying footnote, "Family Visits to Cuba," 29 December 1975, document 306, *FRUS, 1969–1976*, E-11, Part 1: *Documents on Mexico, Central America, and the Caribbean, 1973–1976*.

79. Kissinger telephone conversation with Callahan, 2 March 1976, *KTC*, ProQuest.

80. Scowcroft to Ford, "Kissinger in Lima," 19 February 1976, document 42, *FRUS, 1969–1976*, E-11, Part 1: *Documents on Mexico, Central America, and the Caribbean, 1973–1976*; memorandum of conversation between Kissinger and President Pérez, 17 February 1976, document 396, *FRUS, 1969–1976* E-11, Part 2: *Documents on South America, 1973–1976*; Scowcroft to Ford on Kissinger conversation with President López Michelsen, 23 February 1976, document 274, ibid.

81. Rogers to Kissinger on Eagleburger's 7 February 1976 meeting with García, 10 February 1976, document 307, *FRUS, 1969–1976*, E-11, Part 1: *Documents on Mexico, Central America, and the Caribbean, 1973–1976*.

82. CIA memorandum, "Fidel Castro's Expanding Role as a Broker between the Communist and Third Worlds," 26 February 1976, document 308, ibid.

83. Christine Hatzky, *Cubans in Angola: South-South Cooperation and Transfer of Knowledge, 1976–1991* (Madison: University of Wisconsin Press, 2012), 193–267.

84. CIA quoted in LeoGrande and Kornbluh, *Back Channel to Cuba*, 151–52.

85. Kissinger telephone conversation with Eagleburger, 15 March 1976, *KTC*, ProQuest; Kissinger telephone conversation with Califano, 15 June 1976, ibid.

86. Memorandum of conversation, with accompanying footnote, 15 March 1976, document 310, *FRUS, 1969–1976*, E-11, Part 1: *Documents on Mexico, Central America, and the Caribbean, 1973–1976*.

87. Transcript of WSAG meeting, with accompanying footnote, 24 March 1976, document 311, ibid. For Latin American opposition to unilateral action against Cuba, see the paper developed by the International Security Affairs Office transmitted in Assistant Defense Secretary Harry Bergold to Rumsfeld, 23 March 1976, Cuban Military Intervention in Africa folder, box 3, Richard Cheney papers, GRFL.

88. CIA study, "Cuban Contingencies," not dated but in response to 22 April meeting of WSAG, document 314, ibid.

89. Gleysteen to Rogers, 19 April 1976, document 312, ibid.

90. Acting Secretary of State Charles W. Robinson to Levi, with accompanying footnote, 24 May 1976, document 315, ibid.

91. CIA quoted in Shlaudeman to Kissinger, 22 October 1976, document 321, ibid.

92. Shlaudeman to Kissinger, "Allegations of Complicity in Sabotage of Air Cubana Flight from Barbados," 12 October 1976, document 320, ibid.; Shlaudeman to Kissinger, "Cubana Airlines Crash: Strategy Paper," 22 October 1976, document 321, ibid.; briefing memorandum from Director of the Bureau of Intelligence and Research Harold H. Saunders and Shlaudeman to Kissinger, "Allegations of U.S. Involvement in Cubana Airliner Crash," *FRUS, 1969–1976*, E-11, Part 1: *Documents on Mexico, Central America, and the Caribbean, 1973–1976*; October 1976, ibid.; Shlaudeman to Kissinger, "Cubana Crash Trial and Steps We Can Take to Restore Proper Focus," 29 October 1976, document 323, ibid.

93. Shlaudeman to Kissinger, "Allegations of Complicity in Sabotage of Air Cubana Flight from Barbados," 12 October 1976, document 320, ibid.; Shlaudeman to Kissinger, "Cubana Airlines Crash: Strategy Paper," 22 October 1976, document 321, ibid.; briefing memorandum from Director of the Bureau of Intelligence and Research Harold H. Saunders and Shlaudeman to Kissinger, "Allegations of U.S. Involvement in Cubana Airliner Crash," *FRUS, 1969–1976*, E-11, Part 1: *Documents on Mexico, Central America, and the Caribbean, 1973–1976*; October 1976, ibid.; Shlaudeman to Kissinger, "Cubana Crash Trial and Steps We Can Take to Restore Proper Focus," 29 October 1976, document 323, ibid.

94. Memorandum for National Intelligence Officer for Latin America [unnamed] to Deputy Director of CIA E. Henry Knoche, "Current U.S. Policy Toward Cuba and Related Intelligence Needs," 18 November 1976, document 327, ibid.; DoS to Swiss Embassy in Havana on Hijacking Agreement, 11 November 1976, document 325, ibid.

95. Rabe, *Killing Zone*, 198; Frances Robles, "Luis Posada Carriles, 90, Anti-Castro Warrior, Dies," *NYT*, 23 May 2018, B13.

Conclusion

1. Dean Acheson, *Present at the Creation* (New York: Norton, 1969); Dean Rusk, as told to Richard Rusk, *As I Saw It* (New York: Norton, 1990).

2. Tom Blanton, "Kissinger, Dallek, and Suri in the Gangster Den," *Diplomatic History* 33 (September 2009): 771.

3. Henry Kissinger, *Years of Upheaval* (New York: Simon & Schuster, 1982), 423.

4. Jussi M. Hanhimäki, "An Elusive Grand Design," in *Nixon in the World*, ed. Logevall and Preston, 25–26.

5. Kissinger discussed Chile 122 times over the telephone between 1970 and 1976. *KTC*, ProQuest.

6. Peter Kornbluh, *The Pinochet File: A Declassified Dossier of Atrocity and Accountability* (New York: New Press, 2003); Tanya Harmer, *Allende's Chile and the Inter-American Cold War* (Chapel Hill: University of North Carolina Press, 2011).

7. Telephone conversation between Kissinger and Nixon, 16 December 1971, *KTC*, ProQuest.

8. Jonathan Haslam, *The Nixon Administration and the Death of Allende's Chile: A Case of Assisted Suicide* (London: Verso, 2005).

9. H. R. Haldeman, *The Ends of Power* (New York: Times Books, 1977), 94.

10. Daniel J. Sargent, *A Superpower Transformed: The Remaking of American Foreign Relations in the 1970s* (New York: Oxford University Press, 2015), 96; Mario Del Pero, *The Eccentric Realist: Henry Kissinger and the Shaping of American Foreign Policy* (Ithaca, NY: Cornell University Press, 2010), 148–49.

11. Henry Kissinger, *Years of Renewal* (New York: Simon & Schuster, 1999), 754.

12. Memorandum of conversation between Kissinger and Escovar, 9 June 1976, document 401, *FRUS, 1969–1976 E-11, Part 2: Documents on South America, 1973–1976*.

13. Kornbluh, *Pinochet File*, 230–65; Kissinger, *Years of Renewal*, 754–60.

14. Memorandum of conversation between Kissinger and Balaguer, 6 June 1976, document 355, *FRUS, 1969–1976 E-11, Part 1: Documents on Mexico; Central America; and the Caribbean*; Scowcroft to Ford transmitting Kissinger report on Dominican Republic, undated, document 356, ibid.

15. Stephen G. Rabe, *The Most Dangerous Area in the World: John F. Kennedy Confronts Communist Revolution in Latin America* (Chapel Hill: University of North Carolina Press, 1999), 60.

16. Stephen G. Rabe, *The Killing Zone: The United States Wages Cold War in Latin America*, 2nd ed. (New York: Oxford University Press, 2016), 45.

17. Virginia Garrard-Burnett, *Terror in the Land of the Holy Spirit: Guatemala under General Efraín Ríos Montt* (New York: Oxford University Press, 2010).

18. Arthur M. Schlesinger Jr., *A Thousand Days: John F. Kennedy in the White House* (Boston: Houghton Mifflin, 1965), 769.

19. Stephen G. Rabe, *Eisenhower and Latin America: The Foreign Policy of Anticommunism* (Chapel Hill: University of North Carolina Press, 1988), 85–86.

20. Gary J. Bass, *The Blood Telegram: Nixon, Kissinger, and a Forgotten Genocide* (New York: Alfred A. Knopf, 2013), 344–45.

21. Associated Press, "Argentina Group Identifies 128th Person Taken during 'Dirty War,'" *NYT*, 4 August 2018, https://www.nytimes.com/2018/08/04/world/americas /argentina-dirty-war-disappeared.html.

22. Julie Hirschfeld Davis, "Obama Expresses Regret for U.S. Policies during Argentina's 'Dirty War,'" *NYT*, 24 March 2018, A12. The Donald J. Trump administration has continued to declassify documents on Argentina. Ernesto Londoño, "Declassified U.S. Documents Reveal Details about Argentina's Dictatorship," *NYT*, 12 April 2019, A8; NSA, "Declassification Diplomacy: Trump Administration Turns Over Massive Collection of Intelligence Records on Human Rights and Argentina," *Electronic Briefing Book #669*, 12 April 2019, https://nsarchive.gwu.edu/briefing-book/southern-cone/2019-04 -12/declassification-diplomacy-trump-administration-turns-over-massive-collection -intelligence-records.

23. Walter Isaacson, *Kissinger: A Biography*, with a new introduction (New York: Simon & Schuster, 2005), 10.

24. Hal Brands, *Latin America's Cold War* (Cambridge, MA: Harvard University Press, 2010), 127; Stephen G. Rabe, "Human Rights, Latin America, and the Cold War," *DH* 36 (January 2012): 231–36.

25. Max Paul Friedman, "Retiring the Puppets, Bringing Latin America In: Recent Scholarship on United States–Latin American Relations," *DH* 27 (November 2003): 621–36.

26. Memorandum of conversation between Kissinger and Carvajal, 29 September 1975, document 201, *FRUS, 1969–1976 E-11*, Part 2: *Documents on South America, 1973–1976*.

27. Kathryn Sikkink, *Mixed Signals: U.S. Human Rights Policy and Latin America* (Ithaca, NY: Cornell University Press, 2004), 80–105, 121–47; William Michael Schmidli, *The Fate of Freedom Elsewhere: Human Rights and U.S. Cold War Policy toward Argentina* (Ithaca, NY: Cornell University Press, 2013), 152–55; Lars Schoultz, *Human Rights and United States Policy toward Latin America* (Princeton, NJ: Princeton University Press, 1981), 363; Thomas C. Wright, *State Terrorism in Latin America: Chile, Argentina, and International Human Rights* (Lanham, MD: Rowman & Littlefield, 2007), 118–25. See also Patrick William Kelly, *Sovereign Emergencies: Latin America and the Making of Global Human Rights Politics* (Cambridge, UK: Cambridge University Press, 2018).

28. Jonathan Gilbert, "Argentina Confirms a Deadly Legacy of Dictatorships," *NYT*, 28 May 2016, A8.

29. Jussi M. Hanhimäki, *The Flawed Architect: Henry Kissinger and American Foreign Policy* (New York: Oxford University Press, 2004), 491.

30. Niall Ferguson, *Kissinger, 1923–1968: The Idealist* (New York: Penguin Press, 2015), 24; remarks by Niall Ferguson in Jussi M. Hanhimäki, ed., "Roundtable Review," *H-DIPLO* 18, no. 3 (2016): 25, http://www.tiny.cc/Roundtable-XVIII-3.

31. Daniel J. Sargent, *A Superpower Transformed: The Remaking of American Foreign Relations in the 1970s* (New York: oxford University Press, 2015), 96.

32. Jon Lee Anderson, "Does Henry Kissinger Have a Conscience?," *New Yorker*, 20 August 2016, http://www.newyorker.com/news/news-desk/does-henry-kissinger -have-a-conscience.

33. Mark Atwood Lawrence, "History from Below: The United States and Latin America in the Nixon Years," in *Nixon in the World: American Foreign Relations, 1969–1977*, ed. Fredrik Logevall and Andrew Preston (New York: Oxford University Press, 2008), 286.

34. Roham Alvandi, *Nixon, Kissinger, and the Shah: The United States and Iran in the Cold War* (New York: Oxford University Press, 2014), 175–76; Isaacson, *Kissinger*, 760–63; Barbara Keys, "Henry Kissinger: The Emotional Statesman," *DH* 35 (September 2011): 599–600; Jeremi Suri, *Henry Kissinger and the American Century* (Cambridge, MA: Belknap Press of Harvard University Press, 2007), 270.

35. Memorandum of conversation between Kissinger and Cuadra, 11 June 1976, document 260, *FRUS, 1969–1976, E-3: Documents on Global Issues, 1973–1976* (Washington, DC: GPO, 2009).

Primary Sources

Archives

Jimmy Carter Presidential Library. Atlanta, Georgia
Dwight D. Eisenhower Presidential Library. Abilene, Kansas
Gerald R. Ford Presidential Library. Ann Arbor, Michigan
Lyndon Baines Johnson Presidential Library. Austin, Texas
John F. Kennedy Presidential Library. Columbia Point, Boston, Massachusetts
Richard M. Nixon Presidential Library. Yorba Linda, California
Rockefeller Archives Collection. Pocantico Hills, New York
U.S. National Archives. College Park, Maryland

Electronic Archives

American Presidency Project. http://www.presidency.ucsb.edu/.
Argentina Declassification Project. https://foia.state.gov/Search/Results.aspx
    ?collection=ARGENTINA&searchText=*.
Association for Diplomatic Studies and Training Oral Histories. https://adst.org
    /oral-history/oral-history-interviews/#.Wm9lFLpFw2w&gsc.tab=0.
Chile Declassification Project. https://foia.state.gov/Search/Results.aspx?collection
    =CHILE&searchText=*.
CREST. https://www.cia.gov/library/readingroom/collection/crest-25-year
    -program-archive.
Foreign Affairs Oral History Collection (Arlington, VA: Association for Diplomatic
    Studies and Training, 2000). CD-ROM.
Foreign Relations of the United States, 1969–1976. https://history.state.gov
    /historicaldocuments/nixon-ford.
Kissinger Telephone Conversations. https://proquest.libguides.com/dnsa
    /kissinger1.
National Security Archive. https://nsarchive.gwu.edu/.
Nixon White House Tapes. http://nixontapes.org/.
Presidential Daily Brief. https://www.cia.gov/library/readingroom/presidents-daily
    -brief.
U.S. Overseas Loans and Grants. https://explorer.usaid.gov/reports.html.

INDEX

CPSIA information can be obtained
at www.ICGtesting.com
Printed in the USA
LVHW091923290120
645204LV00010B/23/J